CRIMINAL JUSTICE, LAW ENFORCEMENT AND CORRECTIONS SERIES

VIOLENT CRIME AND PRISONS: POPULATION, HEALTH CONDITIONS AND RECIDIVISM

CRIMINAL JUSTICE, LAW ENFORCEMENT AND CORRECTIONS SERIES

Homicide Investigations
Allan B. Smythe
2009. ISBN: 978-1-60692-258-3

Mass Incarceration and Offender Reentry in the United States
Russell D. Javitze (Editor)
2009. ISBN: 978-1-60692-657-4

Batterer Intervention: Program Approaches and Criminal Justice Strategies
Kerry Healey, Christine Smith, and Chris O'Sullivan
2009. ISBN: 978-1-60692-934-6

Batterer Intervention: Program Approaches and Criminal Justice Strategies
Kerry Healey, Christine Smith and Chris O'Sullivan
2009. ISBN: 978-1-60876-537-9
(Online book)

Digital Surveillance: Laws, Security and Related Issues
Joseph G. Massingale (Editor)
2009. ISBN: 978-1-60692-312-2

Incarceration and the Family: Issues, Effects and Approaches to Successful Reentry
U.S. Dept. of Health and Human Services
2009. ISBN: 978-1-60692-933-9

Policing the Police: Knowledge Management in Law Enforcement
Petter Gottschalk
2009. ISBN: 978-1-60741-765-1

Policing the Police: Knowledge Management in Law Enforcement
Petter Gottschalk
2009. ISBN: 978-1-60876-653-6
(Online Book)

Gun Ownership and the Second amendment
Pjeter D. Baldrige
2009. ISBN: 978-1-60692-226-2

Homicide: Trends, Causes and Prevention
Randal B. Toliver and Ulrich R. Coyne (Editors)
2009. ISBN: 978-1-60741-625-8

Delinquency: Causes, Reduction and Prevention
Ozan Sahin and Joseph Maier (Editor)
2009. ISBN: 978-1-60741-558-9

Violent Crime and Prisons: Population, Health Conditions and Recidivism
Aidan Renshaw and Emelina Suárez (Editors)
2009. ISBN: 978-1-60741-668-5

CRIMINAL JUSTICE, LAW ENFORCEMENT AND CORRECTIONS SERIES

VIOLENT CRIME AND PRISONS: POPULATION, HEALTH CONDITIONS AND RECIDIVISM

AIDAN RENSHAW
AND
EMELINA SUÁREZ
EDITORS

Nova Science Publishers, Inc.
New York

For permission to use material from this book please contact us:
Telephone 631-231-7269; Fax 631-231-8175
Web Site: http://www.novapublishers.com

LIBRARY OF CONGRESS CATALOGING-IN-PUBLICATION DATA

Renshaw, Aidan.
Violent crime and prisons : population, health conditions and recidivism / Aidan Renshaw and Emelina Suárez.
p. cm.
Includes index.
ISBN 978-1-60741-668-5 (hbk.)
1. Violent crimes. 2. Prisons. 3. Prisoners--Health and hygiene. 4. Recidivism. I. Suárez, Emelina. II. Title.
HV6493.R46 2009
365'.4--dc22

2009027061

Published by Nova Science Publishers, Inc. ✦ New York

CONTENTS

PREFACE

Violence is observed in all levels and expressions of biological and social life. However, human violence has the distinction of being greatly altered by the dynamics of individual and group development, which takes place in the context of our world views - view of reality, human nature, the purpose of life, and laws governing human relationships. Criminality is related to deficient skills for resolving interpersonal problems and to deficient behavioral skills in social interaction; therefore, the prevention and/or intervention with training programs in these skills is necessary. Consequently, prison is an institution that strives to combine two different and contradictory goals. On the one hand, its purpose is to isolate individuals that are considered threats to society and to impose an exemplary punishment, and on the other hand it aims at their social reintegration by the means of correction. This new book gathers the latest research from around the globe in the field of violent crime and prisons with topics such as unity building as violence prevention, violence and college students, female inmates attitudes towards same-sex relationships, art therapy in prison and the link between high environmental temperatures and violent behavior.

Chapter 1 - This chapter outlines the claim, now widely accepted among scientists, that there tends to be more crime when the temperature is high. Perhaps the most often-discussed effect of this pattern is that in most or all cities, there tends to be more violent crime in summer months than in cooler months. Other effects of the temperature-violence link have also been reported, such as geographical variation in crime rates: hot places tend to have high rates of violent crime, relative to cool locations. Various types of violence seem to be affected by high temperature: several kinds of violent crimes, but also (often unreported) domestic violence. The authors investigate these claims, and examine various types of evidence on whether or not this hypothesized link between temperature and violence is true. The authors also consider possible explanations for these patterns. Despite much agreement on the existence of a link between temperature and violence, there are several controversies in this field. One issue the authors explore is whether or not violence continues to rise if the temperature gets higher, or whether there is a 'curvilinear' pattern – in which rates of violence tend to decline above a particular temperature. The authors also investigate various mechanisms which have been put forward to explain the observed patterns; in particular, the authors discuss claims that increased prevalence of violence is due to the effects of culture, or due to stress hormones.

Chapter 2 - Studies of the adaptation to prison have been heavily influenced by classic prison sociology. This has meant that the majority of literature on adjustment to imprisonment has focused on adult males and has been described and interpreted against adult male models of adaptation. Though there is some recognition in these studies of the inherent vulnerability of young people because of their age, they tend to examine the stress of incarceration from a universally adult perspective and belief system. For example, there is a presumption that not being able to see friends and family is equally difficult for adults and youth. There does not appear to be a serious consideration of the possibility that youths find certain events uniquely problematic – nor is there a consideration of the possibility that adolescence itself has its own stresses that may be relevant in this setting. Utilizing a decade of research on adolescent males in custody, this chapter will argue the importance of using a development framework to the study of the adjustment of youth in custody. Additionally, it will present data to suggest that for a small but significant proportion of adolescent male youth, "doing time" is extremely difficult.

Chapter 3 - Violence is observed in all levels and expressions of biological and social life. However, human violence has the distinction of being greatly altered by the dynamics of individual and group development, which takes place in the context of our worldviews—view of reality, human nature, the purpose of life, and laws governing human relationships. Three metacategories of worldview—survival-based, identity-based, and unity-based—are identified. The first two categories are conflict-based and conducive to violence. The third category—unity-based worldview—is peace-based and conducive to significant decrease in both occurrence of conflicts and their satisfactory peaceful resolution. It is proposed that with regard to the genesis of human violence and its prevention there is a need for a fundamental paradigm shift of a kind identified by Kuhn with regard to revolutionary periods in the advancement of any given area of science. Current, generally accepted, perspectives on violence make no distinction between human violence and the types observed in other living beings in the arena of struggle for survival and dominance. It is argued that while these forms of violence do exist and have always existed in human life, they are, nevertheless, subject to the dynamics of human individual and group development, which are conscious and deliberate processes, not autonomous and involuntary as in other levels of life. The premises of the chapter are validated by the extensive and intensive Education for Peace Program, which has been implemented in post-war Bosnia and Herzegovina since 2000 and has brought tangible levels of conflict reduction and violence prevention among the participants (80,000 students, 5,000 educators, 120,000 parents) in this post-war highly conflicted society.

Chapter 4 - Criminality is related both to deficient skills for resolving interpersonal problems and to deficient behavioral skills in social interaction; therefore the prevention and/or intervention with training programs in these skills is necessary (Beleña, 1992; Garrido et al., 2006; Redondo, 2008; Ross and Ross, 1995).

The principal objective of this study was to determine the effectiveness, feasibility, and effects obtained by the application of a training program designed and applied by the authors and directed at the fomentation of *interpersonal skills* in a sample of incarcerated women, taking into account quantitative and qualitative response criteria in the dimensions considered, that is, in the face of an interpersonal problem, not only generating as many solutions as possible (quantitative aspect), but also evaluating those solutions as to whether they are ethical and socially permissible (qualitative aspect).

The sample comprised 44 women distributed in two groups: control (N=22) and experimental (N=22). In the first stage of evaluation the women completed the *Progressive Matrices* test of Raven and the *Battery of Interpersonal Skills*, adapted for the criminal population by Báguena and Beleña (1993). This battery evaluates five dimensions: Appreciation of Perspectives, Causal Thinking, Alternative Thinking, Consequential Thinking, and Means-End Thinking. The women of the experimental group, divided into small groups, received a training program in interpersonal skills. The interpersonal skills of both experimental groups were then reevaluated with the post-test.

The results obtained suggest that the situation of incarceration produces a decrease in the interpersonal skill levels of women criminals. The authors cite the degree of effectiveness of our program with a set of direct effects that implied a neutralization or slowing down of this decrease, as well as the improvement of some of the skills. In addition, the program significantly improved the following qualitative components: direct causes, ethical and socially permissible solution alternatives ("what" to do in the face of a problem), solutions for the intragroup, short- and long-term consequences, and the use of ethically and socially permissible means and resources ("how" to solve a problem). Moreover, the need to improve the aspects of the program related to the improvement of "appreciation of different perspectives" (empathy) when facing a problem was demonstrated.

The study also suggests the importance of incorporating in penitentiary institutions programs such as that developed by us, insofar as incarcerated women, upon release from prison, must reintegrate themselves into a social world that demands the mastery of interpersonal skills.

Chapter 5 - In the early 1990s, the fundamental changes in the social system in Poland had begun: the communist regime failed and the new social and economic order had been emerging. This situation offers an opportunity to study the consequences of the turn on the prison system and prisoners, changes within penal institutions, differences between 'totalitarian' prisons and a democratic penal system. The basic idea is to examine the influence of political and social changes on conditions of imprisonment, and to explore the process of institutional adjustment to a free market economy and democratization.

This article presents research on inmates in Poland, with a focus on a prisoner as a rational actor in a penal institution environment. The main issues of the research focus on the consequences of penal reform on the social community of prisoners, especially on social order in the convicts' community, normative system, social relations among inmates and social relations between inmates and correctional staff and the standard of living in confinement.

The results of the research reveal that social relations have changed and a relatively high level of integration among the inmates' community in 'the totalitarian' prison has been displaced with distrust; the social ties are based mainly on interests and 'goods-exchange' relations. The 'old' sub-culture community which controlled social order disappeared. The role of bureaucratization increases significantly. It decreases the rehabilitation function of prisons because the main goal of staff is to respect formal regulations. Bureaucracy redefines the rational rules of acting both for inmates and prison staff. For prisoners it becomes a means to achieve their purposes. The result of the new organizational order is more control on the penal institutions, especially inmates gaining more influence over their lives. The question arises about the consequences of such conditions in correctional institutions for inmates and society.

The analysis is based on data collected in the empirical research carried out in 20 prisons in Poland, on a sample of over 1000 persons.

Chapter 6 - There is an explicit expectation that universities will educate students and a tacit expectation that they will protect those in their care. Unfortunately, universities are seeing high levels of campus violence. This chapter will discuss the prevalence of violence among college students with an eye toward the legal mandates to warn students of imminent danger and the psychological consequences for exposure to violence among college students. The authors will conclude with specific recommendation for college counseling centers, which are most likely to encounter trauma-exposed college students.

Chapter 7 - Since the inception of commercial television broadcasting in the early 1950s, the home screen has been swept with a long line of screened and non-screened programs portraying violent crime. From the *Naked City* and the *Untouchables* in the 1950s and 1960s to the *Sopranos* and *Rescue 911* in the 1990s and 2000s, viewers have been exposed to excessive amounts of violent attacks, interpersonal and collective aggression, gunshots, gory images and even death (Roman, 2005). Even though the direct behavioral effect of prolonged routine exposure to TV violence is not conspicuously large by social science standards (see Bushman & Anderson, 2001; Paik & Comstock, 1994), the academic establishment, along with public figures and public opinion, have been treating the appearance of and the report on violent crime on television broadcasts as a serious problem. Three out of four Americans think that there is a relationship between violence on television and the national crime rate (Saad, 2007), and a majority of the public feel that television crime shows, violent films and television news items about crime contribute a lot to the seemingly high US murder rate (Potter, 2003). Epidemiologists have asserted that television violence is responsible for no less than 10,000 homicide cases in the USA alone (Centerwall, 1989). The late Senator John Pastore has argued that television violence is "a public health risk" (see Cole, 1996, p.15). Newton N. Minow, former Chairman of the Federal Communications Commission (FCC), the federal agency in charge of broadcasting regulation, said the following in a text selected by rhetoric experts as one the twenty-five speeches that changed the world.

Chapter 8 - Psychopathy is a construct that has been robustly linked to violent behavior. Yet, violence encompasses a wide variety of behaviors, which potentially masks more nuanced relationships. In this chapter, the authors review the theoretical and empirical literature between psychopathy and different manifestations of criminal behavior and aggression. In doing so, the authors demonstrate that psychopathic individuals are more likely to engage in (1) violent than non-violent criminal behavior and (2) both proactive and reactive types of aggression. These empirical findings are then discussed in the context of a recent theoretical development that explains these patterns. Finally, the authors discuss how a more detailed understanding of both individual characteristics and behavioral outcomes may yield more promising treatment approaches.

Chapter 9 - This study aims to explore adolescents' assessment of the target in hypothetical scenarios of aggression and to establish any sex differences in adolescent perceptions of the target of these scenarios. An instrument with eight different hypothetical scenarios of aggression was designed. This instrument manipulates the sex of the aggressor, the sex of the target, and the status difference (same vs. different) between the aggressor and the target in each scenario. The instrument was administered to a sample (N = 653) of adolescents aged 14 to 18. A multifactorial repeated-measures design with a 2 x 2 x 2 analysis of variance (ANOVA) was used. Results showed a significant interaction between sex of aggressor, sex of target, and status difference of aggressor and target ($F_{1,560} = 20.329$, $p = .000$). More specifically, results showed that (i) when the aggressor was male, the subjects assessed a female target more positively than a male target, regardless of status difference; (ii) when the aggressor was female, the subjects assessed a male target more positively than a female target, regardless of status difference; (iii) the subjects assessed a target more positively in the scenarios where the aggressor and target were of different sexes; (iv) the subjects assessed a target more positively when the aggressor and the target were of different status; (v) the subjects assessed a target more positively in the scenarios in which the target was a student, either male or female; (vi) compared with females, males assessed the target more positively when the aggressor was a female, when the target was a male, and when the target was a male with unequal status in the relationship; and (vii) females assessed the target more positively when the aggressor was a male and when the target was a female. These findings are discussed in terms of important attitude changes in overcoming the sexist stereotype toward a female target in a situation of aggression within the family; nevertheless, this stereotype has not been completely overcome in other scenarios where aggression takes place.

Chapter 10 - Research on same-sex sexual relationships among female inmates has been a neglected topic until recently. This article examines female inmates' attitudes toward same-sex sexual activity in prison, and analyzes the link between female inmates' viewpoints of same-sex sexual relationships in prison and the length of imprisonment, ethnicity, and the prevalence of such conduct.

Main findings: (a) Most female inmates express negative attitudes towards same-sex sexual relationships in prison; (b) `short-timers` and 'long-timers' define and perceive same-sex sexual relations in prison differently; (c) ethnicity does not affect female inmates' attitude toward same sex sexual relationships.

Chapter 11 - It is well known that, internationally, women's delinquency is lower than the one of men's. However, the last ten years it is observed that women's participation in criminality appears to be on the increase and is mainly detected at specific crimes. This increase can be related to the expansion of opportunities resulted from the new roles adapted by women, as well as to the wider exposure of their actions following their way into public life for professional and social reasons. This exposure enhances the possibilities of their taking part in the mechanisms of the criminal justice award system.

Chapter 12 - HIV-positive inmates in the United States have often been segregated in an attempt to prevent the spread of HIV/AIDS in the nation's prisons. Not surprisingly, this practice generated considerable litigation, including in Alabama where segregation for HIV-positive inmates still exists today. Using Foucault's (1995) theory of carceral power, this article analyzes two class action lawsuits that failed to overturn Alabama's policies of mandatory HIV testing and segregated medical care and housing for HIV-positive inmates. Case One (*Harris v. Thigpen)* challenged the power of the penitentiary, but was unsuccessful because the court deferred to prison authority regarding prison conditions. Case Two (*Leatherwood v. Campbell*) similarly failed in challenging segregated housing for HIV-positive inmates, but did pave the way for modest improvements in housing and medical care. These cases demonstrate how the power of the penitentiary expanded during the HIV/AIDS epidemic in Alabama through legislative fiat, judicial deference, and offender classifications that were deployed to discipline and punish HIV-positive prisoners on the basis of epidemiologic tropes about violence, deviance, and contagion.

Chapter 13 - Prison is an institution that strives to combine two different and contradictory goals. On the one hand, its purpose is to isolate individuals that are considered threats to society and to impose an exemplary punishment, and on the other hand it aims at their social reintegration by the means of correction (Haidou, 2002). Watson and his colleagues (2004) are supportive of Haidou's point of view by drawing attention to the fact that prison's objectives are punishment, correction and successful reintegration. Correction requires that the inmate adjusts to the values, the mores, the mentality, and the subculture of prison, thus resulting in the distortion of his/her personal identity and uniqueness (Paterline & Petersen, 1999).

Chapter 14 - Drug addicted prisoners are in a special situation: they are permanently oscillating between consciousness of reality and preservation of their illusory dreams. One goal of arts therapies in prison consists in developing their capacity to elaborate on a symbolic level and in favouring a better equilibrium between their Ego Ideal and their Superego. If there is no restructuring process of this kind, they risk having a relapse as soon as they are released.

Clinical vignettes will illustrate the therapeutic process and the special function of the arts therapist in prison.

The authors present a comparative study of pictures drawn at the beginning of arts therapeutic treatment. Based on the evolution of the pictorial and literary production, the authors extract the first indicators of a possible relaunch of the subjectivation process.

Our discussion stresses the possibilities but also the limits of arts therapies in prison. The extracted indicators can be useful for future research.

In: Violent Crime and Prisons: Population... ISBN: 978-1-60741-668-5
Ed: Aidan Renshaw and Emelina Suárez

Chapter 1

EXTREME TEMPERATURE AS A CAUSE OF VIOLENCE

John Simister* and Cary Cooper**

* Birkbeck College, University of London, UK.

** Lancaster University, UK

ABSTRACT

This chapter outlines the claim, now widely accepted among scientists, that there tends to be more crime when the temperature is high. Perhaps the most often-discussed effect of this pattern is that in most or all cities, there tends to be more violent crime in summer months than in cooler months. Other effects of the temperature-violence link have also been reported, such as geographical variation in crime rates: hot places tend to have high rates of violent crime, relative to cool locations. Various types of violence seem to be affected by high temperature: several kinds of violent crimes, but also (often unreported) domestic violence. We investigate these claims, and examine various types of evidence on whether or not this hypothesized link between temperature and violence is true. We also consider possible explanations for these patterns. Despite much agreement on the existence of a link between temperature and violence, there are several controversies in this field. One issue we explore is whether or not violence continues to rise if the temperature gets higher, or whether there is a 'curvilinear' pattern – in which rates of violence tend to decline above a particular temperature. We also investigate various mechanisms which have been put forward to explain the observed patterns; in particular, we discuss claims that increased prevalence of violence is due to the effects of culture, or due to stress hormones.

1.1. INTRODUCTION

Many researchers have claimed to find a link between temperature and aggression. This chapter summarises empirical evidence on the effects of extreme temperature on violence, and suggests possible explanations for the observed patterns. We use data from various countries, to confirm strong seasonal patterns in several types of violent crime. This chapter confirms previous claims that violent crime is associated with temperature extremes.

There is evidence from several countries that temperature extremes are associated with violence, including the UK (Semmens et al., 2002: p. 798) and USA: "Field studies clearly show that heat increases aggression" (Anderson, 1989: 74). Temperature-induced violence includes political rebellions/riots, assaults, spouse abuse/domestic violence, manslaughter and murder (Anderson, 1989; Rotton & Cohn, 2001). Rosenfeld's research on USA (cited in Anderson, 1989: p. 79) found violent crimes such as murder significantly higher in (hot) southern cities.

Although there seems widespread agreement about the existence of a link between temperature extremes and crime (some of the evidence is reported in this chapter), there are many aspects which science has not yet solved: for example, what is the shape of the curve relating temperature to aggression? Some writers suggest a 'curvilinear hypothesis': as temperature rises, violence becomes more prevalent, but only up to a certain temperature – after that point, further increases in temperature tend to reduce violence (see Anderson & Anderson, 1984). In section 1.5 below, we discuss the question of whether the relationship between temperature and violence is an inverted-U-shape, or some other form.

Much of this chapter tests the idea that adrenaline and/or noradrenaline explains many, if not all, of the observed seasonal and geographical patterns in violent crime. Our hypothesis is that extreme temperature (especially heat) leads to adrenaline and/or noradrenaline production, which causes aggression. We cannot rule out the possibility that other hormones are involved. As far as we know, the first source to suggest adrenaline and/or noradrenaline (as the cause of crime seasonality) is Simister & Cooper (2005).

1.2. Evidence That Temperature Increases Violence

Different Types of Evidence

There are various ways of analysing data, to assess whether or not violence is related to temperature. This section focuses mainly on crime data, but there are other ways to assess effects of violence: for example, some household surveys ask respondents about domestic violence. In this chapter, we do not report all available evidence: we only attempt to discuss a fraction of the claims that have been published on this topic. It would be a daunting task to list all research: it would need to include numerous academic disciplines (such as criminology, medicine, meteorology, geography, and anthropology). We have not read any research published in a language other than English; and we suspect we have only read a fairly small fraction of relevant research in the English language.

In this paper, all temperatures are "dry-bulb" temperatures, reported in degrees Centigrade (°C). For most charts in this chapter, temperatures are shown between –17°C and +43°C, so we can compare different locations – for example, temperatures are much lower in Alaska than in other locations investigated in this chapter.

Where appropriate, crime rates in this paper are numbers of crimes per year, per 100,000 people. However, this is not suitable for USA, due to the strong time-trend: hence our use of what we call the 'FBI method' for USA crime rates, explained below. Chart 1 uses data on violence expressed as a percentage.

Chart 1. Domestic violence prevalence by average temperature, in various countries.

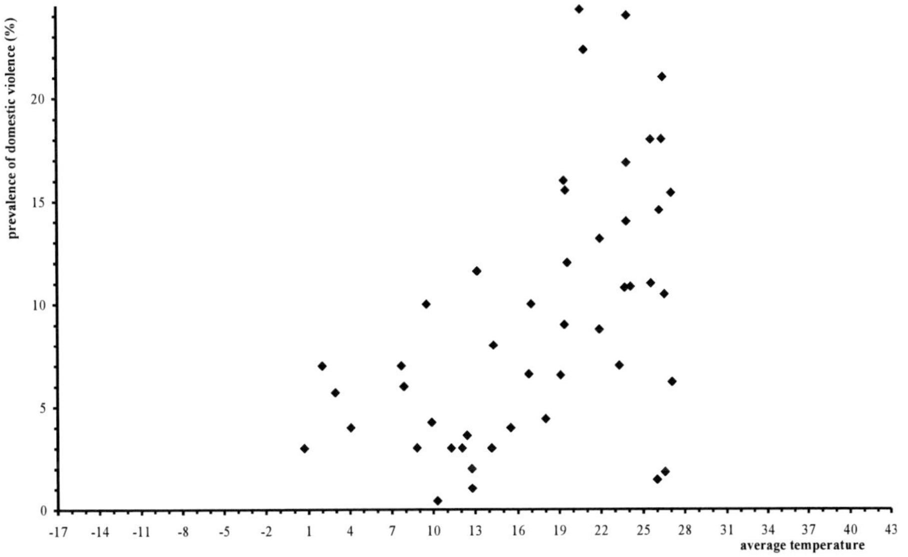

Source: domestic violence data from Ellsberg & Heise (2005); temperatures from CRU (2001).

More Violent Crime in Hot Countries than in Cooler Countries

As an example of a link between temperature and violence, we created Chart 1 based on domestic violence by men against women (sometimes called 'Gender Based Violence'): we use data from Ellsberg & Heise (2005: pp. 13-5), which is a compilation of various studies of domestic violence by different agencies. Temperature data for Chart 1 are annual average temperature at all weather stations in the country, from CRU (2001); we use –17 to +43 °C on the horizontal axis of Chart 1 for comparability with subsequent charts in this chapter. Each point on Chart 1 represents one country.

Chart 1 suggests a link between temperature and domestic violence: there is a tendency for more violence (higher up Chart 1), in countries with a higher average temperature (towards the right hand side of Chart 1). This chart is not entirely persuasive, however: for example, two countries at the bottom-right of Chart 1 have low prevalence of domestic violence, despite having high temperatures. It is plausible that differences in definitions of 'domestic violence' explain some of the variation in prevalence of violence at any given temperature.

More Crime in Hot Regions of Big Countries (e.g. USA, India)

Evidence cited in Anderson (1989) on the link between temperature and crime includes evidence comparing hot with cold geographical areas within the same country. Rosenfeld's research on USA (cited in Anderson, 1989: p. 79) found violent crimes such as murder significantly higher in (hot) southern cities, whereas non-violent crimes such as theft showed no significant north/south difference.

Chart 2. Assault rate versus temperature – USA, 1999 to 2003.

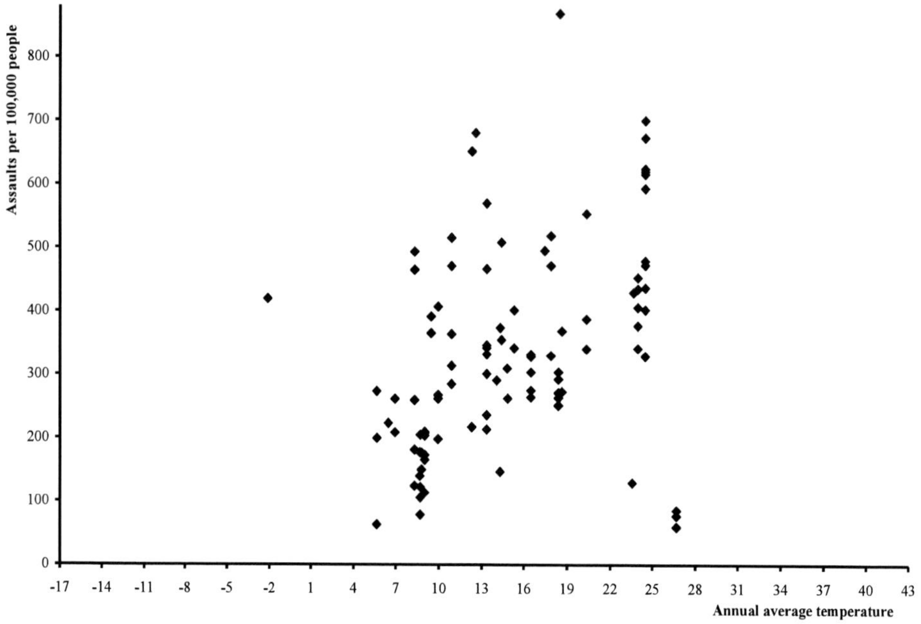

Source: crime data from FBI (2003, & other editions); temperatures from CRU (2004).

An illustration of such evidence on this debate is reported in our Chart 2, which uses USA data on 'aggravated assault' for 1999 to 2003, from FBI (2003, and other editions of the same publication). There is one point in Chart 2 for each city ('metropolitan statistical area'); we exclude a city if it contained under a quarter of a million people in 2002, to reduce the influence of random 'noise'. We average data for 5 years, because we find there is significant year-to-year variation in each location – especially in smaller towns; hence, combining data for 5 years makes the effects of temperature more clear.

Chart 2 suggests an upward trend in crime, as we go from left to right. However, the chart is not very persuasive – for example, there is a cluster of locations at the bottom-right corner of the chart, which are hot and yet have a low crime rate (this cluster is in Puerto Rico: we return to this issue when discussing the 'curvilinear hypothesis', in section 1.5 below). The point nearest the left-hand-side of Chart 2 is Anchorage, Alaska: it has a fairly high rate of assaults (420 per 100,000 people), but is cold (average temperature -2°C), which may suggest violent crimes are more common in cold weather; this issue is discussed below.

More Crime in Hot Years, and in Heat Waves

Anderson (1989) reports evidence of a link between temperature and violent crime comparing hot years with cold years. There tends to be more violent crime in a year which is unusually hot, compared to normal years (at that geographical location). Similarly, violence and murders have been found to increase following 'heat waves', i.e. brief periods of exceptionally high temperatures (McGeehin & Mirabelli, 2001: 185).

More Crime in Summer Months

Many writers claim that temperature is related to seasonal patterns in rates of violent crimes, using studies from several countries (e.g. Jacob & Lefgren, 2003: p. 1561). Anderson (1989) provides an excellent overview of the topic. Describing India, Crowther et al. (1990) wrote "The heat towards the end of the hot season is like a hammer blow; you feel listless and tired and tempers are short. It's said to be the time of year when murders and suicides take place".

To assess seasonal variations in crime, we begin with time-series temperature data from CRU (2004). This website reports data in two files: average temperature, and deviation from average. We wrote a Turbo Pascal computer program (available from the authors on request) to combine data from both files to obtain temperatures for the USA. We use temperature data for latitudes 30 to 35 North, and longitudes 115 to 120 West, i.e. the box which includes Los Angeles, from CRU (2004). These temperatures are averages for each month, and tend to understate extremes of temperature – for example, we expect temperatures to be hottest in mid-afternoon, and to vary from one day to the next, but such extremes are averaged out. We would prefer data on the hottest and coldest recorded temperature in each month at each location, but we have not found such data in sufficient detail. Temperatures are shown in the right-hand scale of Chart 3; the range is from -17°C to 43°C, for comparability with our other charts.

Chart 3. Violent crimes in Los Angeles, 1988 to 2002, by month.

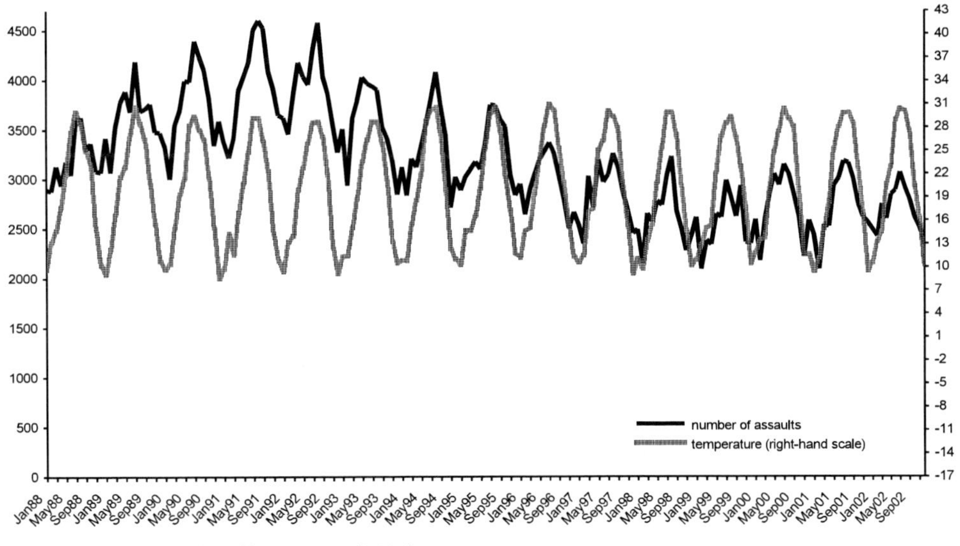

Source: LAPD (2003 and earlier); CRU (2004)

Chart 4. Aggravated assault in USA, 1993 to 1996.

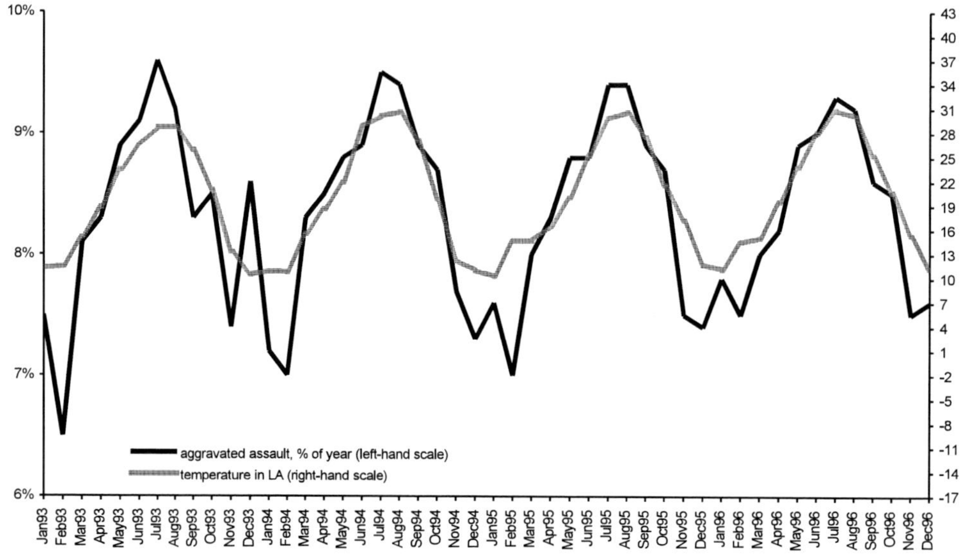

Source: crime rates from FBI (1997); temperatures from CRU (2004).

Chart 3 focuses on crime in Los Angeles (the second largest city in USA: we cannot find monthly crime data for New York, the largest city). We use data on the number of 'aggravated assaults', from LAPD (2003: table 2.3; and all equivalent reports for earlier years on the LAPD website). Chart 3 shows a clear seasonal pattern: the summer months are associated with both high temperatures, and high rates of assaults, hence Chart 3 is consistent with the claim that there tends to be more violence in hot weather. Note, however, that the seasonal variation (more crimes in summer) is not the only pattern in Chart 3: there is also a tendency for crimes to fall from about 1991 to 2002; we wonder if this might be associated with increased ownership of air-conditioners (see 'Less Crime in Temperature-Controlled Environments' section below).

We now consider national USA crime data, for 1993 to 1996 inclusive, from FBI (1997: p. 6). In Chart 4, we use reported crime occurring each month as a percentage of crime for the whole calendar year, this reduces the distraction caused by trends in crime (as seen in Chart 3), and we refer to it as the 'FBI method'. Chart 4 uses the same temperature data source as Chart 3 (but for fewer years). We use Los Angeles temperatures as a proxy for temperatures in the USA as a whole, on the assumption that the hottest month in Los Angeles coincides with the hottest month elsewhere in USA; Michael & Zumpe (cited in Anderson, 1989: p. 86) claim the maximum temperature in Atlanta and Texas occur about 40 days earlier than in Oregon and California, so our assumption is far from perfect (this approximation is simply to demonstrate that seasonality in USA crime appears to have some link with temperatures).

Chart 4 indicates a very clear link between temperature and violent crime, and is generally consistent with Chart 3. In Chart 4, the monthly rate of violent crime varies between about 7% of annual crime (in cold months), to over 9% of annual crime (in hot months). Other researchers have observed the seasonal pattern in Chart 4: for example, FBI (1997: p. 11) wrote "Violent crimes occurred most frequently in July and August. The lowest total was recorded in the month of February". Seasonal patterns similar to Chart 4 are also apparent for murders and for rapes, in our analysis of FBI (1997) data (not reported here).

Chart 5. Monthly temperature and rate of murder/attempted murder, Pakistan, 1980-9.

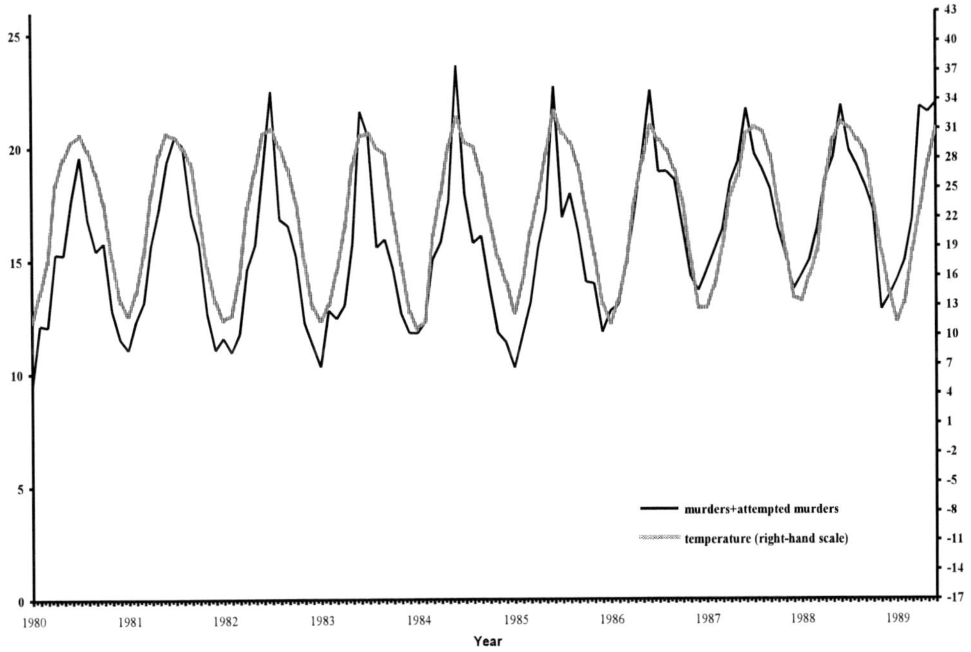

Source: Federal Bureau of Statistics (various editions).

For Chart 5, we assess violence in Pakistan by number of murders plus attempted murders, reported in Federal Bureau of Statistics (various editions). We divide the number of these crimes by our estimate of population each month (based on census data), to give a crime rate per 100,000 people; we divide this by the number of days per month, and multiply by 365 to get annual equivalents (for comparability with cross-section data below). This source (Federal Bureau of Statistics) has data from about a dozen weather stations; but missing values for some weather stations could distort results (e.g. if weather data were missing from a hot area, the Pakistan average might appear to be cool that month). Hence, we use data from only 4 weather stations, which have few missing observations: Karachi Airport (Sindh); Lahore (Punjab); Peshawar (North West Frontier Province); and Quetta (Baluchistan). We calculated the average temperature in each month, for these 4 weather stations.

Chart 5 (like Charts 3 and 4) shows very clear seasonal patterns, in both temperature and violent crime. It is consistent with the claim by many academics that temperature is related to the prevalence of violence, due to some causal mechanism (some possible causes for more violence in hot weather are discussed in section 1.3 below).

Chart 6 is based on Rajasthan, a state in north-west India. It shows clear seasonal patterns in murder rate and temperature; it looks similar to chart 5 above, but there are differences: Chart 6 shows murders, whereas Chart 5 adds data on murders and attempted murders (the left-hand scale for Chart 6 goes up to a crime rate of just over 4, compared to over 25 in the left-hand side of Chart 5).

Chart 6. Monthly temperature and murder rate, Rajasthan (India): 1965 to 1973.

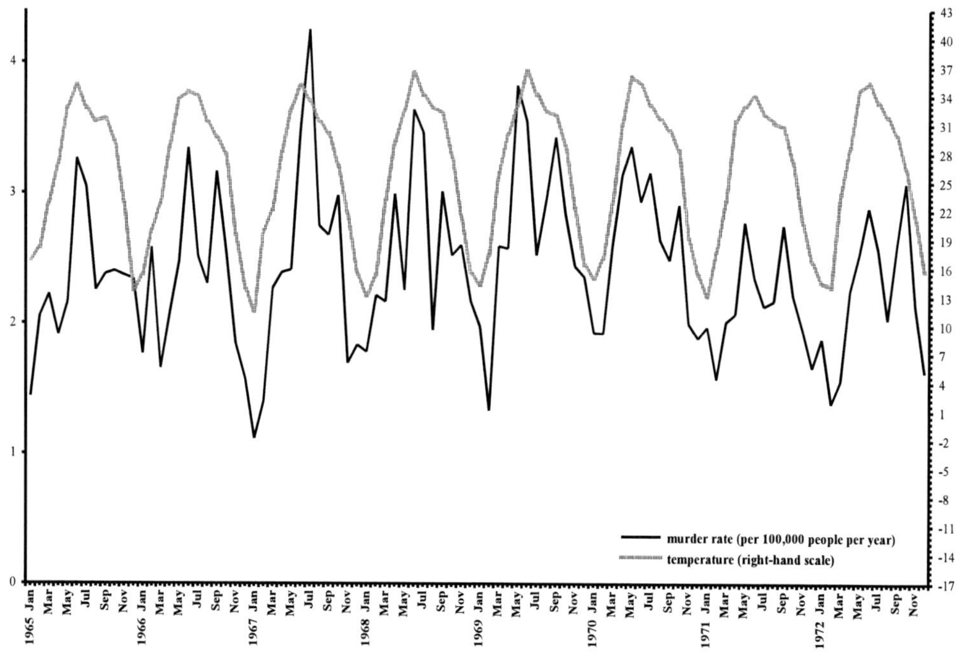

Source: Directorate of Economics & Statistics (1965, & similar up to 1972); CRU (2001).

Crime rates in Charts 3, 4, 5 and 6 are not smooth curves: there are many small vertical "spikes" (increases & decreases from month-to-month), which we consider to be 'noise' due to random factors irrelevant to this chapter. According to the 'Central Limit Theorem', such variations are generally more noticeable in smaller samples; hence, if we had used data from a city smaller than Los Angeles, it would tend to show a pattern less clear than are seen for Los Angeles in Chart 3. Similarly, Chart 5 is a relatively smooth curve for violent crimes; the murder rate in Chart 6 is less smooth, which may be due to the smaller population in Rajasthan compared to Pakistan. This suggests we cannot rely too much on the crime rate in a small town/city (where a few random assaults can noticeably distort the crime rate), and makes us cautious in relying too much on the precise details of Charts 3 to 6. For example, all four of these charts show more crime in hot months; but it is not obvious if they also show evidence of increasing crime rates in the coldest months.

Where possible, it would be desirable for future researchers to study crime and temperature data for city with a large population, to reduce the problem of random 'noise' affecting results. In some respects, it would be desirable to study regional or national data, to increase the sample size; but for a large country (such as USA), this introduces the problem that the temperature in one part of the country may be very different to the temperature in another part of the same country (in the same month).

Chart 7 uses the same crime and temperature data as Chart 3 above; but Chart 7 is a different type of chart to those used earlier in this chapter. To reduce the influence of random variation, the January temperature in Chart 7 is the average temperature of each January in the period 1988 to 2002 inclusive. Similarly, the January crime rate is the average of every

January in the period 1988 to 2002. We use a similar method for each of the other 11 months, February to December.

Chart 7. Aggravated assaults in Los Angeles, 1988 to 2002.

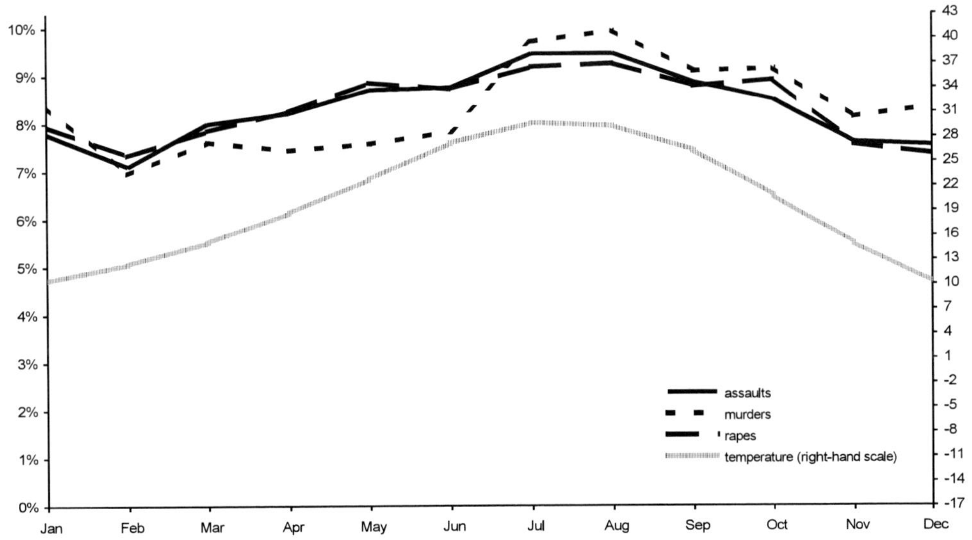

Source: crime rates from LAPD (2003 & earlier); temperatures from CRU (2004).

Chart 3 is complicated by falling crime-rates between 1991 and 2000 (this national decline in U.S. violent crime has been noted by various observers, including FBI, 1997: p. 6); we control for this (for Chart 7), by using the 'FBI method', i.e. reporting each month's crime as a percentage of crime for that calendar year. This method has advantages; but it means our Chart 7 does not show if there is more crime in Los Angeles (Chart 7) than in Alaska (Chart 8, below). Chart 7 suggests a slight increase in crimes in January, and it may seem that temperature-related violence in Los Angeles is associated with extreme cold in winter (as well as with heat in summer); but, as we show below, this interpretation of the effects of cold weather is highly questionable.

A seasonal pattern of aggravated assaults in Los Angeles is clear in Chart 7: the highest number of murders per month tends to be in the hottest months (July or August). Chart 7 also suggests a slight increase in number of assaults in the cold winter months (December and January). However, CRU (2004) reports each temperature as an average for the whole month – averaging daytime and night-time temperatures, so it conceals short-term temperature variations; it could be argued that we should study the temperature at the hottest time of day, on the hottest day of the month (rather than average temperature), rather than using the average temperature for the month. The extreme maximum temperature in Los Angeles is 43°C (NOAA, 1991: p. 9) – far higher than 31°C, the highest temperature shown in Chart 7.

Chart 8 uses Alaska crime data from Johnson (2002, and equivalent reports for 2001 & 2000 from the same website); again, we use the 'FBI method' to remove trends in violent crime, by calculating the average percentage of assaults in January (and other months) for these 3 years. Chart 8 uses temperature data for Anchorage, to represent temperatures for Alaska as a whole (this simplifies the analysis, but makes Chart 8 less reliable). For clarity,

Chart 8 shows only one type of violent crime (assaults); we found murder and rape data for Alaska (not reported here) show a similar pattern to assaults in Chart 8.

Chart 8. Assaults in Alaska, 2000 to 2002, by month.

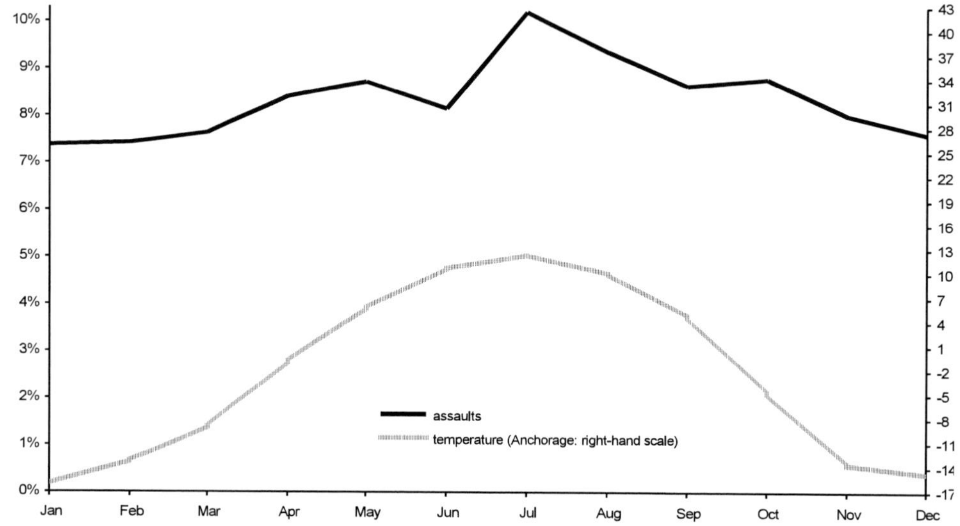

Source: Johnson (2002, and equivalent reports for 2001 & 2000); CRU (2004).

Chart 9. Assaults in Phoenix, 1996 to 2003, by month.

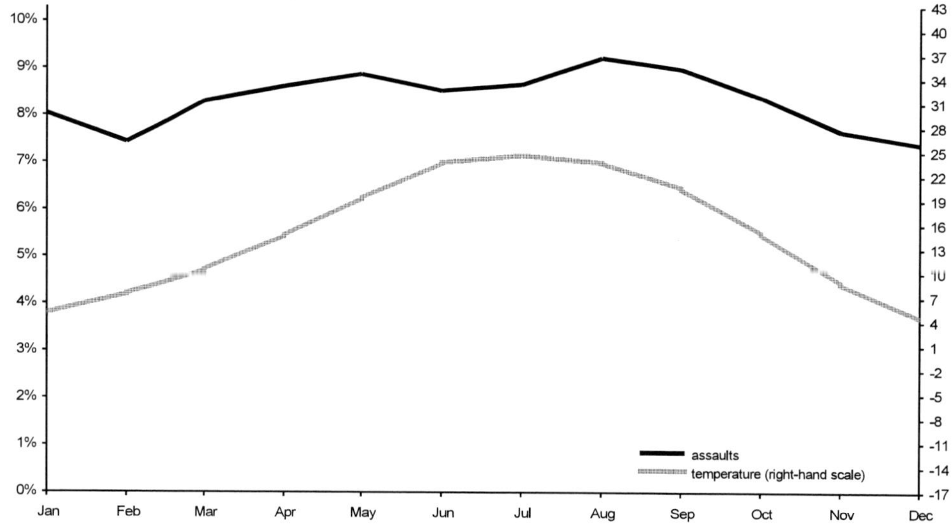

Source: Phoenix Police Department (2004) and CRU (2004).

Chart 8 seems surprising: it shows a clear peak in assaults in July, the hottest month. Alaska is very cold; if extreme temperatures lead to violence, we might expect the crime rate in Alaska to be higher in cold months – but Chart 8 makes it clear that this interpretation is mistaken. Rather, Chart 8 implies crime increases due to excessive heat, even though Alaska is cold relative to the rest of USA. We return to this issue after discussing Chart 9.

Chart 7 above suggests that crime rates in Los Angeles rise in January, when temperatures fall below about 11°C; and crime in July is high in Alaska when temperatures are about 11°C, from Chart 8. Is there something special about a temperature of 11°C? The answer is no, as shown in Chart 9, which examines Phoenix, Arizona. Chart 9 uses the same method as Charts 7 and 8 (but for a different time-period, due to data availability in Phoenix Police Department, 2004). Chart 9 (and similar charts for other U.S. states not included in this chapter) does not show a peak in crime rates at 11°C.

Charts 7, 8, and 9 all show a broadly similar seasonal pattern, in which more violent crimes occur in summer. Of these three charts, Chart 9 is perhaps the least convincing: crime rates vary little between months, and the highest crime-rates appear to be in May and August – i.e. before and after the hottest month. We cannot explain this, but would not wish to put too much trust in Chart 9 because Phoenix is a relatively small city – hence crime data from it is prone to random 'noise'.

So we are left with a puzzle: how can we explain the unexpectedly high crime-rate in Alaska in Chart 8? Because Alaskan summers are not hot, we would expect little summer crime in Alaska. But people generally react to extreme cold by wearing extremely warm clothes; if they enter a heated building without removing enough layers of clothing, they could feel very hot and react aggressively due to adrenaline (or possibly noradrenaline). An alternative explanation for Alaskan violence is acclimatization: perhaps Alaskans get so used to cold weather that they find their summers uncomfortably hot. Alternatively, perhaps Alaskan crime is higher in summer than expected simply due to random variation. More data would be helpful, to settle this issue; thankfully, many government statistical agencies (including, but not limited to, sources of crime data used in this chapter) do excellent work in making crime data available. Each year, more data becomes available to researchers; many websites (such as those in the bibliography for this chapter) are extremely helpful in this respect. Without such data being available, it would be difficult for researchers to make much progress in this topic.

More Crime in the Hottest Part of the Day

Analysis of juvenile crime in 29 USA cities by Jacob & Lefgren (2003: p. 1568) revealed a striking pattern in which the crime rate rises steadily to a peak at about 3 pm, and then falls steadily to the lowest crime-rate at about 6 am, except for a spike around midnight. This suggests aggressive behaviour is more likely in the hottest part of the day (which we think could be 3 p.m.), and least likely at the coldest part of the day (which we assume to be just before dawn: presumably about 6 a.m.); we suspect the 'spike' around midnight may be related to closing time of venues selling alcohol.

Less Crime in Temperature-Controlled Environments

Rotton & Cohn (2004: 295) claim that there tends to be less violent crime in climate-controlled environments. This claim is confirmed by our analysis of the 2005 Egypt

'Demographic and Health Survey', which asked married women respondents 'Does your husband ever … punch you with his fist or with something that could hurt you?' (El-Zanaty & Way, 2006: p. 350). Among households with neither an electric fan nor air-conditioning, 31% of women (662 cases) had been punched, compared with 24% in households with fan but no air-conditioning (4,735 cases), and 8% of households with air-conditioning (208 cases).

As discussed above, Chart 3 is complicated by falling crime-rates between 1991 and 2000. This national decline in U.S. violent crime has been noted by various observers, including FBI (1997: p. 6); it is not clear how to explain this decline. One possible explanation is air-conditioners: if humans can reduce their exposure to extremes of temperature, we would expect a corresponding fall in violent crime rates. The fraction of U.S. homes with no air-conditioning equipment fell from 44% in 1978, to 16% in 2005 (EIA, 2008); hence, increasing ownership of air-conditioning equipment may explain at least some of the falling rate of violent crime.

For Chart 5, we focused on a 10-year period, because this makes the seasonal pattern in violence more obvious. We do not report more recent data here, but our research indicates that if the horizontal axis of Chart 5 is extended to include more recent years, the seasonal pattern is less similar to the seasonal pattern in temperatures up to 1989; it is possible that this is due to more widespread ownership of electric fans or air-conditioning in Pakistan in recent years.

Rotton & Cohn (2004: 281; 279) report that about 13% of USA violent crimes occurred in homes, despite the fact that USA citizens spend about 61% of their time inside their home; perhaps this is because about 93% of southern USA households have air-conditioning, so temperature-induced violence (if it exists) is more likely to occur outside the home than inside.

Is there more Crime in very Cold Weather?

The above discussion of links between violence and temperature concentrated on effects of hot weather. If stress due to extreme temperatures is a cause of violence, as some researchers claim, we might expect more violent crimes to occur in very cold temperatures. Chart 4 above suggests an increase in violent crime in USA generally occurs in December or January – generally the coldest months in the USA. However, evidence from Alaska reported in Chart 8 above casts doubt on the idea of more violence in extremes of cold.

If crime only increased in hot weather, we might interpret this as support for the hypothesis discussed below that adrenaline is a cause of violence (testosterone may also be involved). But if crime increases in both hot and cold weather, adrenaline does not seem sufficient explanation: perhaps noradrenaline could explain increasing aggression in cold weather. Chart 1 suggests that there are more violent crimes in cold months, but this pattern is much less pronounced than the effect of hot weather. Chart 2 suggests the violent crime rate in Anchorage (Alaska) is high because of extreme cold; but this seems incompatible with Chart 8, showing that most crime in Alaska is in summer, despite the fact that Alaska never reaches temperatures most people consider 'hot'. Overall, the evidence for increased violence in extreme cold is not very persuasive – for example, Chart 8 does not suggest a dramatic increase in crime below 11°C. This suggests that we should focus on adrenaline, rather than noradrenaline, as the most plausible cause of violence in hot weather.

It is difficult to test if extreme cold leads to violence, due to availability of data. Rotton & Cohn (2004: p. 297) claim "the NAE model not only predicts an inverted U-shaped function for comfortable and high temperatures, it also predicts the same curve for low temperatures. In other words, as we have previously shown (see Figure 1 in Rotton & Cohn, 2002), the function relating violence to negative affect takes the form of a butterfly curve. However, we have been unable to detect the secondary peak during moderately cold periods that the NAE model predicts in any of our studies". It is quite possible, however, that sufficient data to make a reliable assessment of the possible effects of extreme cold has already been published somewhere; we expect that in future, researchers will be able to answer this question.

In general, we expect people to cope better with cold weather than hot weather: wearing more clothes is an easy way to reduce stress from cold weather (Anderson, 1989). Perhaps we could only detect a link between extreme cold and violence in a poor country, where many people were unable to afford warm clothing.

Relative Temperature, or Absolute Temperature?

A key issue for this research is – can we take 'temperature' directly from a thermometer, or should we consider today's temperature in the light of changing temperature in the last few days or weeks or months? If acclimatisation is important, then perhaps we should consider today's temperature relative to that experienced recently.

The temperature at which violent crimes increases is not identical in each country: Charts 7, 8 and 9 indicate violent crimes rise in summer, but also show that these three locations have very different temperatures. If there were some absolute temperature above which the human body is unable to cope, we would expect a very high crime-rate in Los Angeles, but little or no seasonal pattern in cooler places such as Alaska. We think Los Angeles residents adapt to the range of temperatures they regularly experience, and can cope fairly easily with a temperature of (for example) 20°C – whereas Alaskan residents are not used to temperatures as high as 20°C, and experience stress and increased crime-rates. It seems likely that acclimatisation is central to the way humans cope with extreme temperatures.

Is Rainfall or Humidity, or Wind Speed, Relevant?

Other possible ways to reconcile the divergent results between competing evidence include rainfall and humidity. We expect these to have opposing effects, if temperatures are high: rainfall should reduce stress, because water cools clothes & skin as it evaporates; whereas humidity (without rainfall) should increase thermal stress, because it reduces the human body's ability to lose heat by sweating. Hence rain in summer should reduce thermal stress, but rain in winter could increase stress. The effects of wind, often called 'wind chill', could also be relevant.

Summary

Seasonal patterns in violent crime (such as those shown in Charts 3 to 6) seem persuasive evidence of seasonal patterns in the prevalence of violent crime. Various hypotheses to explain the observed seasonality in violent crime rates have been proposed, and rejected, as explanations - for example:

- violence cannot be explained only by seasonal hunger (e.g. food shortages before harvest-time);
- maximum day length does not correspond to maximum crime rates (Anderson, 1989: p. 86);
- Christmas has been suggested as a cause of increased crime in winter (Anderson, 1989: p. 80); but Pakistan is a mainly Muslim country, and shows a (small) rise in violence around January (Simister & Van de Vliert, 2005).

We think the most plausible explanation for seasonal patterns in violent crime (reported in this chapter) is temperature. In particular, high temperatures each summer seem to be associated with higher rates of violence. The obvious inference is that extreme temperature is the cause, and crime the effect; but we cannot rule out the possibility that the association is spurious, and is the result of intervening variables other than temperature.

When assessing this topic, we need to note the limitations of much previous research in this field – which often uses annual data. Where possible, we encourage researchers to use data which can take account of seasonal variations (monthly data should be sufficiently detailed; but weekly or daily data could have advantages). Most sources of crime data we are aware of use annual data; perhaps the best sources of monthly data for this topic are for locations within the USA, such as Los Angeles (see Chart 3 above). As well as making monthly data available, published crime statistics in cities such as Los Angeles are helpful because they refer to a large city – a large enough population for much of the monthly crime data to be reliable (whereas if a researcher chose to study a small town, we would expect random "noise" to mask the systematic seasonal component in crime statistics).

1.3. Cause of the Link between Temperature and Aggression

Introduction

Section 1.2 provides evidence that there are links between temperature and violence. If we knew why some people are violent, we might be able to reduce violence in future. It would be helpful if we could understand this phenomenon better; in particular, why does extreme heat seem to make people aggressive?

How pleasant or hostile a particular temperature "feels" depends on many factors, include humidity; air movement; clothing; and work intensity. Acclimatization (see Brück, 1989) may also be important – for example, we expect hot weather to be more stressful if the temperature rose dramatically in the last few days.

Machismo Cultures in Hot Countries

Some writers suggest a 'culture of violence' may be responsible for more aggression in areas such as southern USA (the hotter parts of the United States). Nisbett & Cohen (1999) claim that cultural differences explain why homicide is twice as high in small cities in the South and Southwest as the rest of USA. Doyle (2000) claimed that firearms, combined with the Southern 'culture of honor', explain why homicide rates are high in the former Confederate states of USA.

Evidence reported by Van de Vliert et al. (1999), at first reading, seems persuasive to explain why some countries (and some regions within large countries) have more violence. However, there seems to be considerable evidence (from several countries) of seasonal variation in crimes, as discussed in section 1.2 above; cultural explanations seem unable to explain why there is more violent crimes at hot times of day, or in hot months of the year. A cultural explanation also seems unable to explain why there is less crime in air-conditioned homes (Rotton & Cohn, 2004: 295).

Hence, we think it more likely that a cultural explanation is not the true cause of observed patterns in violence. In fact, the patterns found by writers such as Van de Vliert et al. (1999) are generally consistent with medical explanations discussed later in this section, in that hot countries could be more violent because of stress hormones. A 'macho' culture may be an effect rather than a cause (Anderson, 1989: p. 79); the fact that 'macho' cultures are associated with hot countries could indicate that such 'macho' cultures and high violence prevalence are both effects of temperature. In our view, writers who believe in culture as the fundamental cause of high rates of violence need to provide more evidence to justify their arguments – if they can't explain seasonal patterns in crime rates, their arguments seem (in our view) weak and unconvincing. We discuss this further in the conclusion to this chapter.

Psychological Explanations of the Temperature-Violence Link

Previous researchers have proposed psychological explanations of violent crime patterns: more crime in hot countries, and seasonal patterns in crime. Talan (2005) claims that there are two types of aggression: planned violence, such as armed robbery; and unplanned violence, where an aggressor over-reacts to a situation. Talan uses the term 'hot aggression' to refer impulsive violence, without suggesting a link with thermal stress. But the implication is that only certain types of people (for example, people with autism, ADHD, or mood disorders) become violent when under stress; and it is possible that medication could break the link between heat and violence.

Medical researchers have suggested various possible mechanisms to account for the apparent link between temperature and aggression. Anderson (1989) discusses five hypotheses:

- negative affect escape;
- simple negative affect;
- excitation transfer/misattribution;
- cognitive neoassociation;

- physiological-thermoregulatory.

The first four hypotheses are psychological, and inter-related: for example, Anderson (1989: p. 76) suggests the excitation transfer/misattribution hypothesis is a "sophisticated version of the simple negative affect model". But Anderson (1989: pp. 93-4) found these hypotheses don't perform well: "The bulk of the studies strongly contradicted" the simple negative affect model, and the cognitive neoassociation model appears to be contradicted by evidence. Anderson (1989: p. 93) suggested that "the failure of experimental laboratory studies" to confirm any of the four psychological hypotheses suggests we should consider abandoning them. Anderson (1989) did not test the last of the above five hypotheses, because it is too complicated to test; we investigate this (physiological – thermoregulatory) hypothesis below.

Stress Hormones as an Explanation for the Temperature-Violence Link

This part of the chapter focuses on possible medical explanations of observed patterns: more crime in hot countries, and seasonal patterns in crime. We suggest a medical explanation for these seasonal variations in crime rates, based on stress hormones (adrenaline, and perhaps noradrenaline and/or testosterone). The human body generates adrenaline and/or noradrenaline in response to excessive heat; this response to extreme temperature is helpful in keeping the body within safe limits, but it may – as a side effect – lead to violence.

Strain occurs if temperature & other stresses "exceed the body's tolerance threshold" (Mawson, 1999: p. 177). Very hot or very cold weather are stressful to humans, and the human body reacts to extreme temperatures by producing stress hormones (catecholamines). It is vital for a human to keep the blood temperature within a narrow range of temperatures: 37°C is a typical temperature in the inner 'core' of the human body, but brain damage and death can result from a prolonged core temperature above 40°C (Brück, 1999: p. 642). Humans need stress hormones, to cope with the stressful environments in which we live; but stress hormones may have undesirable side effects. For example, adrenaline is associated with aggression.

Temperature extremes, like other forms of stress, cause the human body to produce hormones. We focus mainly on three hormones: adrenaline (also known as epinephrine); noradrenaline (also known as norepinephrine); and testosterone.

- Adrenaline level in the blood is higher in very hot conditions, in both men and women (al-Hadramy, 1989; Jezova, Kvetnansky & Vigas, 1994); but blood adrenaline level is not raised by cold weather (Frank et al., 1997; Sramek et al., 2000). Effects of adrenaline include vasodilation (expanding peripheral blood vessels, which can cool the body); increasing the rate of heartbeat; raising blood pressure; and stimulating respiration – these effects of adrenaline "probably contributing thereby to the regulation of body temperature in mammals" (Barrington, 1983: p. 1081).
- Noradrenaline blood levels are higher in extreme heat or cold, in both men and women (al-Hadramy, 1989; Frank et al., 1997; Jezova, Kvetnansky & Vigas, 1994;

Sramek et al., 2000). In cold weather, noradrenaline has a vasoconstrictor effect – contracting blood vessels, which can reduce heat loss through the skin (Pocock & Richards, 1999: p. 541); noradrenaline also reduces the heart rate, and slightly increases blood sugar level & metabolism (Barrington, 1983: p. 1081). Noradrenaline is associated with 'nonshivering thermogenesis' (Brück, 1999: p. 633).

Simister & Cooper (2005) claim violence is a side effect of stress hormones such as noradrenaline. Links between violence & temperature may reflect the need for humans to keep vital organs within a very narrow temperature range; outside a person's "comfort zone", there are various things he/she can do, such as seeking shade or drinking – but if these aren't sufficient, the body has an emergency response: Kukkonen-Harjula et al. (1989) found more noradrenaline in blood of heat-stressed people. This response to temperature may, in turn, cause violence: Haller, Makara & Kruk (1998) claim noradrenaline causes aggression. Adrenaline prepares a human to run away from, or use aggression towards, a threat. Noradrenaline could have similar effects: research by Kemper (1990: p. 31) suggests a relationship between noradrenaline and "anger, which is a frequent precursor of aggression".

It would be desirable to understand the shape of the curve relating temperature to aggression. Charts 3 and 7 above are consistent with the claim that summer temperatures in Los Angeles, and presumably in many other parts of USA, are stressful. However, we cannot use Chart 4 to assess which temperatures are stressful, because of temperature differences between parts of the USA (the Chart 4 temperatures are for Los Angeles, not for USA as a whole).

Testosterone as an Explanation for the Temperature-Violence Link

Testosterone is a sex hormone. Testosterone levels are found to be higher in summer; Andersson et al. (2003) conclude that air temperature, rather than light level, accounts for this seasonal variation of testosterone in men. It has been claimed that testosterone may cause higher incidence of rape in summer, but Anderson (1989: p. 85) cites evidence casting doubt on this hypothesis: increases in rapes occurs earlier in the year than the rise in testosterone levels.

If testosterone does cause rape, it might be argued that testosterone is a cause of violence in general. However, rape is sexual violence; perhaps sex hormones are related to rapes, whereas other types of violent crime don't have an obvious sexual cause. Even if testosterone were found to be a cause of increased rapes in summer, we are not aware of any evidence that other types of violence are associated with testosterone. Mazur (cited in Kemper, 1990: p. 29) claimed "testosterone affects dominance behaviour but not aggressive behaviour".

Kemper suggests the interaction of noradrenaline and testosterone cause aggression; but testosterone may be an effect – rather than a cause – of violence (Kemper, 1990: pp. 29-33). Testosterone levels are much higher in men than in women (ten times higher, on average, according to Kemper, 1990: p. 134); but there is evidence that "women and men are equal in rates in nonlethal violence" (cited in Kemper, 1990: p. 139), which casts doubt on the importance of testosterone in violence.

Other Hormones as possible Explanations for the Temperature-Violence Link

Apart from adrenaline, noradrenaline, and testosterone (discussed above), other hormones could be related to temperature, at least indirectly: for example, circulating adrenaline can lead to release of ACTH (Adrenocorticotropic Hormone), which can affect the level of glucocorticoids (the group of hormones which includes cortisol) in blood (Barrington, 1983: pp. 1075-6). But Kurina, Schneider & Waite (2004) and others report that cortisol levels usually rise suddenly on waking, and then gradually fall during the day; this does not suggest a strong relationship between cortisol and temperature (we would expect temperatures to be highest about mid-day).

Another possible explanation of seasonal patterns in human behaviour is Seratonin: Preti et al. (2002: p. 477) referred to evidence of circadian and seasonal patterns, and claimed "The intrinsic circadian and seasonal rhythms of some neuronal systems, particularly those of serotonin, involved in the control of mood and impulses, are thought to favour the behavioural rhythms observed". However, we are not aware of any evidence that seratonin causes violence.

Summary

There are various competing explanations for the link between extreme temperatures and violence. Of the hypotheses discussed above, we find the stress hormones noradrenaline and/or adrenaline to be the most plausible. Perhaps the best way to settle this issue is by more medical research: in a temperature-controlled environment, it should be possible to measure blood concentrations of hormones such as adrenaline. Note, however, that ethical problems may be a major obstacle: research should not put the subjects at risk.

1.4. Is Heat-Related Violence Due to High Temperature, or to Acclimatisation?

Introduction

This section considers whether the temperature-crime link is due to temperature, or the rate of change of temperature, or some combination. Humans can acclimatise to different temperatures: for example, a person might learn to cope with (and even enjoy) a summer temperature which would have seemed very unpleasant, if they had suddenly experienced it in winter. But perhaps there is a price to pay for such acclimatisation: it may be stressful to the human body, while this adjustment process is going on. Could such stress lead to aggression and violence?

Possible Links between Acclimatisation and Violence

Acclimatisation is about how people respond to changes in temperature: we might expect hot weather to be more stressful if the temperature rose dramatically in recent days. Studying evidence reported in section 1.2 above, it appears that very high temperatures lead to violence. In Charts 3, 4, 5 and 6, we see a temperature variation shaped approximately like a sine wave – and the crime rate seems to follow a similar shape. Could acclimatisation explain the patterns in Charts 3 to 6? The simple answer seems to be 'no': the highest rate of change for a sine wave is at about the average value, i.e. sin(zero), corresponding to spring (rising temperature) and autumn (falling temperature). If rapidly rising temperature cause violence, we would expect crime rates to peak in spring; but, as shown in Charts 3 to 6, violent crimes are more common in summer than in spring. But beware simple answers: temperatures don't exactly follow a sine wave. There is a drop in murders in Chart 7 (April to June) over a temperature range about 24 to 27°C. Perhaps people find it less stressful when temperatures remain approximately constant: the range 24 to 27°C (Los Angeles) occur in periods when temperatures are not rising quickly. To illustrate this, we report Chart 10 below. It compares temperature with the rate of change of temperature (this graph looks reminiscent of a 'hysteresis' graph, in magnetism). In Chart 10, rate of change is measured by increase in temperature from last month to this month. It would be interesting to consider other time-periods (for example, considering temperature change from day to day); daily and even hourly data are available for some weather stations, such as Pierce College (2008).

Chart 10 is based on the same temperature data as Charts 3 and 7 above; but the time period is limited to the period January 1989 to December 1995 (more points on this Chart would make it harder to interpret). Chart 10 puts the rate at which temperature changed, since the preceding month, on the vertical axis. Points near the top of Chart 10 indicate when the temperature rose quickly (usually in summer); whereas points near the bottom of Chart 10 indicate when the temperature fell quickly (usually in winter) – in one month, the temperature fell almost 10 degrees since the previous month. In Chart 10, months in which temperatures rose fastest (at about 26°C on the horizontal axis of Chart 10) are also among the hottest months. Similarly, the hottest months (about 31°C in Chart 10) were times when temperatures rose. This means we cannot easily separate effects of high temperatures from effects of rising temperatures.

In Chart 10, temperatures rise most quickly when the temperature is about 28°C – at this temperature (typically about April), temperatures sometimes rise about 7°C from one month to the next. By the time we got to the hottest months, though, temperature rise is less dramatic: when temperatures reach 30°C, they usually only increase by a few degrees per month. Los Angeles residents will be acclimatising to the heat in early summer. Hence, if there were a temperature of (for example) 28°C, we might expect Los Angeles residents to cope better when temperatures are falling (in about September: below the horizontal axis in Chart 10), than when temperatures are increasing (about July: above the horizontal axis in Chart 10).

We can investigate crime using Chart 10, by studying the points. We used two sizes of point on Chart 10: bigger points indicate months where crime in that month was more than 8.5% of crime in that year, whereas smaller points indicate crime below 8.5%. Hence for Chart 10, we adopt what we call the 'FBI method', to avoid results being too much influenced by declining trends in violent crime. If acclimatisation from cold weather to hot weather is the cause of violence, we would expect bigger points to be at the top of Chart 10; on the other hand, if very hot temperatures cause high crime rates, the bigger points should be on the right-hand-side of Chart 10. The bigger points are on the right, not the top, of Chart 10; this suggests that acclimatisation is not a major cause of violence (in Los Angeles, at least).

Chart 10. Temperature versus rate of temperature change, Los Angeles,, 1989-1995.

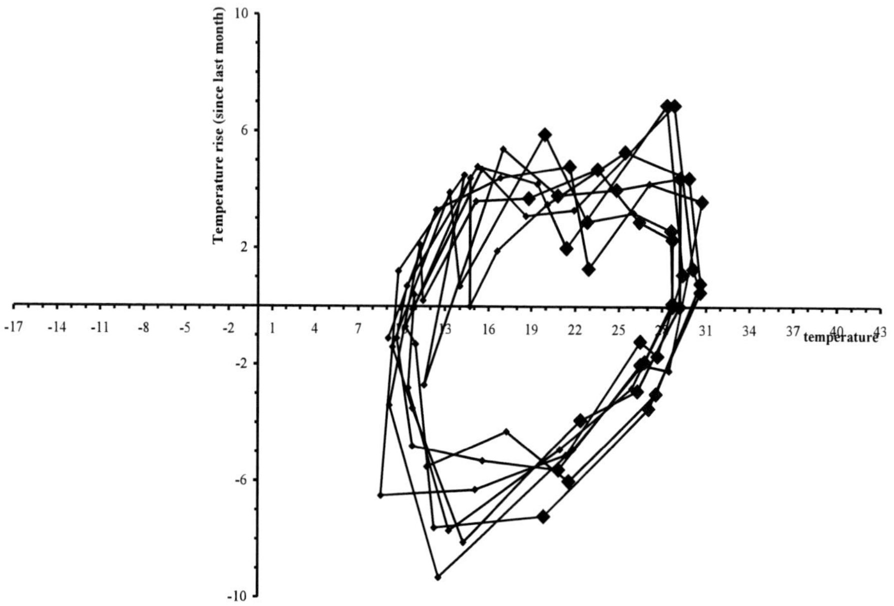

Source: crime rates from LAPD (2003 & earlier); temperatures from CRU (2004).

Regression analysis on the Los Angeles data used in this paper might give more reliable results than the graphical method (analysing Chart 10). However, we do not know exactly how to model this: perhaps acclimatisation takes several months, in which case we would need a complicated equation to estimate thermal stress (in terms of current temperature, and temperature in recent months). There is considerable "noise" in crime data, as shown in (for example) Charts 3 to 6: these mean we cannot describe the shape of the seasonal pattern in violent crimes exactly by using a sine wave. Hence, we cannot tell if acclimatisation has some influence on violence. In principle, a time-series regression technique such as ARIMA might be used to assess if acclimatisation is relevant to crime rates, but practical problems with the data make this a difficult exercise. One of the best datasets we know of for such research is Los Angeles, but it is clear from Chart 3 that temperature does not explain all violent crime: there seems to be a peak in violence about 1991, followed by a steady decline, and this might cause ARIMA regression to give misleading results.

Another way it is possible to investigate acclimatisation is to compare different countries or regions with the same summer temperature, but with different ranges of temperature. An example is Kerala, in south India: it has a high average temperature, but relatively little annual variation – even the winters are warm in Kerala. Researchers have commented that Kerala is more developed than most of India, in terms of liberal attitudes towards women; whereas north-central India has much higher rates of violent crimes against women, and this could be related to the dramatic changes in temperature between winter and summer, in (for example) Delhi, if acclimatisation causes male violence against women.

Medical Evidence on Effects of Acclimatisation

Numerous studies into human physiology have investigated the relationship between acclimatisation and hormones; taken together, this literature suggests we should not expect a simple relationship between acclimatisation and stress hormones. For example, O'Brien et al. (2000: p. 246) report that if a human subject is acclimatised by repeatedly <u>resting</u> in cold air or cold water, causing their skin and core temperatures to fall, the noradrenaline level in their blood tends to rise; but if the subject acclimatised to cold by <u>exercising</u> in cold water, their skin temperature fell but their core temperature did not – and this type of acclimatisation did not raise their noradrenaline level.

Summary

The discussion in this section suggests that it is temperature, rather than changes in temperature, which lead to violence. We need to be careful, however, before dismissing the role of acclimatisation. We think it plausible that acclimatisation is, at least to some extent, causing an increase in crime if the temperature is hot and (in recent days) has risen quickly. In other respects, acclimatisation is useful: if it helps humans to cope with extreme temperatures, then it may be reducing crime rates (compared to what would happen if humans could not acclimatise).

1.5. The 'Curvilinear' Hypothesis, Versus Other Claims

Introduction

This section considers the question of the shape of the curve relating temperature to aggression. Anderson (1989: p. 75) suggests several possible shapes for the curve:

- Inverted-U: aggression is highest at a particular temperature, and then declines.
- M-shaped (two inverted Us): cold or heat cause aggression, but aggression declines at very extreme temperatures.
- Linear: aggression increases steadily as temperature increases.
- J-shaped: aggression is not affected until a critical temperature, above which further temperature rises raise aggression rates.
- U-shaped: there is an optimal range of temperatures, but extremes of heat or cold cause aggression.

One widely-discussed shape of the temperature-versus-aggression relationship is the 'curvilinear' relationship, promoted by – among others – Evert Van de Vliert and his co-authors. The 'curvilinear hypothesis' fits in the 'Inverted-U' pattern in Anderson's list above. Other writers who have investigated the 'curvilinear hypothesis' include Rotten & Cohn (2004: pp. 295-6): "It is important to note that we have not claimed that violence is always a curvilinear function of temperature, as our critics have suggested. We have instead concluded that although there are times when the relationship between temperature and violence is curvilinear, there are also times (e.g., early evening hours) when it is either linear or accelerated by alcohol consumption, and there are even times (e.g., early morning hours) when temperature and violence do not appear to be related."

To assess the 'curvilinear hypothesis', we used data from Van de Vliert et al. (1999), who studied political violence in 136 countries (riots and armed attacks, from 1948 to 1977). We use their violence data to create Chart 11, in which each symbol represents one country. Like Van de Vliert et al. (1999), we calculate logarithms to minimise the distorting effects of very high rates of violence in some countries: Log(1+political crime rate per 100,000) adding 1 because no political crime is reported in some countries (the vertical axis in Chart 11). We use monthly temperature data from Mitchell et al. (2003), calculating the average temperature in all 12 months of the year (whereas Van de Vliert et al. use temperature in the capital city). In the data used to create Chart 11, no riots or assaults (from 1948 to 1977) are reported in three countries, all of which have small populations: Barbados; Central African Republic; and The Gambia. However, these three countries do experience violence, and they might report political violence if we had data for more years. Similar problems apply in other small countries; it may be safer to exclude countries with small populations in future research, to avoid being misled by 'noisy' data.

Chart 11 is similar to that produced by Van de Vliert et al. (1999). Chart 11 seems to show approximately an inverted-V shape, in which violent political crimes tend to become less frequent at high temperatures: it appears to support the 'curvilinear hypothesis'. However, Simister & Van de Vliert (2005) suggest a chart like Chart 11 is unreliable, because it relies on annual data: we cannot tell if most political crimes occurred in summer, or in winter (or at the same prevalence rate in all seasons). Monthly data is required, for us to know if the violence occurred at high or low temperatures. Unfortunately, our investigations suggest that data used by Van de Vliert et al. (1999) is not yet available on a monthly basis (we encourage all providers of crime data to report data for each month of each year, if possible). This problem does not prove Van de Vliert et al. are wrong; but it does mean we can't rely on charts like Chart 11 to show they are correct.

For more evidence, consider USA data in Chart 2, near the start of this chapter: there seems to be non-linear pattern, in which cities with temperatures over about 25°C have very low rates of assaults; this might be considered support for the 'curvilinear hypothesis'. Cities at the bottom right of Chart 2 (at temperatures over 25°C) are in Puerto Rico; they are 'outliers', perhaps because temperatures vary little (from about 24°C in February to 28°C in July-September: CRU, 2004), so Puerto Ricans – if acclimatised – can cope easily with the temperatures. We discuss the issue of acclimatisation in section 1.4 above. But Puerto Rico is unusual in respects other than just temperature, such as being poorer than the rest of USA. Another factor is rainfall: there is more rain in Puerto Rico than in most of USA (for example, June rainfall in Puerto Rico is 184 mm, compared to 69 mm in USA: calculated from Mitchell et al., 2003). Hence, we cannot be confident from data we currently have, whether acclimatisation or rainfall (or something else) is the correct explanation for the anomaly of

Puerto Rico. If we exclude the Puerto Rico cluster, then we lose all locations with temperatures above 25°C, so Chart 2 seems unreliable to assess the curvilinear hypothesis.

Chart 11. Political violence by average temperature, in various countries.

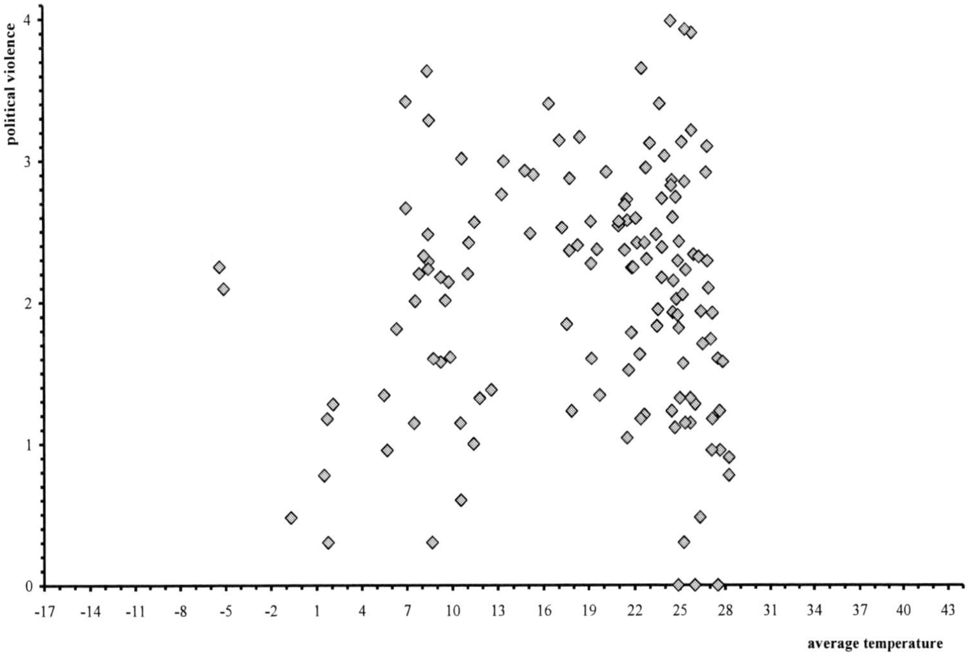

Source: crime data from Van de Vliert et al. (1999); temperatures from Mitchell et al. (2003).

To examine this issue further, we create Chart 12 from Los Angeles data. We consider this the best dataset we have to explore this issue, because Los Angeles is a big city (we would prefer New York City crime data, if it were available, because New York has a larger population – hence there is less likelihood of random variation distorting results). Chart 12 uses the same data as Chart 3, but Chart 12 is a scatter graph rather than a time-series graph.

A glance at Chart 12 suggests a linear graph (with a positive slope); but we think Chart 12 is actually V-shaped, with the minimum level of violence at about 11°C. This optimal temperature will differ from 11°C in other geographical locations, due to acclimatization. Another puzzle is why Los Angeles residents don't acclimatize in such a way that the minimum point of the V-shape is about the middle of Chart 12. But no doubt acclimatization does occur, and this will have affected Chart 12 (we cannot tell what shape Chart 12 would have been, if acclimatization had not occurred). The V-shaped graph in Chart 12 surprised us, because we expected a wide range of temperatures at which humans feel comfortable – suggesting a U-shaped curve. For example, a temperature of 20°C doesn't sound particularly hot, and yet Chart 12 suggests there is more crime at 20°C than at 11°C. Note, however, that a month in which the average temperature is 20°C includes days much hotter than 20°C. Daily data (if available) would be preferable, but still imperfect: temperatures also vary during each day.

Above a set-point (usually a blood temperature around 37°C), the human body's mechanisms promoting heat loss operate; whereas at temperatures below the set-point, heat-conserving & heat-generating systems operate (Pocock & Richards, 1999: p. 541). This suggests we should expect a V-shaped curve in Chart 12. Roberts (1986: pp. 238-9) suggests that for a naked man, 29°C is comfortable (Roberts does not indicate whether a woman has different preferences to a man); Brück (1989: p. 631) suggests a seated, lightly clothed person in 50% humidity will prefer a temperature around 25 to 26°C (but other factors such as work and acclimatization also affect preferences). Humphreys (1995: p. 8) claims that humans prefer temperatures ranging from 17°C to 33°C. These preferred temperatures are all hotter than the minimum-crime temperature in Chart 12, which we think is about 11°C; why are these temperatures so different?

Chart 12. Aggravated assaults versus temperature, Los Angeles (monthly data, 1988-2002).

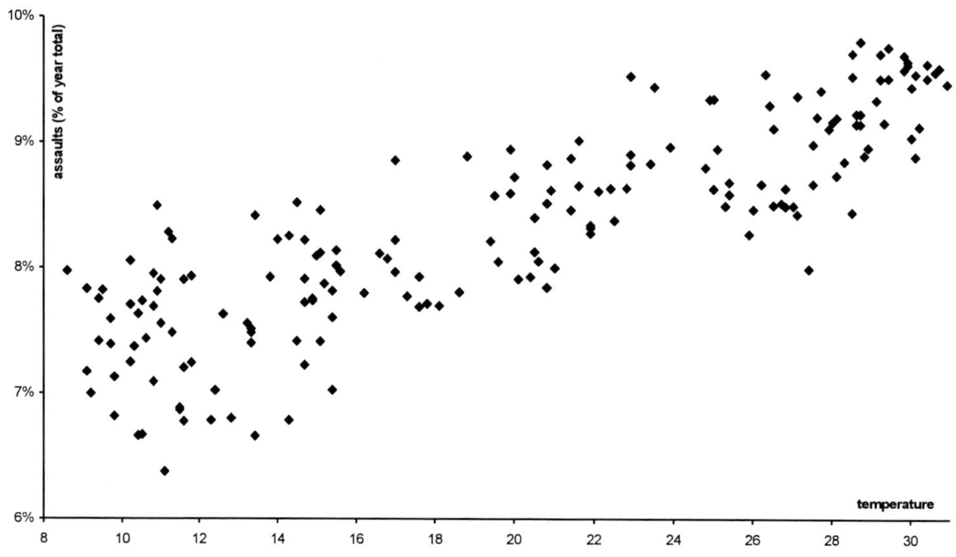

Source: LAPD (2003 and earlier); CRU (2004).

Roberts (1986: pp. 238-9) describes an "efficiency range", in which the body can control temperature by physical means (such as vasodilation and sweating); if the temperature is hotter or colder than this efficiency range, the body augments physical cooling with an emergency response, to increase the metabolic rate. The 'efficiency range' view appears to predict a U-shaped curve in Chart 12; but vasodilation involves adrenaline, so perhaps adrenaline levels rise when temperatures are outside the efficiency range. Roberts (1986: pp. 238-9) suggests the lower end of the efficiency range is about 27°C for a naked man, not much below the optimal temperature of 29°C (Roberts doesn't state the upper end of the efficiency range); the small gap between 27 and 29°C suggests the efficiency range is fairly narrow, and is unlikely to include a temperature as low as 11°C. We suggest the optimal temperature is as low as 11°C in Los Angeles due to a combination of factors including warm clothes, and heated work & home environments.

Our understanding of this topic could be improved by laboratory studies. If a person's blood adrenaline level was measured while the subject was exposed to a wide range of temperatures (while wearing normal clothing), it should be possible to produce a graph to compare with our Chart 12. We do not know of any such research: the nearest we have found is studies which measure adrenaline levels only at very hot or very cold temperatures, and are often complicated by immersion in water or intense exercise.

The shape of the curve in Chart 12 may tell us about the underlying process: Anderson (1989: p. 75) explores four psychology-based explanations for seasonal crime patterns, and suggests they predict an inverted-U-shaped or M-shaped relationship (at very extreme temperatures, aggressors do not confuse irritation due to uncomfortable temperature with irritation caused by a nearby person). Baron & Bell's research (cited in Anderson, 1989: p. 76) suggests a peak in aggression about 29°C. We do not see a fall in crime above 29°C in Chart 12; but Chart 12 doesn't tell us what happens above 31°C, and hence does not convincingly reject Baron & Bell's ideas. It would be interesting if future researchers analyze locations experiencing a wider range of temperatures than Los Angeles, to assess whether crime really does increase below about 11°C, and whether crime rates fall at temperatures over 31°C.

In summary, our evidence from Chart 12 seems consistent with the adrenaline hypothesis, and is difficult to reconcile with psychological models (which generally predict an inverted-U shape graph: see Anderson, 1989). However, we expected the effects of adrenaline to generate a U-shaped curve, rather than the V-shaped curve we found; and our adrenaline hypothesis is only supported if we assume adrenaline is produced over a wide range of temperatures (down to an average monthly temperature of about 11°C in Los Angeles). In addition, assuming adrenaline is not produced at low temperatures, there must be a different cause of aggression (such as noradrenaline) below 11°C.

We now consider the rate (per hundred thousand people, per year) of murders plus attempted murders in Pakistan, in Chart 13, using the same sources of temperature and crime data as chart 5 above. Chart 13 clearly has some 'outliers', i.e. points above or below the general trend. But the general pattern is similar to our Chart 12 above: there is a general increase in murder rates in the hottest months, and no support for the claims of Van de Vliert et al. (1999) of a curvilinear hypothesis.

Previous researchers (such as Brück, 1989: p. 631) discuss many influences on how hot humans feel – including humidity. Perspiration is one way humans keep cool, if the temperature is high; but sweating tends to be less effective if the air is very humid. Chart 13 includes this, as a third dimension: months in which rainfall is over 40 mm (wet months are shown as black, other months as white). Rain seems to have complicated effects on violence. On the right-hand-side of Chart 13, there is less violence in rainy months than in dry months; whereas the opposite effect is seen on the left-hand-side of Chart 13, where there tends to be more violence in months with high rainfall (although some cold & rainy months have low crime rates). In hot weather, rain falling on skin or clothes will cool the body as it evaporates. But in cold weather, the cooling effects of rain can make people too cold, increasing thermal stress. Many wet months are on the right-hand-side of Chart 13, suggesting that wet summers tend to be associated with high temperatures. And we can also observe in Chart 13 that months which are both hot & wet tend to have lower crime rates than would be expected, given their high temperature.

Next, we consider murders in Rajasthan (a state in North-West India), in Chart 14. The horizontal axis uses temperatures from Bikaner, using data from CRU (2001). Chart 14 confirms the impression of Charts 12 and 13 above, that the crime rates seem to keep rising as the temperature gets hotter. Again, this evidence appears to reject the curvilinear hypothesis –

unless the crime rate starts to fall at temperatures well over 30°C, i.e. at temperatures above those experienced in Pakistan.

Chart 13. Murder/attempted murder in Pakistan, by temperature (monthly data, 1980-9).

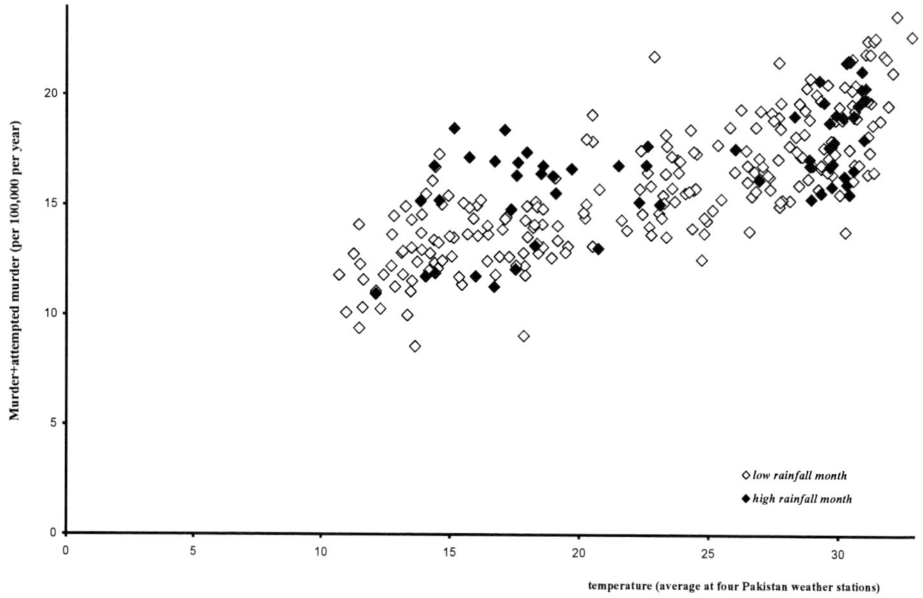

Source: Federal Bureau of Statistics, various editions.

Chart 14. Temperature and murder rate in Rajasthan, India (monthly data, 1964-72).

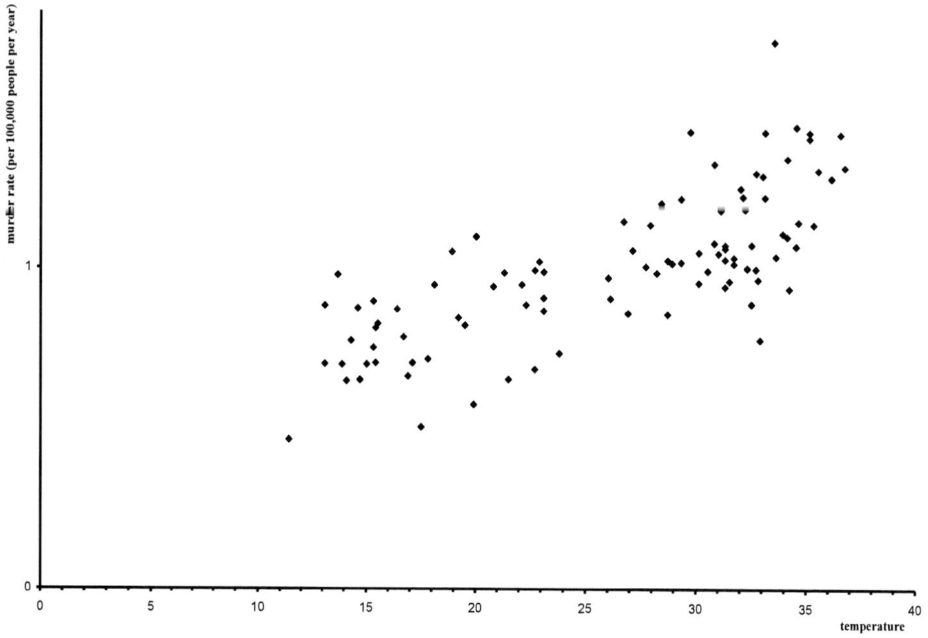

Source: Directorate of Economics & Statistics (1965, & similar up to 1972); CRU (2001).

But Charts 12 to 14 are not necessarily conclusive evidence: we don't have evidence of what happens above about 37°C in Chart 14 (or above about 32°C in Charts 12 and 13) – perhaps there is a fall at temperatures above 37°C. A similar problem applies to the question of whether there are more crimes at very cold temperatures: Charts 13 and 14 don't tell us about temperatures below about 11°C, and even Chart 12 has no observations below 8°C. Nevertheless, Charts 12 to 14 all seem to reject the 'curvilinear hypothesis': they seem to show a relationship between temperature & violence which is fairly close to being linear, at least for the temperature range 8°C to 37°C.

Summary

This section considered the possibility of 'curvilinear' effects of temperature on violent crime rates. Charts 12, 13 and 14 offer fairly persuasive evidence that the pattern is a monotonic, rather than curvilinear, relationship between temperature and violence. But there are reasons to question this interpretation: there may be some non-linear patterns in some of Charts 12, 13 and 14 (e.g. there seems to be a fall in violence if the Los Angeles temperature is about 27°C in Chart 12). Also, there may be a decline in violence if the temperature rose above the range of temperatures shown in Charts 12, 13 and 14, i.e. more than about 37 °C.

1.6. Conclusion

Introduction

This chapter discusses evidence on the hypothesis that violent crime rates vary from month to month in a seasonal pattern, and this evidence is consistent with the hypothesis that the seasonal pattern is caused by temperature. We think these seasonal patterns are due to the side effects of stress hormones (which the body generates to cope with thermal stress): we interpret our findings in terms of the effect of thermal stress, and hence of stress hormones, in causing impulsive and violent behaviour.

Culture of Masculinity

What should we make of the claim by Van de Vliert et al. (1999), that the link between temperature and violence is a result of masculine, or perhaps 'macho', culture? The discussion in section 1.3 above appears to dismiss their claims – a culture-based theory can't explain seasonal changes such as more crimes in summer, or more violence at hot parts of the day; and it can't explain why air-conditioned homes are less prone to violence. Evidence of a link between temperature and violence in section 1.2 can all be explained by a medical approach (e.g. based on adrenaline and/or noradrenaline); a cultural theory can explain some, but not all, of the section 1.2 evidence. It may surprise readers, then, to find that we still think writing by Van de Vliert and his collaborators is among the most exciting work ever published in this field. Why are we impressed?

A key point about Van de Vliert et al.'s work is that it does not conflict with medical explanations of the temperature – violence link. It is entirely plausible that if extreme temperatures lead to violence, they may also lead to 'machismo' (also called 'macho') attitudes and a culture of masculinity. Given the mass of evidence provided by Van de Vliert et al., and other researchers, it seems probable that masculine cultures are indeed associated with hot countries. We suggest the causal chain shown in Figure 1 is a plausible explanation for the evidence discussed in this chapter.

Hence, the cultural patterns observed by Van de Vliert et al. (1999) could be interpreted as confirmation that there is indeed a medical response to very hot weather. This is not particularly surprising, because the evidence of a link between temperature and violence is overwhelming (see section 1.2). But work by Van de Vliert et al., and by other researchers discussed in section 1.3, tells us that violence is not an isolated effect independent of other aspects of human behaviour: rather, it is part of the way of life for many people in hot countries. Perhaps 'cultural masculinity' can help us to understand violence – for example, it gives us insights into the thought processes of violent people.

Another insight from the 'culture of masculinity' approach is where thermal stress is likely to influence various aspects of human life. It is straightforward to identify which locations to study, i.e. very hot places – and geographical science is very clear on this. Many atlases include a climate-based map – perhaps the most famous of these is the Köppen climate classification system (Wikimedia, 2008). This classification suggests there are several hot regions on earth, one of which is a band across northern Africa. In these regions, the 'culture of masculinity' suggests we should expect to see effects of male violence. An example might be female seclusion (where married women are not permitted to leave their home without their husband's permission): over 95% of women in Kano (northern Nigeria) are secluded (Callaway, 1984: p. 431); seclusion of wives by husbands has also been observed in northern India (Jejeebhoy, 1998: p. 303), and in Brazil (Russell-Wood, 1978: p. 69). It is possible that female seclusion is part of the effect of very high temperatures, in the northern regions of these three countries – perhaps originating in a system intended to protect women from violence from male strangers, but resulting in women being financially dependent on their husband (hence, according to many writers, female seclusion is harmful to women's interests).

However, human behaviour is complicated – consider, for example, 'macho' culture in Latin America. Some writers claim that many Latin American men have 'machismo' values, which expects men to be aggressive; and that many women have 'Marianismo' values – in which women should be submissive, like the mother of Jesus. But female submission is not the only possible outcome: "among females, the destructive syndrome of *marianismo* (submissiveness towards males, passive acceptance of destiny) may be replaced by *hembrismo* – the assertive and independent woman" (Cuadrado & Lieberman, 2002: p. 3). In hot parts of Latin America, it seems feasible that some women are made more aggressive by high temperatures; whereas other women may be intimidated by their husband, as a result of his (temperature-induced) aggression.

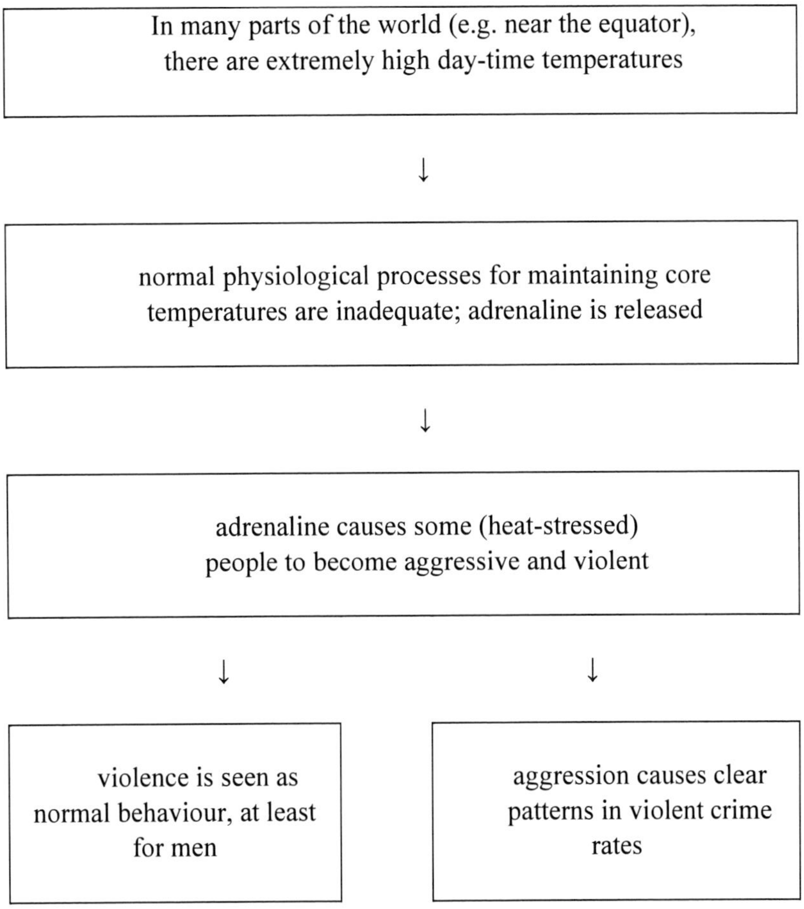

Figure 1. Possible sequence of cause and effect.

Medical Research

We think there is strong evidence that adrenaline is involved in raising aggression in summer. But we cannot tell if adrenaline and/or noradrenaline also causes violence in winter, or whether testosterone is also implicated in violent crimes. Testosterone is associated with the sex drive, so some observers might interpret rape statistics as indicators of the effects of testosterone; or perhaps rape is more a form of violence against women, than a sexual act. Our research using USA data (not all reported here) suggests that seasonal patterns of rape are very similar to seasonal patterns in other types of violent crimes (such as murders, assaults, and robberies). Chart 7 is an example of such evidence, for Los Angeles.

Ethical problems prevent some types of research (for example, it would be impossible to inject every citizen of a city with noradrenaline, to see if the homicide rate rose); hence, epidemiological research seems appropriate. We encourage the FBI and other agencies to make monthly crime data available for as many cities and/or states as possible, to help criminologists investigate these issues further. More information on the time-of-day crime occurs would also help. Household surveys such as Demographic & Health Surveys can tell us more about domestic violence.

Of course, thermal stress is no excuse for violence: no reasonable person would carry out murder, rape, or similar violence at any temperature. But we advise people to be aware of the increased risk of violence when the temperature is unusually hot (compared with temperatures usually experienced in that location). This problem, and hence our advice, applies to every country.

Implications

Although humans tend to react violently to thermal stress, people can learn to control this response (Kemper, 1990: p. 133); it may be appropriate to make the public aware of the dangers of high temperatures. Perhaps violence can be reduced if schools & workplaces explain the effects of extreme temperatures (and how to spot warning signs). Every school child in a hot country could be taught about how extreme temperatures can lead to aggression and violence. Teachers should also point out the harmful aspects of 'machismo' culture, such as the belief that a man must always be ready to defend his property and his wife from other men, by threats or use of violence. To reduce domestic violence, girls and women can be taught how to diffuse anger in men, by use of counselling techniques.

Anyone likely to experience extreme heat should behave responsibly, e.g. drink water, to protect other people around himself/herself. People living in very hot climates can help to protect themselves from becoming victims of violence by being aware of the risks, for example by avoiding controversial discussion with other members of their family on hot days. Police need extra staff on duty, for demonstrations & protests on very hot days; and political demonstrations in hot countries should be timed to avoid mid-day and/or hot summer days.

The increased use of electric fans and air-conditioning is a helpful trend, in protecting people from violence; perhaps they should be installed in more public buildings and private homes. However, we need to be aware that such equipment is expensive to run (for poor families); can put strain on electricity generating stations; and adds to the global warming problem. Another approach worth considering is for architects to design buildings which are less prone to feeling excessively hot in summer, for example by improved use of passive ventilation (relying on convection currents, rather than electric fans, to provide air movement).

More quantitative scientific research is needed into the effects of extreme temperatures on human physiology, and on societies. But more qualitative research is also essential, if we are to understand the cognitive processes which adrenaline (and perhaps noradrenaline) appear to generate. Violence is a problem in every country; but humans can learn to reduce the size of the problem.

1.7. References

al-Hadramy, M. S. (1989). Catecholamines in heat stroke. *Military Medicine, 154 (5: May)*, 263-4.

Anderson, C. A. & Anderson, D. C. (1984). Ambient temperature and violent crime: tests of the linear and curvilinear hypothesis, *Journal of Personality and Social Psychology,46 (1: Jan)*, 91-7.

Anderson, C. A. (1989). Temperature and aggression: ubiquitous effects of heat on occurrence of human violence. *Psychological Bulletin, 106 (1: Jul)*, 74-96.

Andersson, A. M., Carlsen, E., Petersen, J. H. & Skakkeback, N. E. (2003). Variation in levels of serum inhibin B, testosterone, estradiol, luteinizing hormone, follicle-stimulating hormone, and sex hormone-binding globulin in monthly samples from healthy men during a 17-month period: possible effects of seasons. *Journal of clinical endocrinology and metabolism, 88 (2: Feb)*, 932-7.

Barrington, Ernest, J. W. (1983). Hormone, *Encyclopaedia Britannica, 8*, 1074-88, Chicago, Helen Hemingway Benton.

Brück, K. (1989). Thermal balance and the regulation of body temperature, in R. F. Schmidt, & G. Thews (Eds.), *Human physiology* (2nd edition), Berlin, Springer-Verlag.

Callaway, B. (1984). Ambiguous consequences of the socialisation and seclusion of Hausa women. *The Journal of Modern African Studies, 22 (33)*, 429-50.

Crowther, G., Finlay, H., Raj, P. A. & Wheeler, T. (1990). *India: A Travel Survival Kit.* Hawthorn, Victoria: Lonely Planet.

CRU, (2001). temperatures file 'cruwlda2.txt', downloaded on 16th November 2001 from www.cru.uea.ac.uk/advance10k/climdata.htm (this file is no longer available at CRU).

CRU, (2004). temperatures files 'absolute.dat' and 'crutem2.dat', downloaded on 13th March 2004 from www.cru.uea.ac.uk/cru/data/temperature/

Cuadrado, M. & Lieberman, L. (2002). Traditional family values and substance abuse: *the Hispanic contribution to an alternative prevention and treatment approach*, New York : Kluwer Academic / Plenum Publishers.

Directorate of Economics & Statistics (1965). *Quarterly digest of economics & statistics*, Jaipur: Government of Rajasthan.

Doyle, Roger, (2000). By the numbers: *the roots of homicide*, Scientific American, October 2000.

EIA. (2008). 'Table 2.6: Households with selected appliances and types of main heating fuel, selected years, 1978-2005', U.S. government's Energy Information Administration, downloaded 13th December 2008 from www.eia.doe.gov/emeu/aer/consump.html

Ellsberg, M. & Heise, L. (2005). Researching violence against women. *a practical guide for researchers and activists*, Washington DC: World Health Organization, PATH. Downloaded on 13th December 2008 from www.path.org/files/GBV_rvaw_complete.pdf

El-Zanaty, Fatma & Way, Ann (2006). *Egypt Demographic and Health Survey 2005*. Cairo, Egypt: Ministry of Health and Population, National Population Council, El-Zanaty and Associates, and ORC Macro.

FBI (Federal Bureau of Investigation) (1997). *Uniform crime reports for the United States*, 1996, U.S. Department of Justice, Washington D.C.

FBI (Federal Bureau of Investigation) (2003). *Uniform crime reports for the United States*, 2002, U.S. Department of Justice, Washington D.C.

Federal Bureau of Statistics (various editions), Monthly Bulletin of Statistics, Government of Pakistan, Karachi.

Frank, S. M., Higgins, M. S., Fleisher, L. A., Sitzmann, J. V., Raff, H. & Breslow, M. J. (1997). Adrenergic, respiratory, and cardiovascular effects of core cooling in humans. *American Journal of physiology, 272 (Feb: 2 Pt 2)*, R557-62.

Haller, J., Makara, G. B. & Kruk, M. R. (1998). Catecholaminergic involvement in the control of aggression: hormones, the peripheral sympathetic, and central noradrenergic systems, *Neuroscience and Behavioral Reviews, 22(1)*, 85-97.

Humphreys, M. A. (1995). Thermal comfort temperatures and the habits of hobbits, In F. Nicol, M. Humphreys, O. Sykes, & S. Roaf (Eds.), Standards for thermal comfort: indoor air temperatures for the 21st century, London, SPON.

Jacob, Brian, A. & Lefgren Lars (2003). Are idle hands the devil's workshop? Incapacitation, concentration, and juvenile crime. *American Economic Review, 93 (5: Dec)*, 1560-77.

Jejeebhoy, S. J. (1998). Associations between wife-beating and fetal and infant death: impressions from a survey in rural India, *Studies in Family Planning, 29 (3)*, 300-308.

Jezova, D., Kvetnansky, R. & Vigas, M. (1994). Sex differences in endocrine response to hyperthermia in sauna. *Acta Physiologica Scandinavica, 150 (3: Mar)*, 293-8.

Johnson, K. (2002) Crime reported in Alaska 2002, Department of Public Safety, downloaded on 1st April 2004 from www.dps.state.ak.us/OnlineLibrary/htm/cria2002.pdf.

Kemper, Theodore, D. (1990). *Social structure and testosterone*, New Brunswick: Rutgers University Press.

Kukkonen-Harjula, K., Oja, P., Laustiola, K., Vuori, I., Jolkkonen, J., Siitonen, S. & Vapaatalo, H. (1989). Haemodynamic and hormonal responses to heat exposure in a Finnish sauna bath. *European Journal of Applied Physiology and occupational Physiology, 58(5)*, 543-50.

Kurina, Lianne, M., Schneider, Barbara & Waite, Linda, J. (2004). Stress, symptoms of depression and anxiety, and cortisol patterns in working parents. *Stress and Health,20 (2: April)*, 53-63.

LAPD, (2003). Statistical digest 2000, Los Angeles Police Department, downloaded on 12th December 2003 from www.lapdonline.org.

Mawson, A. R. (1999). Stimulation-induced behavioral inhibition: a new model for understanding physical violence, Integrative physiological and behavioral science. *the official journal of the Pavlovian Society, 34 (3: Jul-Sep)*, 177-97.

McGeehin, Michael, A. & Mirabelli, Maria, (2001). The potential impacts of climate variability and change on temperature-related morbidity and mortality in the United States. *Environmental Health Perspectives, 109 (supplement 2: May)*, 185-9.

Mitchell, T. D., et al. (2003). *A comprehensive set of climate scenarios for Europe and the globe*, including gridded datasets, downloaded on 7th June 2005, from www.cru.uea.ac.uk/~timm/cty/obs/TYN_CY_1_1.htm

Nisbett, R. E. & Cohen, D. (1999), *Men, honor and murder*, Scientific American, Summer, 1999.

NOAA (National Oceanic and Atmospheric Administration), (1991). *Climates of the world*, Asheville, North Carolina: U.S. Department of Commerce.

O'Brien, C., Young, A. J., Lee, D. T., Shitzerm A., Sawkam M. N. & Pandolf, K. B. (2000). Role of core temperature as a stimulus for cold acclimation during repeated immersion in 20°C water. *Journal of Applied Physiology, 89*, 242-50.

Phoenix Police Department, (2004). *Statistics for reported crimes - district*, downloaded 2nd April 2004 from www.ci.phoenix.az.us/haht-bin/hsrun/payf/CRIMGRIDP/Stateld/C2eTxLQU25HNwQsAchTxfBoO3oeSE-4Nb3/HAHTpage/HS_selectdate

Pierce College, (2008). *Temperature archive*, Los Angeles Pierce College weather station, downloaded 13th December 2008 from data.piercecollege.edu/weather/temperatures.html

Pocock, G. & Richards, C. D. (1999). *Human physiology: the basis of medicine*, Oxford: OUP.

Preti, A., Miotto, P., De Coppi, M., Petretto, D. & Carmelo, M. (2002). Psychiatric chrono-epidemiology: its relevance for the study of aggression, *Aggressive behavior*, *28 (6)*, 477-90.

Roberts, M. B. V. (1986: 4th edition). *Biology: a functional approach*, Nelson: Walton-on-Thames.

Rotton, J. & Cohn, E. G. (2001). Temperature, routine activities, and domestic violence: a reanalysis. *Violence and Victims*, *16 (2: Apr)*, 203-15.

Rotton, J. & Cohn, E. G. (2004). Outdoor temperature, climate control, and criminal assault: the spatial and temporal ecology of violence. *Environment and behaviour*, *36*, 276-306.

Russell-Wood, A. J. R. (1978), Female and family in the economy and society of colonial Brazil, In A. Lavrin (Eds.). Latin American women: historical perspectives, *Contributions in women's studies Number 3*, Westport CT: Greenwood Publishing Group.

Semmens, Natasha, Dillane, Jennifer & Ditton, Jason, (2002). Preliminary findings on seasonality and the fear of crime. *British Journal of Criminology*, *42 (4: Aut)*, 798-806.

Simister, John & Cary Cooper, (2005). Thermal stress in the USA: effects on violence and employee behaviour. *Stress and Health*, *21*, 3-15.

Simister, John & Evert Van de Vliert, (2005). Is there more violence in very hot weather? Tests over time in Pakistan and across countries worldwide. *Pakistan Journal of Meteorology*, *2 (4)*, 55-70.

Sramek, P., Simeckova, M., Jansky, L., Savlikova, J. & Vybiral, S. (2000). Human physiological responses to immersion into water of different temperatures. *European Journal of Applied Physiology*, *81 (5: Mar)*, 436-42.

Talan, Jamie, (2005). Cooling hot aggression. *Scientific American Mind*, *16 (2)*, 7.

Van de Vliert, Evert, Shalom H. Schwartz, Sipke E. Huismans, Geert Hofstede & Serge Daan, (1999). Temperature, Cultural Masculinity, and Domestic Political Violence: A Cross-National Study. *Journal of Cross-Cultural Psychology*, *30*, 291-314.

Wikimedia, (2008). 'World map of Köppen – Geiger climate classification', http://en.wikipedia.org/wiki/Image:World_Koppen_Map.png downloaded 12th December 2008.

In: Violent Crime and Prisons: Population...
Ed: Aidan Renshaw and Emelina Suárez
ISBN: 978-1-60741-668-5

Chapter 2

UNDERSTANDING EXPERIENCES OF INCARCERATED ADOLESCENT MALE YOUTH: THE IMPORTANCE OF A DEVELOPMENTAL FRAMEWORK

[1]Carla Cesaroni* and [2]Michele Peterson-Badali
[1]University of Ontario Institute of Technology.
[2]University of Toronto.

ABSTRACT

Studies of the adaptation to prison have been heavily influenced by classic prison sociology. This has meant that the majority of literature on adjustment to imprisonment has focused on adult males and has been described and interpreted against adult male models of adaptation. Though there is some recognition in these studies of the inherent vulnerability of young people because of their age, they tend to examine the stress of incarceration from a universally adult perspective and belief system. For example, there is a presumption that not being able to see friends and family is equally difficult for adults and youth. There does not appear to be a serious consideration of the possibility that youths find certain events uniquely problematic – nor is there a consideration of the possibility that adolescence itself has its own stresses that may be relevant in this setting. Utilizing a decade of research on adolescent males in custody, this chapter will argue the importance of using a development framework to the study of the adjustment of youth in custody. Additionally, it will present data to suggest that for a small but significant proportion of adolescent male youth, "doing time" is extremely difficult.

Keywords: Young offenders, custody, prison, adjustment.

* Assistant Professor, Faculty of Criminology, Justice and Policy Studies, University of Ontario Institute of Technology, 2000 Simcoe Street North, Oshawa, Ontario L1H 7K4, Canada. (905)721-8668 Ext 2517, Fax (905) 721-3372. carla.cesaroni@uoit.ca

INTRODUCTION

The majority of literature on adjustment to imprisonment has focused on adult males. Though there have been a number of significant studies on subgroups within the prison population, for example young adult males (Harvey, 2007) or aging prisoners (Crawley & Sparks, 2005), the experiences of other groups, including women and youth, have generally been ignored (Liebling, 1999). Kruttschnitt and Gartner (2003) suggest that much of the early research on women's adaptation to incarceration was heavily influenced by classic prison sociology. This meant that women's experiences were described and interpreted against male models of adaptation. Similarly, research on adolescent males has also focused largely on how closely youths' patterns of adjustment mirror that of older men, with little regard to important differences between the two groups. Peer-on-peer victimizations have tended to be the focus of the majority of studies on the adjustment of adolescent males to custody[1]. The importance of familial relationships, peer relationships, and 'bullying' have been seen as important, not because of the critical role these have in developmental processes, but because of presumptions emanating from adult studies of adjustment to incarceration, including the 'inevitability' of male violence and the formation of 'subcultures' in reaction to the deprivations and stresses of prison life – key themes of classic sociological studies of adult adjustment (see for example Bottoms, 1999; Feld,1981; McCorkle, 1993; Poole & Regoli,1983).

In this chapter we review several literatures that, together, have informed the development of a research program aimed at understanding the adjustment of youth in custody. We begin by discussing the existing literature on young people's adjustment in prison, followed by a review of the adult prison adjustment literature and the models of prison adjustment arising from that research. A brief review of the literature on normative adolescent development is followed by a summary of the 'risk and resilience' framework of child and adolescent adjustment that arises from the developmental psychopathology literature. Next, we present the results of several studies that are premised on the assumption that we can better understand the adjustment of young people in custody when we consider the sociological models emanating from the adult prison literature *together* with the developmental psychopathological approach. The implications of the findings for research and policy are discussed.

Adjustment of Youth in Custody

The adjustment of youth in custody is typically studied from a typological perspective, with different 'types' of youth and the way in which they 'do time' described in detail (see for example Bartollas, 1976; Ireland & Monaghan, 2006;Shields & Simourd, 1991). Often these typologies are reflections of prison sub-cultures that are described in the adult prison literature and, as in the adult literature, they are presumed to result from the 'deprivations' of prison life. Though there is some recognition in these studies of the inherent vulnerability of young people because of their age, youth incarceration is generally examined from an adult perspective and belief system. In many studies of incarcerated youth there is a tendency to describe age as only a small aggravating factor in terms of the stress of, and adjustment to, prison life, with little consideration of the possibility that youths would find certain events uniquely problematic. For example, there is a presumption that time has the same relative meaning and weight for a youth as an adult. There is little consideration of the possibility that adolescence in *itself* presents stresses that may be relevant in this setting (e.g., the fact that establishing a stable, integrated identity is a central task of adolescent development that can be disrupted by an onerous, overly restrictive, institutional environment; Greve, Enzmann & Hosser, 2001). Thus, rarely are relationships and environment placed within a developmental context.

There is often a presumption that not being able to see friends and family is equally difficult for adults and youth. However, in contrast to adults, incarceration is likely the first significant period many young people have spent away from family, friends and home communities. Indeed, a custodial sentence may increase disengagement from family, pro-social peers, and familial/social values at a critical stage in youths' development (Steinberg, Chung Len & Little, 2004). With respect to relationships *within* the institution, the existing literature includes discussions of the initial formation of inmate solidarity and resistance against institutional life, with little reflection on the social dynamic of adult guards versus youthful inmates (e.g., the fact that, for youth, the inmate-staff power imbalance is exacerbated by the power dynamic of adult versus adolescent). Notable exceptions to this approach are studies by Harvey (2007)[2] and Lane, Lanza-Kaduce, Frazier and Bishop (2002).

There is also a strong presumption in much of the literature that there is relatively little variation in the way in which youth experience custody. For example as Bartollas (1982, p.165) suggests that "*All* youths experience the stresses of the loss of liberty, the coerciveness of a punishment-oriented environment, and the deprivations of caring relationships they would have in their home." Individual characteristics of young offenders have largely been ignored except to delineate typologies, to predict 'victim' versus 'bully' status, and to describe the frequency of victimization (see for example Connell & Farrington, 1996; Dyson, Power & Wozniak, 1997; Edgar & O'Donnell, 1998; Ireland, 2005; Mutchnick & Fawcett, 1991).

Violence in custody

One of the most studied aspects of adjustment in custody is prison violence. Many studies of adults presume that violence in prison is inevitable, not only because men find themselves in a prison environment but because they are men. For youth there appears to be a parallel presumption: that violence is inevitable because they are *young* men. There is little attention given to the developmental significance of peer/social status or, as has long been recognized in the developmental psychology literature, that boys tend to externalize pain and despair (Katz, 2001). In addition, discussions regarding the inevitability of violence in youth custody facilities, like those in the adult literature, focus on the important role of masculine cultures and institutional atmospheres where toughness, status and aggression are an inevitable part of doing time (Bartollas, 1982; Bishop, 2000; Feld, 1981; Johnson, 1978; Maitland & Sluder, 1996; O'Donnell & Edgar, 1998; Wright, 1991). However, there is little recognition of the

---

[1] The terms 'custody' and 'prison' are used interchangeably.

[2] Harvey's study is based on 18 – 20 year old young adults, rather than adolescents but his in-depth work pays careful attention to the ways in which young people's adaptation differs from that of adults.

fact that for adolescent males, unlike adult males, this preoccupation with maleness may be about *establishing* masculinity as opposed to reconfirming it. There is little consideration that perhaps physical assertions of strength and tests of masculinity that often lead to male bonding and an inmate solidarity of sorts (Jewkes 2005) which help to establish adolescent masculine identity in a way that is acceptable amongst ones peers.

Sim (1995) provides a critique of the focus on masculine culture and violence in the prison literature, suggesting that there are many acts of cooperation among adult inmates. Similarly, within the youth custody literature, with a few exceptions (see for example Clarke-McClean, 1996; Feld, 1981) there is also a general absence of reporting of acts of cooperation, which is not to say that they do not exist, only that they tend not to be the focus of research attention.

The literature on the victims of peer-on-peer violence in youth custody facilities -- unlike its adult counterpart – often highlights the long-term negative effects of victimization on psychosocial outcomes (Maitland & Sluder, 1998; McCorkle, 1993). This same literature suggests that victimization, fear, and negative outcomes would seem stronger for adolescents than for adults (Maitland & Sluder, 1996; McCorkle, 1993; O'Donnell & Edgar, 1998; Poole & Regoli, 1983; Windzio, 2006).

Finally, although a number of studies note the consistency of the negative correlation between age and violence in prison, (Bottoms, 1999; MacKenzie, 1987; McShane & Williams, 1989; Wright, 1991), only a few propose a developmental explanation. Notable exceptions include Johnson (1978) and Bishop (2000), who recognize that the prison world exaggerates adolescent concerns regarding peer pressure, and MacKenzie (1987), who argues that youth prison violence can be accounted for by five related developmental factors. First, youth are less aware of the consequences of their actions. Second, as individuals mature they "age-out" of violence and anti-social/violent behavior becomes less of an option. Third, violence is a youth's impulsive reaction to stress. Fourth, aggression may be a sign of immature coping ability, and fifth, for most youth, in and out of prison, peer victimization is more likely a reality than for adults. Though these observations are true for youth in prison, they can also be seen as developmental phenomena that characterize adolescent males generally. For example "... imprisoned youth are similar to other youths in their immaturity, vulnerability, and lack of decision making abilities." (Bortner & Williams, 1997, p.xiii).

Youth adjustment beyond prison

Although much of the research on youth in custody has focused on peer-on-peer victimization, more recent studies have examined youth adjustment in terms of recidivism or post release success (see for example van der Laan, Vervoorn, van der Schans & Bogaerts, 2008). This research mirrors more recent research on adult inmates and a focus on 'risk' as it relates to recidivism and the impact of the 'new penology'. As Simon (2000, argues, there has been a switch from an interest in the 'society of captives' and the state's role in rehabilitation, to a focus on 'responsibilization' – making individuals responsible for their own actions, the consequences of their actions, and ultimately, their own rehabilitation. Within the youth literature, this approach has led to a focus on the social and psychological characteristics of youth in custody and recognition of the high incidence of familial adversity and emotional, behavioral and mental disorder in incarcerated youth (Bortner & Williams, 1997; Duclous et al, 1998; Ulzen & Hamilton, 1998). However, it has also been argued that this perspective has led some authorities responsible for young inmates to attribute maladjustment to custody as being predicted by the 'weaknesses' of individual youth (Goldson, 2005, 2006;Vandergoot, 2006) rather than systemic problems. Our research calls into question the ethos of punishment and responsibilization (i.e., children need to be treated as adults when they do something wrong) that currently prevails when you having difficulties within state run institutions.

Feminist scholarship has highlighted how using a male standard or male 'yardstick' is inadequate in explaining women's adjustment to prison. Similarly, we argue that using an *adult* male standard may be inadequate for explaining *adolescent* male youths' adjustment to prison. However, the adult literature may still be an appropriate point of departure because of its important contribution to the general study of prison life. This study of prison life has included the recognition of the unique environment and culture of prison life and the fact that doing time requires acclimatization and adaptation. In addition, the adult literature suggests possible predictors of adjustment to institutional life.

Research on Adult Adjustment in Prison

The 1950's through to the late 1970's has been described as the golden age of prison research (Kruttschnitt, Gartner & Carbone, 2002), an era in which "prison sociology was emerging as a highly productive field for both theory building and positive policy application" (Simon, 2000, p.287). During this era sociological studies described the prison as a world set apart: one with unique cultures, demands, and processes.

The 'prisonization effect'

Clemmer (1940, p.299) argued that every man who enters the penitentiary undergoes the prisonization effect, or the "taking on in greater or lesser degree of the folkways, mores, customs and general culture of the penitentiary." He suggested that susceptibility to the prisonization effect was affected by an inmate's personality, the kind and extend of relationships outside of the prison walls, the affiliation with prison groups, and whether or not the inmate accepted the dogmas and codes of the prison culture.

Wheeler (1961) took up Clemmer's idea of prisonization and developed it further. Perhaps Wheeler's greatest contribution to our understanding of the prisonization effect was his description of the amelioration process that occurs as inmates adjust to prison life. According to Wheeler, there is evidence that, from an inmate's perspective, it is the length of time remaining that is the most crucial temporal aspect of prison adjustment. This contrasts with Clemmer (1940), who suggested that time already served was critical.

Wheeler (1961) argued that how quickly the prisonization process occurs for an individual inmate is a function of inmate involvement and time remaining in the institution. He suggested that for some inmates there is a particular pattern of adjustment – a U-shaped curve that has its lowest point during the middle period of institutional confinement. In particular, he described how proximity to the community in terms of entering or exiting the prison contributes to the prisonization effect for this group of prisoners: stress is highest when the inmate first enters prison and again when he prepares to exit, but is felt less acutely during the course of an inmate's sentence.

Over the past several decades a number of studies have supported Wheeler's theory regarding prisonization, a process that implies adherence to a prison sub-culture, is inmate centered, and is anti-staff/anti-institution. Recent studies confirm a slow and gradual amelioration in levels of stress over time and suggest that most inmates feel the stress and difficulties of entry into prison, regardless of previous prison experience. For example, Zamble and Porporino's (1988) longitudinal study of 300 Canadian federal inmates is interesting because the authors concede that though prison may not have any long term emotional effects, most prisoners experience an elevated level of suffering and distress when they first enter a custodial institution.

Deprivation, importation, and interactionist models of prison adjustment

The adult prison literature is important in describing the initial stress and adjustment to a custodial institution. It is also significant for its attempts to describe what makes prison culture distinct and what may predict inmate distress and adjustment. For example, Gresham Sykes' (1958) landmark book "The Society of Captives" makes a substantial contribution to the adult prison literature not only because of the richness in which the author describes prison life and prison sub-cultures, or his coining of the phrase 'pains of imprisonment', but because of his development of the 'deprivation model' of prison adjustment. Sykes (1958) argued that it is the depriving conditions of the prison itself that cause the stress and difficulties associated with entry into prison life. He suggested that aspects of prison life exert a negative influence on inmate attitudes, values, and modes of interaction. The prisonization effect first described by Clemmer, and later by Wheeler, is described by Sykes in terms of prison countercultures – 'argot roles' which inmates take on as a response to specific problems posed by imprisonment. Sykes (1958) argues that the formation of sub-cultures is a *coherent response* to the depriving conditions of imprisonment.

The deprivation model of prison adjustment dominated most adult prison studies through the 1960's. A change in correctional management styles and shifting demographics of the prison population in the United States throughout the 1960's and 1970's, however, meant increases in inmate violence and a change in earlier preoccupations with prisonization (Goodstein & Wright, 1989). Beginning with ex-offender John Irwin and sociologist Donald Cressey, a new 'importation' model of prison adjustment was proposed, which suggested that inmates' pre-prison experiences in the outside world are pivotal in understanding the social system of prison (Irwin & Cressey, 1962). Irwin and Cressey suggested that the manner in which prisoners adjust to the deprivations of imprisonment is a function of adaptive patterns learned on city streets, and is not functionally related to the prison structure.

It is now recognized that the prison experience is too complex to be a single model and requires an integrated approach (Crewe, 2007; Hochstetler, DeLisi, 2005; Lawson, Segrin & Ward, 1996; Liebling, 2003). Current research on prison adjustment recognizes the necessity of viewing prison adjustment from an interactionist perspective, in which a combination of inmate characteristics and environmental factors contribute to individual outcomes (Kruttschitt, Gartner & Carbone, 2002). However, Liebling (2003) suggests that importation and deprivation factors may play different roles in prison-induced stress and adjustment.

In addition, recent studies suggest there is no single pattern of adjustment to prison life and indeed, inmates may chose to withdraw, rebel and resist against prison, or even conform (Crew, 2007). As Crew (2007) argues, the majority of prisoners find ways to adjust that do not involve extreme resistance or complete acquiescence, but combine several strategies. However, recent research has also illuminated the fact that for a minority of inmates, the initial distress experienced at entry into prison never fully disappears (Liebling, 2003; Zamble & Porporino, 1988). Subsequent studies have also identified more clearly the negative consequences of the inability to cope with the prison stress, including self-inflicted injury, depression, illness, psychiatric commitments, suicide, and antisocial behavior (Hochstelter, Murphy & Simons, 2004; Ivonoff, 1992; Johnson, 1976, 1987; Liebling, 1999, 2003; Liebling, Durie, Stiles & Tait, 2005; Toch & Adams, 1989).

Implications of the adult literature for youths' adjustment to incarceration

It is important to note that processes that may be part of the 'routine' stress of entry into prison may have unique meanings for youth. For example the relegation to a child-like status during an age that is about individuation and independence and control may increase conflict between adult guards and youth in the same way it does between adolescents and their parents. Eccles et al. (1993) suggest that some of the negative psychological changes associated with adolescent development result from a mismatch between the needs of developing adolescents and the opportunities within their social environments. The authors discuss why an early shift from elementary school to high school is harmful for vulnerable youth. An analogous situation may be the removal of vulnerable youth from their home community to a custodial facility:

> In light of these needs, the environmental changes often associated with junior high school seem especially harmful in that they emphasize competition, social comparison and ability self-assessment at a time of heightened self-focus; they decrease decision making and choice at a time when the desire for control is growing; they emphasize lower level cognitive strategies at a time when the ability to use higher level strategies is increasing; and they disrupt social networks at a time when adolescents are especially concerned with peer relationships and may be in special need of close adult relationships outside of the home.
>
> (Eccles et al., 1993, p.94).

As Clemmer (1961, p.710) suggested four decades ago, young offender institutions "...are likely to receive a larger number of offenders whose frames of reference are not solidified, and who may thus be more susceptible to peer-group influence." In addition, Clemmer (1961, p.710) suggests that even within youth facilities, "A less negative inmate culture may still produce the prisonization response."

As in the case of adults, an adjustment model for youth that focuses purely on the prison environment itself or on young people's demographic characteristics may be inadequate to explain their adjustment to custody. There are certainly a number of clues within the adult literature that suggest similar processes in youths' adjustment to prison. What is generally lacking in both the adult and youth literature is recognition of the fact that there are also likely important differences. Attention to research on 'typically developing' adolescents may shed some light on this issue.

Change and Adjustment in 'Normal' Adolescents

With the exception of infancy, adolescence is characterized by more rapid changes than any other period in the life cycle (Smetana, Yau, Restrepo & Braeges, 1993). It is a developmental period in which the individual is confronted not only with dramatic physical changes, but also with a series of complex and inter-related developmental tasks such as autonomy from parents, establishing sexual relationships and developing an occupational identity (Seiffge-Krenke, 1993). The number of physical, psychological, and sociological influences brought to bear on the individual at this stage in development poses its own unique kind of stress (Hendren, 1990).

For some, the number of rapid changes in adolescent development stimulates further growth while for others changes may be overwhelming and lead to problems (Peterson, Kennedy & Sullivan, 1991). In addition, there are 'sensitive periods' at which certain stressors have profound impacts (Arnold, 1990). Changes during adolescence can either be normative, those experienced by all adolescents, or non-normative, those that occur at unpredictable points in the life course such as the divorce of a parent (Rice, Herman & Peterson, 1993). Non-normative events that occur during a developmental transition may interact with normative events to amplify or moderate their effects (Rice, Herman & Peterson, 1993). The absolute number of changes an adolescent might experience is directly related to negative outcomes (Peterson, Kennedy & Sullivan, 1991). Pre-existing psychological symptoms and pre-existing life stressors may create special vulnerability for youth during the transition through adolescence (Ge, Conger & Elder, 2001).

Friendships during adolescence become more intense, enter increasingly into the daily lives of youth, and pose new demands (Seiffge-Krenke, 1995). In addition to the emotional support friendship provides, consensual validation, identification, and modeling are important processes operating among friends at this age (Seiffge-Krenke, 1995). Research suggests that adolescents who identify highly with their peer group report fewer problems with developmental tasks and get more support from peers in coping with these tasks (Shulman, 1993). In addition, because peer relations influence various elements of self-perception, active rejection by peers may be related to feelings of distress (Seiffge-Krenke, 1995). Unpopularity is one of the most common, and most potent, sources of distress for children from school-entry age on (Maccoby, 1983). In a study by Moran and Eckenrode (1991) social stress in friendship relationships accounted for significant variance in stress in adolescents aged 14 and younger, though not for older (15 – 18-year-old) adolescents.

It is important to bear in mind that some youth face extremely adverse life conditions in addition to the 'regular' stresses of adolescence. These conditions include poverty, a climate of violence, or familial homelessness (Gore & Colten, 1991). A complex set of factors and mechanisms seem to influence which youth are able to rise above adversity.

Risk and Adjustment

Norman Garmezy (1983) and Michael Rutter's (1983) research on risk and resilience in children came at a time when stress in children was under-researched. By studying the impact of hospital admissions, births of siblings, and parental divorce on the stress levels of children, the authors were able to argue that stressful events in childhood may lead to short-term psychosocial disturbances. Key amongst their early findings were a) most stressors that produce psychiatric disorder involve some sort of loss, disappointment or disturbed interpersonal relationships, b) it is the sheer number of events that occur to a child during a unit of time that cause distress and disturbance (Rutter, 1983), and c) contextual, situational factors are important. Much is dependent upon the interactions that a child has with significant adults in new settings, whether hospital, institution or foster care (Garmezy, 1983).

Stated simply, risk factors are "...those factors which if present increase the likelihood of a child developing an emotional or behavioral disorder in comparison with a randomly selected child from the general population (Kimichi & Schaffner, 1990). They refer to a broad range of *chronic*, or ongoing, features that characterize a child, his or her relationships, or his or her environment (e.g., poverty). They can be distinguished from stressors, which are defined as more *acute* events such as parental death or divorce, or a child's hospitalization.

Research since Rutter and Garmezy's original research has reconfirmed that it is not the occurrence of a particular risk factor but the cumulative, or additive, effect of multiple risks that produce consistently negative outcomes (Burt, Resnick & Novick, 1998; Smith, Lizotte, Thornberry, & Krohn, 1995). Furthermore, Rutter (1983) suggests that acute stressors and risk factors in isolation predispose towards disorder, but when combined they increase the effects of negative outcomes in a *non-linear* manner. Thus, the combination of chronic vulnerabilities and acute stressors is much more powerful (and therefore potentially more debilitating) than even the additive effects of the risks and stressors (Hauser & Bowlds, 1990). Gore and Eckenrode (1994) suggest that the significance of an acute stressor must be seen in the context of risk factors, or chronic stressors, for the event to have meaning. In other words, stressful life events act as antecedents to negative outcomes only when in the presence of risk factors (Ruffolo, 1998). However, in this regard it is important to note that children with multiple life traumas usually differ in many respects from their peers who have fewer acute stressors (i.e. they also have a wider range of chronic risk factors or disadvantage; Rutter, 1983).

High risk, or vulnerability, in children is associated with a high incidence of negative social and mental health outcomes, including delinquency, teenage pregnancy, school dropout, depression, and suicide (Cowan, Cowan & Schultz, 1996). Three critical antecedents appear to be linked consistently to adolescent problem behaviors: *family environment* (family dysfunction including alcoholism, violence, abuse, and lack of parent support and involvement), *poverty*, and *neighborhood institutional inadequacy* (including institutions such as schools and health care systems; Burt, Resnick & Novick, 1998).

Incarceration, Risk, Stress and Adjustment

Incarceration is for many troubled individuals, adult or adolescent, a potentially damaging hardship within a life already filled with trauma and adversity (Hoschstetler, Murphy & Simons, 2004). Given that, as a group, incarcerated young offenders are characterized by multiple forms of familial, socio-emotional, and academic disadvantage (Bortner & Williams, 1997) it is foreseeable that a custodial sentence could act as an acute stressor in the lives of vulnerable youth, with potentially negative consequences.

Despite a growing literature within the developmental psychopathology field on the impact of risk factors in childhood and adolescence on both short-term and long-term psychosocial outcomes, there is relatively little research on the relationship of these factors to the adjustment of incarcerated young offenders. Noteworthy exceptions to this include work by Biggam and Power (1999, 1997), Gover (2000), Maitland and Sluder (1996, 1998), and Martin, Sigda, and Kupersmidt (1998). Biggam and Power's (1997) study of the structure and function of social support in a group of incarcerated young offenders and Maitland and Sluder's (1996) study of the general well being of youthful inmates and related institutional, social, psychological and individual variables (e.g., victimization experiences, fear of victimization, prison support and correctional experience) provide important evidence for the influence of factors associated with institutional risk, social relations, and social skills on the adjustment of youth in custodial facilities. However, while these studies focus on institutional functioning, they do not attempt to draw conclusions or connections regarding pre-existing vulnerabilities.

Gover's (2000) study on previous child maltreatment and youth adjustment within custodial institutions and Martin, Sigda, and Kupersmidt's (1998) study of the effect of family and neighborhood violence on depressive symptomatology among incarcerated youth have provided important insights into the influence of pre-existing factors that are associated with adjustment. These studies examined how several risk factors were individually related to psychosocial adjustment. However, there remains a paucity of research that examines the adjustment of young offenders from a multiple, or cumulative risk, perspective.

The Integration of Two Important Literatures

Over the past decade we have attempted to integrate sociological/criminological theory on adult prison adjustment with developmental psychological theory on adolescent risk and stress. We have utilized adult models of prison adjustment – the importation and deprivation frameworks – as a methodological basis for analysis, in conjunction with adolescent models of risk or vulnerability to stress. In this context, it is important to note that within the criminological – as in the forensic psychology – literature, the term 'risk' is often used to describe an actuarial approach to the prediction of recidivism and institutional misconduct (e.g., in terms of an individual's 'risk to reoffend'). This use of the term is different from the way it has been discussed in the earlier 'risk and adjustment' section of this chapter. While there is overlap between those characteristics that place young people at risk for poor psychological and psychosocial outcomes and those that predict criminal justice outcomes such as post release failure, the models that underlie the developmental psychopathology and criminological approaches are quite different. We take a developmental psychopathology approach to examine the impact of risk factors on young offenders' psychosocial adjustment in custody. In order to avoid confusion in terminology and theory we will use the term "vulnerability" to discuss both pre-existing and institutional factors that predispose young people to – or place them 'at risk' for – negative outcomes.

Our Research on Prison Adjustment in Youth: An Integrated Perspective

As part of a research program aimed at understanding the adjustment of incarcerated youth, the discussion in this chapter draws on data from two studies of adolescent male youth in custody and detention facilities and outlines the goals and preliminary findings of a third, ongoing, study. The goal of our first study (Cesaroni & Peterson-Badali, 2005) was to examine the contribution of both pre-existing vulnerabilities – an importation model – as well as institutional vulnerabilities – a deprivation model – to youths' psychosocial adjustment while in custody. In addition to examining these two important models of prison adjustment, Study 1 tested the prediction that it is the accumulation of vulnerabilities that predicts (lack of) adjustment in youth (i.e., a cumulative risk perspective). Anecdotal reports of institutional staff, together with literature on adult prison adaptation, suggests that inmates' functioning improves as the stresses of the initial 2-3 week 'settling in' period subside (Adams, 1992; Liebling, 1999; McCorkle, 1993; Wheeler, 1961; Zamble and Porporino, 1990). In order to control for the effects of this initial adaption to custody only youths who had been in a facility for at least three weeks participated.

Building from Study 1, a primary purpose of the second study was to examine predictors of youths' adjustment both during the settling in period and once they had transitioned to the daily routine of the institution (Cesaroni & Peterson-Badali, in press). Thus, employing a short-term longitudinal design, we examined youth at the beginning of their custodial stay and again 2 – 3 weeks later. Secondly, we aimed to test the non-additive – or potentiating – model of (mal)adjustment: that the *interaction* of pre-existing vulnerabilities and institutional stressors contributes uniquely to youths' adjustment beyond the combination (addition) of the two individual measures.

METHOD

Sample

The sample for Study 1 consisted of 113 youths recruited from 11 different secure custody (N=60) or open custody (group-home like; N=53) facilities in Ontario, Canada (see Cesaroni & Peterson Badali, 2005).[3] Participants ranged in age from 13 to 19 (M = 15.1, SD = 1.05) at the time of the interview[4]. In Study 2, the Time 1 sample consisted of 100 12- to 17-year-old (M = 14.8, SD = .84) males interviewed at 11 secure custody or open custody facilities in southern Ontario, Canada. Of the youth who participated in the Time 1 interview shortly after entering custody, 74 participated in follow-up interviews. There were no significant differences between the initial and follow-up samples with respect to either the background characteristics or the main variables of interest. In accordance with the study aims, many participants had relatively little experience in custody; 34% were "first timers" and a further 22% had only one other custodial stay.

Demographics for the two studies are noted in Table 1. In both studies, black and Aboriginal youth are overrepresented relative to their frequency in the population.[5] Although many of the respondents in both studies were charged with a violent offense, in Study 2,

---

[3] At the time of data collection, 75% of all custodial sentences in Ontario were open custody sentences (Gannon, Mihorean, Beattie, Taylor-Butts and Kong, 2005).

[4] Canada's youth justice legislation applies to young people age 12 to 17, inclusive.

[5] Blacks comprise 2.5% of the Canadian population and 3.4% of the population of the province of Ontario. Aboriginals comprise 3.8% of the Canadian population and 2% of the population of the province of Ontario.

which did not include youth in secure custody or secure detention, only 34% had violent charges compared to 66% in Study 1, which included youth in secure custody. Violent offences included murder, manslaughter, sexual assault, assault with a weapon, aggravated assault, assault, robbery and various weapons offenses. Charges for respondents also included property offenses and administration of justice offenses, such as breach of probation and failure to appear. Almost half of the respondents in all three samples were first charged with an offense at the age of 12, which is the youngest age at which a person can be charged with a criminal offense in Canada.

Table 1. Sample Demographics (Percentages).

	Sample 1 (N=113)	Sample 2 (N= 100)
Age		
12	0	1
13	6	4
14	21	22
15	48	55
16+	38	18
Race		
Black	18	18
Aboriginal	17	6
White	67	59
Asian	6	3
Other	5	34
Types of Charges		
Violent offences	66	34
Drug offences	4	8
Property Offences	73	69
Administrative offences	70	71
"Other" offences	15	17

Procedure

The procedure in all studies followed a similar format. The first author made an initial visit to a facility, giving a brief talk about the study to all potential participants. Youths who indicated interest in participating were given the name of one staff member with whom they could speak. This same staff member also acted as the liaison between the interviewer and the facility, thereby minimizing the involvement and knowledge of other staff regarding which youths had participated. The first author carried out all of the interviews. A formal consent protocol was read to each participant outlining the purpose of the study, the interview's risks and benefits to the participant, and the limits of confidentiality. Each respondent was told the facility would neither punish them nor give them special treatment for participating. Each respondent was also advised that some questions might make them uncomfortable and they were free to refuse to answer any question if they chose, without fear of reprimand. Interview questions were administered verbally, with each interview taking approximately an hour.

Measures

Our interview protocol has evolved over the past decade. While the majority of the instrument has remained consistent across studies, there are differences between protocols to accommodate new questions of interest and new populations. For example, in our most recent survey of youth held in pre-trial detention, questions have been added regarding youths' understanding of their rights while in detention, relationships with staff and peers, and concerns around masculinities. As described below, the primary measures in all studies include vulnerability (both chronic and acute), as well as psychosocial adjustment.[6]

Pre-existing vulnerability

Youth responded to a questionnaire that included a number of vulnerabilities taken from the developmental psychopathology literature (Burt, Resnick & Novick, 1998; Farrington, 2000; Garmezy, 1983; Gore & Eckenrode, 1994; Loeber & Farrington, 1997; Rutter, 1983) as well as items derived from the Juvenile Survey Instrument: National Evaluation of Juvenile Correctional Facilities (Evaluation Research Group, 1997). The measure included items that probe instability in living (e.g., number of moves in the past year, contact with child welfare services), school-related problems (e.g., school suspensions, academic performance), drug and alcohol use (e.g., frequency), criminal justice contact (e.g., police stops, court appearances), and delinquent friendships (e.g. number of friends with history of trouble with the law, having friends who have been in custody or detention).

The measure was extended in subsequent studies to include items from the sociological literature on prior traumatic events and lifetime stress (Turner, Wheaton & Lloyd, 1995; Wheaton, 1990; Wheaton, Roszell & Hall, 1997). Youth responded on a five-point scale (1=Never; 2= Once or Twice 3= 3-4 Times 4= More than 4 times) to 21 questions addressing traumatic events, including whether their parents had died, been incarcerated, been unemployed for long periods of time, had substance abuse problems or struggled with mental illness, whether youth had witnessed violence in his home or community, and whether they had ever been frightened by something they witnessed, or been abandoned or neglected.

In addition, a 19-item inventory assessed enduring or chronic stress, to which youth responded on a three-point scale (1=Not true; 2= Somewhat true; 3=Very true). Though common measures of chronic stress were used as a guideline for developing items (see for example, Turner, Wheaton & Lloyd, 1995; Wheaton 1990; Wheaton, Roszell & Hall, 1997), these inventories tend to be designed for and administered to adults and therefore reflect issues that are more likely to be indicative of the chronic stress focus of adult lifestyles (i.e. work, marriage, debts etc.). Therefore items were developed to better reflect adolescent

[6] In addition to psychosocial adjustment, we have measured youths' self-reported adjustment to custody and/or detention using common institutional standards: violations of institutional rules resulting in infraction reports or separation from others. However, in neither of our completed studies have pre-existing or institutional vulnerability been related to these measures of institutional adjustment, suggesting that institutional measures of behavior may not be a valid indicator of how a youth is feeling or adjusting to a facility. Perhaps this is not surprising given that infractions capture a range of behaviors from violence to simple noncompliance. It is also possible that participants' reports are not a reliable measure of compliance or misconduct. However, 'official' (i.e., staff) documentation of prison misconduct may be equally unreliable, as evidence indicates that official records underestimate infractions such as physical bullying (Dyson, Power & Wozniak, 1997), as well as more mundane victimization or minor harm (e.g. threats, verbal abuse, exclusionary behavior; O'Donnell & Edgar, 1999).

concerns and stresses. Items fell into five areas – *general problems* (e.g., too much is expected of me by others, I don't have enough money to buy the things other kids have), *family* (e.g., my parents don't understand me, my parents don't show me enough affection), *peer relations* (e.g., other kids tease or bully me for the way I look, speak or dress), *health* (e.g., I have a health problem that keeps me from doing things), *school* (e.g., I don't get along with my teachers, I wish I did better in school) and *residence* (e.g., I wish I could move away from my neighborhood).

In order to develop an overall measure of vulnerability, items from the aforementioned instruments were combined into seven vulnerability domains: School, Drugs and Alcohol, Delinquent Friends, Criminal Justice Contact, Family Adversity, Lifetime Trauma/Stress, and Chronic Stress. A total 'pre-existing vulnerability' index score was then created by summing these seven scales.

Institutional vulnerability

Institutional vulnerability was probed using items – including peer-on-peer violence, staff relations and feelings of well-being while in detention – derived from a number of studies on youth in custody and detention (see for example Maitland & Sluder, 1996; Evaluation Research Group, 1997; MQOL survey – Measuing Quality of Life Survey in Liebling; 2004; Liebling et. al. 2005; and items from Pathways to Desistance Study, Mulvey, 2006). Items derived from Maitland and Sluder's (1996) Fear of Victimization Scale and Prison Stresses Scale were administered in all three studies in order to explore vulnerability within the institution. Items that probed peer-on-peer violence amongst inmates and their peers were of particular interest, including: 'How safe do you feel in this prison?', 'How much do you worry that you'll be attacked during this sentence?', and 'Do you feel the chance of being attacked in this prison is low, medium, or high?' In order to measure prison stress, youth were asked to rate the difficulty of a number of aspects of prison, including missing freedom, missing family and friends, strip searches, and lack of privacy. Several items measuring institutional peer relationships were also administered: 'How many friends do you have in this prison?', 'Do you spend most of your free time in this prison alone or with friends?', and 'If you were going to be attacked, could you count on friends to help?' (Maitland & Sluder, 1996).

Psychosocial adjustment in prison

To obtain information on the socio-emotional behavioral functioning of participants, Achenbach's (1991) Youth Self Report (YSR) was administered. The YSR is a widely used self-report measure of both social competence and behavior problems in youth 11-18 years of age. Reliability and validity of the YSR have been extensively documented in both clinical samples and school-aged youth from the general population (Achenbach, 1991). Each behavior problem item is rated on a 3-point scale (1= 'Not True', 2 = 'Somewhat True' or 3 = 'Very True'). The Internalizing scale, comprised of withdrawn behaviors (e.g., I refuse to talk, I am under-active), somatic complaints (e.g., aches and pains without known medical causes), and anxious/ depressed behaviors (e.g., I am sad, I am too fearful or anxious) was used to measure psychosocial adjustment. The decision to focus on internalizing arises in part from findings suggesting that staff at custodial facilities may be less successful at identifying internalizing difficulties than externalizing problems ('acting out' behaviors). In addition, we chose not to focus on externalizing, which comprises aggressive, delinquent, antisocial and oppositional behaviors, because these characteristics describe the vast majority of incarcerated youth.

RESULTS

Levels of Vulnerability and Adjustment Difficulties Characterizing Youth in Custody

According to Achenbach's (1991) norms, approximately 16% of the general population of young people show significantly concerning levels of internalizing behavior (defined as falling in the Borderline-Clinical or Clinical range). In contrast, in both Study 1 (23%) and Study 2 (25%), internalizing behaviors are somewhat overrepresented in incarcerated youth.

In addition, as anticipated, youth in each of our samples report multiple forms of familial, socio-emotional, and academic disadvantage including instability of living, difficulties in school, substance abuse problems, delinquent friends, contact with child welfare authorities, and witnessing violence (see Table 2). Though the presence of multiple forms of pre-existing vulnerable has remained consistent across studies, the qualitative data being collected in our current study speaks to the increasing presence of gang violence and gang activity in our respondents' neighborhoods. It has signaled the importance in future surveys of including items that probe gang involvement. Following is one example of a young man's response to whether he had ever witnessed violence in his neighborhood:

> Everything - swearing, fighting, shooting, people being put on fire, people buried alive - it's like a movie - it's crazy- sometimes I think this is a movie - this shit is only in made up stories...I lost one of my children at 8 months old - I was carrying her in my arms and I was shot at and she was shot (dead) that's why you cannot get attached to people - I hate to say it but that is why I can't get attached to my 3 kids I have now or my baby mother - that's life - you can't dwell on it -- you have to accept it and move on…

Table 2. Percentage of Youth Reporting Pre-existing Vulnerabilities.

	Sample 1 (N=100)	Sample 2 (N=100)	Sample 3 (N = 137)
Moved 2-4 times in past three years	60	44	59
Suspended from school	78	79	75
Uses Drugs	79	89	84
Uses Alcohol	78	77	66
Friends in trouble with police	76*	97	95
Children's Aid involvement	59	57	52
Removal from family**	_	32	28
Parents been to prison**	_	39	40
Witness violence or someone killed in neighborhood**	_	72	88

* 9% of youth in this sample said they had no friends.

**These questions were not part of first survey

When asked “Have you ever lived in a war or been present for a political uprising?” a surprising number of youth in our current studied answered, “my neighborhood is a war zone”.

Pre-existing Vulnerability is Related to Psychosocial Adjustment in Custody

Based on their pre-existing vulnerability index scores, participants in our first two studies were divided into low, medium, and high pre-existing vulnerability groups. Consistent with expectations, in both Study 1 and Study 2, one-way analyses of variance indicated that self-reported difficulties in psychosocial adjustment were significantly greater for those in the high vulnerability group compared to participants in the medium or low vulnerability groups (see Figure 1). Thus, consistent with an importation model of adjustment, youth who entered a facility with high levels of vulnerability were more likely to have difficulties with adjustment.

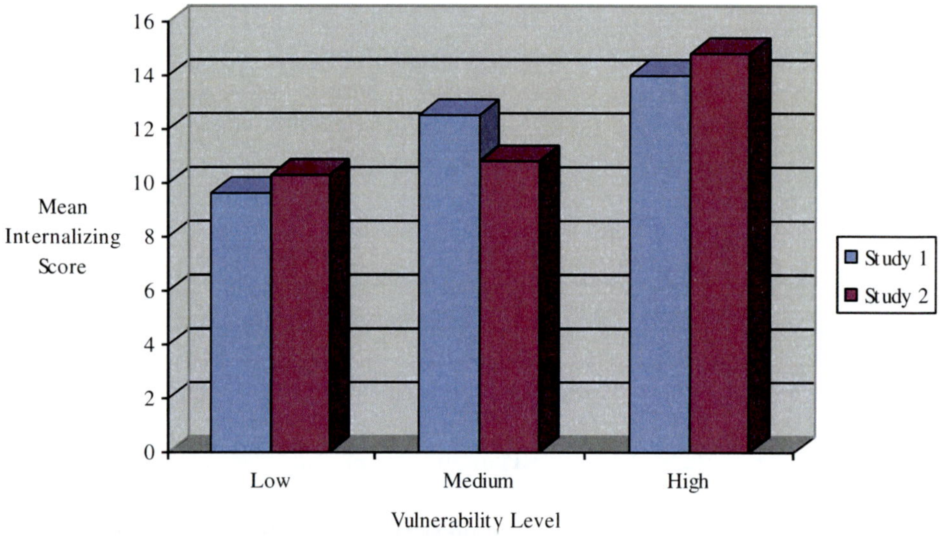

Figure 1. Youths' Raw Internalizing Scores as a Function of Pre-existing Vulnerability Level.

Institutional Variables Also Predict Psychosocial Adjustment

In terms of the significance of institutional vulnerability, our research to date has underscored the importance of internal support and friendship to young people’s psychosocial adjustment. In Study 1, institutional risk was explored in terms of perceptions about victimization and peer relationships within the custody facility. Perceptions of safety, including a youth’s worry about whether he might be attacked by another inmate or what he thought the chance of an attack by another youth was, were found to be critical to his sense of well being. Friendships also seemed to play a critical role in the general well being of youth. Fully half of the respondents who reported having no friends within the institution were characterized by borderline-clinical or clinical levels of internalizing, compared to only 19% who reported having even a few friends or 16% who reported having many friends ($\chi 2$ (2, 111) = 9.7, p < .05). Similarly, almost half (41%) of the youth who reported experiencing conflicts with other young offenders as "moderately" or "very" hard had borderline-clinical or clinical levels of internalizing compared to 17% who reported conflicts as "not hard" and 21% who reported conflicts as "a little hard" ($\chi 2$ (2, 111) = 6.1, p < .05). When respondents were asked whether friends would help if they were attacked, those youth who indicated that friends would *not* help were more likely to have borderline or clinical levels of internalizing scores (44%), than those who indicated that friends would assist them (18%; $\chi 2$ (1, 107) = 6.9 p < .05). In sum, many types of difficulties with peer relationships in custody seem to play a critical role in adjustment.

In Study 2, three summed scales were created to represent institutional vulnerability domains of Prison Stresses, Internal Support, and Fear.[7] There were significant relationships between two of the measures of institutional vulnerability and psychosocial adjustment. Youth who reported a high level of prison stress, F (2, 100) = 9.37, p. <.001) and who felt that they did not have much peer support in the institution, F (2, 100) = 5.05, p. <.01, were more likely to report being anxious, depressed or withdrawn than those with low levels of stress and high support.

Taken together, these results are consistent with a deprivation model of adaptation, suggesting that there is something unique about the prison environment that influences patterns of adjustment. What is interesting is that these findings suggest there is a differentiation between specific aspects of the prison environment (e.g., fear of victimization vs. social support).

Comparing the Contributions of Pre-Existing and Institutional Vulnerability to Psychosocial Adjustment

Study 1 and Study 2 employed two different analytical strategies for understanding the relative contribution to adjustment of pre-existing and institutional variables. However, both suggest that pre-existing vulnerabilities (and an importation model of adjustment) and institutional vulnerabilities (and a deprivation model of adjustment) contribute to young people's psychosocial adjustment in prison.

For Study 1, in order to examine the relationship between both pre-existing factors and institutional factors and psychosocial adjustment, a hierarchical regression analysis was carried out with internalizing raw scores on the YSR as the outcome variable. The pre-existing vulnerability total scores were entered in the first step of the analysis, and in Step 2 the institutional factors were entered. In Step 1 the model was significant in predicting internalizing scores, F (1, 107) = 6.75, p < .05 and pre-existing risk factors predicted 6% of the variance. The model remained significant at Step 2, F (7, 100) = 11.06, p < .01, accounting for 47% of the variance in internalizing scores, and was significantly improved by

[7] An institutional vulnerability index was not created as there is no evidence from prison literature that institutional vulnerabilities work in the same (cumulative) manner as pre-existing vulnerability.

the addition of the institutional risk measures. Four institutional risk factors significantly predicted internalizing: worry of attack, chance of attack, conflict with other inmates, and how inmates chose to spend their free time (alone or with friends).

As mentioned above, Study 2 explored the potentiating effect on adjustment of combining pre-existing vulnerability with institutional stressors. In other words, we wished to examine whether the combination of the two types of risk predicted greater maladjustment than would be expected by simply adding them together. In order to compare the relative contribution of pre-existing vulnerabilities and institutional vulnerabilities to youths' adjustment when they first entered custody, a two-step regression analysis was performed. The first model, which included both pre-existing vulnerabilities and institutional vulnerabilities (prison stresses, internal support, and fear), was significant and explained 37% of the variance in adjustment at Time 1. Both pre-existing vulnerability and prison stresses emerged as significant individual predictors of adjustment. The addition of the interaction between pre-existing vulnerability and prison stresses at Step 2 added significantly to the model (p. <.05), which accounted for 41% of the variance in psychosocial adjustment scores. Again, both pre-existing vulnerability and prison stresses, as well as the interaction term, were significant predictors of internalizing. Thus, youth with high levels of *both* pre-existing vulnerability and perceived prison stress experienced poorer self-reported adjustment than those who scored high on either vulnerability or stress (but not both) or neither variable. Neither internal support nor fear predicted psychosocial adjustment at either step of the model.

Taken together, the results of these studies: (a) support *interactionist* criminological theories of prison adaptation (i.e., those that emphasize both importation and deprivation factors as important in adjustment), (b) indicate that the *accumulation* of pre-existing vulnerabilities (i.e., high vulnerability scores) predicts poorer psychosocial adjustment (higher levels of internalizing), which is consistent with a cumulative risk model, and (c) support the developmental psychopathology assertion that the *combination* of risks and stressors (in this case pre-existing vulnerability and institutional stresses) results in poorer psychosocial functioning than would be predicted by simply adding these predictors.

Comparing Predictors of Adjustment during and after the 'Settling-in' Period: Do the Same Variables Matter?

As mentioned above, we also wanted to explore whether the factors that predict custodial adjustment during the initial settling in period are the same as those that predict adjustment once youths have been in the custodial environment for several weeks. This is an important question as poor adjustment to pre-trial detention or a custodial sentence at any stage of a young person's incarceration negatively affects both discipline and youth's capacity to take advantage of available programming. Two sets of analyses explored this question. In the first, we examined whether pre-existing and institutional vulnerabilities measured at entry into custody would continue to predict youths' adjustment at Time 2. In the second we examined youths' Time 2 adjustment on the basis of concurrent (Time 2) measures of vulnerability and stress.

Taken together, the results of these analyses suggest that different variables predict adjustment at entry into custody and later on as youths spend more time in custody. Pre-existing vulnerability was a consistent predictor of adjustment at both the initial and follow up points. This is not surprising since this scale measures historical (and thus static) vulnerabilities with which a youth 'walks into' a custody facility. In contrast, there were differences in the dynamic factors that predicted initial adjustment to custody versus youth adjustment following the settling in period. For example, prison stresses, though an important predictor of psychosocial adjustment at Time 1, was not a strong predictor of internalizing at Time 2. In terms of the deprivation hypothesis, the finding suggests that there are some institutional vulnerabilities – such as stress – that are always present, but that some youth are able to manage or cope with them over time so they become less related to their functioning. This is consistent with research on adult inmates (Adams, 1992; Liebling, 1999; Wheeler, 1961; Zamble and Porporino, 1988).

Interestingly, although the level of internal support youth reported at Time 1 did not predict Time 1 adjustment, it was a moderately important predictor of adjustment at Time 2. Therefore the level of support youth can garner from front line staff and peers at entry into custody may have increasing importance as a youth spends more time in an institution. In contrast, while Time 1 fear did not predict Time 2 adjustment, youths' level of fear at Time 2 was a significant predictor of adjustment at Time 2. Thus, it is a young person's current level of fear that predicts adjustment. This is an interesting finding given that prison stress appears to become less important as a youth spends more time in a facility. It suggests that life within the institution, particularly peer relations, becomes increasingly important as worries and concerns about being isolated from the outside world (which are reflected in the prison stresses scale) recede.

Youths' Adjustment in Pre-Trial Detention

The purpose of the third, ongoing, study is to examine the adjustment of adolescent males in secure pre-trial detention facilities and to compare their adjustment to our previous findings on adolescent boys serving post-sentence custodial terms. Sentenced populations and detention populations have often been studied separately, not only because of a difference in seriousness of charges but because it is believed that remand is a unique time of severe stress and uncertainty. Studies of both adults and youth in detention often focus on the negative effect that detention has on the outcome of a case in court. Those who are detained are more likely to plead guilty, be convicted if tried, and to receive a prison sentence (Fagan & Guggenheim, 1996; Moyer & Basic, 2006). There is evidence to suggest however, that in addition to negative legal outcomes, detention may present possible negative psychological outcomes for young people. Remand is a highly stressful time for most detainees, but especially for youth, because of fear of the unknown (including the uncertainties of charge, conviction and sentencing), the distrust of an authoritative environment, a lack of control, and isolation from family and significant others (Hayes, 2000). Youths, who are especially dependent on structure, activity, family support and staff interaction, may be particularly prone to boredom, bullying, a high rate of infractions, and at the extreme, suicide (Liebling, 1999).

We also continue to examine the theoretical frameworks of importation, deprivation, and cumulative risk in relation to adjustment to detention. In part, this involves measurement development and refinement. For example, the consistency of our findings regarding the contribution of pre-existing vulnerabilities to adjustment has given us confidence in the validity of the scale used in our previous studies. However, findings from these same studies suggest that the model for institutional vulnerability is likely complex and requires further development. To that end, we have included new items to measure institutional vulnerabilities, including items that tap into internal support and relationships between staff and youth, and youth and peers. A primary goal of this study is to develop and test an overall 'institutional vulnerabilities' index analogous to our measure of pre-existing vulnerabilities. This will allow us to examine whether, as with pre-existing vulnerabilities, the developmental psychopathology model of cumulative risk also applies when considering risks and stresses within an institution.

Consistent with our emphasis on viewing adjustment to incarceration through a developmental lens, in our current research we have begun to explore youths' perception of masculinities – their sense of emerging from boyhood into manhood against the backdrop of adult institutions and processes. In this regard, one of the themes that has surfaced to date is youths' preoccupations with appearing "mature" and not like a "stupid kid" especially vis-à-vis interactions with staff. Following is a typical narrative:

> just be more mature about it - people see you are more mature you get more respect - I don't want to see any of the guys from here on the road...(they are) immature kids (They) try to make fun, try to rap, stupids jokes - stuff you laugh at when you are 12 - certain, desprespctful ways they talk about women...

Despite the desire to be (or at least appear) mature, preliminary analyses support Katz's (2001, p.207) assertion that "boys are not men". Indeed, demonstrating seemingly 'adult' behavior (e.g., a violent crime) is not an indicator of a youthful offender being more sophisticated or mature than his peers (Zimring & Fagan, 2000). Many of the youth we interview still share youthful preoccupations. They talk about the importance of negotiating friendships within the institution, about missing girlfriends, about crying when they are alone, and about being homesick. The following is typical of a young person whose incarceration experience is the first real moment away from home:

> Having to be away from my family for a really long time – when I got here I was up in my room I wouldn't come downstairs. I stayed up in my room and cried; I could not handle it – I didn't want to associate with anyone – the police holding cell was crappy – it's not that bad (now) but I've never been away from my family for this amount of time and I am not used to it – I've never even gone camping before with or without... I've just been at home with my family the whole time – I can stay away for a weekend that is only two days.

Their future plans/dreams following release might be those of any 13 or 15 year old: to go to McDonalds, or to a hockey game, to go to a local amusement park for the first time, to attend university. In our continuing attempt to place young people's experience within a developmental context, we feel that our qualitative data will add enormously to our understanding.

Implications for Research and Practice

Our research on youth in custody and detention to date has been an attempt to understand patterns and predictors of adjustment. We have endeavored to integrate sociological/ criminological theory on adult prison adjustment with psychological theory on adolescent stress. We have utilized adult models of prison adjustment – namely the importation and deprivation models – as a methodological basis for analysis in conjunction with developmental psychopathology models of risk. This integrated model has helped us explore the contributions of pre-existing vulnerabilities *and* institutional vulnerabilities to adjustment. Most of our analysis to date has been quantitative in nature. However, our interviews with youth have also involved a great deal of informal discussion about their lives, including their life in the institution. Our ongoing study gathers this type of qualitative data in a systematic fashion. It complements the quantitative protocols we have used to date and in so doing, will provide a broader, richer understanding of the experiences of youth in custody.

Gover, MacKenzie and Armstrong (2000) argue, "Identifying juveniles with high anxiety levels, whether it was caused by institutional conditions, past experiences, or a combination of both, would allow treatment staff to direct attention to those who experienced negative emotional reactions to confinement" (p.451). Our research suggests that pre-existing vulnerabilities are a strong and consistent predictor of difficulties in adjustment throughout a youth's time in custody. Though institutional staff cannot change a young person's past experiences, knowing which youth enter the facility with high levels of pre-existing vulnerability may be useful in determining levels of institutional support.

In addition, one of the central findings of our research confirms that institutional vulnerabilities appear to be separate predictors of adjustment. Prison stresses which many inmates feel at entry into custody (missing freedom, missing family and friends, missing certain activities) are aspects of adjustment to custody that unfortunately, are not something that the institution can control. As most front-line staff are likely aware however, many youths learn to manage the traditional difficulties associated with entry to custody.

There are however, important predictors of prison adjustment over which staff may have some control. Internal support and levels of fear appear to play an important role in adjustment behaviors. Developmental research on adolescent adjustment suggests that one of the most important predictors of adolescent adjustment is perceived support in relationships with significant others (Scholte, van Lieshout & van Aken, 2001). Our research confirms this finding, suggesting that internal support within the institution appears to play a critical role in adjustment to custody the longer a youth spend time in an institution.

Many front-line staff that often felt overwhelmed by their day-to-day duties. They often feel that they have little impact on youth with whom they work with. Nevertheless the vast majority of our respondents over the past decade have said that there were staff that they could talk to about their problems, that the presence of staff made them feel safe and believed that if a fight broke out staff would stop it. Perhaps one of the most encouraging findings of our research has been the discovery of the important role that staff can play in shaping a young person's custodial stay. Staff it would seem may play a critical role in shaping a healthy institutional environment. This finding we feel should be integral to the development of best practices for youth in custody or pre-trial detention.

REFERENCES

Achenbach, T. M. (1991). *Manual for the Youth Self-Report and 1991 Profile*. Burlington, VT: University of Vermont Department of Psychiatry.

Adams, K. (1992). Adjusting to prison life. In M. Tonry (Ed.), *Crime and justice: Vol. 16. A review of research,* (pp. 275-359). Chicago: University of Chicago Press.

Arnold, E. L. (1990). *Childhood Stress* New York: John Wiley and Sons.

Bartollas, C. (1982). Survival problems of adolescent prisoners. In R. Johnson & H. Tock (Eds.), *The pains of imprisonment* (pp. 165-179). Beverley Hills, CA: Sage Publications.

Bartollas, C., Miller, S. J., & Dinitz, S. (1976). The exploitation matrix in a juvenile institution. *International Journal of Sociology of Law, 4*, 257-270.

Biggam, F. H. & Power, K. G. (1999). Social problem-solving skills and psychological distress among incarcerated young offenders: The issue of bullying and victimization. *Cognitive Therapy and Research, 23(3)*, 307-326.

Biggam. F. H. & Power K. G. (1999). Suicidality and the state-trait debate on problem solving deficits: A re-examination with incarcerated young offenders. *Archives of Suicide Research, 5(1)*, 27-42.

Bishop, D. M. (2000). Juvenile offenders in the adult criminal justice system. In M. Tonry (Ed.), *Crime and Justice: Vol. 27. A review of research* (pp. 81-167). Chicago: University of Chicago Press.

Bishop, D. M., Frazier, C. E., Lanza-Kaduce, L. & White, H. G. (1998). *Juvenile transfers to criminal court study: Phase I final report*. Washington, D.C.: U.S. Department of Justice, Office of Juvenile Justice and Delinquency.

Bortner, M. A. & Williams. L. M. (1997). *Youth in prison: We the people of unit four.* New York: Routledge.

Bottoms, A. E. (1999). Interpersonal violence and social order in prisons. In M. Tonry & J. Petersila (Eds.), *Prisons* (pp. 205-281). Chicago: University of Chicago Press.

Burt, M. R., Resnick, G. & Novick, E. R. (1998). *Building supportive communities for at-risk adolescents*. Washington, DC: American Psychological Association.

Cesaroni, C. and Michele Peterson-Badali. (2005). Young offenders in custody: Risk and adjustment. *Criminal Justice and Behavior, 32(3)*, 251-277.

Cesaroni, C. and Michele Peterson-Badali. (In press). Understanding the adjustment of incarcerated young offenders: A Canadian Example. *Youth Justice.*

Clarke-McLean, J. G. (1996). Social networks among incarcerated juvenile offenders. *Social Development, 5(2)*, 7-21.

Clemmer, D. (1940). *The prison community*. New York: Holt, Rinehart & Winston.

Connell, A. & Farrington, D. (1996). Bullying among incarcerated young offenders: developing and interview schedule and some preliminary results. *Journal of Adolescence, 19*, 75-93.

Cowan, P. A., Pape Cowan, C. & Schulz, M. S. (1996). Thinking about risk and resilience in families. In E. M. Heatherington, & E. A. Blechman (Eds.), *Stress, Coping, and Resiliency in Children and Families.* (pp. 1-38). Mahwah: NJ: Lawrence Erblaum.

Crawley, E. & Sparks, R. (2005). Hidden Injuries? Researching the Experiences of Older Men in English Prisons. *The Howard Journal, 44(4)*, 345-356.

Crewe, B. The sociology of imprisonment. In Y. Jewkes (Ed.), *Handbook on Prisons* (pp. 123 -151) Portland: Willan Publishing.

Duclos, C. W., Beals, J., Novins, D. K., Martin, C., Jewett, C. & Manson, S. M. (1998). Prevalence of common psychiatric disorders among American Indian adolescent detainees. *Journal of American Academy of Child and Adolescent Psychiatry, 37(8)*, 866 -873.

Dyson, G. P., Power, K. G. & Wozniak, E. (1997). Problems with using official records from young offender institutions as indices of bullying. *International Journal of Offender Therapy and Comparative Criminology, 41(2)*, 121-138.

Eccles, J. S., Midgley, C., Wigfield, A., Buchanan, C. M., Reuman, D., Flanagan, C. & Iver, M. D. (1993). Development during adolescence: The impact of stage-environment fit on young adolescents' experiences in schools and in families. *American Psychologist, 48(2)*, 90-101.

Edgar, K. & O'Donnell, I. (1998). Assault in prison: The victim's contribution. *British Journal of Criminology, 38(4)*, 635-650.

Evaluation Research Group, University of Maryland. (1997). *Juvenile Survey Instrument: National Evaluation of Juvenile Correctional Facilities.* Author: Maryland.

Fagan, J. & Guggenheim, M. (1996). Preventive detention and the judicial prediction of dangerousness for juveniles: A natural experiment. *The Journal of Criminal Law and Criminology, 86(2)*, 415-449.

Farrington, D. (2000). Explaining and preventing crime: The globalization of knowledge. *Criminology, 38*, 1-25.

Feld, B. (1981). A comparative analysis of organizational structure and inmate subcultures in institutions for juvenile offenders. *Crime and Delinquency, 27*, 336-363.

Garmezy, N. (1983). Stressors of childhood. In N. Garmezy, & M. Rutter (Eds.), *Stress, coping and development in children,* (pp. 43-85). New York: McGraw Hill.

Ge, X., Conger, R. D. & Elder, G. H. (2001). The relationship between puberty and psychological distress in adolescent boys. *Journal of Research on Adolescence, 11(1)*, 49-70.

Goldson, B. (2005). Child Imprisonment: A Case for Abolition. *Youth Justice, 5(2)*, 77-90.

Goldson, B. (2006) Damage, Harm and Death in Child Prisons in England and Wales: Questions of Abuse and Accountability. *Howard Journal, 45(5)*, 449-467.

Goodstein, L. & Wright, K. N. (1989). Inmate adjustment to prison. In L. Goodstein, & D. L. MacKenzie (Eds.), *The American Prison,* (pp. 229-251). New York: Plenum Press.

Gore, S. & Colten, M. E. (1991). Adolescent stress, Social relationships and mental health." In M. E. Colten, & S. Gore (Eds). *Adolescent Stress: Causes and Consequences*, (pp. 1-14). New York: Aldine de Gruyter.

Gore, S. & Eckenrode, J. (1994). Context and process in research on risk and resilience. In R. J. Haggerty, L. R. Sherrod, N. Garmezy, & M. Rutter (Eds.), *Stress, risk and resilience in children and adolescents,* (pp. 19-63). Cambridge: Cambridge University Press.

Gover, A. R., MacKenzie, D. L. & Armstrong. G. S. (2000). Importation and Deprivation Explanations of Juveniles' Adjustment to Correctional Facilities. *International Journal of Offender Therapy and Comparative Criminology, 44(4)*, 450-467.

Gover, A. R. (2000). *Influence of Child Maltreatment on Juveniles' Psychological Adjustment Within Correctional Institutions.* Diss. University of Maryland, 1999.

Greve, W., Enzmann, D. & Hosser, D. (2001). The stabilization of self-esteem among incarcerated adolescents: Accommodative and immunizing processes. *International Journal of Offender Therapy and Comparative Criminology, 45(6)*, 749-768.

Harvey, J. (2007). *Young Men in Prison: Surviving and Adaptation to Life Inside*. Portland, Willan Publishing.

Hauser, S. T. & Bowlds, M. K. (1990). Stress, Coping and Adaptation. *At the threshold: The developmental adolescent* (pp. 388 - 413). Cambridge, MA: Harvard University Press.

Hayes, L. M. (2000). Suicide prevention in juvenile facilities. *Juvenile Justice, 7(1)*, 24-33.

Hendren, R. L. (1990). Stress in Adolescence. In L. Eugene (Ed.), *Childhood Stress* (pp. 247-264). New York: John Wiley and Sons.

Hochstetler, A. & DeLisi, M. (2005). Importation, deprivation, and varieties of serving time: An integrated-lifestyle-exposure model of prison offending. *Journal of Criminal Justice, 33(3)*, 257-266.

Hoschstetler, A., Murphy, D. S. & Simons, R. L. (2004). Damaged goods: Exploring predictors of distress in prison inmates. *Crime & Delinquency, 50(3)*, 436-457.

Ireland, J. L. & Monaghan, R. (2006). Behaviours indicative of bullying among young and juvenile male offenders: A study of perpetrator and victim characteristics. *Aggressive Behaviour, 32(2)*, 172-180.

Ireland, J. L. (2005). Psychological health and bullying behaviour among adolescent prisoners: a study of young juvenile offenders. *Journal of Adolescent Health, 36(3)*, 236-243.

Irwin, J. & Cressey, J. (1962). Thieves, convicts and the inmate culture. *Social Problems, 10(2)*, 142-155.

Ivanoff, A. (1992). Background risk factors associated with parasuicide among male prison inmates. *Criminal Justice and Behaviour, 19(4)*, 426-436.

Jewkes, Y. (2005). Men behind bars: "Doing" masculinity as an adaptation to imprisonment. *Men and Masculinities, 8(1)*, 44-63.

Johnson, R. (1978). Youth in crisis: Dimensions of self-destructive conduct among adolescent prisoners. *Adolescence, 13(51)*, 461-482.

Katz, J. (2001). Boys are not men: Notes on working with adolescent males in juvenile detention. In D. Sabo, T. A. Kupers, & W. London (Eds.) *Prison Masculinities*. Philadelphia: Temple University Press.

Kimchi, J. & Schaffner, B. (1990). Childhood protective factors and stress risk.. In L. E. Arnold (Ed.) *Childhood Stress* (pp. 475-500). New York: John Wiley and Sons.

Kruttschnitt, C. & Gartner, R. (2003). Women's imprisonment. In M. Tonry (Ed.), *Crime and Justice: Vol. 30. A Review of Research* (pp. 1-81). Chicago: University of Chicago Press.

Kruttschnitt, C., Gartner, R. & Carbone, K. (2002, Nov.). *Women's styles of doing time and their adjustment in two different prison settings.* Paper presented at American Society of Criminology, Chicago.

Lawson, D. P., Segrin, C. & Ward, T. D. (1996) The relationship between prisonization and social skills among prison inmates. *The Prison Journal, 76(3)*, 293-309.

Liebling, A. (1999). Prison Suicide and Prison Coping. In M. Tonry, & J. Petersilia (Eds.), *Prisons: Crime and Justice A Review of Research* (pp. 283-359). Chicago: University of Chicago Press.

Liebling, A. (2003, Nov.). *Legitimacy, Prison Suicide and the Moral Performance of Prisons.* Paper presented at American Society of Criminology, Chicago.

Liebling, A. (2004). *Prisons and Their Moral Performance*. Oxford: Oxford University Press.

Liebling, A., Durie, L., Stiles, A. & Tait, S. (2005). Revisiting Prison Suicide: The Role of Fairness and Distress. In A. Libeling and S. Maruna (Eds.), *The Effects of Imprisonment*, (pp. 209-231). Portland: Willan Publishing.

Loeber, R. & Farrington, D. P. (1997). Never too early, never too late: Risk factors and successful interventions for serious and violent juvenile offenders. *Studies on Crime and Crime Prevention*, 7, 7-30.

Maccoby, E. E. (1983). Social-emotional development and response to stressors In N. Garmezy, & M. Rutter (Eds.), *Stress, Coping and Development of Children,* (pp. 217-234) New York: McGraw-Hill.

MacKenzie, D. (1987). Age and adjustment in prison: Interactions with Attitudes and Anxiety. *Criminal Justice and Behavior*, *14(4)*, 427- 447.

Maitland, A. S. & Sluder, R. D. (1996). Victimization in prisons: A study of factors related to general well-being of youthful inmates. *Federal Probation*, *60*, 24-31.

Maitland, A. S. & Sluder, R. D. (1998). Victimization and youthful prison inmates: An empirical analysis. *The Prison Journal*, *78(1)*, 55-73.

McCorkle, R. C. (1993). Living on the edge: Fear in a maximum security prison. *Journal of Offender Rehabilitation*, *20(1/2)*, 73-91.

McShane, M. D. & Williams III, F. P. (1989). The prison adjustment of juvenile offenders. *Crime and Delinquency*, *35(2)*, 254-269.

Moran, P. B. & Eckenrode, J. (1991). Gender differences in costs and benefits of peer relations during adolescence. *Journal of Adolescent Research*, *6*, 396-409.

Moyer, S. & Basic, M. (2006). Pre-Trial Detention Under the Young Offenders Act: A Study of Urban Courts. Ottawa: Department of Justice Canada.

Mulvey, E. (2006). *Pathways to Desistance Study.* Pittsburgh: University of Pittsburgh School of Medicine.

Mutchnick, R. J. & Fawcett, M. (1991). Group Home Environments and Victimization of Resident Juveniles. *International Journal of Offender Therapy & Comparative Criminology*, *25*, 126-142.

O'Donnell, I. & Edgar, K. (1998). Routine victimization in prison. *Howard Journal of Criminal Justice*, *37*, 266-279.

Peterson, A. C., Kennedy R. E. & Sullivan, P. Coping with adolescence. M. E. Colten & S. Gore (Eds.) *Adolescent Stress: Causes and Consequences*. (pp. 93-110). New York: Aldine de Gruyter.

Poole, E. D. & Regoli, R. M. (1983). Professionalism, role conflict, work alienation and anomie: A look at prison management. *Social Science Journal*, *20(1)*, 63-70.

Rice, K. G., Herman, M.A., & Peterson, A. C. (1993). Coping with challenge in adolescence: a concepetual model and psycho-educational intervention." *Journal of Adolescence*, *16*, pp. 235-251.

Ruffolo, F. (1998). Coping strategies and well-being during adolescence and early adulthood." Diss. Ontario Institute for Studies in Education of the University of Toronto.

Rutter, M. (1983). Stressors of childhood. In N. Garmezy & M. Rutter (Eds.), *Stress, coping and development in children,* (pp.1- 41). New York, NY: McGraw Hill.

Scholte, R. H. J., van Leishout, C. F. M. & van Aken, M. A. G. (2001). Perceived relational support in adolescence: Dimension, configurations, and adolescent adjustment. *Journal of Research on Adolescence*, *11(1)*, 71-94.

Schulman, S. (1993). Close relationships and coping behavior in adolescence. *Journal of Adolescence, 16*, 267-283.

Seiffge-Krenke, I. (1993). Coping behavior in normal and clinical samples: more similarities than difference? *Journal of Adolescence, 16*, 285-303.

Seiffge-Krenke, I. (1995). *Stress, coping and relationships in adolescence.* Mahwah, NJ: Lawrence Erlbaum.

Shields, I. W. & Simourd, D. J. (1991). Predicting predatory behaviour in a population of incarcerated young offenders. *Criminal Justice and Behaviour, 18*, 180 -194.

Sim, J. (1995). Tougher than the rest? Men in prison. In T. Newburn, & B. Stanko (Eds.), *Just boys doing business: Men, masculinities and crime,* (pp. 110-117). New York: Routledge.

Simon, J. (2000). The 'society of captives' in the era of hyper-incarceration. *Theoretical Criminology, 4(3)*, 285-308.

Smetana, J. G., Yau, J., Restrepo, A. & Braeges, J. L. (1991). Conflict and adaptation in adolescence. In M. E. Colten & S. Gore (Eds.), *Adolescent Stress: Causes and Consequences,* (pp. 643-654). New York: Aldine de Gruyter.

Smith, C., Lizotte, A. J., Thornberry, T. P. & Krohn, M. D. (1995).Resilent youth: Identifying factors that prevent high-risk youth from engaging in delinquency and drug use. *Current Perspectives.*

Steinberg, L., Chung Len, H. & Little, M. (2004). Re-entry of young offenders from the justice system: A developmental perspective. *Youth violence and juvenile justice, 2(1)*, 21-38.

Sykes, G. M. (1958). *The society of captives: a study of a maximum security prison.* Princeton, N.J.: Princeton University Press.

Toch, H. & Adams, K. (1989). The disturbed violence offender. London: Yale University Press.

Ulzen, T. & Hamilton, H. (1998). Psychiatric disorders in incarcerated youth. *Youth Update, 16*, 4-5.

Vandergoot, M. E. (2006). Justice for Young Offenders: Their Needs, Our Responses. Saskatoon, SK: Purich Publishing Ltd.

Wheaton, B. (1990). Life transitions, role histories and mental health. *American Sociological Review, 55*, 209-223.

Wheaton, W., Roszell, P. & Hall, K. (1997). The impact of twenty childhood and adult traumatic stressors on the risk of psychiatric disorder. In I. H. Gotlib, & B. Wheaton (Eds.), *Stress and adversity over the life course: Trajectories and turning points,* (pp. 50-72). New York: Cambridge University Press.

Wheeler, S. (1961). Socialization in correctional communities. *American Sociological Review, 26*, 697-712.

Windzio, M. (2006). Is there a deterrent effect of pains of imprisonment?: The impact of social costs of first incarceration on the hazard rate of recidivism. *Punishment & Society, 8(3)*, 341-364.

Wright, K. (1991). The violent and victimized in the male prison. *Journal of Offender Rehabilitation, 16(3)*, 1-25.

Zamble, E. & Porporino, F. J. (1988). *Coping, behavior and adjustment in prison inmates.* New York: Springer-Verlag.

Zimring, F. E. & Fagan, J. (2000). Transfer policy and law reform. In J. Fagan & F.E. Zimring (Eds.), *The Changing Borders of Juvenile Justice: Transfer of Adolescents to the Criminal Court,* (pp. 407-424). Chicago: University of Chicago Press.

In: Violent Crime and Prisons: Population... ISBN: 978-1-60741-668-5
Ed: Aidan Renshaw and Emelina Suárez

Chapter 3

UNITY BUILDING AS VIOLENCE PREVENTION: A CALL FOR A FUNDAMENTAL PARADIGM SHIFT

H.B. Danesh *
International Education for Peace Institute (EFP-International)
Interpersonal Skills: Effects of a Training Program on Quantitative and Qualitative Response Criteria in Incarcerated Women Criminals

ABSTRACT

Violence is observed in all levels and expressions of biological and social life. However, human violence has the distinction of being greatly altered by the dynamics of individual and group development, which takes place in the context of our worldviews—view of reality, human nature, the purpose of life, and laws governing human relationships. Three metacategories of worldview—survival-based, identity-based, and unity-based—are identified. The first two categories are conflict-based and conducive to violence. The third category—unity-based worldview—is peace-based and conducive to significant decrease in both occurrence of conflicts and their satisfactory peaceful resolution. It is proposed that with regard to the genesis of human violence and its prevention there is a need for a fundamental paradigm shift of a kind identified by Kuhn with regard to revolutionary periods in the advancement of any given area of science. Current, generally accepted, perspectives on violence make no distinction between human violence and the types observed in other living beings in the arena of struggle for survival and dominance. It is argued that while these forms of violence do exist and have always existed in human life, they are, nevertheless, subject to the dynamics of human individual and group development, which are conscious and deliberate processes, not autonomous and involuntary as in other levels of life. The premises of the chapter are validated by the extensive and intensive Education for Peace Program, which has been implemented in post-war Bosnia and Herzegovina since 2000 and has brought tangible

* H.B. Danesh, M.D., F.R.C.P. (C) is the founder and director of the International Education for Peace Institute (EFP-International) with programs in Bosnia and Herzegovina (EFP-Balkans), Canada (EFP-Canada), Switzerland (EFP-International), and the United States (EFP-America). He is a retired professor of psychiatry and conflict resolution. This article is a revised segment of an unpublished manuscript—Fever in the World of the Mind: On the Causes and Prevention of Violence—one of a series of publications in the Education for Peace Program. The manuscript was partially funded by a research grant from the United States Institute for Peace.

levels of conflict reduction and violence prevention among the participants (80,000 students, 5,000 educators, 120,000 parents) in this post-war highly conflicted society.

INTRODUCTION

In September 2000, a comprehensive two-year pilot program of Education for Peace was introduced into all classes and to all students of three primary and three secondary schools, one of each, in three different Bosnia and Herzegovina (BiH) cities—Banja Luka, Sarajevo, and Travnik. The pilot project involved some 6,000 students, 400 teachers and 10,000 parents/guardians from Bosniak (Muslim), Croat (Catholic), and Serb (Orthodox Christianity) backgrounds who represented the three main ethnic populations of BiH that were engaged in the devastating 1992–1995 civil war. With the successful completion of the pilot project, the program was subsequently introduced to an additional 106 schools with a total of 80,000 students, 5,000 teachers and school staff, and tens of thousands of parents/guardians. The project now, at the behest of the Government of BiH and the International Community in that country, is being gradually introduced to all 2,200+ BiH schools, involving 1.5 million students and 110,000 educators.

The EFP curriculum is based on the concept of unity presented in this chapter and which forms the basis of the Integrative Theory of Peace (ITP). ITP holds that the most effective approach to dealing with human violence is to create peaceful environments—home, school, community, national, and the world. It further states that peace is the outcome of inclusive and ever-widening circles of unity in the context of diversity.[1]

Since its inception, the EFP Program has demonstrated the validity of its main premise that human conflict and violence can best be understood and prevented when the participants are helped to systematically investigate their own respective individual and group worldviews, make conscious and deliberate effort to discard their conflict-based worldviews and replace them with unity-based worldviews, and implement that inclusive worldview in their personal, professional, and community life. For the past nine years (2000–2008) the EFP Program has been focused on assisting BiH educators, parents/guardians, community leaders, and policy-makers in their efforts to provide new generations of young leaders and citizens in their country with the knowledge, skills, and motivation to resolve their conflicts peacefully and to prevent occurrence of violence in and between their respective ethnic communities. The outcome of this endeavor, thus far, has been extremely promising and positive (see Appendix I), and its findings merit serious consideration by those concerned with the task of peaceful resolution of human conflicts and effective, sustainable prevention of human violence.[2] This is particularly important as EFP Programs are now being gradually introduced to schools in Canada and the United States, and other countries in several parts of the world that are currently considering its implementation. This chapter describes concepts of unity, worldview, peace building, and violence prevention, which constitute the core components of ITP and EFP within the broad framework of peaceful conflict resolution and effective violence prevention.

THE CHALLENGE

Violence is one of the most puzzling and costly aspects of human life; and, as yet, no universally satisfactory and compelling approach for its understanding and prevention has been proposed. The premise of this chapter is that human violence has its genesis in the interface between human biological, psychological, social, and spiritual aspects of life in the context of our personal and collective worldviews. Everything that we humans think, feel, and do, as individuals and in groups, is shaped by our "worldviews"—our view of reality, human nature, the purpose of life, and human relationships. Worldviews, in turn, are shaped by interface between our hereditary and genetic endowments, mental and emotional capacities, moral and ethical principles, and our unique life circumstances and experiences.

The faces of violence are many. They include self-mutilation and suicide, injury to others and homicide, persistent conflicts and wars, cruelty to animals, and destruction of nature and property. However, in recent times both the extent and intensity of human violence have increased dramatically. The twentieth century has by far been the most violent period in human history. Two World Wars and many extremely destructive regional wars; the Holocaust; Hiroshima and Nagasaki; the political purges of the Stalin era; the Cultural Revolution in China; several major regional wars, deprivations imposed and cruelties committed by the more powerful and the wealthy on the abject masses in Africa, Asia, and the Americas; and religious, racial, and ethnic conflicts throughout the world are among the most well-known examples of violence during the 20th century. Now in the 21st century international terrorism has been added to the list. There are yet other virulent forms of violence that continue to plague humanity in both poor and rich countries and in all segments of the society, notably violence against women, children, the poor, those with physical or mental challenges, minorities, and the underprivileged. In short, violence is found in every culture and stratum of human society.

RESEARCH ON VIOLENCE

In its 28 July 2000 edition, the prestigious journal *Science* [3] reviewed some of the most generally accepted theories and discourse on the causes of violence and attempts at its prevention. The editorial, "Violence: A New Frontier for Scientific Research," refers to the role of guns, drugs (particularly crack cocaine), and the state of economy as the main causes for the rise of interpersonal violence in the United States of America in the mid-1980s and its subsequent decline in the 1990s. The editorial also refers to the need for research in the "biological underpinnings of individual violent behavior," "parenting styles," community and environmental attitudes towards violence, and "situational dynamics" such as gun possession.[4] The editorial by Alfred Blumstein, professor of public policy and management at Carnegie Mellon University, is an accurate reflection of the prevailing perspectives on violence. It is at once broad but not comprehensive, informative but not insightful, and promising but not hopeful.

The introduction to the special section on violence also begins with a statement that reflects the most commonly accepted views on both the nature and causes of human violence. It reads: "From the neighborhood bully berating a meek classmate to the rhesus macaque screaming at a rival, displays of aggression are the weapon of choice throughout the animal kingdom for asserting dominance, challenging a higher ranking individual, or laying claim to food, water, and other resources…."[5] This statement makes the assumption that human aggression has the same underlying causes as animal aggression. It sees aggression as a necessary and unavoidable dimension of human life. It asserts that the purpose of human aggression, like that of the rhesus macaque, is to establish dominance over others, to win victory over competitors, and to use aggression for obtaining the requisites for survival and pleasure. The statement also indirectly asserts that these issues—dominance, victory, survival, and pleasure—are the primary objectives of human life, just as they are for all members of the animal kingdom.

A large number of researchers aim to understand the biological and physiological roots of violence. This body of research deals with experiments on animals, study of biochemistry and brain anatomy, and the effect of various drugs on the work of the brain as they relate to violence. The article "Searching for the Mark of Cain" by Martin Enserink begins with a report on various studies focused on the impact of alcohol on mice and the observation that 25% of inebriated mice become violent.[6] The thinking behind such research, according to Klaus Miczek of Tufts University, is that such studies are relevant to "a society in which alcohol figures in two out of every three violent crimes."[7] The article also refers to research performed on the relationship between violence and serotonin, the Y chromosome, and the hypothalamus respectively. Research has demonstrated that serotonin, a neurotransmitter, has a significant role in the development of a number of conditions including violence, depression, and eating disorders. The article points out that "[n]umerous studies have found that aggressive animals, including humans, on average have lower levels of a serotonin metabolite—which is thought to reflect lower serotonin levels in the brain—in their cerebrospinal fluid (CSF)."[8] Other research corroborates these findings.[9] However, the article does not clarify whether violence decreases the level of this serotonin metabolite or that the low serotonin level consequently causes violence. Likewise, the results of research on the human brain, particularly the prefrontal cortex, have suggested certain possible anomalies in the brains of violent individuals. However, these findings are not by any means conclusive. Even if there were clear evidence of a physiological change in the brain of violent individuals, this fact alone will not help much in reducing the degree and scope of human violence.

Based on their studies on animals, other researchers have postulated that humans are a violent species. In a review article, Frans B. M. de Waal, an expert on conflict resolution in nonhuman primates, puts forward the notion that aggression is not an antisocial instinct in primates; rather, it is "a tool of competition and negotiation." The article's main conclusion is that "human aggressive conflict is subject to the same constraints known of cooperative animal societies."[10] Richard J. Davidson and colleagues "posit that impulsive aggression and violence arise as a consequence of faulty emotion regulation. Individuals vulnerable to faulty regulation of negative emotion are at risk for violence and aggression."[11] The authors then suggest that research on the "neural circuitry of emotion regulation" may show the way for prevention of human violence.

In October 1999 and September 2000, a set of different perspectives were put forward by the participants in the two public symposia organized by the Program on Negotiation at Harvard Law School. Frans de Waal stated that the current research "looks at aggression not as a product of an inner drive, but as one of the options that exists when there's a conflict of interest."[12] He further stated "people may claim, 'We are aggressive by nature'—I say we shouldn't delude ourselves about how aggressive we are. We can breed pit bull terriers to be aggressive; we can breed mice to be aggressive; and while I hope no one will ever do it, we could probably breed people to be aggressive."[13] Like de Waal and William Ury, the other main speaker at the same symposium, anthropologist Brian Ferguson, discarded the widely popular and accepted notion of humans as killer apes put forward by Raymond Dart, and popularized and further developed, respectively by Robert Ardry and Desmond Morris, the author of *The Naked Ape* (1969).

In 2002, the World Health Organization (WHO) issued its first comprehensive review of violence and its impact on the health of individuals and societies alike. The report identifies violence as a major public health challenge, reviews the existing literature on violence, identifies various forms in which violence occurs, and makes recommendations for action by governments and social institutions. The report begins by stating:

> No country or community is untouched by violence. Images and accounts of violence pervade the media; it is on our streets, in our homes, schools, workplaces and institutions. Violence is a universal scourge that tears at the fabric of communities and threatens the life, health and happiness of us all. Each year, more than 1.6 million people worldwide lose their lives to violence. For everyone who dies as a result of violence, many more are injured and suffer from a range of physical, sexual, reproductive and mental health problems. Violence is among the leading causes of death for people aged 15–44 years worldwide, accounting for about 14% of deaths among males and 7% of deaths among females....Because it is so pervasive, violence is often seen as an inevitable part of the human condition—a fact of life to respond to, rather than to prevent.[14]

However, the report, while offering relative optimism in the face of a colossal challenge, falls short in offering a definitive and effective remedy for the dilemma of human violence. "Violence is not inevitable" it declares and states that we "can do much to address and prevent it. The world has not yet fully measured the size of this task and does not yet have all the tools to carry it out. But the global knowledge base is growing and much useful experience has already been gained."[15] However, to the question: "What can be done to prevent violence?" WHO offers a very general and vague answer:

> There is no simple or single solution to the problem; rather, violence must be addressed on multiple levels and in multiple sectors of society simultaneously. Based on the perspective provided by the ecological model, violence prevention programmes and policies can be targeted at individuals, relationships, communities and whole societies, and delivered in collaboration with different sectors of society in schools, workplaces, other institutions and criminal justice systems. Violence prevention is most likely to be successful if it is comprehensive and scientifically based. In general, interventions that are delivered in childhood and those that are sustained over time are more likely to be effective than short-term programmes.[16]

A qualitatively different view of human violence is proposed in the *Seville Statement on Violence*, drafted by leading scientists from around the world during the UN International Year for Peace in 1986. The statement drew its conclusions from scientific arguments based on evolution, genetics, animal behavior, brain research and social psychology. Since then many scientists have scrutinized the statement; however, its main theses remain valid. The

Seville Statement on Violence focuses on the two of the "most dangerous and destructive activities" of human species—violence and war—and offers its conclusions in the form of five propositions, asserting that "it is scientifically ***incorrect*** to say that":

1. "we have inherited a tendency to make war from our animal ancestors."
2. "war or any other violent behaviour is genetically programmed into our human nature."
3. "in the course of human evolution there has been a selection for aggressive behaviour more than for other kinds of behaviour."
4. "humans have a 'violent brain'." And,
5. "war is caused by 'instinct' or any single motivation." [17]

The interesting thing about this brief review of causes of human violence is that different scientists reach diametrically opposite conclusions about the same subject—human violence—even though drawing from the same pool of scientific data and knowledge.

These are only a few examples of a continually expanding discourse on the nature of human violence and the search for its prevention. They point to the diversity of views among researchers and scholars on the causes of violence and how it could and should be dealt with. However, none has offered a definitive answer to the dilemma of human violence. In fact, despite all the efforts to better understand and prevent violence, it is evident that such efforts are not producing the desired results. Violence, committed by individuals and groups, continues to increase in its intensity, frequency, and scope. Wars have persisted and have become more deadly and destructive. Terrorism has emerged as another devastating expression of human violence. The rate of avoidable deaths related to poverty in an increasingly more prosperous world has not abated, and the number of needless deaths due to preventable diseases continues to be devastatingly high. In an increasingly more interrelated world, interreligious and interracial conflict and discord persist, and violence against women, minorities, and the abject poor is unacceptably prevalent. These conditions demand that we review the nature of our individual and collective worldviews, in general, and the researchers' worldviews, in particular, and consider the phenomenal impact of worldview on the manner in which we, in general, and scientists, in particular, understand and approach the phenomenon of human violence.

Worldview and Violence

We all have a worldview, and we all operate within the parameters of our worldview. The concept of worldview used here refers to our view of reality, human nature, purpose of life, and laws governing human relationships. Worldviews develop in the context of life experiences, cultural norms, and constant challenges and opportunities that life presents to individuals and communities of people. As such, our respective worldviews both shape and justify our thoughts, feelings, and actions. It is this self-containing character of worldview that renders it extremely influential in all human affairs, whether conflicted or peaceful in nature. Therefore, in order for us to better understand the causes of human violence and to identify the requirements for creation of harmonious and peaceful life conditions, we need to better understand the nature and type of worldviews we hold and within whose frameworks we operate.

The concept of worldview, at one level, is metaphysical because it deals with the individual's and group's perspectives on human nature, life purpose, and moral/ethical principles that govern human relationships. These issues are at once intellectual, emotional, and spiritual in nature and deal with both temporal and transcendent human needs. Worldviews are formed in the course of life through the influences of the family, culture, education, environment, and various life experiences. Our worldviews develop in a passive manner, and unless we make a deliberate effort to understand and if necessary change them, they continue to form our approach to all aspects of life, usually at a subconscious level. However, when our worldviews fail to adequately explain and deal with serious challenges and crises, we are then forced to review and, if necessary, change them. And this, in my opinion, is our current situation with respect to the issue of human violence. We now need to look seriously at the prevailing worldviews and their role in creating the framework within which we both conduct our research on violence and interpret our findings. I have elsewhere discussed the concept of worldview and have identified three metacategories of worldview—survival-based, identity-based, and unity-based.[18]

Throughout human history, the *survival-based* (or authoritarian-based) worldview has been, and currently remains, the most prevalent mindset. It views the world as a dangerous arena of force, domination, and subjugation, and has as its main objective the security and survival of oneself and one's group, which quite frequently occurs in the context of conflict and violence. The *identity-based* worldview has as its main focus the issue of individual and group identity formation and assertion, usually in the context of relationships characterized by power-struggle, survival of the fittest, and considerable conflict. The *unity-based* worldview is the hallmark of the coming of age of humanity and has as its main objectives creating interpersonal, intergroup, and global relationships based on mutual trust and cooperation within the parameters of equality, justice, unity, and peace.

The first two of these worldviews have always been, and continue to be, the most prevalent in all societies and correspond respectively with the developmental stages of childhood and adolescence that are highly conflict-prone. Therefore, it is not surprising that conflict and violence have forever been considered as the inevitable and inherent aspects of human nature and necessary for the survival of the species. I argue that as humanity evolves on the path of its development and enters its age of maturity, it will begin to adopt unity-based worldviews, and, as a result, the occurrences of conflict and violence will gradually but decidedly decrease. The process of transition of many societies in the past two centuries away from authoritarian and dictatorial forms of relationships and governance to those of individualism and adversarial democratic practices is a clear demonstration of the dramatic alteration in the prevailing worldviews. The transition to an identity-based worldview has gained momentum since the Second World War and now is the predominant worldview being promulgated by Western Societies and international agencies such as the United Nations. While replacement of authoritarian-based worldviews with identity-based worldviews is a major step forward in the advancement of humanity, it is by no means the end of the process of human individual and collective development. The process of humanity's progression is ongoing and ever-advancing.

Both authoritarian-based and identity-based worldviews revolve around the issue of power in human relationships. Authoritarian-based worldviews are founded on the principles of control and the oppressive use of power. These worldviews are highly prone to conflict and violence, and usually generate dictatorial and hierarchical modes of relationships and governance. Identity-based worldviews are also based on the concept of power as the main instrument for arrangement of human individual and group relationships. However, in this framework, power is more equitably distributed and human affairs are conducted within the politics and dynamics of power balance, competition, winning, losing, and compromise. Identity-based worldview promotes individualism, nationalism, and other exclusive group-identities. These modes of relationship are conflict-based by nature and can easily degenerate into protracted conflict and even violence.

The unity-based worldview, which is now slowly emerging as a framework for various types and levels of human relationships, is fundamentally different from the other two metacategories of worldview. The central focus and prerequisite of the unity-based worldview is unity, not power. Expressed differently, within the framework of unity-based worldview, individual and group power and empowerment are obtained through the establishment of ever-expanding circles of unity in the context of diversity.

RESEARCHERS AND THEIR WORLDVIEWS

There is no doubt that research, conducted within the parameters of the scientific method, is the most valuable and surest avenue for understanding the causes of human violence and its prevention. However, because scientific research takes place within the parameters of the worldview of the researcher, it is essential that in formulating our hypotheses, choosing our research modalities, and interpreting its outcome, we consider the worldview within which that research is conducted and its conclusions are reached. In his groundbreaking book *The Structure of Scientific Revolution*, Thomas Kuhn points to the relationship between worldview of the researcher and the scientific conclusions reached within its parameters. He states that the development of science has alternating 'normal' and 'revolutionary' phases. The normal phase is the process of accumulation of more knowledge within the existing paradigm. However, gradually as the prevailing worldview or 'paradigm' (in Kuhn's terminology) loses its capacity to explain all issues under consideration, a revolutionary phase in that discipline of science begins by the introduction of a totally new, and usually very different, paradigm. In the opening paragraph of the ninth chapter of this book, Kuhn asks, "What are scientific revolutions, and what is their function in scientific development?" He then provides this concise, clear answer: "[S]cientific revolutions are…those non-cumulative developmental episodes in which an older paradigm is replaced in whole or in part by an incompatible new one."[19]

The prevailing views on human violence can be summarized under two broad categories: biological/genetic and environmental/learning. The biological/genetic category sees violence as an inevitable and even necessary component of human nature. The environmental/learning category emphasizes the primacy of the role of learning and environment in the appearance of human violence. However, many students of human violence consider it to be *both* genetically determined and environmentally caused. Nevertheless, these concepts of violence, alone or in unison, have not provided either convincing formulations on the nature of violence or offered truly effective approaches for its prevention. The existing paradigms see conflict and violence as inevitable and, even necessary, aspects of human life in the context of conflicting interests, limited resources, and survival imperatives. They neither adequately explain the genesis of human violence, nor offer satisfactory solutions on how to prevent its occurrence.

The main reason for this inability, in my view, is the fact that the prevalent worldviews—authoritarian (survival)-based and identity-based—that inform the existing paradigms of violence are conflict-based. They either emphasize the view that the world is a dangerous arena of fight for survival and security, and/or promote the notion that life is an ongoing process of competition and power struggle in quest of superiority and victory. Both these mindsets are conflict-based and violence-prone and together account for most, if not all existing paradigms that inform the prevailing views and approach to the issue of human violence and its management. Clearly, a new worldview—a fundamental paradigm shift—for understanding violence is required.

I posit that human violence is the outcome of the violation of the primary law governing all life and relationships—unity. Life takes place in the context of unity-based relationships and when the law of unity is violated, conflict and violence ensue. Science is the process of discovery of relationships within material entities (physical sciences) and living organisms (biological sciences) and between humans (social sciences). In order to understand the causes and prevent the occurrence of human disunity and its consequent conflict and violence, we need to study them within the framework of the "unity paradigm."

The Unity Paradigm

Certain inviolable and therefore essential laws, whose violation makes the continuation of life problematic or even impossible, govern life. Among the most crucial laws of life is the law of unity. Unity is the primary law of life. Everything that exists is the outcome of the operation of the law of unity. At the physical level, the law of unity ensures order and stability in the manner in which subatomic particles, atoms, molecules, stars, and galaxies cohere and operate in a harmonious and integrated manner. At the biological level, the very process of creation and continuation of life is dependent on the proper operation of the law of unity. The same is true at the social level. Families are happy, healthy, and stable when unity exists between all its members. Communities of people prosper and are safe in the context of unity, and nations advance in every area when peace is present. At all levels of human life—intrapersonal, interpersonal, intergroup, and international—unity, not conflict, is the fundamental operative and creative force. "Unity is a conscious and purposeful condition of convergence of two or more unique entities in a state of harmony, integration, and cooperation to create a new and evolving entity or entities, usually, of a same or higher nature."[21] Conflict is, simply, the absence of unity.

A review of dominant contemporary thought on issues of the nature and dynamics of life reveals an amazing omission—a total disregard for the law of unity. Current psychological, social, and political theories pertaining to practically every aspect of human life have conflict as their starting point. These theories consider struggle and competition as the necessary and inevitable processes of life; regard conflict as the unavoidable outcome of the struggle on behalf of oneself or one's group; and accept violence as its expected outcome under certain circumstances. Galtung and Jacobsen comment that "[c]onflict, incompatible goals, are as human as life itself; the only conflict-free humans are dead humans" and that "war and violence are like slavery, colonialism, and patriarchy; however, they come and they go."[21] Muldoon states that "[c]onflict is the spice that seasons our most intimate relationships," and "it is woven into the fundamental fabric of nature."[22] Dahrendorf states that "[conflict is] the great creative force of human history,"[23] and Coser in his analysis of the results of social conflict concludes "that conflict often leads to change. It can stimulate innovation, for example, or, especially in war, increase centralization."[24] Freud, in *Civilization and Its Discontents* (1931), moves beyond the issue of conflict and boldly asserts that "[t]he tendency of aggression is an innate, independent, instinctual disposition in man....it constitutes the most powerful obstacle to culture."[25] According to these theories, conflict and aggression are inherent and essential qualities of being human. However, it is important to note that several concepts and approaches to conflict resolution such as "super-ordinate goals,"[26] "cooperative conflict resolution,"[27] "principled negotiation,"[28] and "conflict transformation,"[29] seek to bring more cooperative, positive, and caring dimensions to the current understanding of conflict and its resolution. Similar attempts at finding a new approach to the issue of conflict and violence are also being made within the education community.[30]. It is important to note that all of these concepts and strategies are still formulated according to the notion that conflict is an intrinsic, inevitable, and necessary aspect of human nature and life. In other words, the intellectual and emotional paradigm within which the scholars, researchers, and practitioners interested in issues of human conflict and violence operate is skewed in favor of the inevitability of both. The inevitability of conflict and violence is taken for granted. Therefore, the question that concerns these experts is how to create a less conflicted and violent world and not how to create peaceful world, which by definition is violence-free. Peace is not the absence of war. Peace is the ultimate outcome of unity in the context of diversity, justice, equality, and freedom. Our objective, therefore, should not be merely to find ways of decreasing incidence and intensity of violence. This, as our world today and history demonstrate, is a futile effort in the context of prevailing dominant conflict-based worldviews. In fact, history demonstrates that both the scope and intensity of violence—against others and against the environment—have dramatically increased as we have developed greater knowledge and skill to create instruments of violence, crime, and war. However, in spite of this monumental increase in our destructive capacities and activities, we have neither changed our conceptualization of human conflict and violence nor altered our approach to them.

I propose that a fundamental paradigm shift from conflict-based to unity-based worldviews is required in order to alter the present impasse with respect to human violence. At the core of this paradigm shift to unity are five premises:

- Unity is the main law of existence and life;
- Unity—as opposed to uniformity—is only possible in the context of diversity;
- Conflict is the absence of unity;
- Violence is the outcome of violation of the law of unity'
- Effective conflict resolution and violence prevention is only possible by creating ever-enlarging and all-inclusive circles of unity.

Therefore, the main objective of research on human conflict and violence should be aimed at identifying those dynamics and processes that are conducive to the optimal development of unity at all levels: intrapersonal, interpersonal, intergroup, and international. Healthy human development is a conscious, deliberate, and flexible process that, at the individual level, begins with the predominance of the conflict-prone biological processes of infancy and childhood, traverses through the turbulent and conflicted biological and psychosocial phase of adolescence and early adulthood, and eventually arrives at the creative and generative age of maturity operating according to the law of unity.

A similar process of development is observable in the history of all societies and cultures. According to this developmental framework, it is evident that the world of humanity today is divided into two major camps—those societies that are operating according to the survival-based worldviews and those that are permeated with identity-based perspectives. Authoritarian, violent, and oppressive leaders predominantly rule the first group that comprises all so-called developing countries and a few others. The second group—the so-called developed countries—administer their social and political life according to adversarial, multi-party, democratic practices, fueled by their fervor to prove themselves superior over others and to win in the arena of competition and the survival of the fittest. The first group—authoritarian societies—are oppressed and violent, while the second group—adversarial democratic societies—are highly conflicted and easily prone to violence. There is, however, a growing awareness that we cannot afford to continue to administer the affairs of humanity along these two tried and failed approaches. New models of organization of human world, conducive to cooperation, harmony, and strict regard for the rights of all people, including the primary rights for safety, security, freedom, and peace, are urgently needed. These new approaches, by definition, need to be based on the fundamental foundations of unity—that there is only one human race and that the welfare of the whole body of humanity and all its individual members is totally interconnected.

The unity paradigm provides a framework within which various theories of conflict—biological, psychological, and social—can be accounted for and the diverse expressions of our humanness can be understood within a developmental framework. Unity is at once a scientific and a spiritual phenomenon. One of the primary strengths of science seeks truth in its search for understanding the laws of nature. And among the most important functions of religion is its articulation of universal truths that govern all human conditions and relationships. Both these tasks—search for truth and articulation of standards of truth—are among the most important qualities of the phenomenon of unity. Unity encompasses reality in all its expressions—material, biological, intellectual, artistic, and spiritual. It reconciles science with religion and offers the broadest framework for research into all human phenomena, including conflict and violence.

UNITY AND VIOLENCE

Because the conceptual framework of the researcher's worldview shapes both the focus and the method of research, and because conflict-based worldviews are the predominant frames of reference in the contemporary biological and social sciences, theories of violence are formulated based on the concept of inevitability and necessity of conflict. The researcher's psyche does not function in a vacuum. It is an active, conscious, and searching entity that is continuously interacting with its internal and external environments within the parameters of the worldview of the researcher. Thus, it is not surprising that within the prevalent conflict-based worldviews, the phenomenon of human violence emerges as being unavoidable, albeit not always acceptable.

Human violence is a universal and ubiquitous phenomenon. The individual who kills another person with a handgun is violent, but indirectly so too are the owners of the companies that manufacture guns, the technicians and scientists who design such items, the society that encourages and glorifies the use of guns in human interactions, the businesses who sell guns, and the politicians who advocate the right to possess guns in the name of self-defense, security, freedom, democracy, and human rights. All these individuals and institutions are engaged in a complicated web of human violence. It is because of this ubiquitous presence of violence in human history and in the contemporary world that we first need to answer a fundamental question: "Are humans by their very nature violent?" An affirmative answer to this question would dramatically reduce the burden on us to find a solution for human destructive tendencies and violence. If indeed we are inherently violent by nature, then the best we could do is to find more effective ways of managing human violence and decreasing its destructive impact, while at the same time accepting violence as an unavoidable aspect of being human.

However, if our answer to the question "Are humans by nature violent?" is negative, then we need to clearly explain the causes of our past and present violence. We need to offer convincing proof that we humans can indeed free ourselves from those dynamics and processes that render us violent. We need to begin the task of creating violence-free environments—homes, schools, communities, nations, and world—and usher in the long sought-after age of peace. These issues are now being questioned frequently by researchers and scientists dealing with human violence. The challenge to the deterministic view on human violence is gaining momentum.

Here, we are dealing with the ephemeral nature of theoretical formulations of violence. One of the strengths of the scientific approach is that it is open to change. As Kuhn noted, once new evidence proves the fallacy of previous paradigms about a given phenomenon, science ultimately abandons its previous frameworks and explanations, and adopts new paradigms, often at odds with previous ones. However, while the field of science is open to change, scientists, like all human beings, function within the parameters of their respective worldviews and are not easily open to new conceptual frameworks. Notwithstanding this fact, in the face of alarming escalation of human destructive powers, the need for an all-inclusive, comprehensive, and integrative approach to the issue of human violence has never been more urgent and universally acknowledged.

Humans are, at once, similar to and distinct from animals. At the biological level, there are many similarities between humans and some higher primate animals. At the core of these similarities are the instincts of self-preservation and need gratification. In the context of threatening environments with scarce resources, these two powerful instincts are frequently accompanied by varying degrees of conflict and aggressive behavior. The underlying dynamics of biologically determined aggression are instinctual and autonomic, and their intensity and frequency are determined by environmental variations. However, as human cognitive (knowledge), emotive (love), and conative (will) powers expand and develop, a higher level of self-knowledge and understanding develops, a greater capacity for cooperation and love is achieved, and the ability to have mastery over one's biological and environmental forces and processes is greatly enhanced. Eventually, some individuals transcend the limitations imposed on them by the conflict-prone biological, environmental, and psychological processes, and arrive at a state best described as a state of *authentic unity*—intrapersonal, interpersonal, and intergroup. This state is that condition which employs the powers of the human mind (knowledge, love, and will) for the refinement of human character, introduction of justice and fairness in human relationships, civilizing of human communities, and betterment of human life in all societies. As such, the concept of *authentic unity* encompasses all aspects of human reality—biological, psychological, social, moral, and spiritual—and considers the developmental and hierarchical stages of human ability to control and eventually transcend its aggressive impulses. These stages are depicted in the following diagram:

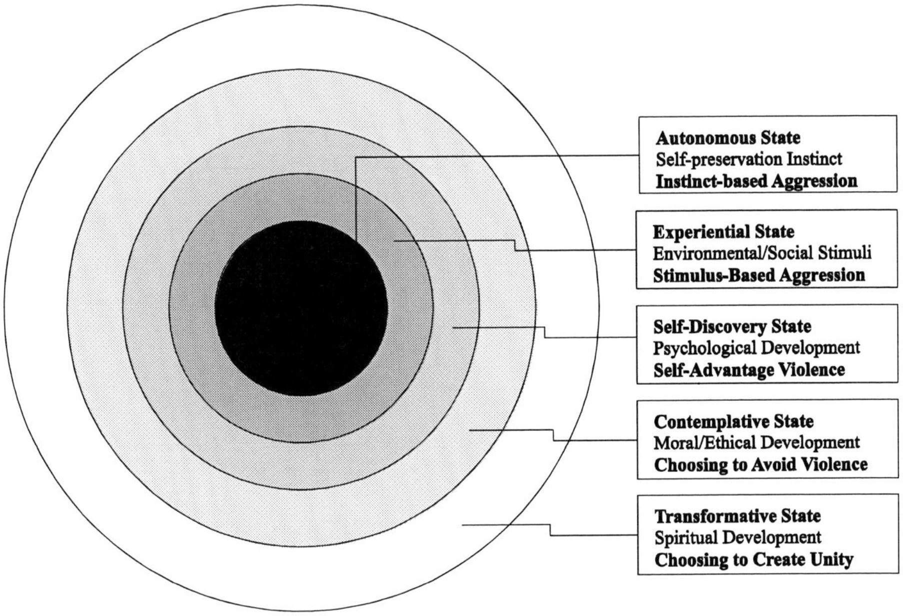

Figure 1. Human states of being and their impact on the presence or absence of aggression, violence, and peace

The five existential states depicted in this diagram identify the various conditions of human life observable in individuals and societies. In the autonomous and experiential stages, aggressive human behavior is displayed in basically the same form and for the same reason as we find in animals. However, in the third stage (self-discovery state), the aggression impulse is replaced by violence, which in the fourth stage (contemplative) is either given moral and ethical legitimacy or rejected as an immoral, unethical condition. In either case this process is an intentional product of human psychological processes such as planning and executing acts of violence and war, or developing psychosocial, moral, and ethical strategies for prevention of violence. In the transformative state we begin a new, dramatically different approach to the issue of human violence. In this state, individuals and groups focus on perspectives, principles, and practices that create unity, with peace as its finest outcome. These conditions of aggression, violence, and peace are all aspects of human life and history that are inarguably best understood when studied within an integrative unity-based paradigm.

THE CHOICE

With respect to the issues of conflict and violence we are on the horns of a dilemma. Our current theories and formulations about the genesis of human conflict (particularly intractable conflict) and violence seem to be lamentably inadequate for helping us to significantly decrease their occurrence. And our sincere and considered efforts to deal with conflicts peacefully and to prevent occurrence of violence at interpersonal, community, and international levels have little positive results. Conflicts persist, and episodes of violence are becoming more frequent and deadly. [31] However, we continue to approach human conflict and violence within the same, already proven inadequate, formulae. And this is at the core of our dilemma. This chapter presents the outline of a new formulation of both the nature and dynamics of human conflict and violence and extends an invitation to academics, researchers, and practitioners in the field of conflict and violence to seriously consider this new approach. This is an extremely difficult choice because it requires a fundamental paradigm shift on our part, a shift that negates our much cherished perspectives and insights, requiring us to replace them with diametrically opposite notions. It calls upon us to consider unity rather than conflict as the primary operating force in human relationships. It asks us to seriously investigate our closely held views that inform our own approach to life and to our work and to ensure that our worldviews neither consider conflict as a given nor disregard unity as irrelevant. These challenges and choices need to be met, and this brief chapter intends the start of a fresh discourse on them.

APPENDIX I

COMMENTS ON THE EDUCATION FOR PEACE PROGRAM IN BOSNIA AND HERZEGOVINA

In May 2002, the Government of Bosnia and Herzegovina, through its Mission to the United Nations in New York, addressed an open letter to the Special Session of the United Nations General Assembly on Children (8–10 May 2002), describing the pilot EFP Program in the six BiH schools, stating that "the results of this program have been very positive," and concluding their letter with this statement:

> The children all over the world are in need of peace and security. On the occasion of the Summit devoted to the children, we recommend this program [EFP] to all the nations for consideration, as a model of society oriented towards peace, cooperation, and development.

The following excerpts from the March 6, 2006 letter of Ambassador Douglas Davidson, Head of the BiH Mission of Organization for Security and Co-operation in Europe (OSCE) provides a summary of evaluation of the EFP Program in BiH prepared by the Education Department of OSCE. This organization is mandated by the International Community to assist and oversee the process of education reform in BiH:

The Education for Peace Program, which has been developed from the outset with the full involvement of educators and parents throughout Bosnia and Herzegovina, has proven its effectiveness as a model for peace education….Its pilot program, which began in September 2000, yielded such significant results that half-way through the first year it gained the recognition and endorsement of the Ministry of Foreign Affairs, all thirteen Ministries of Education, all eight Pedagogical Institutes, the Mission of Bosnia and Herzegovina to the United Nations, the Office of the High Representative (OHR), and, soon thereafter, my own Mission as well. The Government of Bosnia and Herzegovina, through its educational authorities, then requested that this program be extended throughout the country….

EFP engages young people in an in-depth examination of the universal principles of peace in every subject of study and teaches them to apply these principles in their daily lives and in society at large. Drawing on modern, interactive teaching tools, which it trains participating teachers to use in their classrooms, EFP assists young people to develop critical thinking skills and modes of thought in order to encourage and enable them to help create a badly-needed culture of peace and inter-ethnic understanding in Bosnia and Herzegovina. EFP thereby contributes significantly to the overall reform of education in Bosnia and Herzegovina. To date, an estimated 80,000 students as well as 5,000 teachers, staff members, and school administrators have been actively involved. If one adds participating parents to this sum, one can say that more than 100,000 citizens of Bosnia and Herzegovina have benefited from the EFP program.

In a comprehensive external evaluation of the EFP Program by two peace education experts commissioned by the Swiss Development and Cooperation Agency—the main financial sponsor for the introduction of the EFP Program into 100 BiH schools—the following conclusions were reached:

There seems to be little doubt that the project has had great impact on many of the participants, both on teachers, support staff, administrators and students involved. The most important impact seems to have been on the personal level, the meeting of people across nationalities and languages. The evaluation team heard several touching stories from teachers about their own experiences and the experiences of parents and children gained especially during the pilot phase of the project….

It may be concluded from the evaluators' observations and comments that the programme is generally well received by Bosnian pupils, teachers and authorities. Psychological elements such as 'bringing people together in an atmosphere of trust' as well as a number of didactical innovations are recognised by the evaluators. EFP has achieved positive impact not only among teachers and students but has had effects on the families of participants as well.

The following are few randomly chosen comments from among several hundred teachers, students, and parents/guardians participating in one of the research projects on the EFP Program in BiH. These reports are from members of all three ethnic populations of BiH—Bosniak (Muslim), Croat (Catholic), and Serb (Eastern Orthodox)—and are presented here as narrated by the individuals themselves:

75. Support Staff

I have been working in this school for eight years. There have never been more changes seen in the pupils and the staff as this past year, since the project "Education for Peace" was implemented. The relation of the pupils toward each other is completely different, especially toward us, the support staff. The greatest changes in the school happen during certain events.

The school is cleaned, the performance is prepared, and the assignments are written—all in the sign of peace and freedom. That is how it should be. The children should live in peace and freedom. It is surely better now for all of us. The days when Sanna and Alma [EFP-Balkans Staff] are in our school are especially different, and these are the changes that I experience as something special.

21. Student

The most important thing that happened to me is that I made new friends in other schools. I can contact them whenever I want to. This project helped me to learn a lot about EFP. Children in the whole world need peace. All people do. Since I began to participate in this project, I became a better person. I think this is a unique project as it teaches us how to create non-violent surroundings in our homes, schools and the whole country....

19. Parent

First I would like to say that I am glad that EFP has chosen the school of my children. I am glad that my children have a chance to be educated in a civilized way, and that they learn to resolve their and their friends' conflicts in a diplomatic manner. But most important thing is that finally children's voices can be heard through the Students Council....As a parent, I notice a quiet and peaceful atmosphere among the children on the way from home to the school. My children are very communicative and relaxed for their age, but they are smart and "mature" in their thinking. They make nice and enlightening decisions. Everything they learn in the school, they implement in their lives (at home, with the friend and outside). This all means that your project had a positive impact on them. Peace is essential for everything. Thank you.

73. Member of EFP Student Club

I would be the happiest person if Education for Peace started before 1992. And that it was first recognized by those who were carrying guns that year. Many parents, children, godfathers, friends and acquaintances would have changed their opinions and would have walked alive today.

Since March 2005, Education for Peace is present in our schools. This education has positive impact on us, primary school students, and it guides us to [a] nice and free future. We are just children eager for a nice life, eager for new insights and for associating with any type of nationality and religion. Since March, my heart is ruled by tolerance for all religions, races and nationalities. We are all someone's children whose parents want peace that you are teaching us about.

71. Principal

The implementation of the EFP Project has contributed to the democratization of educational and upbringing process in our school. Talking to teachers, one can conclude that most of them have accepted the way of incorporation of the EFP program contents into the syllabi prescribed by the curriculums. The peace ceremonies have special impact on all participants, where pupils' creativity in preparation of the presentations becomes prominent. The Regional Peace Ceremony and workshops organized within it have their special upbringing function. The children fit very quickly in the group consisting of children from different schools and discuss the creation of the culture of peace with the children of different nations and ages. The children make new friendships with the pupils from other schools. Since this ceremony left very positive impression in the pupils, it would be very useful to organize more often socializing among children and visits to other schools. The most important issue from the beginning of the EFP Project implementation is that there is no skepticism among the teachers, pupils and parents in relation to the implementation of the EFP program goals and the creation of the culture of peace. On the contrary, there is large interest for participation in the Project and wish to implement the Project in the future.[32]

REFERENCES

[1] The Integrative Theory of Peace (ITP) was formulated by H. B. Danesh and first described in H. B. Danesh, Towards an Integrative Theory of Peace Education, *Journal of Peace Education, 3.1,* (March 2006), 55-78.

[2] For details of the EFP Program see: Danesh, H.B. (2006). Towards an integrative theory of peace education. *Journal of Peace Education, 3.1* (March), 55-78., (2002) Breaking the cycle of violence: Education for Peace. *African civil society organization and development: re-evaluation for the 21st Century.* (New York, United Nations), September 2002., (2007). Education for Peace: the pedagogy of civilization. In Z. Bekerman & C. McGlynn (Eds.), *Addressing Ethnic Conflict through Peace Education: International Perspectives.* New York: Palgrave Macmillan., (2008). Creating a culture of healing in schools and communities: An integrative approach to prevention and amelioration of violence-induced conditions. *Journal of Community Psychology, vol. 36, No. 6*, 814-832 (August 2008).,(2008) Conceptual Foundations of Education for Peace: An Introduction, included in *Educating for Civilization of Peace,* Edited by Sara Clarke-Habibi, EFP Press, Vancouver, 6-15., (2008) Unity-Based Peace Education, included in the *Encyclopedia of Peace Education)* edited by Monisha Bajaj, Charlotte North Carolina, Information Age Publishing. 147-156.

[3] *Science* 289. 5479 (July, 2000), 497-684.

[4] Ibid. 545.

[5] Ibid. 569.

[6] Ibid. 575–79.

[7] Ibid. 575.

[8] Ibid. 575.

[9] See for example: M. Virkkunen et al. "Serotonin in Alcoholic Violent Offenders," *Ciba Foundation Symposium, 194(1995)*, 168-182. M. Virkkunen & M. Linnoila, "Serotonin and Glucose Metabolism in Impulsively Violent Alcoholic Offenders," in D.M. Stoff & R.B. Cairns, eds., *Aggression and Violence.* Mahwah, NJ: Lawrence Erlbaum, 1996, 87-100. E. F. Coccaro & R. J. Kavoussi, "Neurotransmitter Correlates of Impulsive Aggression." in Stoff, & Cairns, eds., *Aggression and Violence*, Mahwah, NJ: Lawrence Erlbaum, 1996, 67-86.

[10] Frans de Waal. *Science, 289, 5479,* (July, 2000), 586.

[11] Richard J. Davidson, *Science, 289, 5479,* (July, 2000), 591-94.

[12] Frans de Waal. in *Must We Fight?*, William L. Ury, editor, A Publication of the Program on Negotiation at Harvard Law School and San Francisco: Jossey-Bass 2002, 24.

[13] Ibid. 25.

[14] World Health Organization. (2002). *World Report on Violence and Health: Summary,* Geneva, p. 1 http://www.who.int/violence_injury_prevention/violence/world_report/en/.

[15] Ibid. 36.

[16] Ibid. 25.
[17] NESCO, The Seville Statement,1986) http://www.unesco.org/cpp/uk/ declarations /seville.pdfsearch='seville% 20statement%20on%20violence).
[18] For more readings on the concept of worldview see: H. B. Danesh, "Towards an Integrative Theory of Peace Education," *Journal of Peace Education, 3.1,* (March2006), 55-78. H. B. Danesh, "Breaking the Cycle of Violence: Education for Peace. *African Civil Society Organization and Development: Re-evaluation for the 21st Century,* New York: United Nations, September 2002. H. B. Danesh, "Education for Peace: The Pedagogy of Civilization," in Z. Bekerman, & C. McGlynn (Eds.), *Addressing Ethnic Conflict through Peace Education: International Perspectives,* New York: Palgrave Macmillan, 2007., (2008). Creating a culture of healing in schools and communities: An integrative approach to prevention and amelioration of violence-induced conditions. *Journal of Community Psychology, vol. 36*, No. 6, 1-19 (2008)., S. Clarke-Habibi, (2005). "Transforming Worldviews: The Case of Education for Peace in Bosnia and Herzegovina," *Journal of Transformative Education, 3.1*, 33-56.
[19] Thomas Kuhn, (1962). The Structure of Scientific Revolutions, Chicago: University of Chicago Press, 91.
[20] Danesh, H. B. & Danesh, R. P. (2002). Has Conflict Resolution Grown Up? Toward a New Model of Decision Making and Conflict Resolution, *International Journal of Peace Studies*, *7.1*, 67.
[21] Johan Galtung & Carl. G. Jacobsen, (2000). *Searching for Peace: The Road to TRANSCEND.* London: Pluto Press, vii.
[22] Brian Muldoon, (1996). *The Heart of Conflict.* New York: Perigree, 9.
[23] Ralf Dahrendorf, (1958). Toward a Theory of Social Conflict, Journal of Conflict Resolution, *2*, 170-83.
[24] Coser as sited in: Paul Wehr, (2001). *Conflict Theory and Analytic Sociology*, University of Colorado at Boulder Department of Sociology course chapter. http://spot.colorado.edu/~wehr/40RD2.TXT.
[25] For other perspectives on human aggression and violence see: Floyd Matson, (1976). *The Idea of Man,* Delacorte Press, The quotation on aggression by Freud appears on page 36 of this book.
[26] See for example: M. Deutsch, (1973). *The Resolution of Conflict: Constructive and Destructive Processes*, New Haven: Yale University Press., Johan Galtung, and Carl G. Jacobsen, (2000). *Searching for Peace: The Road to TRANSCEND,* London: Pluto Press., Stephen Worchel, (1986). The Role of Cooperation in Reducing Intergroup Conflict, in Stephen Worchel and W. G. Austin, (Eds.), *Psychology of Intergroup Relations*, Chicago, Nelson-Hall, 288-304.
[27] See for example: M. Deutsch, (1994). Constructive Conflict Resolution: Principles, Training and Research, *Journal of Social Issues*, *50*, 13-32., Johnson, D., Johnson, R. & Tjosvold, D. (2000). Constructive Controversy: The Value of Intellectual Opposition. In M. Deutsch, & P. T. Coleman, (Eds.), *The Handbook of Conflict Resolution: Theory and Practice*, San Francisco: Jossey-Bass.
[28] Roger Fisher, Bruce Patton, and William Ury. (1991). *Getting to Yes: Negotiating Agreement without Giving In.* 2d ed. New York: Penguin Books.

[29] See for example: Bush, R. A. B. and Folger, J. P. (1995). *The Promise of Mediation*, San Francisco: Jossey-Bass., J. P. Lederach, (1995). *Preparing for Peace: Conflict Transformation across Cultures*. Syracuse: Syracuse University Press.

[30] See for example: *Journal of School Health.* Special Theme: "School Connectedness—Strengthening Health and Education Outcomes for Teenagers," multiple authors, *vol. 74*, number *7*, September 2004.

[31] For sobering statistics on violence refer to the following to sources, which provide a glimpse of the extent of human violence in our times: http://www.thepeacealliance.org/files/outreach_material/stats_violence.pdf , http://users.erols.com/mwhite28/warstats.htm (both accessed on 8 September 2008)

[32] For more reports, evaluations, and activities of EFP refer to: www.efpinternational.org

In: Violent Crime and Prisons: Population…
Ed: Aidan Renshaw and Emelina Suárez
ISBN: 978-1-60741-668-5

Chapter 4

INTERPERSONAL SKILLS: EFFECTS OF A TRAINING PROGRAM ON QUANTITATIVE AND QUALITATIVE RESPONSE CRITERIA IN INCARCERATED WOMEN CRIMINALS

***María Ángeles Beleña*[*], *María José Báguena*[*], and *María de la Paz Toldos*[**]**
[*]Departamento de Personalidad, Evaluación y Tratamientos Psicológicos. Facultad de Psicología. Universidad de Valencia (España).
[**]Escuela de Negocios y Humanidades. Instituto Tecnológico de Estudios Superiores de Monterrey (ITESM), Campus Guadalajara, Jalisco (México).

ABSTRACT

Criminality is related both to deficient skills for resolving interpersonal problems and to deficient behavioral skills in social interaction; therefore the prevention and/or intervention with training programs in these skills is necessary (Beleña, 1992; Garrido et al., 2006; Redondo, 2008; Ross and Ross, 1995).

The principal objective of this study was to determine the effectiveness, feasibility, and effects obtained by the application of a training program designed and applied by the authors and directed at the fomentation of *interpersonal skills* in a sample of incarcerated women, taking into account quantitative and qualitative response criteria in the dimensions considered, that is, in the face of an interpersonal problem, not only generating as many solutions as possible (quantitative aspect), but also evaluating those solutions as to whether they are ethical and socially permissible (qualitative aspect).

The sample comprised 44 women distributed in two groups: control (N=22) and experimental (N=22). In the first stage of evaluation the women completed the *Progressive Matrices* test of Raven and the *Battery of Interpersonal Skills*, adapted for the criminal population by Báguena and Beleña (1993). This battery evaluates five dimensions: Appreciation of Perspectives, Causal Thinking, Alternative Thinking, Consequential Thinking, and Means-End Thinking. The women of the experimental group, divided into small groups, received a training program in interpersonal skills. The interpersonal skills of both experimental groups were then reevaluated with the post-test.

The results obtained suggest that the situation of incarceration produces a decrease in the interpersonal skill levels of women criminals. We cite the degree of effectiveness of our program with a set of direct effects that implied a neutralization or slowing down of this decrease, as well as the improvement of some of the skills. In addition, the program significantly improved the following qualitative components: direct causes, ethical and socially permissible solution alternatives ("what" to do in the face of a problem), solutions for the intragroup, short- and long-term consequences, and the use of ethically and socially permissible means and resources ("how" to solve a problem). Moreover, the need to improve the aspects of the program related to the improvement of "appreciation of different perspectives" (empathy) when facing a problem was demonstrated.

The study also suggests the importance of incorporating in penitentiary institutions programs such as that developed by us, insofar as incarcerated women, upon release from prison, must reintegrate themselves into a social world that demands the mastery of interpersonal skills.

1. INTRODUCTION

1.1. Criminality and Psychosocial (or Interpersonal-Social) Competence

Criminality is related to deficient skills for resolving interpersonal problems and to deficient behavioral skills in social interaction. Existing research shows inconsistent results due largely to the conceptual and methodological disparity that affects the area of interpersonal skills (Pelechano, 1996, 2000). Therefore, tackling the study of interpersonal skills demands, from the start, that one ascribe oneself to a specific conceptualization of these skills due to the broad theoretical and procedural-evaluative range that exists in the field. In our case, the conceptual and evaluative aspects have been gathered by Pelechano (1984, 1985, 1986, 1989, 1991, 1996), who suggests that interpersonal skills form part of a hierarchically structured social intelligence in which social competence and interpersonal recognition form two significant, clearly differentiated nuclei.

In this theoretical framework it is assumed, through rational analysis and the corresponding review of the literature, that in every interpersonal problem there exists a series of independent dimensions that can be isolated and evaluated. Concretely, these dimensions are the ability to appreciate perspectives different from one's own, the ability to generate different solution alternatives for the same problem, the ability to attribute causes of interpersonal problems, the ability to predict consequences, and the ability to articulate measures to achieve an end.

The theoretical position that we followed is the social-cognitive. That is, in this study our objective was to discover and foment the cognitive processes and dimensions that shape effective interpersonal behavior. It was hypothesized that criminal women present deficits in adequate interpersonal skills, a lack that impedes both their achievement of socially valuable goals and their capacity to face and efficiently manage themselves in the interpersonal-social world.

In addition, another question to point out refers to the fact that many studies have been carried out with criminals who have been detected and institutionalized, a situation that does not permit the discounting of the effect of "differential apprehension" (the least skillful criminals are those who come to be institutionalized), nor does it permit the discounting of the possibility that it is imprisonment that deteriorates interpersonal skills. Currently, the most accepted conclusion is that criminals are a heterogeneous group in terms of their social competence (Veneziano and Veneziano, 1988) and that many, though not all, could benefit from programs of interpersonal-skills training; this is a very widely developed intervention modality that has generated interesting results (Beleña, 1992; Garrido et al., 2006; Redondo, 2008; Ross and Ross, 1995).

1. 2. Social Intelligence and Interpersonal Skills

At a general level we are working within the framework of a model of multiple intelligences (based on Gardner's model, 1993) in which Pelechano (2000) proposes that interpersonal skills are located in the nucleus of an aspect of social intelligence called interpersonal intelligence.

1.2.1. Social intelligence

The ***social intelligences*** refer to the group of capacities necessary for social coexistence and interpersonal relationships. Pelechano (2000) differentiates two large groups:

(i) One group is called **socioinstitutional** and refers to the elements of competence that are directly related to "institutional" social functioning and, therefore, closely related to social success.
(ii) The second group is called **sociopersonal** and refers either to the relationship of an individual with himself or herself, or to the relationships of an individual with other individuals in a small group that involves direct contact among the persons in the group.

A diagram of what is understood by "social intelligence" is found in Figure 1 (taken from Pelechano, 2000).

Sociopersonal intelligence is understood as the competences and capacities in which interpersonal elements and human factors matter more than economic or institutional factors at the time of comprehension and concrete action; that is, it has to do with "success or personal recognition". The following components, at the least, should be differentiated:

(1) Intrapersonal intelligence refers to the individual and is characterized by at least the following components: capacity for self-knowledge, personal wisdom (components of traditional "practical wisdom" and ethical components in the search for happiness), strategies for and styles of coping with personal problems in different contexts (love, health, friendship), intrapersonal skills or dimensions of intrapersonal problem-solving, nonaggressive personal assertiveness, and spiritual knowledge, or the capacity for spiritual analysis in extreme situations (for example, the loss of loved ones or one's own death).

We are going to look in more detail at some of the aspects that we consider more relevant:

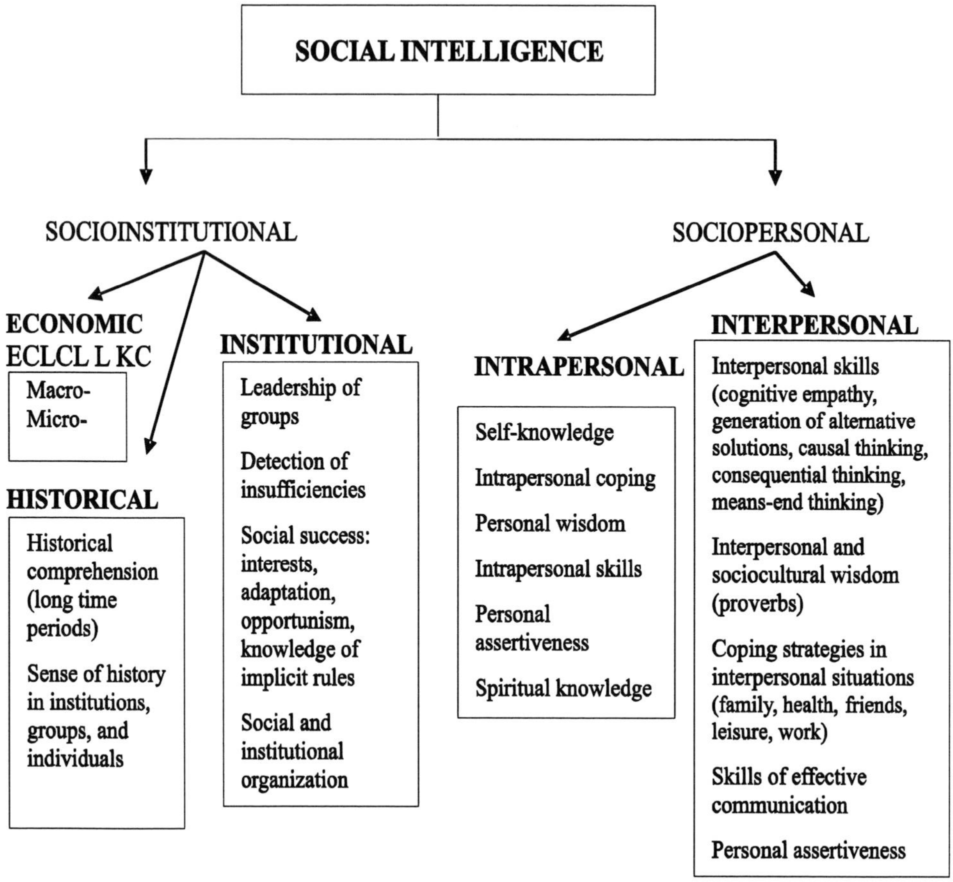

Figure 1. Social intelligence (Pelechano, 2000).

(a) *Self-knowledge* refers to the volume and precision of the knowledge of one's own realistic abilities for the achievement of a task, the facility to carry out an analysis of one's own psychological states. It refers to the capacity of being conscious of one's own feelings and of rejecting self-deceiving strategies. This self-knowledge not only refers to the emotional life but can also refer to basic aspects of personal functioning, to different life contexts, and to concrete and changeable states and/or situations of life.

(b) *Nonaggressive personal assertiveness* refers to personal security with respect to private questions, removed from both self-deception and denial of one's own feelings.

(c) *Spiritual knowledge* refers to the aspect of individual transcendence (through work performed during life, one's offspring, or belief in a future life), of the meaning of the life that one is living and of the place that each human being occupies in the world in which he or she lives. Spiritual knowledge refers to the belief that every human becomes the author of his or own biography in the book of his or her life, a situation that has advantages (being the protagonist) but also disadvantages (being responsible for writing and for the results of what he or she has written).

(d) *Intrapersonal coping* refers to the concrete ways that people deal with their own problems—their coping strategies. Here we find the coping activities directed at (i) solving the problem (such as self-knowledge, separating oneself from the problem to better define its characteristics and the possibilities of a solution), or directed at (ii) alleviating emotion (denial, blaming of others, etc.).

The other two aspects, *personal wisdom* and *intrapersonal skills*, will be treated later within the context of interpersonal intelligence. In the case of intrapersonal intelligence, the objective is the solution of one's own problems, concerning the individual; in the case of interpersonal intelligence, the objective is the solution of problems that an individual has with others.

(2) Interpersonal intelligence refers to the world of interpersonal relationships; it brings with it recognition by others and inspires confidence and personal closeness. Interpersonal intelligence is characterized by at least the following components: dimensions of skills for solving interpersonal problems, strategies and styles of coping with interpersonal problems, and historical-cultural wisdom.

We are going to look at these components in more detail:

(a) Dimensions of skills for solving interpersonal problems

(i) Non-aggressive assertiveness in social interaction implies a lack of belligerence with those who surround us and with whom we interact; it prevents the development of anxiety.

(ii) Skills for the development of effective communication are those skills that transmit desired information to the receiver. These skills include listening skills, appropriate use of silence, coherence between the content of the message and the emotion expressed, avoidance of repeating arguments without advancing the communication, lack of concern for who has the first and last word, etc.

(b) *Coping strategies and coping styles* refer to forms of action, thought, and emotion in stressful situations. One group of coping strategies and styles has been mentioned previously, oriented to (i) the solution to the problem (search for information about and solutions to concrete problems) and another group oriented to (ii) the modification of emotions (in the case of not being able to solve the problem, one would have to develop it emotionally and cognitively in a different way).

(c) *Interpersonal and sociocultural wisdom.* Wisdom is defined as an expert knowledge and correct judgment in practical questions of life. Pelechano (2000) proposes five criteria to evaluate the quantity and quality of knowledge required to successfully face difficult problems in life: (i) knowledge of the facts that define situations; (ii) procedural knowledge directed at solving problems (how to think about and act on problems); (iii) contextualization within the life cycle, that is, framing the facts within the corresponding context in order to define and isolate them; (iv) possession of a relative and flexible value system; and (v) consciousness and capacity to cope with uncertainty in the face of problems. In addition, as far as "wisdom" refers to interpersonal and intrapersonal relationships, there is an enormous deposit of it in the collection of Spanish proverbs.

In the following section we are going to deal especially with the interpersonal skills necessary for effective coexistence and relationships, and for the prevention of antisocial behavior.

1.2.2. Interpersonal skills

Next we present the different dimensions of interpersonal skills contemplated in Pelechano's model (1989, 2000). In addition, correlational-descriptive hypotheses that have been found in non-criminal populations will be shown.

1. *Appreciation of Perspectives (AOP).* The first dimension to be pointed out is the *appreciation of perspectives other than one's own* with the goal of being able to perceive, identify, and/or contemplate, from each perspective, the type of problem and the characteristics it possesses. This is a rational dimension that is needed to avoid dichotomous true/false thinking when dealing with interpersonal problems. This dimension forms part of the processes, primarily cognitive, that are used in taking into consideration the "other" as a person and partly overlaps with the cognitive component of empathy.

Among interpersonal skills, empathy deserves a special mention for having given rise, in itself, to a rich tradition of research. Again, we find ourselves with a concept with multiple meanings (Romero et al., 1999), to which cognitive components (the capacity to recognize the thoughts or feelings of others) have been attributed. The distinction between cognitive and affective empathy is very relevant, given that it has been seen that criminals do not necessarily score low in cognitive empathy (Pelechano, 2000), but do score low in affective empathy (Romero, 1996). Emotional reaction when faced with the suffering of others appears vital in determining prosocial or antisocial behavior. Knowing the feelings of others does not necessarily inhibit a subject from doing them harm if this knowledge lacks affective depth; that is, a high level of cognitive empathy can even facilitate criminal action (for example, it would help in planning more effective crimes) if the subject is not "infected" by the discomfort of his or her victims.

2. *Causal Thinking (CT).* A second dimension has to do with the *attribution of causes* of interpersonal problems. In our case, the search for and attribution of causes is restricted to interpersonal problems. In the conceptualization that we follow, the search for plausible and possible causes matters as much as or more than the discovery of the actual cause of the problem.

3. *Alternative Thinking (AT).* A third dimension is *generating different solution alternatives* when faced with a problem. This search for different solutions is independent of the ethical acceptability of the alternative proposals; solutions would be looked for to open perspectives and options for courses of action and for analysis of the situation from a single position (in this sense, *Alternative Thinking* is somewhat contradictory to *Appreciation of Perspectives*). This dimension is also a factor of flexibility that should offer guidelines for behavior that correlate negatively with social rigidity.

4. *Consequential Thinking (COT).* A fourth dimension is, following the suggestion of Spivack's group (Spivack and Shure, 1974), the *prediction of consequences* of one's own and/or others' actions on oneself and on others. This dimension is of interest to be able to establish courses of action. It forms part of the conceptual device necessary for decision making and/or the putting into action of decisions adopted.

5. *Means-End Thinking (MET).* A fifth dimension has been identified as the *articulation of means for the achievement of ends*. In the analysis of a problem, in addition to everything said previously, the following is important: the elaboration of a plan of action that includes not only the main points to resolve but also the prediction of possible obstacles, subproblems that may appear and that must be resolved, and finally, the articulation in one's plans of both linear and resourceful means that permit one to predict and be able to satisfactorily resolve situations that present themselves. This dimension, of all of those isolated up to now, is the dimension that most resembles that which is called in isoprocedural models "problem solving."

These dimensions of interpersonal skills are considered to be the fruit of learning; they modify their structure throughout the life of the human being as he or she socializes and integrates within a given culture. In this way, the importance and explanatory weight that these skills possess for social behavior vary as a function of the level of development of the skills. Given these aspects, a strategy of intervention based on the psychology of learning is defended, with the goal of eradicating the deficits that provoke and/or promote an interpersonal problem. Furthermore, the strategy deals with dimensions that do not overlap with academic intelligence or with the temperamental variables of personality psychology, although the dimensions can maintain relationships with these two aspects (Pelechano, 1991b, 1993).

In addition, in this work categories of "qualitative" response in relation to interpersonal skills have been dealt with, a fact that contributes to put between parentheses the fact that the models of "deficit" traditionally accepted in the area of intelligence are the only possible models (Pelechano, 1996). This means that, although in part, as has been seen previously in the literature, a deficit in interpersonal skills in the criminal population is talked about generically (i.e., Gaffney, 1984; Gaffney and McFall, 1981, in Ward and McFall, 1986; Hains and Rian, 1983; Ross, 1987), correcting these deficits may or may not be desirable in the function of the sociocultural context, of existing structural relationships among the diverse components of the intelligences, and of the level of personal development. The importance of the aspect that we are dealing with is illustrated by Pelechano (1996) in the case of adolescents at great risk of becoming juvenile delinquents.

2. METHOD

2.1. Sample and Design

In a stage of initial evaluation (pre-test) a sample of women criminals institutionalized in the Penitentiary Center of Seville II (Spain) (N = 44) completed the Battery of Interpersonal Skills for criminal adult women (BIS-CW). Then 22 of them (experimental group) received training in cognitive skills for solving interpersonal problems (training in dimensions), leaving the other 22 to form the control group. Finally, an evaluation using the post-test for both groups took place after an interval that varied between 9 and 12 months. Both groups were similar in terms of age, socioeconomic level, and time in prison. On the other hand, while the control group was for the most part composed of reoffenders, the experimental group contained some women who had committed more serious crimes.

2.2. The Battery of Interpersonal Skills: Qualitative Response Criteria

The Battery of Interpersonal Skills, which we adapted for criminal adult women and which has served as a criterion of therapeutic change, is made up of five semi-structured tests of character that refer to situations that involve interpersonal problems. Taking into account the work of Bethencourt (1989), within each test problematic situations have been included, such as the following:

(a) Equal at the level of family, work, neighborhood, friends, strangers.
(b) Before authority figures at the level of family, work, and public authorities, and in situations of illness. In this section, the relationships of subordination had to do with both superiors and inferiors, both indirect and direct relationships, and in which the protagonist could play a role both as actor and as observer.

Each of the tests permits the execution of a quantitative correction that is represented by the total score that a person obtains through the responses that he or she gives when faced with the problematic situations, independent of any type of qualification in relation to the given response (e.g., to what extent the response implies elements that are not socially or ethically permissible, whether the responses reflect thoughts and feelings with a positive or negative affective tone, etc.). The response categories that follow arose from a process of discussion among a specialist consultant and three judges who are knowledgeable of the theoretical and procedural aspects implied by the tests.

The dimensions of interpersonal skills and the categories of analysis employed are described as follows:

(1) ***Appreciation of Perspectives*** other than one's own is the ability to perceive, identify, and/or contemplate from each perspective the type of problem and the characteristics it possesses. For this dimension, the following response categories were taken into account:

Total score in *Appreciation of Perspectives (AOP)*

Positive emotional component (PEC). This corresponds to the sum of the women's responses to each of the 15 problem situations that reflect the detection of positive feelings and/or thoughts in others (e.g., responses like "I want her to feel calm," or "It doesn't matter, since the other one likes her the same").

Negative emotional component (NEC). This is similar to the previous category, but in this case the identification of negative feelings and/or thoughts in others is considered (e.g., "She'll think that the other one doesn't like her," or "She'll feel very sad and deceived").

(2) ***Causal Thinking*** is understood as the capacity to search for and attribute causes to interpersonal problems. In this case, the search for plausible and possible causes matters as much as or more than the discovery of the actual cause of an interpersonal problem. In the case of this dimension, the following response categories were considered:

Total score in *Causal Thinking (CT)*

Direct causes (DC). This corresponds to the sum of the women's responses to each of the 15 problem situations which reflect the immediate causes of the problem (e.g., responses like "Because the others forgot to tell her about it").

Indirect causes (IC). This is similar to the previous category, but in this case the remote causes of a problem are considered (e.g., "Because they haven't talked to her for a long time" or "Because they know that she never has anything to drink").

Personal responsibility (PR). This corresponds to the sum of those responses of causes that show that the woman attributes a personal responsibility to the problem situations posed (e.g., "Because Margarita is really annoying").

External responsibility (ER). This is similar to the previous category, but this category considers those responses of causes that show that the woman attributes an external responsibility or sociological interpretation to the problem situations (e.g., "Because in that office they go to lunch in shifts").

(3) ***Alternative Thinking*** is conceived as the ability to generate alternative possible solutions when faced with a problem of interpersonal relations. The following categories were considered:

Total score in *Alternative Thinking (AT)*

Ethically and socially permissible solutions (EPS). This refers to the sum of nonaggressive and nonviolent alternative solutions given for each of the 15 problem situations (e.g., responses like "He could try taking her for a walk or to the movies to get her mind off it").

Solutions for the intragroup (SI). This category considers those responses that are solutions for the intragroup, in the sense of being solutions relative to the reference group of the protagonist of each of the problem situations (e.g., "Start other conversations that are interesting for everyone").

Solutions for the exogroup (SE). This is similar to the previous category, but in this case the solutions for the external group that is not the reference group of the protagonist of the problem situation is counted (e.g., "Join others who don't always talk about the same thing").

(4) ***Consequential Thinking*** is the prediction of consequences of actions for oneself and for others that is used to establish courses of action. This dimension forms part of the conceptual system necessary to make decisions and/or execute actions decided on. The following categories were considered:

Total score in *Consequential Thinking (COT)*

Direct consequences (DCO). This corresponds to the sum of the responses given by the women which indicate immediate consequences. In short, the responses given to the question What could happen next? in each of the 15 problem situations are considered (e.g., responses like "She might discuss it with the other person," or "She might talk to the boy and make plans for another day").

Indirect consequences (ICO). This is similar to the previous category, but in this case the responses that imply indirect or long-term consequences are taken into account, such as responses to the question What will happen further in the future? (e.g., "In the end she did well because the boy wasn't worth it").

(5) ***Means-End Thinking*** takes into account that in the analysis of a problem it is important to elaborate a plan of action that includes not only the main points to resolve, but also the prediction of possible obstacles that might appear and that must be resolved. The following categories were taken into account:

Total score in *Means-End Thinking (MET)*

Ethically and socially permissible means (EPM). This corresponds to the sum of the responses of the women to each of the 15 problem situations which indicate ethically and socially permissible means and procedures and, as in the case of the dimension of alternative thinking, it deals with responses that are not violent or aggressive, nor added to an aggressive response (e.g., responses like "She should make friends with the waiter and get him to introduce her to the man").

In total, 12 qualitative response criteria and 5 quantitative response criteria have been employed to demonstrate the immediate effects of the training.

We think that few instruments exist that have focused and been validated specifically for this population, and this gap should be filled quickly. We have presented a battery that covers an important area of the personal functioning of women criminals: that of their interpersonal relations and their ways of viewing the social-interpersonal world. We strive to know in order to intervene, and intervene in order to help in the most effective way. But we will present this intervention later when we show the results of the intervention program that was used.

2.3. Description of the Intervention Program Developed: Integrated Training Program in Seven Stages

The women who composed the experimental group, divided in small groups, received a training program in *Cognitive Skills for the Solution of Interpersonal Problems (training in dimensions).* The sessions of the program took place with groups of 7-8 women with two therapists who took turns on alternate days in the roles of therapist and cotherapist. The program consisted of 33 sessions of approximately one hour, of which the last 5 were follow-up support sessions.

The program is one of training in interpersonal skills developed from the fusion of two types of previous programs: of stages of solution (based on an isoprocedural tradition of the psychology of thought) and of training in dimensions (based on a heteroprocudural tradition that claims that different processes exist for the solution of impersonal problems and the solution of interpersonal problems). From this basis a seven-stage program was developed in which the dimensions of interpersonal problem solving in the corresponding stages were included. In this way, the two types of programs were integrated into one more-complex program in which seven periods can be differentiated. At the same time, a series of conceptual blocks can be differentiated within each period. A number of different sessions are dedicated to each stage in function of the type of problem to be dealt with and the level of progress of the participants. This program has been applied individually to several types of patients with successful results: patients on hospitalized hemodialysis, those with anxiety of diverse etiologies, and those with flashbacks due to amphetamine psychosis (Pelechano, 1995). In its group version, this program has been applied to the elderly, to advanced-stage cancer patients, and to diabetics, as well as to primary-school-aged children for the modification of attitudes toward the integration of disabled children.

In our study, the training program posed problematic situations of the daily life of these women (the subjects); situations from both within and outside the prison context were used. In this way, problems with family relationships, with husbands or boyfriends, with sons and daughters, in the penitentiary, at work, etc. were analyzed, with the aim of promoting solution strategies on the part of the women.

During the training sessions, at least the following learning strategies were employed: modeling, social reinforcement, rehearsal of behavior through role plays in experimental situations, and brainstorming. The order of training for each of the dimensions had the following sequence: *Appreciation of Perspectives*, *Causal Thinking*, *Alternative Thinking*, *Consequential Thinking*, and *Means-End Thinking*. A detailed analysis of the training program is found in Beleña (1992) and Báguena and Beleña (1996).

Next we present a general outline (a summary-guide) of the program sessions, taking into account that the corresponding exercises for each unit of content, as well as the demands in any aspect, substage, or section of the outline must be appropriate to the objectives, the conditions of the participants, and the time available.

Units 1 and 2: *Initial contact and general objective*. The objective of these units is for the members of the group to understand the purpose of the sessions of the program, learn something about each of the individuals that make up the group, learn to converse by taking turns and create a warm group atmosphere.

Units 3, 4, 5: *Identification of problematic interpersonal situations.* The objective is to identify aspects involved in recognizing problematic interpersonal situations through identifying those feelings that are associated with having problems and through requesting information from the women about their experiences with problematic situations.

Units 6, 7, 8, 9: *Appreciation of Perspectives.* The general objectives of the activities and exercises of these sessions are to identify problems in others, to identify states of mind in general from verbal and nonverbal messages, and to put oneself in another's place in order to see a situation from the other's point of view. Specific objectives are the following: (i) to identify aspects involved in recognizing problematic interpersonal situations through identifying those feelings that are associated with having problems; (ii) to understand that before and/or after a personal problem, different people feel different emotions and have different conceptions of the problem; and (iii) to try to achieve the perception of feelings in interpersonal situations.

Units 10, 11, 12, 13: *Causal Thinking.* The general objective of these sessions is to find the causes that have produced an interpersonal situation, since a situation can have multiple causes. The activities and exercises carried out aim to achieve an appropriate use of temporal sequencing in the ordering of interpersonal phenomena. It is assumed that both conflictive emotional states and those of personal well-being have a history that is necessary to know and take into account.

Units 14, 15, 16, 17: *Alternative Thinking.* The general objective of the sessions dedicated to this dimension is that the women learn to think of as many different solutions as possible for the daily interpersonal problems that are presented. The emphasis is on the generation of alternatives more than on the evaluation of their appropriateness. The objective is to get across that in interpersonal problems there is always more than one alternative for a solution; more than one action can always be taken, and those actions can be positive. The dynamic of the sessions centered on this dimension is that the therapist presents interpersonal problem situations to the women and asks them to share all of the ways that occur to them to resolve the problems.

Units 18, 19, 20, 21: *Consequential Thinking.* The general objective of these sessions is to guide the women to think about what will happen next if a concrete solution is put into action. They are encouraged to cite all the consequences that they can for a given solution. Then they are asked to evaluate the different solutions. The dynamic of these sessions is that the therapist reads a solution that the women have given in previous sessions and the dialogue must involve questions about the consequences: consequences for oneself, for others, and in the short and long term. Once the consequences derived from the solutions for each situation have been determined, the therapist reviews them and emphasizes those solutions that, in the judgment of the women, are and are not appropriate, so that it becomes clear that we can have many solutions for a problem, but that before putting them into action, we must take the consequences into account.

Units 22, 23, 24, 25: *Means-End Thinking.* The general objective of these sessions centers on the details and elaboration of one particular solution, specifying the concrete steps that must be taken into account to articulate a given solution. The focus is on detailing step by step the means necessary to reach the goal. The objective is to learn how to overcome obstacles and use alternative means in case we come up against insurmountable barriers.

Units 26, 27, 28: *Synthesis activities.* The general objective of these sessions is to put into practice each of the five dimensions of interpersonal skills that have been trained and that make up the program of training in dimensions.

Units 29, 30, 31, 32, 33: *Support sessions.* The objective is to reinforce everything that was learned throughout the training to achieve a better consolidation. There are five support sessions every two weeks after the last sessions of training; therefore, these sessions take more time than previous sessions. The general structure of each session involves a summary of the whole process.

This is a program in which cognitive mediators are trained together with willful and conscious motor responses—the action. A fundamental premise of the cognitive model lies in the educational nature of its orientation to treatment: the best way to reeducate criminals is through direct and systematic teaching of the personal resources necessary to live more effectively and in a more dignified manner. And so, it is claimed that a considerable deficiency in socialization (of the values, attitudes, and reasoning skills that are required for social adjustment) in criminals can be compensated for in the majority of cases.

At this moment a question arises: Is prosocial training capable of improving responsibility, competence, and maturity in persons with cognitive deficits? We are sure of the affirmative answer to this question, given that the main objective of this training is precisely to modify, with a broad range of techniques, some of the individual characteristics that delay the development of maturity and responsibility, such as impulsiveness, lack of consideration of the consequences of actions, egocentric thinking, lack of ability to conceive of alternatives in the solution of interpersonal problems, and lack of consideration of the impact of behavior on other persons.

3. RESULTS

3.1. Internal Consistency

		Pre-Test				Post-Test			
		Control		Experimental		Control		Experimental	
Variables	No. Items	N	α	N	α	N	α	N	α
AOP	15	22	.97	22	.98	22	.94	22	.96
PEC	15	22	.75	22	.91	22	.83	22	.76
NEC	15	22	.94	22	.94	22	.90	22	.88
CT	15	22	.96	22	.92	22	.95	22	.92
DC	15	22	.94	22	.90	22	.93	22	.86
IC	15	22	.87	22	.82	22	.87	22	.88
PR	15	22	.79	22	.39	22	.72	22	.57
ER	15	22	.89	22	.84	22	.87	22	.86
AT	15	22	.83	22	.84	22	.89	22	.80
EPS	15	22	.84	22	.82	22	.82	22	.81
SI	15	22	.68	22	.77	22	.75	22	.64
SE	15	22	.52	22	.26	22	.57	22	.01
COT	15	22	.95	22	.97	22	.91	22	.97
DCO	15	22	.91	22	.95	22	.80	22	.95
ICO	15	22	.93	22	.96	22	.89	22	.95
MET	15	22	.96	22	.93	22	.82	22	.94
EPM	15	22	.96	22	.93	22	.83	22	.94

Figure 2.

3.2. Results at the Quantitative and Qualitative Level

3.2.1. Analysis of means and differences between and within groups (intragroup)

The effects of the training were determined for the five dimensions (at the quantitative level). The results appear in Figures 3, 4, and 5:

Figure 3 presents the means, standard deviations, and tests of differences in the pre-test between the control and experimental groups in the variables of interpersonal skills.

Before the training, both groups were homogenous with respect to the five dimensions of interpersonal skills evaluated. None of the differences reached the usual significant level of .05.

Figure 3. Comparison of averages in the pre-test: Control and experimental groups.

Figure 4 presents the intragroup differences (pre-test–post-test) for the control group (left) and experimental group (right).

The results suggest that these skills diminished considerably in the control group during the time of incarceration. All of the intragroup t-tests were significant, the means being higher in the pre-test than in the post-test. In the case of the experimental group we found that this decrease was not relevant and that the training even produced an improvement in *Alternative Thinking* (-2.00; $p > .05$).

Pre-Test	Control GP.		Experimental GP.		
Variables	M	SD	M	SD	T
AOP	101.73	35.23	110.55	43.19	-0.74
CT	56.68	20.96	64.23	15.75	-1.35
AT	50.59	10.18	55.95	9.80	-1.78
COT	79.05	27.31	97.73	39.24	-1.83
MET	67.64	36.62	62.45	18.62	0.59

Figure 3. Note: AOP=Appreciation of Perspectives; CT=Causal Thinking; AT=Alternative Thinking; COT=Consequential Thinking; MET=Means-End Thinking; M=mean; SD=standard deviation; t=Student's t-value

Figure 3 presents the means, standard deviations, and tests of differences (t-tests) in the post-test between the control and experimental groups in the variables of interpersonal skills.

	Control GP.		Experimental GP.	
Variables	T	LS	T	LS
AOP	3.71	.001	0.86	/
CT	6.00	.001	0.06	/
AT	3.80	.001	-2.00	.05
COT	2.43	.05	0.34	/
MET	2.76	.01	-1.15	/

Figure 4. Note: AOP=*Appreciation of Perspectives*; CT=*Causal Thinking*; AT=*Alternative Thinking*; COT=*Consequential Thinking*; MET=*Means-End Thinking*; t=Student's t-value; ls=level of statistical significance achieved by the difference

Figure 4. Intragroup pre-test–post-test differences for the control and experimental groups.

Post-Test	Control GP.		Experimental GP.		
Variables	M	SD	M	SD	t
AOP	77.09	18.35	103.32	30.64	-3.44**
CT	40.14	14.67	64.05	15.66	-5.23***
AT	42.36	9.65	59.86	7.73	-6.64***
COT	64.64	16.08	95.68	31.35	-4.13***
MET	48.45	10.46	68.68	20.52	-4.12***

Figure 5. Note: AOP=*Appreciation of Perspectives*; CT=*Causal Thinking*; AT=*Alternative Thinking*; COT=*Consequential Thinking*; MET=*Means-End Thinking*; M=mean; SD=standard deviation; t=Student's t-value; ** = p <.01; *** =p <.001

	Control Group				Experimental Group			
	Pre-Test		Post-Test		Pre-Test		Post-Test	
Variables	M	SD	M	SD	M	SD	M	SD
PEC	25.27	10.67	21.82	9.67	23.05	15.86	27.82	11.62
NEC	76.45	28.04	55.27	17.09	87.91	29.93	75.50	24.45
DC	38.59	16.04	23.23	11.67	43.27	11.85	44.77	11.25
IC	18.09	5.82	16.91	5.08	20.95	6.40	19.27	19.27
ER	25.50	12.65	19.36	10.34	29.73	11.93	29.91	11.84
EPS	34.36	7.12	28.82	6.25	41.05	7.40	42.41	6.65
SI	40.90	7.96	32.18	7.62	46.18	8.47	48.77	6.81
DCO	41.77	13.19	33.36	7.61	49.77	21.88	50.64	15.51
ICO	37.27	15.69	31.27	9.31	46.14	21.36	45.05	16.90
EPM	66.36	35.67	46.73	10.90	61.86	18.70	67.55	20.08

Figure 6. Note: PEC=positive emotional component; NEC=negative emotional component; DC=direct causes; IC=indirect causes; ER=external responsibility; EPS=ethically and socially permissible solutions; SI=solutions for the intragroup; DCO=direct consequences; ICO=indirect consequences; EPM=ethically and socially permissible means

Figure 5. Comparison of means in the post-test: Control and experimental groups.

In this case, the results are more striking since the experimental group obtained means significantly higher in all of the dimensions of interpersonal skills than did the control group, with levels above .001.

Figure 6. Means and standard deviations of qualitative variables of interpersonal skills.

Next the **qualitative results** obtained are presented, understanding by "qualitative" the rigorous use of models of quantitative analysis on the responses of the women in the Battery of Interpersonal Skills and how the training affected (or not) these qualitative aspects.

Figure 6 presents the means and standard deviations in the pre-test and post-test of the control and experimental groups in the qualitative variables of the Battery of Interpersonal Skills. Figure 6 presents the tests of differences (Student's t-test) of the pre-test (left), control and experimental intragroup (center columns) and the post-test (right).

In general, our results suggest that the training appears to have been effective in slowing down the deterioration of interpersonal skills that seems to occur in incarcerated female criminals. To a large extent, the situation of incarceration appears to be responsible for this deterioration. The dimensions of *Means-End Thinking* and *Alternative Thinking* were most benefited by the training.

Leaving aside the general question of whether the effects of training or the deterioration of interpersonal skills were higher or lower in some women than in others, we want to point out other findings that we consider of interest.

	Pre-Test	Intragroup (Pre-Test–Post-Test)		Post-Test
		Control Group	Experimental Group	
Variables	t	t	t	t
PEC	0.55	1.28	-1.40	-1.86
NEC	-1.31	4.11***	2.15*	-3.46***
DC	-1.10	7.57***	-0.56	-6.23***
IC	-1.55	1.16	1.38	-1.41
ER	-1.14	3.58***	-0.09	-3.15**
EPS	-3.05**	4.43***	-0.87	-6.98***
SI	-2.13*	4.66***	-1.50	-7.61***
DCO	-1.47	2.89**	-0.24	-4.69***
ICO	-1.57	1.72	0.31	-3.35***
EPM	0.52	2.88**	-1.08	-4.27***

Figure 7. Note: PEC=positive emotional component; NEC=negative emotional component; DC=direct causes; IC=indirect causes; ER=external responsibility; EPS=ethically and socially permissible solutions; SI=solutions for the intragroup; DCO=direct consequences; ICO=indirect consequences; EPM=ethically and socially permissible means; * = $p < .05$; ** = $p < .01$; *** = $p < .001$

Figure 7. Qualitative variables of interpersonal skills: Test of differences (Student's t-test) of the pre-test (left), control and experimental intragroup (center columns) and the post-test (right).

These results show the following:

i. Before any type of training was carried out, the groups were homogenous in all the variables of interest except in the two corresponding to the test of *Alternative Thinking*: EPS (ethically and socially permissible solutions; t = -3.05) and SI (solutions for the intragroup; t = -2.13). In these two variables, the experimental group performed significantly better.
ii. The means and standard deviations fell considerably in the control group from the pre-test to the post-test, so it could be said that the women in this group "homogenized toward the bottom," or deteriorated, during the period of incarceration. In other words, the penitentiary situation appears to have considerably influenced some of the components of interpersonal intelligence of the women. This deterioration was significant in the following: the identification of feelings and thoughts with a negative affective tone (NEC), the search for and attribution of direct causes and identification of short-term consequences (DC and DCO), external responsibility (ER), ethically and socially responsible solutions and means (EPS and EPM), and solutions for the intragroup (SI).
iii. As for the experimental group, the intragroup differences show that the training appears to have maintained the women at their initial levels of interpersonal

intelligence. The most evident result suggests a decrease in the negative emotional component (NEC) accompanied by an increase, although not significant, in the identification of positive feelings and thoughts (PEC).

iv. The comparison of post-test means of the control and experimental groups shows significant differences in favor of the experimental group in all of the variables except that of the positive emotional component (PEC; $t = -1.86$, $p > .05$) and the search for and attribution of indirect causes (IC; $t = -1.41$; $p > .05$). The two differences found in the positive emotional component (PEC) in the pre-test not only maintained but doubled and tripled their values.

4. Conclusion

(i) At the level of general interpretation, we see that the training significantly neutralized or slowed down the deterioration of the women's interpersonal skills which the situation of incarceration appears to have produced. It's advisable to point out, with respect to the set of the variables that give rise to significant results, that while a considerable decrease in the means and in the variability from the pre-test to the post-test was detected in the control group, in general the reduction of the variability tended to be associated with a slight increase in the means of the experimental group. In this sense, it is based on this that we affirm that the intervention carried out impeded the "homogenization toward the bottom" of interpersonal skills that was seen in the women who made up the control group.

(ii) The significant results obtained after the training of socially and ethically permissible solutions and means (EPS and EPM) have special importance given the characteristics of the sample of women in this study: criminal women. If women are incarcerated, it is because in one way or another they have transgressed social norms to satisfy a series of needs and personal goals. The problem in general is not in the existence of such needs and personal goals (we are not talking about psychopathic women) but in the types of means and solutions that they adopt to satisfy those needs and goals. Nevertheless, if the punishment (incarceration) given for the use of solutions and means that are not ethically and socially permissible possesses an immediate benefit for society (to free from all types of aggression others who are also in the society), this punishment does not seem advantageous in the long term for such a society, nor does it recall the role of socio-environmental conditions in the origin of the crime. The simple incarceration of women, without being accompanied by an adequate rehabilitation in the area of socio-personal intelligence, has in our judgment little sense of solidarity, if not little social sense. It can be said that the training developed by us at least prevents women from "forgetting" the types of solutions and strategies that society demands.

(iii) Considering the five rational dimensions of interpersonal skills contemplated by the Battery of Interpersonal Skills, the results of this qualitative analysis point to the fact that the greatest success was obtained in the area of *Consequential Thinking*, as the women identified both direct and remote consequences of a problem of interpersonal relations posed to them. Inversely, the results obtained suggest that the training program should include more work on sessions corresponding to the identification of thoughts and feelings in others. Despite this, we would like to comment in more detail on the results relative to the qualitative variables considered in the *Appreciation of Perspectives*— positive emotional component (PEC) and negative emotional component (NEC) — centering the discussion on (iiia) the differential perceptions of the women in the identification of positive and negative feelings and/or thoughts, and (iiib) the failure of the training, particularly in the category of negative thoughts and/or feelings (NEC).

(iiia) The polarization between PEC and NEC (observe the averages reached by the groups in the pre-test and the post-test in each of these categories respectively) reflects that the appreciation of perspectives of the criminal woman lay fundamentally in the identification of negative feelings and thoughts. This finding represents the logical and expected consequence when the biographies of these women, and not just the prison context, is considered. Davis (1983) emphasizes the relationships that the appreciation of perspectives maintains with aspects such as social functioning, self-esteem, and sensitivity toward others. In agreement with these assertions, the social functioning characteristic of the women in our study results in unrewarding interpersonal relationships that are accompanied by poor self-esteem and a sensitivity to the negative experiences of others. Thus the predominance of the excessive identification of negative feelings and/or thoughts, as apposed to positive, can be seen to a certain extent as a normal result.

(iiib) In relation to the above, the question arises as to how the results (although not statistically significant) obtained in these variables (PEC and NEC) in both groups should be evaluated. Although the decrease in negative feelings in the prison context was common to both groups, it was more pronounced in the group that received training, and it was only in this group that the identification of positive thoughts and/or feelings in others increased. This aspect deserves special attention in subsequent studies.

(iv) Additionally, the training clearly increased the search for and attribution of direct causes for interpersonal problems (DC). This increase was consistent with a decrease in the identification of negative feelings and/or thoughts; the correlation between both variables decreased in the experimental group from the pre-test ($r = 0.64$) to the post-test ($r = 0.36$), while the opposite effect was produced in the control group (coefficients of 0.41 in the pre-test and 0.67 in the post-test). Likewise, the results obtained in *Causal Thinking* require a more thorough consideration of the exercises in the program dedicated to the recognition of possible indirect causes of interpersonal problems.

(v) As for the increase that the training promoted in the number of solutions for the intragroup (SI), it is difficult to judge at the level of this study the significance that such a result could have. At the moment, finding alternative solutions that are adaptive, although only for the intragroup, points in the direction of improving this dimension of thought or generation of alternatives.

We would like to stress two points. First, the training program developed by us is feasible for application in the context of the penitentiary institution. Second, we want to highlight the fact that the training program generally produces beneficial effects, at least in the short term. The effectiveness in statistical terms, although minor depending on perspective from which they are viewed, is suggestive as far as providing information about the components of the program that should be improved. Along with the goal of improving the program, research should be continued with follow-up studies that establish the effectiveness of the program in terms of therapeutic benefits that are more long-term. These two considerations invite the incorporation of this type of program into the routine practice of penitentiary institutions, with the goal of contributing to the complicated task of social reintegration.

Finally, we consider that the results obtained permit us to be optimistic with respect to the social usefulness of our work. It is undeniable that the training carried out has produced positive effects. Given these considerations, we believe that this type of training should be incorporated into the routines of prisons, because sooner or later these women will be reincorporated into a society that demands the management of interpersonal skills. By working with these skills, the goal is not just to teach women to offer concrete solutions to specific problems posed to them, but to give these incarcerated women general strategies (cognitive and behavioral skills) to apply to all problematic situations. They need to recognize that problematic situations are part of daily life and that it is possible to face these situations effectively most of the time. And there is no doubt that both of these realizations are symptoms of maturity and responsibility.

It might be thought that these interpersonal skills arise spontaneously during the educational process; however, this is an erroneous assumption. Young people need not only to learn the inferential and critical thinking that permits them to be competent in mathematics, science, and other subjects of the school curriculum, but also to learn the cognitive strategies for adequate social integration. And there is no doubt that among the most important skills of social competence are the skills of knowing how to detect and generate solutions to problems, to predict the consequences of one's actions, to put oneself in another's place when making a decision, and to put into practice guidelines of adequate behavior for social relations. The adaptation of the person to his or her surroundings will arise as a result of possessing and putting into practice this collection of socially and culturally positive characteristics. A person who is responsible and committed to his or her environment and accepted by that environment is a person with a high probability of being socially adjusted. We should not forget that people with all of these attributes must learn them; people are not born socially well-adapted or maladapted. The final result can be considered the success or failure of the socialization process.

5. References

Báguena, M. J. & Beleña, M. A. (1993). Habilidades interpersonales en mujeres delincuentes internas. Un estudio de evaluación. *Análisis y Modificación de Conducta, 63*, 5-27.

Báguena, M. J., & Beleña, M. A. (1996). Programa de entrenamiento en dimensiones de habilidades interpersonales para mujeres internas en cárceles de cumplimiento. In V. Pelechano (dir.), *Habilidades interpersonales. Teoría mínima y programas de intervención* (Vol. III, pp. 632-692). Valencia: Alfaplús.

Beleña, M. A. (1992). *Personalidad y habilidades interpersonales en la delincuencia femenina adulta: evaluación y tratamiento*. Tesis Doctoral. Universitat de València.

Beleña, M. A. & Báguena, M. J. (1992). Habilidades interpersonales: Efectos de un programa de entrenamiento en mujeres delincuentes internas. *Análisis y Modificación de Conducta, 61,* 751-772.

Bethencourt, J. M. (1989). *Evaluación de habilidades interpersonales en adultos.* Tesis Doctoral, Facultad de Filosofía y Ciencias de la Educación. Universidad de La Laguna.

Davis, M. H. (1983). Measuring individual differences in empathy: Evidence for a multidimensional approach. *Journal of Personality and Social Psychology, 44,* 113-126.

Gaffney, L. R. (1984). A multiple choice-test to measure social skills in delinquent and non-delinquent adolescent girls. *Journal of Consulting and Clinical Psychology, 52,* 911-912.

Gaffney, L. R. & McFall, R. M. (1981). A comparison of social skills in delinquent and non-delinquent adolescent girls using a behavioral roleplaying inventory. *Journal of Consulting and Clinical Psychology, 49,* 959-967.

Gardner, H. (1993). *Multiple intelligences. The theory in practice.* Nueva York, Basic Books.

Garrido, V., Stangeland, P. & Redondo, S. (2006). *Principios de criminología.* Valencia: Tirant lo Blanch.

Hains, A. A. & Ryan, E. B. (1983). The development of social cognitive processes among juvenile delinquents and nondelinquent peers. *Child Development, 54,* 1536-1544.

Pelechano, V. (1984). Inteligencia social y habilidades interpersonales. *Análisis y Modificación de Conducta, 10, 26,* 393-420.

Pelechano, V. (1985). Inteligencia social y habilidades interpersonales: Evaluación y validación. *Evaluación Psicológica, 1 (1-2),* 159-188.

Pelechano, V. (1986). Inteligencia y habilidades interpersonales: La excepcionalidad en el tratamiento de un tema. *Análisis y Modificación de Conducta, 12, 33,* 317-346.

Pelechano, V. (1989). Ejes de referencia y una propuesta temática. In E. Ibáñez, & V. Pelechano (Dirs.), *Psicología de la Personalidad,* (pp. 265-329). Madrid: Alhambra.

Pelechano, V. (1991a). Inteligencia y habilidades interpersonales: Un diseño de modelo de trabajo y algunas hipótesis contrastables. *Psicologemas, 10,* 205-248.

Pelechano, V. (1991b). *Habilidades interpersonales en ancianos: Conceptualización y evaluación.* Valencia: Alfaplús.

Pelechano, V. (1993). *Inteligencia sociopersonal: conceptualización y promoción.* Ponencia presentada en "Modificabilidad cognitiva y programas de enriquecimiento instrumental" (Madrid, 17 septiembre).

Pelechano, V. (1995). Habilidades interpersonales: conceptualización y entrenamiento. In M.D. Calero (Comp.), *Modificación de la inteligencia* (pp. 131-181). Madrid: Pirámide.

Pelechano, V. (1996). *Habilidades interpersonales. Teoría mínima y programas de intervención*: Vol. 1. Valencia: Alfaplús.

Pelechano, V. (2000). Competencias de Personalidad. En V. Pelechano (Coord), *Psicología Sistemática de la Personalidad,* (pp. 343-427). Barcelona: Ariel.

Redondo, S. (2008). *Manual para el tratamiento psicológico de los delincuentes.* Madrid. Pirámide.

Romero, E. (1996). *La predicción de la conducta antisocial: Un análisis de las variables de personalidad.* Tesis Doctoral. Universidad de Santiago de Compostela.

Romero, E., Sobral, J. & Luengo, M. A. (1999). *Personalidad y delincuencia: Entre la biología y la sociedad.* Granada: Grupo Editorial Universitario.

Ross, R. R. (1987). Prevención de la delincuencia a través del entrenamiento cognitivo. In V. Garrido, & B. Vidal del Cerro (comps.), *Lecturas de pedagogía correccional,* (pp. 135-148). Valencia: Nau Llibres.

Ross, R. & Ross, R. (1995). *Thinking straight. Reasoning and rehabilitation program for delinquency prevention and offender rehabilitation.* Ottawa, Canadá: Air Training and Publications.

Spivack, G. & Shure, M. B. (1974). *Social adjustment of young children.* Hillsdale: Jossey-Bass.

Veneziano, C. & Veneziano, L. (1988). Knowledge of social skills among institutionalized juvenile delinquents. *Criminal Justice and Behavior, 15,* 152-171.

Ward, C. I. & McFall, R. M. (1986). Further validation of the Problem Inventory for adolescent girls: Comparing caucasian and black delinquents and non-delinquents. *Journal of Consulting and Clinical* Psychology, *54*, 732-733.

In: Violent Crime and Prisons: ...
Ed: Aidan Renshaw and Emelina Suárez
ISBN: 978-1-60741-668-5

Chapter 5

SOCIAL ORDER IN POST-COMMUNIST PRISONS: THE STUDY OF PRISONS IN POLAND

Barbara Pabjan[*]
Wroclaw University, Poland

ABSTRACT

In the early 1990s, the fundamental changes in the social system in Poland had begun: the communist regime failed and the new social and economic order had been emerging. This situation offers an opportunity to study the consequences of the turn on the prison system and prisoners, changes within penal institutions, differences between 'totalitarian' prisons and a democratic penal system. The basic idea is to examine the influence of political and social changes on conditions of imprisonment, and to explore the process of institutional adjustment to a free market economy and democratization.

This chapter presents research on inmates in Poland, with a focus on a prisoner as a rational actor in a penal institution environment. The main issues of the research focus on the consequences of penal reform on the social community of prisoners, especially on social order in the convicts' community, normative system, social relations among inmates and social relations between inmates and correctional staff and the standard of living in confinement.

The results of the research reveal that social relations have changed and a relatively high level of integration among the inmates' community in 'the totalitarian' prison has been displaced with distrust; the social ties are based mainly on interests and 'goods-exchange' relations. The 'old' sub-culture community which controlled social order disappeared. The role of bureaucratization increases significantly. It decreases the rehabilitation function of prisons because the main goal of staff is to respect formal regulations. Bureaucracy redefines the rational rules of acting both for inmates and prison staff. For prisoners it becomes a means to achieve their purposes. The result of the new organizational order is more control on the penal institutions, especially inmates gaining more influence over their lives. The question arises about the consequences of such conditions in correctional institutions for inmates and society.

The analysis is based on data collected in the empirical research carried out in 20 prisons in Poland, on a sample of over 1000 persons.

---

* bpabjan@uni.wroc.pl Institute of Sociology, University of Wrocław, ul. Koszarowa 3, 51-149 Wrocław, Poland

Introduction

The fall of the communist regime and the introduction of democracy and a market economy in Poland that started in 1989 had extensive consequences for the Polish correctional system. The main causes of the transition of the penitentiary system are the modification of the law and institution of new penal policy. In this chapter I will concentrate on the social and cultural aspects of change in the prison system which followed the appearance of new policy, new law and—what is most important—the effects of their implementation. But first, let me outline the theoretical perspective which is the background for data introduced here.

Linkages among a penal system, a state and a society must be taken into consideration to understand the present situation in prisons in Poland. An idea that social order links up the system of punishment was expressed at the very beginning in social sciences: for Marx class structure and economic system influenced both crime and punishment, whereas for Durkheim it established 'moral boundaries' in a society and thus helped to sustain social order. The perspective which serves as a general framework in this chapter is closer to the Marxist approach and based on the assumption that the mechanism of punishment and prison system imprint social order, especially class structure and power relations. In addition, I address the role of culture (values and norms) and a functional explanation referring to the purpose of penalty control for the functioning of the system. Culture is, in a sense, the widest framework within which social action takes place, it creates meaning in all aspects of social life; for instance, certain values create a climate of opinion (e.g. crime fear), and the penal institutions, as well as politicians, must work in this climate. Whether in a direct or indirect manner, values affect also the structural determinism.

Many scholars who analysed the punishment under the capitalism system found they more or less continue the Marxist approach: they stress that the system of punishment reflects the interest of the dominant class [Rusche Kirchheimer 1968 (1939); Quinney 1974, 1980; Garland 1990; Reiman 1998 (1979); Shelden 2001]. A prison as a social institution is part of a society, and it reflects a social order and culture of the society [Garland 1990; Morris, Rothman 1995]. Consequently, studying prisons cannot be separated from the analysis of a social system itself. The social history of criminal justice reveals the influence of a social system on a penal system [Sykes 2007 (1958); Shelden 2001; Garland 1990; Hagan & Peterson 1995; Weiss & South 1998].

The comparison of penal systems in different types of societies shows both parallelism and distinction: we can find many similarities such as the effects of confinement, the structure of the prison population, the structure of crimes. It proves that a prison as a type of social institution has some universal features, but on the other hand one can expect culture and organizational differences. The confrontation of the conditions of confinement in democratic and totalitarian states also reveals some similarities and differences. I try to examine here the standpoint that the basic function of the penal system is the same both in a communist and in a democratic state: to keep control over a society, to employ the prison for political ends, to sustain power and to support social order in the interest of the dominant class. Power (gaining and preserving power) becomes the interest of public institutions. Being public institutions, prisons and criminal justice are used by the state as a tool of control over a society. However, the dominant ideology presents punishment as an institution that serves a society: citizens believe that prisons and criminal justice serve their interests (security). The role of criminal justice was perfectly explained by Reiman, and I refer here to the idea expressed in his work, *The Rich get richer and the poor get prison.* In fact, there is a hidden conflict of interest among citizens, state and penal system. We can find an analogy between the model of the prison system and the state: evidently, the communist state had more extensive control over society and the level of penalization was high. The prison system had two functions: it served as the institution of criminal justice and sustained political control over society. What makes the *difference* between the democratic and totalitarian model of penalty is the *degree* of each type of control and *how* the penal system implements the function of control over a society. It is strictly connected to *mechanisms of power*: to win elections in a democracy has become easier by using the fear of crime in a society and maintaining power through the suppression of opponents (authority institutions in a totalitarian state). Crime control is used to legitimate decisions against the freedom of citizens. But not only are the mechanisms of power important to understand a prison system. Formal crime-control institutions, as all institutions, first of all act in their own interests, and not in the interests of other social organisations or citizens.

The mass media has a special role in the process of gaining power: they are used to create social panic, a stereotype of crime and to uphold irrational, emotional attitudes to crime. Media supports the philosophy of punishment as revenge and influence (or even determine) the contemporary discourse on crime and punishment.

The fear of crime in public opinion expresses in part the lack of knowledge about the social conditioning of crime and the process of society penalization—for instance, there is no connection between the crime rate and incarceration rate, the number of prisoners grows whereas the crime rate does not. The public's fear of crime then is irrelevant to reality. The main factors of public discourse manipulation are: the use of the stereotype of crime in the media for the purpose of winning attention and shock, and the use of crime fear by politicians to win attention, popularity and to gain political support. Thus, the penal system is employed for political ends and involved in the manipulation of media for the benefit of a particular political party.[1]

The empirical data show a lot of similarities in the mechanisms of criminal justice and the penal system in a democratic and totalitarian state. For instance, the structure of the incarcerated population reveals that both in a democratic and a totalitarian state, penal systems control 'the dangerous' classes (in the first case underclass, and in the second political opposition). The prison population consists of the poor and uneducated people, for the most part. This phenomenon is well known for researchers of Western penitentiary systems, who claim that the criminal justice system is much more repressive for the underclass than for 'the white collars" or generally the rich. [Weiss, South 1998: 3]. Therefore the difference between a 'totalitarian prison' and a 'democratic prison' is the *degree* of the control and the methods of controlling people by the authorities and public institutions.

Incarceration as a form of punishment has been criticised for a long time. The debate on the form of the penal system, which started in the 1960s, leads us to important conclusions on the features of imprisonment in modern societies: rehabilitation appeared to be an illusion; a

[1] A good example is the former ministry of justice in Poland Zbigniew Ziobro, who gained extreme popularity and social support promoting a restricted penal policy.

penal system is in crisis and attempts to reform it have failed; it is not rational and not effective. Garland describes the condition of a penal system as "continuing crisis and disruption in a penal system which no longer takes seriously the rehabilitative values and ideologies". In spite of conclusive evidence presented in debates against the rationality of imprisonment, it has little influence on law enforcement [Garland 1990].

The purpose of this chapter is to explore selected issues related to social change in the prison system in Poland. I examine the main features of contemporary prisons in Poland and I try to analyse to what extent they are intentional results of policy and to what extent they are 'unexpected' results of 'social laws' of the total institution, regularities of social behaviour and inevitable dynamics of social life.

The main issue of this chapter is social order in prisons in a 'new' democratic society. The transition from totalitarian to democratic state is often regarded as the background of change in a penal system, however, the specific form of total institution and mechanisms of democracy tend to support the conservation of 'the old' social system in prisons. The question is to what extent the system has changed and what are the new features of penal institutions?

From the sociological point of view the most interesting indicators of a social order of prisons are social structure of the incarcerated population, social relations inside prisons, the normative system of prison community, the organisational and legal aspects (the implementation of new law) of a penal institution. In short, new law regulations give convicts more rights and provide more humanitarian treatment: enable contact with relatives, respect different kinds of material and psychical needs (e.g., religious), support special care and therapies for the sick and the alcohol and drug addicted, and in general give more privileges during incarceration.

These indicators are at the same time the fundamental sociological issues that explain the social reality of confinement and the profile of a penal system. I present some results of the research showing the features of a social order and culture (norms and values) of a prison society: social relations (especially increasing of transactional type of social relationships and decrease of human solidarity), strategies of acting, daily activities and work attitudes, also attributes of social structure.

Methodological Note

The analysis is based on the data collected in the empirical research carried out in 20 prisons in Poland, from 2003 to 2006. The research was carried out inside prisons and it is based on direct contact with inmates and prison staff. Different techniques were used in this study: both quantitative and qualitative survey, in-depth interview, observation and regular focus interviews lasting for two years in two prisons. In this chapter I present a part of the collected data that come from two inquiries: a survey on a sample of over 1000 persons, and interviews on a sample of 434 prisoners (made in three prisons). Also some data from qualitative research will be used to illustrate some conclusions. The sample is not a random and representative one because of restricted access to the respondents. All analysis concerns the sample and when applied to a broader context is regarded as the supposition of explanation of the discussed social process.

The main issue of this chapter is social order in prisons in a 'new' democratic society. The transition from totalitarian to democratic state is often regarded as the background of change in a penal system, however, the specific form of total institution and mechanisms of democracy tend to support the conservation of 'the old' social system in prisons. The question is to what extent the system has changed and what are the new features of penal institutions?

From the sociological point of view the most interesting indicators of a social order of prisons are social structure of the incarcerated population, social relations inside prisons, the normative system of prison community, the organisational and legal aspects (the implementation of new law) of a penal institution. In short, new law regulations give convicts more rights and provide more humanitarian treatment: enable contact with relatives, respect different kinds of material and psychical needs (e.g., religious), support special care and therapies for the sick and the alcohol and drug addicted, and in general give more privileges during incarceration.

These indicators are at the same time the fundamental sociological issues that explain the social reality of confinement and the profile of a penal system. I present some results of the research showing the features of a social order and culture (norms and values) of a prison society: social relations (especially increasing of transactional type of social relationships and decrease of human solidarity), strategies of acting, daily activities and work attitudes, also attributes of social structure.

THE PRISON POPULATION IN POLAND

Table 1. The source of data: Eurostat. 2008

Country	**Rate of imprisonment per 100.000 population, average per year 2004 to 2006**	
USA	496	2004-2007
Estonia	329	
Latvia	308	
Lithuania	231	
Poland	218	
Czech Republic	183	
Slovakia	170	
Romania	169	
Liechtenstein	163	
Hungary	155	
Luxemburg	150	
Bulgaria	145	
UK: England & Wales	144	
Spain	142	
UK: Scotland	136	
Portugal	121	
Austria	109	
Netherlands	103	
the former Yuogoslav Republic of Macedonia	98	

Table 1. Continued

Germany	95	
France	95	
Greece	91	2005-2006
Belgium	90	
Italy	88	
Turkey	86	
Switzerland	81	
Sweden	80	
UK: Northern Ireland	78	
Croatia	77	
Malta	76	
Ireland	75	
Cyprus	75	
Denmark	73	
Finland	69	
Norway	66	2003-2005
Slovenia	56	
Iceland	40	

One of the specific features of the post-communist penitentiary system is relatively high level of imprisonment compared to the average imprisonment rate in Western European countries: the average rate of imprisonment per 100,000 population per year 2004 to 2006 in the post-communist countries was 200[3], whereas in Western European countries it was 99 (table 1). However, in the beginning of transformation the number of prisoners dropped from around 100,000 to 40,000 .

European democratic countries have a lower imprisonment rate than non-democratic countries and to some degree this difference might be used as an argument that the penitentiary system is closely related to the political system: most totalitarian states or unstable democracies have a high incarceration rate. But this does not act as a rule, the well known case is the penal system in the USA: the imprisonment rate in 2000 was 478, in 2006 it was 501, and in 2007 it was 506 (prisoners under state or federal jurisdiction); the incarceration rate that includes all inmates held in state or federal public prison facilities or in local jails is even higher: in 2000 it was 684, in 2006 it was 751, and in 2007 it was 756 per 100,000 residents [West, Sabol 2007]. The example of the USA proves that a democratic country does not create a more liberal penal system automatically, and that conditioning of a correctional institution is more complicated. The culture is one of the most important factors that influence the penal system: each society has different conception of punishment (how people should be punished and for what). It is the culture that shapes the policy of public institutions, but the most important agent is the interest of political institutions and 'power mechanisms' in democracy. The cases of the USA and Poland, and the history of prisons as well, show that a prison system depends on a social order and that power institutions, law enforcement and a penal system are involved in the execution of the elites' interest. The question arises what is the meaning of high rate of imprisonment besides that it indicates the level of penalisation in society?

[3] The mean counted without extreme values (Slovenia and Iceland).

Incarceration rate is 'the simple' indicator how the penal system works. Studying changes in size of incarcerated population shows that the imprisonment in Poland is relatively high except seasonal fluctuation (figure 2 shows changes in the Polish prison system during the past 75 years). From 2004 to 2006 the national imprisonment rate in Poland was 218 per 100,000 population, so it was and still is one of the highest in Europe (table 1 shows that Poland has the fourth place in the ranking). After the temporary decrease in the number of prisoners in 1989–1990, there had been a continuous increase of the incarceration rate in Poland during the period 1995–2006. Since 1990 the number of inmates has doubled (see figure 1). In 2008 (December 31) there were 82,785 persons in custody and prisons (80,272 males and 2,513 females; 8,926 people held in police custody, and 73,859 in prisons.), which is 0.3% of the whole adult population. In 2008 there were 28,824 prison officers and 1016 civilian workers [CZSW 2008]. The structure of prison units' capacity shows that small- and medium-size units are dominating in the Polish penal system (capacity from 100 up to 400 persons, see fig. 4). It is worth noting that many prisons are located in small- and medium-size towns and such locations have important consequences for the organizational culture of an institution. A small town prison is usually the biggest working place and relatively attractive for the local population for at least two reasons: the stability of employment and comparatively high salaries. From a sociological point of view, such a situation creates pressure on the local labour market and local communities to use the prison penal complex as a strategic work place. Thus, the prison becomes in the first place a 'big enterprise, which means that local interests may become more important than the goals of penal policy, for instance in selecting candidates for the staff. The higher the unemployment in a local labour market is, the stronger the pressure of local establishment that may contradict penal policy.

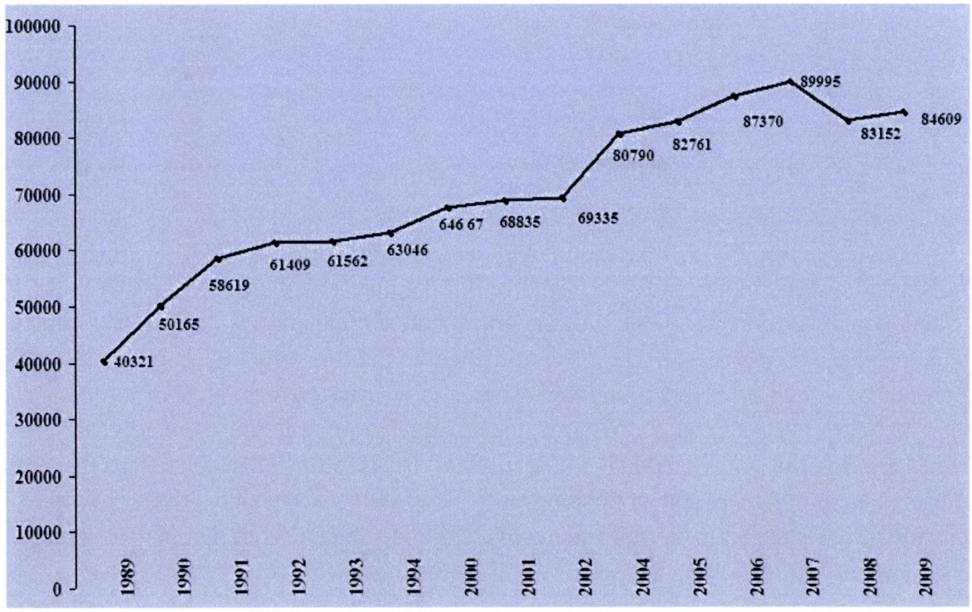

Figure 1. Number of inmates in Poland 1989-2008. Source of data CZSW 1989-2009.

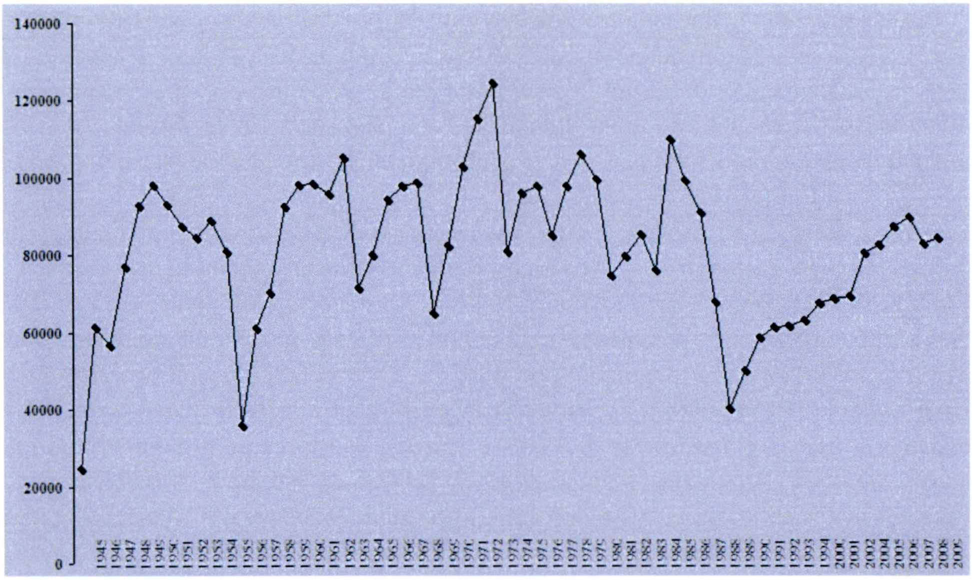

Figure 2. Number of inmates in Poland, 1945-2009. Source of data: CZSW 1989-2009 and Platek 1998.

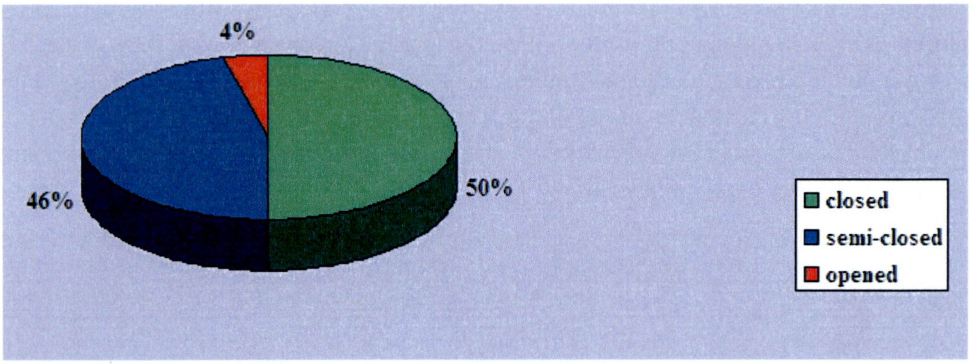

Figure 3. The structure of prison population by type of prison, Dec. 31, 2008. Source of data: CZSW 2008.

Women are only 3% of the prison population in Poland; since 1989 the level of women imprisoned has been more or less the same, and it is rather low (compared to that in the USA or South America for instance). Half of the incarcerated population is held in 'closed prisons' which are the more restricted type of confinement[5]. The age structure is rather typical: the proportion of young offenders is the highest as it is in most prisons: 44% of the inmates are under 30 years old (see fig. 5). What is interesting is the structure of recidivism: 51% of inmates are first-time convicted and 45% are recidivists (see fig. 3), which means that there is quite high mobility in prison population and 'new' persons become prisoners. These two indicators: high proportion of first-time convicted and the increasing number of inmates are the symptoms of intensifying the penalization in Polish society.

[5] Inmates stay for 23 hours inside the cells.

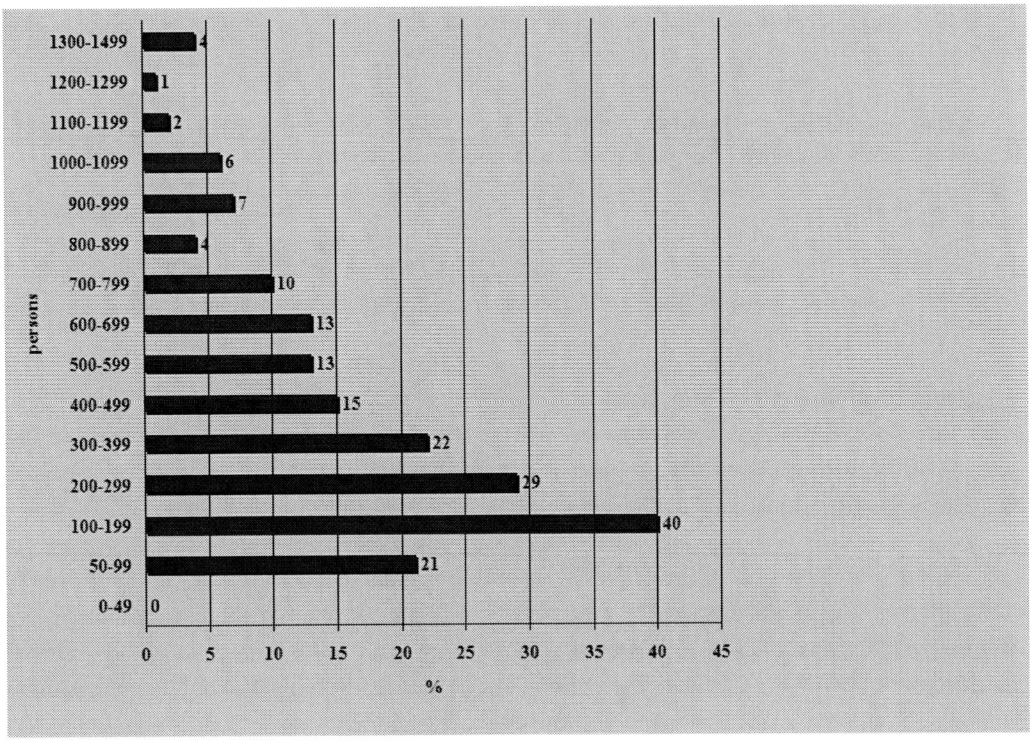

Figure 4. The capacity of penitentiaries, 2007. Source of data CZSW.

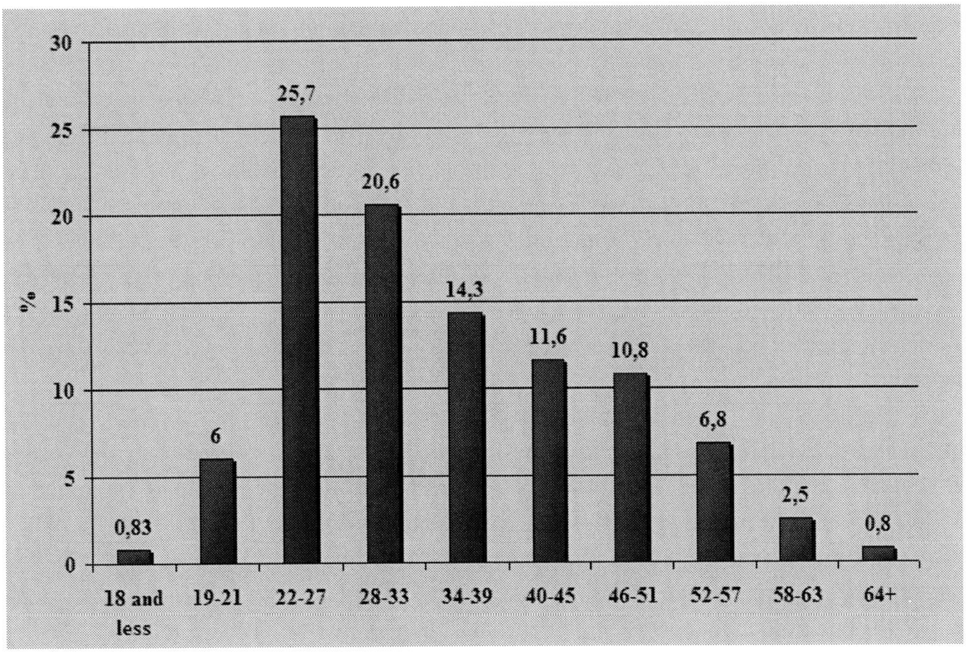

Figure 5. The structure of prisoners population by age of prisoner. 2008. Source of data: CZSW 2008.

According to present regulations the standard of living are regarded today as the fundamental rights of inmates:

> "Living conditions in a prison are among the chief factors determining a prisoner's sense of self-esteem and dignity. The quality of accommodation, how sleeping is arranged, what and where prisoners eat, what they are allowed to wear, whether they have ready access to sanitary facilities all have a tremendous influence on a prisoner's feeling of wellbeing. Even where physical conditions are adequate, restrictive practices, such as having to ask a guard to gain access to the toilet, may have a very negative impact on prisoners' mental health." [Custodial and non-custodial measures. The Prison System. Criminal Justice Assessment Toolkit. United Nations. New York, 2006].

Overcrowding is one of the causes of deterioration of the living conditions and it appears to be the constant problem in prisons because it has appeared ever since prisons came into being. Overcrowding is serious problem in Polish prisons. Since the mid of the 1990s an average occupancy rate oscillated around 110-120% (in 2006 and 2007 – 120%). In the survey presented here the quality of living space perceived by inmates was measured: the average number of persons in the cell was 6[7] and the average capacity of the cell estimated by prisoners was 16 square meters[8]. In the end of 2008 the number of inmates decreased and occupancy rates was 101% which was the consequence of two factors, first is the policy of the new more liberal government (PO) who declared less restricted penal policy comparing to right wing government of PiS[9]. The second is general tendency to release more inmates in the end of each year (which might be the side effect of organizational management; releasing inmates is the only way to control the periodical increase in prison population). Thus, the number of prison units has not changed, but available space has changed. Due to constant overcrowding much of additional space in the prison units such as common rooms were transformed into cells.

The problem of prison crowding has been discussed in many perspectives, but the research result addressing the influence of crowding on inmate misconduct is equivocal. Some empirical studies lend support to a thesis that overcrowding is the reason of violent behaviours. The deprivation model is responsible for quite a popular opinion that crowding leads to the increased level of inmate misconduct [Franklin, Franklin, Pratt 2006]. I believe this is the simplification of the problem. Conditions in Polish prisons confirm rather those theories that stress no direct connections between overcrowding and riots. In spite of difficult conditions there is no increase in the violent behaviour of inmates (except occasional protests in particular prisons).

The efficiency of a penal system appears to be even worse when we realize that the huge number of convicted persons are awaiting for place in prisons to carry out their penalty: in 2004 it was 25.000, in 2006 it raised up to 46.000 and now this group is estimated around 50.000 persons (whereas the present incarcerated population is around 76.000). This congestion of a penal system puts into question the possibility of swift and certain punishment broadly discussed in the theory of penal policy. What is more it may have yet unrecognised consequences for the perception of punishment in Polish society.

---

[7] In the sample N=1011.

[8] In the sample N=731.

[9] PiS (Law and Justice) was the ruling party in 2005-2007, in 2007 PO won elections and introduced new policy.

The restricted penal policy in Poland causes together with overcrowding the shortage of prison staff. Especially penitentiary officers shortages result in reduced interactions with inmates, and consequently less control and less influence on their behaviour. Guards (a security section) and educational officers (a rehabilitation section) who have direct control over inmates usually must deal with the number of persons that exceeds capability of proper control and communication. Namely, one person must oversee from 50 (in a small prison) to over 100 inmates (in a big unit), while the proportional amount should be about 30 persons maximum. Bureaucracy is the other problem indicated by the staff, especially by the education officers. Penitentiary officers are overloaded with bureaucracy: as it was stressed by one of the officers: *Instead of talk to inmates I have to fill in lots of forms and write reports, there are so many papers that I have no time even to get to know them, not mention to fix their problems* (an educational officer, the category of prison: closed, with population over 1000).

Most of the everyday routine duties of educational officers concern mainly organizational and legal matters of inmates and due to lack of time, bureaucracy and overcrowding they do not have time to perform tasks that could be called the rehabilitation of inmates. The administration of prisons manage with overcrowding in the simplest possible way: first, more persons were admitted into existing cells, and when capacity of cells was exceeded and then all available space such as common rooms were transformed into cells. Consequently, there is not enough space for inmates to carry on any activity (cultural, sport, etc) and leisure has became a problem.

Overcrowding is in fact the side effect of a penal policy and the philosophy of punishment and jurisdiction. We lack in Poland a serious debate on the idea of punishment (how to punish and for what purpose?). The general tendency in penal policy is the escalation of penalisation. The most spectacular example is the bill of counteraction of drug addiction (introduced in 1997, with changes in 2000 and 2005). It says that possession of drugs is a subject to penalty of detention up to three years. The possession of small amounts of drugs is prohibited and punishable with a fine, or restriction of liberty or a detention up to one year, and possession of great amount of drugs is subject to penalty of detention from six months up to eight years [Article no 62]. The practice of penal jurisdiction and police statistic show that such regulations caused the intensification of imprisonment among Polish citizens. Thus, the consequence of the bill is the increase in drug-convictions: the number of drug crime is expanding: in 2001 there were 29.230, and in 2005 – 59.356 drug crimes. In 2004 they were about 8% of all crimes. The structure of drug convictions reveals the mechanisms of law enforcement which is determined by public institutions' interest and the elites of power: who want to gain the support of public opinion by establishing more rigorous law which is regarded as the way to cope with criminality. Crimes which are the easiest to find become the subject of penalisation and that is the cause of penalisation increased. In addition it may be use by police 'to improve' the statistics of efficiency. The data prove such phenomena are 'the' case in Poland: in 2004 the majority (40%) cases of drug crime was possessing of drugs, and 30% drug dealing, at the same time as much as 71% of instituted proceedings were for drug possessing and only 10% for drug dealing. Grave drug crimes such as drug production, smuggling and turnover are only 6, 2% of total drug convictions [data of Police Head Office]. What we observe here is the growth of penalisation of social life. Similar process has happened in the USA penal policy and caused the spectacular increase in number of incarcerated persons.

The crucial issue here is involving a penal policy into power mechanisms in democracy: politicians use it to win elections and it is not only the case of Poland, populism is found very often in many countries. A punitive system is not rational, because imprisonment is expensive and yet a system allows for confinement of too many persons for light convictions. As figure 6 shows the majority of inmates have short term sentences, and as many as 26% of prisoners are serving less than one year sentence, 44% of them are serving the sentence from one year up to 3 years, and there is only 7% of long-term punishment (over 10 years). Such a structure of sentences arises the question about rationale of a punitive policy and criteria of using confinement as punishment in the case of small-scale crimes (if one assumes that short term sentence is proper punishment for small offences). Isolation for slight crimes is inadequate and irrational, because it is expensive for the state and minor criminals (at least many of them) do not threat a state or citizens. A penal system, being a bureaucracy, acts by force of inertia, routinely, and overuses this form of punishment, and in those cases rationale of punishing has been lost.

The additional reason of expanding penalisation may be connected to the age and tenure of judges. In Poland the post of a judge is quite often held by relatively young persons with a short tenure and assessors[10]. Young judges have lower status in a professional circle, and we may presume that the lower the status has a judge, the more he/she conforms to the norms of an institution, and he/she may predicate severe sentences as the result of conformity than an old judge. It is a strategy typical for those persons who have a low position in the structure of institution, or more general in a group, if they are intent on advancement.

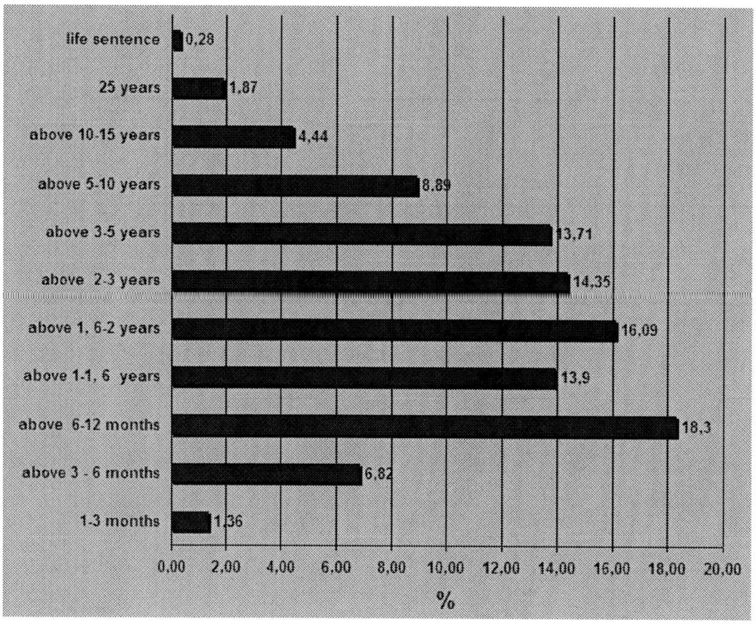

Figure 6. The structure of inmate population by term of punishment. 2007. Source: CZSW 2007.

[10] An assessor is the position of candidate for a judge in Polish jurisdiction; this post is not independent and it is prone to pressure of superiors in an institution. Fortunately, at present this function is being cancelled.

An attempt to introduce the penal reform in Poland shows lack of an effective and coherent penal policy. In 2004 the bill introducing an alternative way of punishment was written: the system of electronic monitoring of inmates (so called electronic bracelets) designed for small-scale crimes[12]. In 2006 it was discussed in the parliament. The work upon this project goes very slowly and the idea itself raises many controversies among lawyers, politicians, practitioner and even prisoners. The project is still being discussed and right now, after five years, the application of the electronic monitoring of inmates is being tested in practice. Anyway, until now the problem of overcrowding has not been resolved and imprisonment is the main form of a penalty enforced in Polish punitive system.

Similar conclusion follows the analysis of structure of inmates' offences in Poland (see table no 2). Grievous crimes are not the most frequent reasons of convictions: there are more inmates convicted for offences against family and traffic (17%) than for offences against life and health (11,4%). The question arises which type of crime should be punished by confinement and which not? Some offence could be regarded as qualified for other kind of punishment than incarceration. It seems to be more universal problem of societies where prison is used as the only possible mean of control and the main type of sentence.

Table 2. The structure of offences by categories. Source: CZSW 2007

main category of crime	detailed category	2007		
				%
offence against life and health	homicides	5132	9710	
	other	4578		11,40%
sexual offence	rapes	2284	3631	4,30%
	others	1347		
offence against family	family violence	4840	6951	8,20%
	alimony	2043 2,4%		
	others	68		
offence against property	thefts	6081	44791	52,40%
	burglary	13212		
	robbery	15621		
	others	9877		
economic offence, forgery		1052		1,30%
traffic offence		7657		9%
offence against freedom		1238		1,50%
offence against public order		1717		2%
offence against justice		2195		2,60%
other		6168		7,30%
together (convicted and sentenced)		85417		100,00%

The economic condition of prisons in Poland is rather poor. There are little investments in the infrastructure of prison units. The number of penitentiary units has remained unchanged for many years while the number of inmates has increased significantly. In 2000 there were

[12]-Legislative Commission of the Senate, the bill of 19th May 2004.

70 custodies with 21,271 persons and 86 prisons with 40,902 inmates. In 2007 there were still 70 custodies with 13,324 persons and 85 prisons with 76,272 inmates.

Many of the prison buildings are old. In the west region of Poland where most survey were carried out many units are simply the former German prisons built in the 19th century and their infrastructure is in deficient technical condition. Let's give some examples of the standard of living: in many cells toilets are not sufficiently separated in cells, there is lack of ventilation of cells and not enough space for living. In 2009 there was a plan to built a new penal complex but due to savings in Ministry of Justice this idea was postpone (there are only two exceptions: lately built the modern units in to towns: Piotrków Trybunalski opened in 2003 and in Opole Lubelskie; the second was opened very lately 5 October 2009).

A decision to increase financing to develop penal institutions is unpopular for most of governments and politicians because Polish society has rather hostile attitudes towards prisoners, which is not surprising. Thus, resolving the problem of 'uncontrolled' expanding of incarceration becomes difficult in a democratic society, because a penal policy involved in politics is used as a tool in election campaign. It means that in democracy where the penitentiaries are more dependent on mechanisms of power it is more probable that a penal policy is not influenced by the professional management but it is prone to politicians' populism.

Such organizational and poor economic conditions of a penal system makes impossible to implement in practice any form of correctional programmes. I do not mean rehabilitation as the intrinsic element of a penal system, I would rather agree with those who treat a prison as an institution that shapes anti-social attitudes and its main role is to isolate criminals from a society. But to treat an imprisonment as isolation only without any attempt to shape some attitudes or at least organizing a life inside prisons should be regarded as the failure of justice. Penitentiary institutions should not be idle, they must give opportunities for those who are 'willing to rehabilitate', whatever it means, but first of all they must apply the confinement as a mean of punishment 'more carefully'.

The general conclusion is that the contemporary penal system in Poland is ineffective in great extent and does not fulfil properly its function. In democracy politicians use a penal policy as a tool of gaining power and actually they act against the interest of citizens: a chance for incarceration grows for all citizens who paradoxically approve such policy.

Work in Prison

Work was obligatory outside as well as inside prisons in Poland during the communist period. The situation changed in the 90ties, because in a free market society work has become a privilege. As many researchers show work is one the factors which cause a reduction in crime [Berk, Kenneth & Lenihan, Rossi 1980, Crutchfield & Pitchofrd 1997, Sampson & Laub 1993, Thorneberry, Christenson 1984]. Of course work is not the only crime reducing factor, other important agents are family status and education. The meaning of work is often perceived as an indirect element which creates social identity, specific social milieu and supports conformity to dominant social values. Work during incarceration has additional function: it fills out the time.

In his classic work David Clemmer notices that it is only an assumption that "education of the prisoner in habits of work will tend to reform him". He claims that work is less important than leisure just because there is not enough work for prisoners (and never will be enough) and it is impossible to employ the entire populations of prisoners. Clemmer compares the labour of prisoners to labour in open market where also not entire population is employed. It means, asserts Clemmer, that idleness is a natural phenomenon in prisons and should be expected [Clemmer 1958]. After nearly seventy years his opinion is still true but only for prisons in democratic states and in a free market. Comparing penitentiaries in totalitarian and democratic state we can notice an interesting paradox: considering accessibility to prison labour only (not its quality or conditions) prisons in totalitarian state were more effective then prisons in democratic state; totalitarian authority forced inmates to work; in democratic society prisoners are excluded from labour market by society and mechanisms of free market (like free competition). However the case of privatisation of prisons in the USA proves that in specific conditions prisoners' labour may stimulate the developement of economy because prison appeared to be very profitable business and inmates are treated as cheap labour force (and this explains why number of the incarcerated people has increased in the USA) [Shelden 2001: 269-283].

Although work was obligatory in totalitarian prisons (as well as in forced-labour camps which is the other form of punishment in totalitarian states) it did not rehabilitate prisoners. Considering the data, the assumptions on rehabilitation through work is rather doubtful, however labour in prisons has lots of advantages and lack of work has long term consequences such as disappearance of important features: the capacity for labour, habits of industry and ability for social activity and self—organising. Idleness evokes inactivity, and helplessness. These symptoms appear generally among unemployed people, especially as the result of a long term unemployment. Given that, a prison administration should offer work for as many inmates as possible. It must be stressed that in case of high unemployment in labour market the work for prisoners becomes privilege, they compete with 'citizens' and they loose as they are the underclass and they are excluded from the labour market. In such situation the only work that is available is work inside penitentiaries. However the needs of workers in a particular unit is limited, about 10-15 % of population can be hired for the maintenance of prison. Again, work inside prison walls is for the privileged. In fact, when access to labour is restricted work becomes a valuable reword in an institution and at the same time it becomes an important mean of formal and informal control in prisons.

Let's first analyse some data on employment in prisons in Poland. In general, minority of inmates work in Polish prisons. Market economy excluded most of the enterprises where prisoners worked during the communist period [Platek 1998]. Especially during the 90ties unemployment in prisons was common. Until 2006 there had been the high rate of unemployment in Poland (oscillating around 15%-20%), in such a difficult labour market prisoners were the last to get the opportunity to work. In the period 1989-2005 majority of inmates who worked were hired inside penitentiary units for prison maintenance (clearing, kitchen, rebuilding and fixing etc.). Only the small part of prison population was hired in the outer enterprises as contracted workers. Prisoners were (and still are) paid low salaries: in 2008 the average salary was 468PLN monthly, and it was about 2,5 less than the minimum salary in Poland that year which is about 281 Euro[13]. Thus, the work of prisoners is a kind of

[13] The latest approximate currency was 1Euro=4PLN, or 3,75$ if 1$=3PLN.

exploitation of almost free manpower, nevertheless if an inmate gets paid for work he /she is still satisfied. The growth of employment has started in 2005 and for the last 3 years there have been significant improvement. In the period 2005-2008 due to decreasing unemployment in Poland the rate of working prisoners raised from 12,3% in 2004 to 34,9% in 2008 (see table no3), and even some employers were striving for prisoners as employees. This was due to lack of the workforce on the labour market in 2008. The prognosis for the forthcoming year of economic stagnation is unfortunately pessimistic: the unemployment is expected to increase, so we may expect also the unemployment in prisons is going to enlarge. Accordingly, if the conditions of the labour market influence employment in prisons, it reveals strong connections between the condition of society and economy and a penal system.

The level of education of prisoners is poor and most of the inmates are low qualified workers, for instance only 3% of the sample had qualified profession, the rest was more or less qualified simple workers, which is typical for most prison populations. As figure no 7 shows 36,5% of the inmates in the sample had the lowest possible education level, which does not provide any profession; 43,3 % of them graduated from a vocational training school, this kind of school ensures an occupation but does not allow to get higher education directly); only 16,3% had the secondary education and 2% higher (while 14% of population had higher education , 21% primary, 23% basic vocational and 33% secondary in 2005).

Table 3. The employment rate in Polish prisons—source CZSW

The employment rate in Polish prisons	
2004	12,3%,
2005	28% ,
2006	31,6%,
2007	34,4%
2008	34,9%

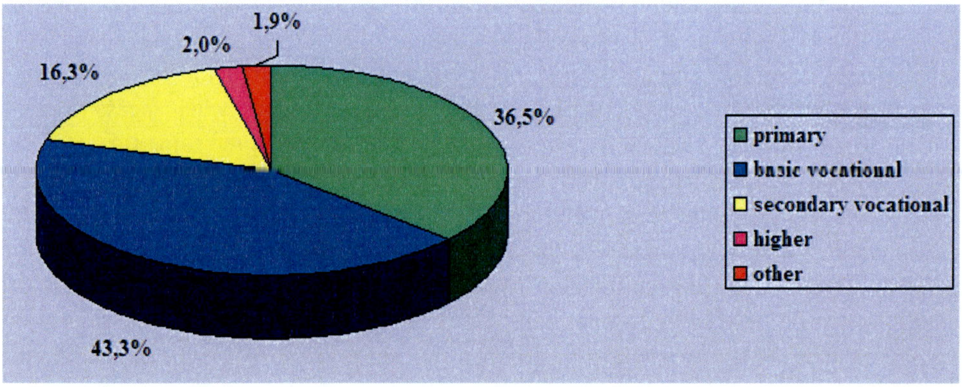

Figure 7. Education of prisoners in the sample. N=1031.

Other issue is work attitude among inmates. If they appreciate work then it might be use as a mean of control and a way of influencing the inmates. In the survey the attitudes toward work among prisoners were examined. In the sample of 1072 inmates 53% have ever worked and 47% have never worked during serving a prison sentence. The 'official' reason of unemployment in prisons is the lack of work. Inmates asked about reason of not working gave the same reason: for 61% of respondents lack of work was the main reason; however it is not true that all inmates want to work: 9% of inmates confessed they just do not want to work.

Table 4. The reasons not to work

The reasons not to work	Answers		% of observations
	N	%	
laziness	55	8.1%	8.6%
lack of work	391	57.8%	61%
low salary	22	3.3%	3.4%
does not want to work for free	28	4.2%	4.4%
other (administrative reasons)	180	26.6%	28.1%
multiple answers N=	676	100.0%	105.5%

One of the purposes of the study was to describe and explain rules of behaviour in terms of subjective definitions of social situation using framework of rational theory. In this theoretical framework the types of behaviour are different strategies, an inmate has his/her objectives and calculate the cost of achieving them. The reasons or motivations are here the objectives of acting and they are chosen with regard to possible advantages or disadvantages. What are the motivation to work from the point of view of the inmates? *'To spend time quickly'* was the most often cause that inmates gave (47,%). It is obvious that *time* becomes a problem in prison, especially for those who cannot organized any activity for themselves. Work is time-consuming activity and it is organised by an institution. In this respect the results of the survey are similar to conclusion of Clemmer about the role of work in prisons: that financial motive is less important then leisure-time reduction [Clemmer 1958]. It is an understandable reason due to very low salaries. The second popular motive of work was '*to get the pass, parole*' or other institutional advantages. This type of answer is the indicator of rational strategy of inmates who calculate the costs of their behaviours in a correctional institution (losses and profits). This kind of strategy lies in the estimation of whether it is

Table 5. The reasons to work

The reasons to work	Answers		% of observations
	N	%	
to spend time quickly	360	27.1%	47.9%
to get the pass, parole	323	24.3%	43.0%
to earn money	287	21.6%	38.2%
to forget (about the prison)	237	17.8%	31.5%
to get profession	102	7.7%	13.6%
because my colleagues go	16	1.2%	2.1%
other	5	.4%	.7%
multiple responses N	1330	100.0%	176.9%

worth it to work because work is perceived by a prison staff as the symptom of conformity to a social system and the way of rehabilitation (the other symptom is having regular contacts with family). Thus, prisoners work to get rewards, a positive 'stigma' in the institution and take advantage of that. Being 'a working person' does not necessarily mean that a particular inmate has accepted the social values of labour.

Another reason to work is to forget (about staying in prison). In a way, it is somehow similar with the first motif—to spend time quickly, but it reveals the harshness of incarceration for inmates, that is why it was more frequently mentioned by women. As it is known, women suffer emotionally much more from incarceration than men do. We may suppose that work has slightly different function for women however this standpoint needs further investigation to be confirmed because the proportion of women in the sample is rather small. In turn, men more often gave such reasons of work like to spend time quickly and to earn money.

Work is the central element of special social programs of re-adaptation designed for prisoners or ex-prisoners (such programs have been popular in EU within the EQUAL project[14]). The data on work attitudes and professional career of inmates suggest such work-programs becomes highly problematic. First, they are expensive, because many inmates need special security service and protection during the work. Secondly, inmates are low qualified work force so 'the enterprises of prisoners' would not be competitive on the market comparing to other firms and the available job for prisoners and ex-prisoners would be of low status and of low income. To maintain workplaces for the incarcerated the state would have to financially support them. In spite of low effectiveness such programs are quite popular in the social policy and programs financed by the EU institutions. Third, as the survey proved, many inmates are not interested to participate in such programs so it is difficult to shape the pro-social attitudes among prisoners through the implementation of work- projects.

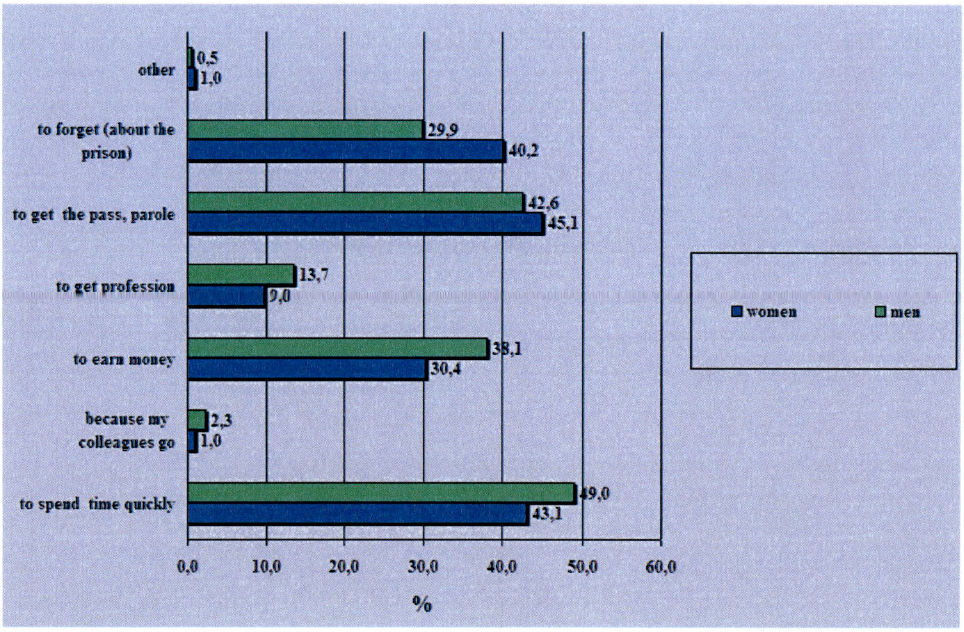

Figure 8. The reasons to work: differences between men and women, N= 724.

[14] EQUAL is a program to promote social activity designed to reduce inequalities in different areas of society.

Here are data that support above arguments: the results of survey[15] which tested the introduction of work-programme for persons leaving the prisons put into question the rationality of this kind of solutions. I intended to investigate motivation to work in respondents' lives. Especially with regard to their general attitudes towards work. In order to reveal the meaning of work the inmates answered the questions requiring a choice between two alternatives: between non-material values and money. It is clear that an income is one of the basic motif of work, but the interesting problem is what are other values of work and how important they are in comparison to money? The results suggest that financial aspect of work is fundamental, which is not surprising, and only one feature appeared to be more important for inmates than money: the stability of job – 53,4% of respondents preferred a regular and less paid job in comparison to 46,6% of prisoners who chose a casual and better paid job. Other features of work: safe work, light work, interesting work were less valued than money: 88% requested inmates favoured hard work and better paid than light but with low salary, 60% chose less interesting job but better paid than interesting and with low salary, 67% wanted dangerous work with high salary more than safe job with low salary (fig. 9,10,11,12). However it is not so obvious - at least for some persons- whether hard or risky work is negative or positive.

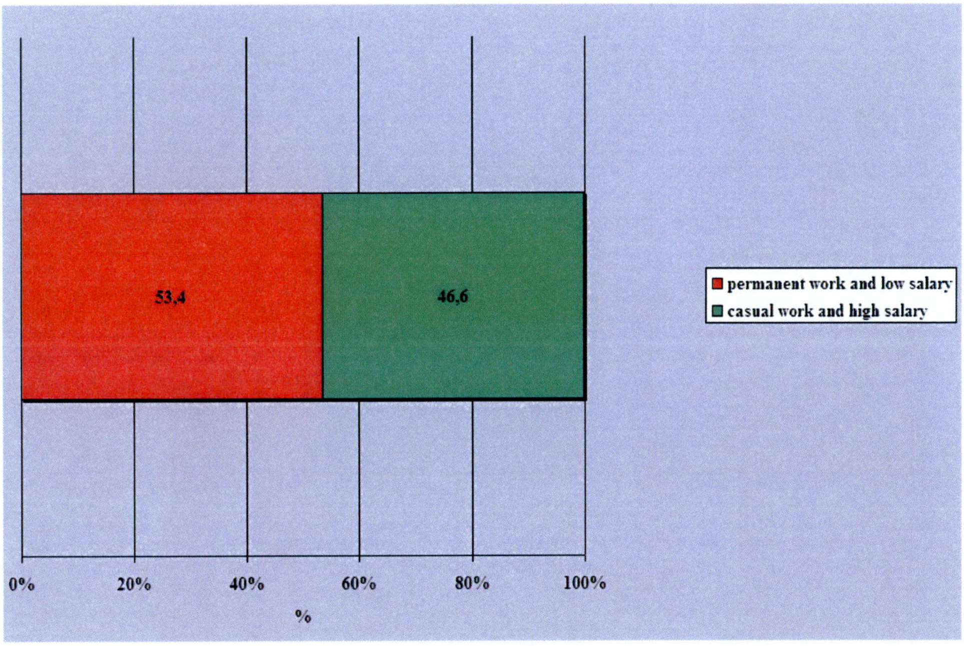

Figure 9. Material and non material values of work: stability of work, N=434.

15 This survey was a part of separate project and was carried on sample of N=434 persons in 3 prisons.

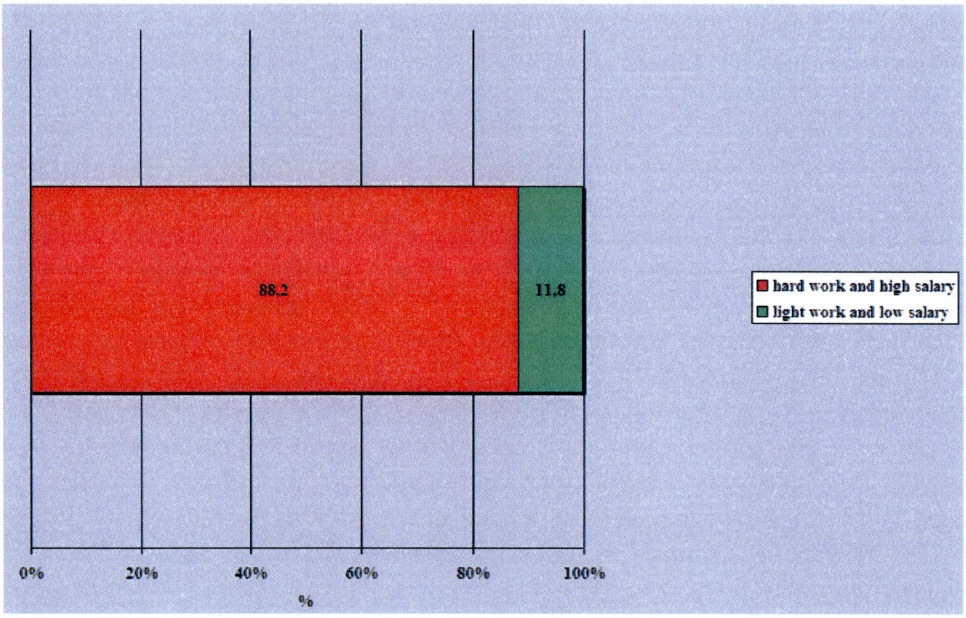

Figure 10. Material and non material values of work: hard and light work, N=434.

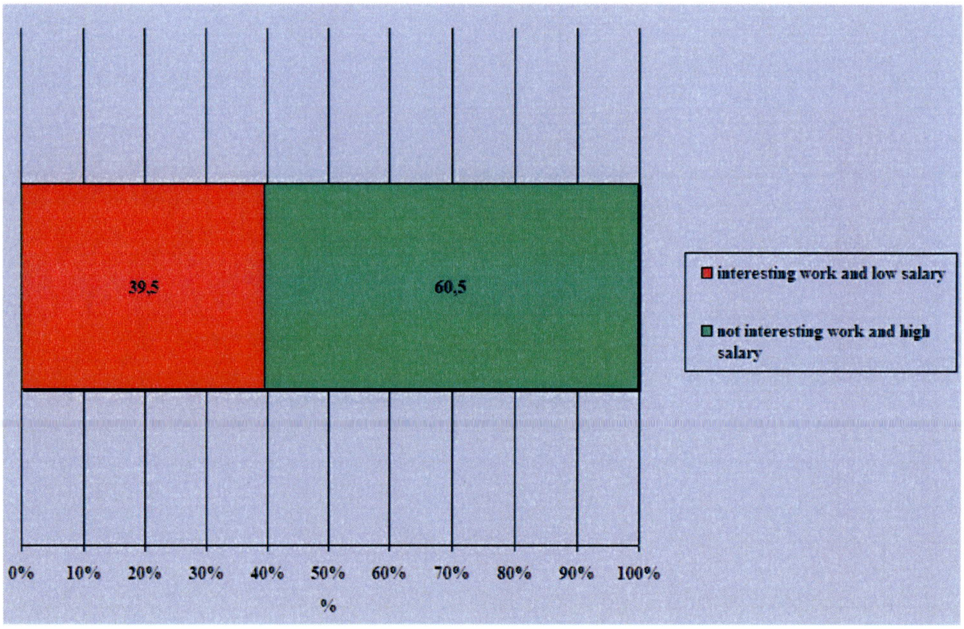

Figure 11. Material and non material values of work: interesting work, N=434.

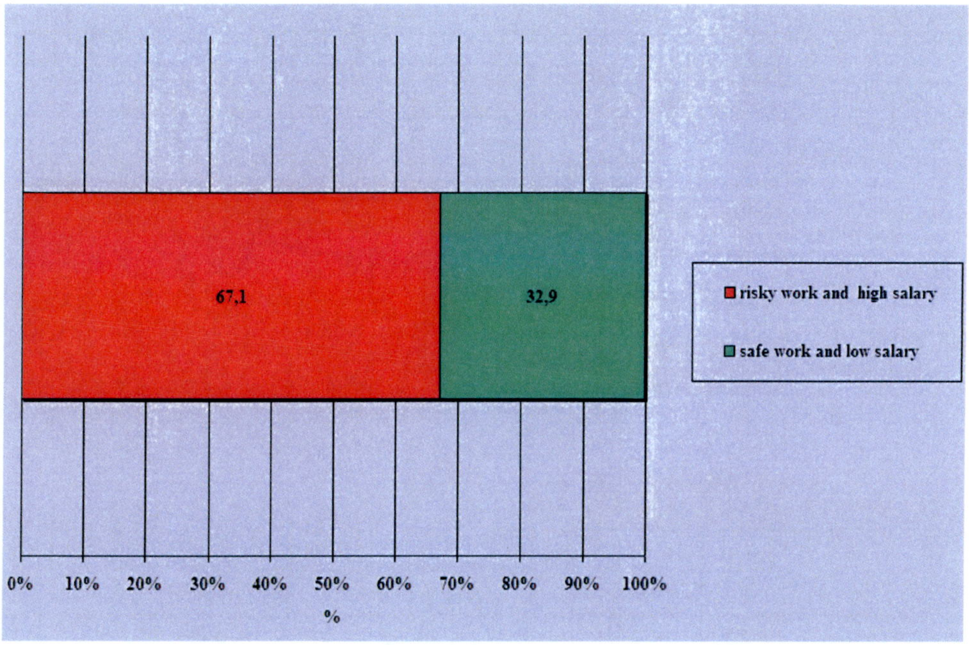

Figure 12. Material and non material values of work: danger, N=434.

It is worth to note that the higher income had the inmates while working before their incarceration, the more often they esteemed the material values of work. Permanent work appeared to be more valuable for persons with lower income. This data shows that attitudes towards work are shaped in the life course and those inmates who were involved in a criminal career are generally less interested in work. Persons with high salary have great expectations of income whereas most of jobs offered for prisoners are low paid. Prisoners (assuming they are rational) who made a living by crime regard work as a poor source of money simply because they earn more money from crime than from work. Considering their poor education and lack of professional background, the acceptable level of income for those people cannot be satisfied by job offers available on labour market. We may expect this type or prisoners would refuse to work and they are likely to return to crime. In the survey those prisoners who confessed to make a living by crime admitted that the reason they chose doing crime was not lack of work but possibility to earn quickly much money illegally (see figure no 13).

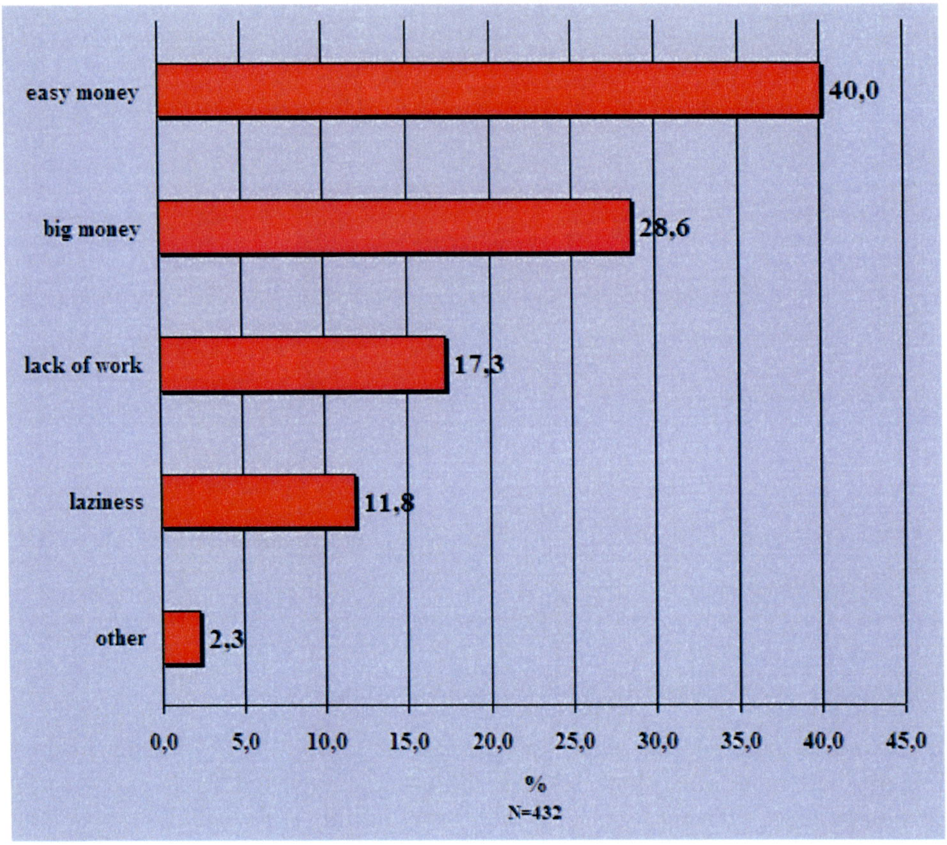

Figure 13. Reason for crime as a source of money.

The question arises how effective is work as a way of rehabilitation and re-adaptation for persons whose income aspirations are disproportionate to qualifications? The answer seems to be obvious.

Concluding, work in contemporary Polish prisons is mainly time consuming activity but not the mean of influence on inmates treated as the change of attitudes . The main problem is lack of labour especially the work that would facilitate the social adaptation through improving skills and encouraging to return to legal labour market.

Idleness and Leisure Time

The time is constant problem for inmates and for a management, especially in the case of high unemployment as it was mentioned. What then do inmates do if most of them do not work? Asked about their 'leisure' time most respondents pointed at the types of activities they do very often and often: *thinking about family, talking to other inmates and thinking about future after prison.* It is worth to note that holding a televison-set in a cell has become common in Polish prisons and is quite a simple inidicator of libaralisation in penitentiaries and inmates spent quite a lot of time watching television. All of these are rather passive kind of activity and first of all **not** organised by the institution. It means that prison hardly control the activity of inmates in their leisure hours.

Table 6. Leisure time activity of inmates

	never		seldom		often	
	frequency N	% of N in raw	frequency N	% of N in raw	frequency N	% of N in raw
thinking about family	6	,6%	75	7,6%	901	91,8%
talking to other inmates	9	,9%	172	18,1%	770	81,0%
thinking about the future after imprisonment	29	3,0%	176	18,4%	753	78,6%
watching television	16	1,6%	282	28,8%	682	69,6%
writing letters	20	2,1%	305	31,9%	631	66,0%
reading	36	3,8%	296	31,1%	621	65,2%
sport	104	11,7%	252	28,4%	530	59,8%
walking	14	1,5%	351	38,6%	544	59,8%
other	83	27,9%	54	18,2%	160	53,9%
playing games	89	10,0%	382	43,1%	415	46,8%
working	322	37,9%	214	25,2%	313	36,9%
learning	358	45,9%	238	30,5%	184	23,6%
drawing, painting etc.	427	52,8%	213	26,4%	168	20,8%

Again, leisure is an universal and an old problem of imprisonment discussed long ago in the work of Donald Clemmer. According to Clemmer the most important function in prison is organization of cultural and recreation activities because it is recreation, and not work, that is the most effective way to influence inmates. As Clemmer wrote: *"in my hypothetical prison the most important employee is the director of recreation and activities. More important is he than the industrial superintendents, than the chaplains, than the teachers, than the doctors. He must by trained, highly skilled, a leader, and an executive"* [Clemmer 1958: 277]. Clemmer meant to develop social skills through leisure time activities, teaching inmates to spend and organize their spare time. It is much more promising to encourage prisoners to take part in such activities with high motivation and first of all it is possible to organise *inside* the prison walls. The belief that work as such improves prisoners is rather an element of ideological thinking. In totalitarian prisons the inmates were forced to work but it did not improve the re-education in a penal system.

Concluding, idleness seems to be the essential problem in Polish prisons. The administration does not supply enough labour or other daily activity. Minority of inmates work or perform any activity that could be considered as educative. In consequence, the institutional influence on prisoners decreases and the influence of informal groups possibly increases.

Social Relations in Prison

When we examine a prison from a sociological perspective our concern is with social relations, in other words, the social reality consists of network of interactions. The other sociological assumption is that a social order emerges from social relations that are ruled by the system of norms and values.

The important features of the prison community in contemporary Polish penitentiaries are the modification of social relations both among the inmates and between the staff and the inmates. The new type of social relations constitutes less coherent social order in prisons.

If we take into account the social relation in wider context, we notice that the type of social order and cultural pattern interweave shaping the form and meaning of social relations. Rooted deeply in history of Polish society culture has structured the individualism and lack of social trust. The appearance of free market has reinforced his feature of Polish culture.

Relations of the Inmates and the Staff

Communist prisons were much more oppressive due to very poor living conditions, restricted contacts with 'the world outside the walls', overcrowding and hostile relations between prison staff and inmates. One of the specific features of 'democratic prisons' is the change in staff attitudes toward inmates, the other is the level of staff education and professional background. At the beginning of the social transition almost 40% percent of the staff left and was replaced by new personnel [Platek 1998]. At present majority of the staff was hired after 1990. The level of education of prison staff has been improved significantly. In 2003 the regulation of Ministry of Justice restricted the admission for the service only for persons who have secondary and university education, the same act encourages personnel to improve qualification through promotions for better educated officers [Dz.U.03.14.142]. The crucial point in the process of transition was introducing the new profile of a correctional officer whose main role was to rehabilitate (educate). According to the same act the correctional staff must have professional education: MA degree in humanities. As a result, more and more prison staff have the MA diploma in rehabilitation, pedagogy, sociology, psychology. Furthermore, penitentiary units must hire psychologists who offer different kinds of therapies. What is interesting, there is rather sceptical attitude towards psychologists among inmates; they quite often confuse this profffesion with psychiatrist and regard psychotherapy and visits in psychologists' office as stigmatised and destined for weak or ill persoms and for that reason they are not open for contact with them.

The profile of mentality and the behaviour patterns of custodians who are better educated have changed. Better educated correctional officers, especially in humanities, more often supports an idea of rehabilitation and treats inmates in more humanitarian and subjective way. They also better understand the causes of criminality and the influence of prison on incarcerated persons. Consequently, one can expect the social relations between the prison staff and the prisoners have improved.

How then relations with custodians are perceived by inmates? Do they see them as rather friendly or rather hostile? 64% of inmates described their relations with prison staff as indifferent, nearly 22% defined them as friendly and very friendly, and for 10% they are unfriendly (see table below). The data allow to draw a conclusion that social relations between the staff and the prisoners had really improved, the minority of inmates have hostile feelings for the staff. In such an antagonistic institution as a prison is indifference can be regarded as rather expected and positive type of social emotion. However one must remember that this was sensitive question, and some of the respondents hid their real emotions that were probably more negative.

Table 7. Relations of inmates and the staff

Relations of inmates and the staff perceived by the inmates		frequency	%	% valid values
	I hate them	41	3,8	3,9
	I do not like them	67	6,1	6,4
	I don't care for them	696	63,7	66,9
	I like them just a little	208	19,0	20,0
	I like them very much	29	2,7	2,8
	total	1041	95,2	100,0
	missing values	52	4,8	
total N=		1093	100,0	

STRATEGIES OF BEHAVIOURS IN SOCIAL RELATIONS

Social Relations between the Inmates and the Prison Staff

An important issue was to discover accepted rules of behaviour that influence the social environment of a prison and the research to a large extent was concerned with strategies[16] of preferable behaviours. I intended to examine the social conditions of the most preferred strategy in such an environment as a prison. Motivations for choosing the strategy are diverse, and this diversity reveals the potentially interesting social foundation of inmates' behaviour. Conformity is a typical social reaction in a total institution that is why the level of conformity was examined. The results show that strategy much preferred is conformity towards the staff and nonconformity towards other prisoners. It appeared that conformity towards the staff was the strategy the inmates favoured most: 71,7% of respondents accepted this strategy (38,3% strong conformity[17] and 33,4% moderate conformity). Non-conformity is less approved strategy and was chosen by 28,2% of the sample (9% persons chose strong nonconformity and 19,1% moderate nonconformity) (see figure15).

Analysing the criteria of choosing particular strategy allows studying structural determinants and the culture of inmates. In this perspective the criteria are defined as the values and strategy as the goal–orientated behaviour. Yet, further analysis is required to explore how these goals (values) are socially constructed. Here I just focus on the majority and the minority strategies and their short explanation.

16 Strategy here means a pattern of behavior to achieve important goals (values).
17 It concerns conformism in the conflict situations.

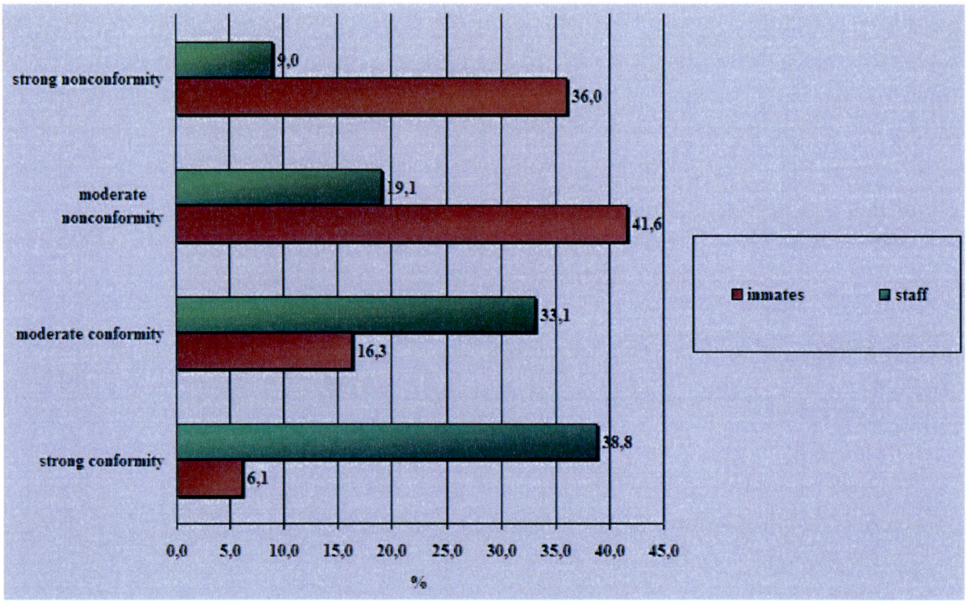

Figure 14. Attitudes towards the prison staff and inmates— conformity.

Prison as a social system supports calculative approach because it is based on system of punishments, rewards and control nearly in all aspects of human behaviour. Consequently, a prisoner learns that there is a reward or punishment for almost every action. Furthermore, it is an isolated social system. All these constraints allow to compare prison environment with game situations and for that reason I apply the categories of rational choice theory to describe human behaviours in a prison world. The basic problem was to distinguish the types of calculations and the level of risk acceptance in social relations. Six types of strategies in social relations between the inmates and the prison staff were taken into account on the basis of data:

1. calculation to minimise institutional costs (avoiding behaviour that is punished by an institution);
2. calculation to minimise social costs (avoiding behaviour that may lead to conflicts in social relations);
3. calculation to maximise institutional reward (the aim of behaviour is formal reward form an institution);
4. calculation to maximise social rewards (the purpose of behaviour is good informal relation with prison administration);
5. normative reasons – the element of dominant normative system (good relation with people is autonomous value);
6. subculture norm - nonconformity as an element of s prison code (there is a norm: avoiding any contacts with the staff).

First two are rather passive and low-risk strategies, while next two are active and high-risk strategies. Most of the surveyed inmates chose a low-risk strategy: to minimise institutional cost (40,6%) and minimise social costs (22,8%) (see table no 8). In prison institutional costs of behaviour are involved in formal control and punishment system, while social cost are related to informal relations and social control in prison groups. The social relations in a prison society can be seen as network where every link has its costs and gains: if you are in good relations with custodians, it means you may be in bad relations with prisoners. What is significant, having good relations with staff arouses suspicion of collaboration. Thus, the strategy to minimize the social cost is specific for those inmates who are orientated to minimum cooperation with a penal institution which enables them to preserve good relations with other inmates. Such a strategy is a distinctive feature of majority and it is an attempt to reconcile the requirements of an institution and a prison community, and to optimize the dilemmas which often accompany conflicted relations in total institutions.

The interesting case is the strategy of the subculture group. From the sociological point of view the phenomenon of subculture needs special attention, especially the transformation of subculture in Polish prisons. If we compare the prison strategies we see the difference between the behaviour of members of subculture and other inmates. The strategy chosen by subculture group members is normative, non-calculative strategy and it is minority strategy - only 7,3% of inmates indicated normative subculture strategy.

Closer analysis of inmates behaviour supports the argument that the old form of subculture vanished, and the new type of subculture need to be redefine. The key issue to understand the new sort of group behaviour is to explore the underlying motifs of normative declaration typical for the members of subculture groups. Is normative strategy really non-calculative as the inmates declared? Looking at the inmates' way of justification more carefully we can suspect that under normative declarations lie calculations: there were many indicators in the data that subculture groups in fact use calculative strategies but tend to present them as normative. First argument for that is quite obvious: conformity to group norms gives advantages while nonconformity results in some costs (and the inmates did talk about these consequences). Secondly, the cost is not only the group rejection and breaking off social ties which was the case in the 'old subculture groups', the consequence is the exclusion from interests groups and the costs of it can be even measured by money and the access to valuable goods.

Many inmates-informants, who were previous member of subculture community mentioned the economic interest as the main value of the present subculture membership. They confirm that subculture has changed and the fundamental difference is normative system: the new subculture is so different that they believe it is not the same type of subculture community.

Of course within sociological perspective subculture is a social phenomenon that has some universal features and can be found in social groups as their immanent feature. In other words, there is always subculture in well-established social groups (what stems from the definition of a social group). What are important then are the differences: the very important elements of 'the old' subculture group were the high level of integration (solidarity), the strong social control and above all values. The reason to be together was 'the fight against prison staff' which was interpreted by subculture members as fight against the communist state and the communist system in general. Thus, the motivation of inmates' behaviours were strictly normative and ideologically embedded. The present subculture community has no clear and commonly professed ideology. The shared features of the new and the old subculture groups are informal hierarchy and organization with strong social control, and they are also universal attributes of social group organisation.

What are the characteristics of the new 'subculture group'? As our informants said the primary goal of new subculture groups was money (mainly from drug dealing inside custody); and the same opinion share both the inmates and staff informants. They do not comply with the normative rules, for instance, quite often there were opinions that being a member of subculture group is a matter of having money and '*one can buy a membership in subculture"*, it is possible to buy a subculture membership even if a candidate was convicted for stigmatised crimes such as sexual offences, or violence against children.

The strong nonconformity to prison staff and conformity to inmates is specific for those prisoners who are orientated to criminal groups and prison life and it is an indicator of advanced process of prisonization. Such attitudes of convicts are more involved in the prison reality and strongly orientated towards the prison values and community. The cost of this kind of strategy is the reduction of chances for parole and better treating by the prison administration and penal jurisdiction.

Table 8. Strategies of inmates towards the prison staff

Inmates strategies in social relations with the prison staff [18]	Answers		Observations
	N	%	%
calculation to minimise the institutional costs	344	35,9%	40,6%
calculation to minimise social costs	193	20,1%	22,8%
calculation to maximise institutional costs	121	12,6%	14,3%
calculation to maximise social costs	116	12,1%	13,7%
normative reasons good relation as value	36	3,8%	4,3%
subculture norm (avoid contact with staff)	62	6,5%	7,3%
other	86	9,0%	10,2%
Multiple responses. N	958	100,0%	113,1%

Risky strategies due to high cost of decisions are less popular: 14,3% examined persons chose the strategy *to maximise institutional costs* and 13,7% *to maximise social costs*. The cost of the first one is accusation of collaboration with prison staff, and the cost of the other is intentional conflicts with personnel in order to gain respect and social reputation. The strategy *to maximise social costs* in relations with prison administration is specific for those inmates who are orientated to collaboration with correctional institutions with the purpose of receive minor benefits in every-day prison life and the advantages from penal institution. As it is easy to guess it is not accepted by those inmates who believe in solidarity among prisoners, or treat penal institution as 'an enemy'. The price of this strategy is the punishment from other inmates. Similarly, the cost of strategy *to subordinate to subculture norms* is similar to strategy *to maximise the social cost*. The difference between those two strategies results from the type of social group identification, not the type of calculation, and they both are high-risk strategies.

The research on risk behaviour proved so far that this is the universal feature of human behaviour: in general people tend to avoid risk situations. However, deeper interviews with

[18] The strategies were reconstructed from answers to closed and open questions where respondents had to choose one way (strategy) of behaviour among several other and then had to justify and explain their motives.

the inmates showed an interesting fact: for those who preferred high risk strategy the definition of risky situation is different: from their point of view the strategy they prefer is not high-risk behaviour. It seems to be an interesting aspect of understanding human behaviour especially in examining how people understand their situations and how they perceive the social reality they live in.

What are the conclusions of analysing strategies that inmates tend to support? Unfortunately, I cannot compare these results with similar data concerning communist prison community, but fragmentary evidence and qualitative data from informants suggest that the dominant type of relation has shifted towards less conflict relations between inmates and the prison staff. As to type of strategies (low risk versus high risk) one may suppose it remains unchanged due to more universal conditionings of human behaviour (as rational choice theory proved): whatever conditions of decisions are people tend to avoid risk situations. Another facet rather general in prisons is the intrinsic contradiction between convicts and prison staff. In total-institutions the conflicts of interests between inmates and personnel is unavoidable but the level of conflicts and antagonisms depends on the culture of institution that is on the style of managing the prison, the accepted rules of behaviour of staff, respected norms and values and the way a correctional institution defines its goals.

The other problem that appeared during the research was the high level of bureaucracy inside the organization and its influence on social relations between inmates and staff. Bureaucracy determines strongly the strategies of behaviours. Prisoners have recognised 'the rules of bureaucracy' quickly and they apply them efficiently to achieve their goals. For instance, they write letters of complaint against the custodians about poor health care, or substandard living conditions. Some of the prisoners manifested extremely high activity in complaining. Such phenomenon exposes the new feature of contemporary 'democratic prison': it is bureaucratic institution with all the features described by M. Weber. It means that prisoners who use bureaucracy to some extent gain control over their situation – for instance, they have the right to complain. It gives them the possibility to re-act with penal institution and evoke the system of institutional control which is typical for democratic system (such as ombudsman or Human Rights Watch) and it was not possible in totalitarian prisons. Such conditions make social relations more complicated because the relations between custodians and convicts are much more balanced than in totalitarian prisons in which staff had supremacy.

An interesting result disclosed while interviewing the staff: comparing the stress level of the inmates and the staff, it appeared the personnel is in bigger stress than the prisoners, mainly because bureaucracy appears to be oppressive for the staff, but not for the inmates. If a prisoner complains about treating, it will cause the troubles for a prison officer who has to explain the relevance of the accusation but not to a complaining inmate. Of course, many convicts do not take such actions to avoid expected informal pressure of the staff (they may be afraid of 'revenge') Thus, one would say, the case of 'democratic' prisons could be treated as the example to verify the theory of Max Weber, who stressed that bureaucracy – in some degree - supports the weaker positions in social structure because it is the mean of influence independent on those who have power. It seems that this point of view is quite reasonable, but considering the social reality of total institution we may suppose that the convicts estimate the price of complaint and presume it is high cost action (because it might elicit the retaliation) which probably quite often prevent them form using bureaucracy against prison administration.

The Social Relations Among the Inmates

The similar typology of strategies can be used to describe relations among inmates. The research focused on types of interactions among prisoners. As it was explained earlier, nonconformity is the dominant strategy in relations among convicts (see figure 15). The reasons for that are the consequences of conformity and non-conformity for the social situation of a prisoner: the one who is conformist has low social position in social structure, the one who is non-conformist has higher position. The social structure in prison is hierarchical. There is a hierarchy in the cells and in the whole community. The struggle for privileges is quite obvious in a structural realm and non-conformity allows one to gain more power and independence. It is also connected with perception of conformity as 'mental weakness'. In other words, conformity supports the social process of creating social structure in a prison community.

Strategies of establishing relations were reconstructed form the inmates' answers in which they explained the motifs of their behaviours and they are as follows:

1. the strategy to keep or gain a social position (low in case of conformity and high in case of nonconformity)
2. the competitive strategy - instrumental strategy: instrumental treating of social relations in order to get individual profits, egoistic interest is priority.
3. the cooperative strategy: mutual interests are respected, exchange of goods, mutual support in order to gain collective profits.
4. the strategy to reduce costs concentrate on avoiding costs of social relations such as punishments, conflicts; relations with other inmates are perceived as dangerous and troublesome. It is necessarily to limit contacts to in-group (e.g. in a cell) to minimize the risk of costs.
5. the strategy to defend an identity and independency of individual ("*you have to be yourself*"); nonconformity in situation of social pressure on opinions, norms etc. this strategy is related to the first one, but the social role and social personality in social structure is emphasized.
6. the strategy of social isolation: it is based on weak relations with other inmates, or even lack of relations, and lack of trust.

Table 9. Strategies of social relations among inmates

strategies of social relations among inmates	answers		% observations
	N	%	
to defend the identity and independency of individual	287	28,7%	31,9%
to reduce costs of social relations	262	26,2%	29,1%
cooperative strategy	140	14,0%	15,5%
strategy of social isolation	136	13,6%	15,1%
strategy to keep or gain social position (low/high)	84	8,4%	9,3%
the competitive strategy: instrumental treating of social relations	31	3,1%	3,4%
other	59	5,9%	6,5%
total N multiple answers	999	100,0%	110,9%

Another important matter is the condition of the community of captives treated as the type of a (small) society. The crucial issues are the sorts of social ties, the structure of interests, the normative rules and the level of social cohesion and integration – all these factors determine in what way the community act as a social entity. The data suggest that the examined prison communities have rather weak social ties, conflicted interests, feeble normative rules and they are closer to the state of disintegration, than integration (considering that any social situation of community is rather continuum than constant).

The strength of social cohesion measured by types of social bounds diverse in sample. It appears that there are two main types of social relations: indifference and companionship - 40,9% of the sample represents indifference (the indicator was the answer *I don't care for them* to describe the social ties among inmates), and 40,% - companionship (here the indicator was the answer *they are just colleagues, I like them*). The companionship is surely not friendship understood as closer relation, it is based on mutual help in demands of everyday life. 14,8% of respondents declared they have strong social ties with other convicts, and almost 4% described the relations as hostile (see table below). Considering the strength of social bounds only companionship can be classified as moderate whereas it is possible to interpret indifference as lack of tie, or in best case as very weak one.

Table 10. Type of relations with inmates in the cell

How would you describe the relations with other inmates?	frequency	%	% valid values	
we are very close, they are like my family	32	2,9	3,2	strong social ties
they are very good friends, I like them very much	116	10,6	11,6	
they are just colleagues, I like them	403	36,9	40,3	companionship moderate social ties
I don't care for them,	409	37,4	40,9	weak social ties - indifference
I do not like them they are just other inmates	34	3,1	3,4	lack social ties
they are completely strangers to me, I hate them	4	0,4	0,4	
other	2	0,2	0,2	
total	1000	91,5	100,0	
missing values	93	8,5		
total N=	1093	100,0		

The empirical evidence suggest that age is very important variable that moderate social bounds in a prison community. The younger inmates (under 26) more often preferred closer relations with prisoners in a cell. The older the prisoners, the more often they have indifferent relations with other inmates. This is rather general feature related to change of of membership in groups: for older generations family ties replace the role of friend group relations.

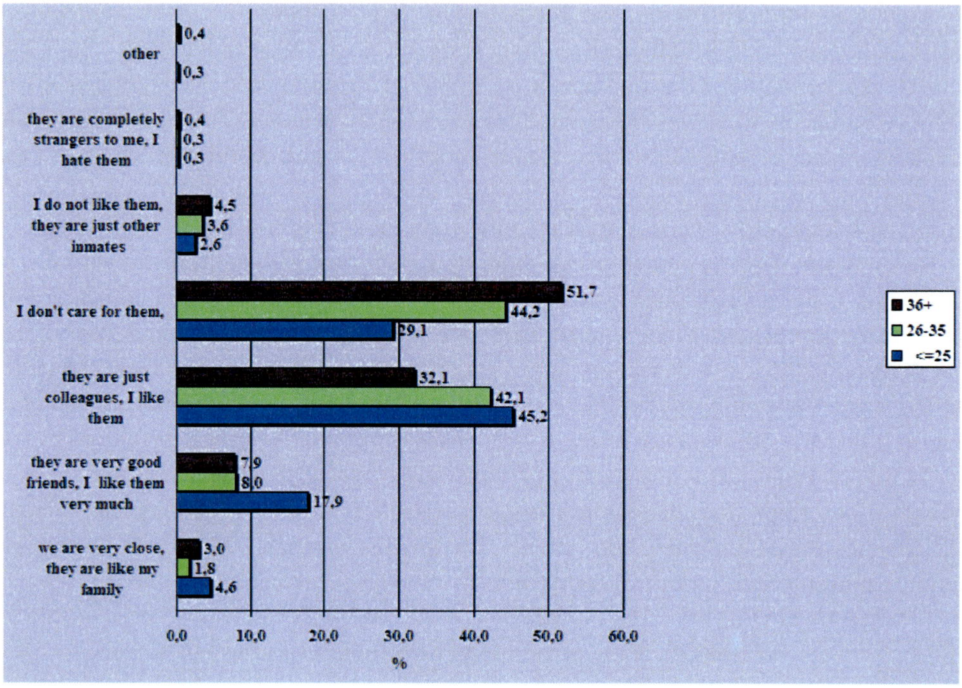

Figure 15. Social relations among inmates in cell by age group, N=949.

The intensity of conflicts and stress is typical for all total institutions, due to confrontational social milieu, lack of space, social and psychical deprivation. The question is to what extent we may explain the specific property of interactions of as the result of social conditions in democratic prison system? What might throw more light on this problem is analysing the differences in character of interactions in different social milieus.

First, let's compare relations between the staff and prisoners to relations among inmates. As data suggest social relations between the staff and the prisoners are better than among the captives. Social relations among inmates are confrontational. In the survey I tried to measure the rules of everyday behaviour and the prison code. Several questions were asked to measure this dimension of social life in prison. Many answers of the prisoners indicated that social relations especially their negative characteristic and conflicts, or possibility of conflicts are the primary problems of everyday life. One of the question was to measure the perceiving of egoism among captives: majority of the respondents (62,3%) saw the relations among inmates in the cells as egoistic, and only ¼ had different opinion. Comparing the relations between the prisoners and the staff and among the convicts one can see the difference: the inmates prefer conformity towards prison staff but nonconformity in relations to each other (see figure 15). Nonconformity in social relations means that individuals must compete with each other, and the reason of nonconformity in a prison society is to defend the interest and the social position, as it was mentioned before. Being a conformist is the indicator of the low status in the group structure. Again, this is rather typical feature of group behaviour in different social settings, but in the case of a prison group there is the difference between the type of relation and the level of conformity to personnel and other inmates: two dominant preferred strategies are *moderate nonconformity to convicts* and *conformity to institution*. It suggests that relations among inmates are rather hostile.

The distribution of answers for another question (*with whom it is worth to have good relations in prison?*) shows that more inmates think that it is more important to have good relations with other inmates then with custodians (see table below). An interpretation of this result is not easy and obvious but also other data describing the nature of inmates relations support the interpretation that interactions among prisoners are trouble spot and more confrontational in comparison to relations with prison staff and this is one of the new characteristic in Polish penitentiary units after introducing democratic reforms.

Table 11. Relations with significant persons

With whom it is worth having good relations in prison?	Answers		% observations
	N	%	
prisoners	374	35,4%	41,0%
staff	264	25,0%	28,9%
everybody	191	18,1%	20,9%
nobody	69	6,5%	7,6%
professionals who work in prison (nurse, doctor etc.)	26	2,5%	2,9%
prisoners who work in prison (in the kitchen)	16	1,5%	1,8%
persons outside the prison (family)	6	,6%	,7%
other	110	10,4%	12,1%
multiple responses N	1056	100,0%	115,8%

I asked the respondents to formulate useful advice for a newcomer (how to survive in prison). One of the 'good rules' for everyday life was to adjust to others and stay passive which means not to step out of line, have proper—no conflict—relations with everybody (47.2% persons expressed such a rule, and it was 55.6% of all observations in multiple responses question.) The minority preferred strong involvement either in subculture groups or in total institution: only 3% of the respondents thought that a good way to survive is to join the subculture groups or any strong social group, and about 7% of the sample expressed the tenet: to conform total institution which means to obey formal regulations, participate in therapies or different treatment programmes and other activity appreciated by the administration of institution such as work. In my opinion these results lead to the inference that social bounds are week and the basic strategy of surviving prison is moderate isolation. Other data also confirm such deduction: the inmates were asked to name "problems of everyday life' by pointing out the things need to be changed and the most annoying thing. In first case prisoners indicated mainly the standard of living (overcrowding, poor living conditions, boredom, lack of contact with family). The second questions revealed that negative relations among prisoners are one of the biggest problem (see figures 16, 17).

The suggestion based on presented data would be as follows: the democratic prison transformed social relations in such a way that social cohesion and social ties have weakened in a prison society, for some convicts relations with other inmates are indifferent and for some they are even hostile. Many of them cooperate with correctional institution and have relatively proper relations with custodians. Thus, oppressive relations in totalitarian prison turned into rather neutral and bureaucratic. Futhermore, money is one of the strongest factor that forms social relation.

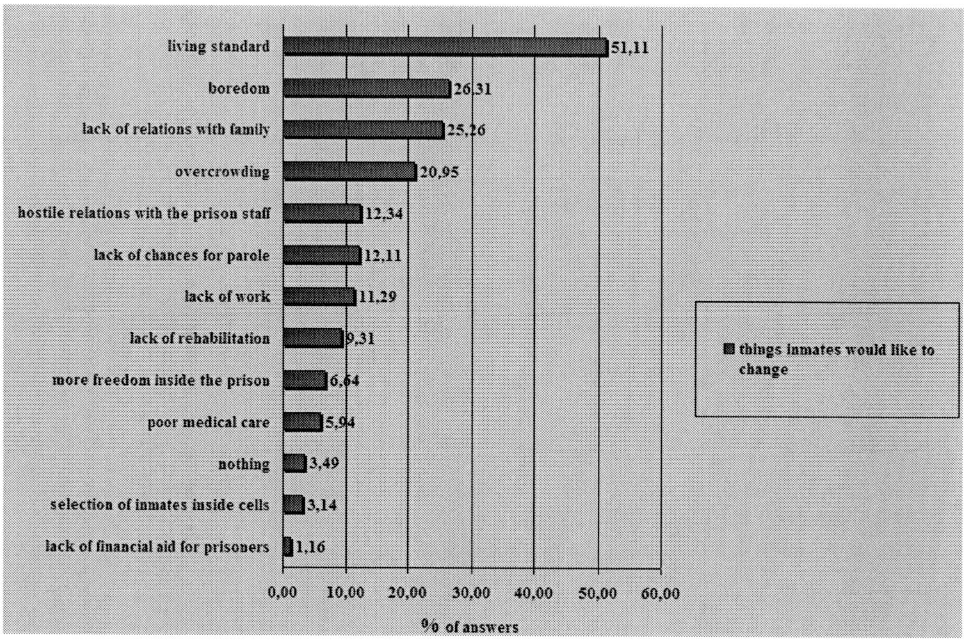

Figure 16. The changes expected by prisoners. N=859

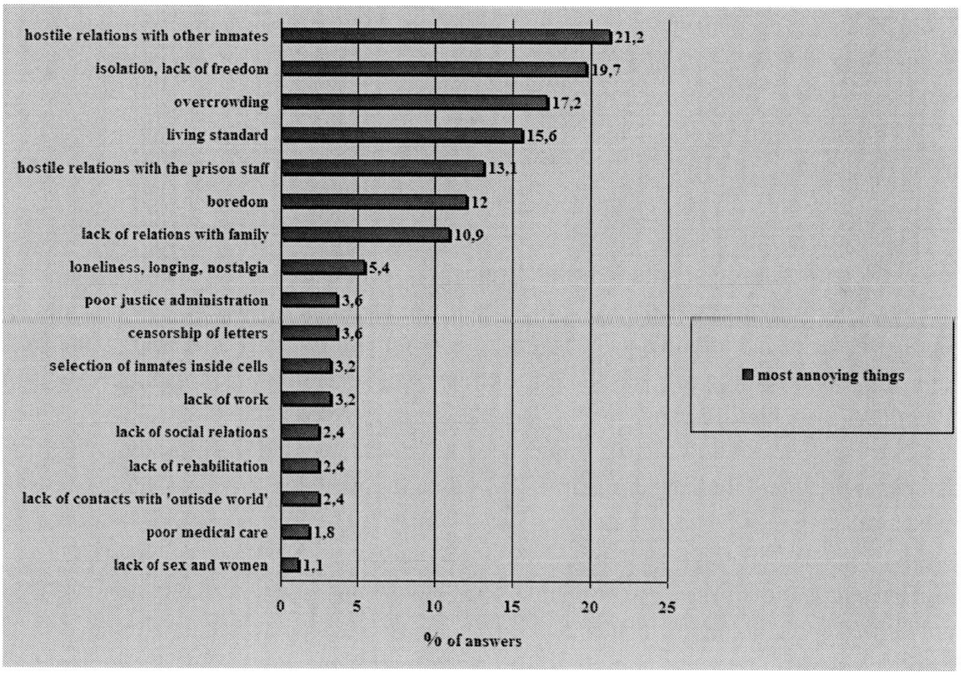

Figure 17. The most annoying thing for prisoners. N=949

Empirically well-grounded 'social law' says that threat changes functioning of groups and communities: it induces in-group integration, strengthens social ties, increases the level of cooperation, and reduces conflicts. Such processes is 'social reaction' for the oppressive conditions of total institutions and they can be found in subculture groups in prisons or in any cohesive social group. But the level of threat and oppression in prisons depends on social conditions inside penal institutions and the model of penal policy in given society, as I was trying to demonstrate. The connection between a social system and a penal system seems to be significant and allows to propose the line of reasoning: less solidarity and weaker social ties are the consequences of a market society, a free market society is regarded to support individualism, competitiveness and even egoism which destroy social bounds. The same social forces that are typical for a free market society influenced social relations inside prisons and destroyed social cohesion. To some degree this important theoretical claim seems to be justified on the empirical ground, nevertheless it needs further investigation, especially a comparison of data coming from different types of the penal systems would be useful to verify it[19].

Social Order and Structure in Prison Community

Social structure is an important aspect of social reality within the sociological (structural) perspective since it is regarded as powerful determinant of human behaviour. The social structure is treated here as the foundation of the social order, and the other important element is the normative system. *The Prison Community* by D. Clemmer and *Society of Captives* by G. Sykes are pioneering works which describe functioning of the social order in prison. Clemmer explains basic social processes in prison groups using classical notions of micro sociological analysis: dominant group, group behaviour, social control, and normative system. Sykes tried to describe the prison as a social system, including living conditions, formal organisation of prison, "the pains of incarceration", the influence of prison on inmates, criminal subculture (to mention just few issues from rich analysis of Sykes). He stress the role of interaction among inmates and guards and inmates when he wrote: "in this interactions we can begin to see the realities of the prison social system emerge" [Sykes 2007: 6]. He also saw the relationships between the prison and social system, prisoners are influenced by "larger society" and "they bring with them the attitudes, beliefs, and values of this larger world. The prison, as a social system, does not exist in isolation any ore than the criminal within the prison exists in isolation as an individual Sykes 2007: 9]

I refer here to their studies: the explanatory categories used by these authors seem to be universal in sociological analysis and useful for examining a social order in prison.

The reconstruction of social order is a challenge which I do not intend (and I am not capable of) to do in this short paper. My intention is to present only some aspects of social structure and normative system, and focus on question what does form social structure in the present prison community? As it was pointed, normative system is a crucial part of social order. System of values, attitudes and beliefs, and behaviour patterns of inmates found

[19] The data concerning prisons from the totalitarian period in Poland would be of great importance for deeper understanding the connections between prison and its social surroundings although there is not enough reliable research from that time.

expression in the so-called inmate code which sustains the order in prison community. So far much have been written about convict code and we have extensive knowledge on it so we must now examine what occurs to convict code in actuality, that is in the process of prison transformation in Polish penitentiaries . Of course, to accept the rules does not mean to comply with them. It is clear that rules are always broken but what is interesting and unpredictable is the extent they are respected in reality and I would like to focus here on this issue then. As it was already mention the extent in which the code is respected has changed: it seems, according to respondents' accounts more and more norms are not respected and not obeyed. It was examined already in this chapter when subculture transformation was discussed. One of the spectacular examples is the breakdown of one of the strongest rule, namely loyalty. In order to achieve individual interest the convicts cooperate with custodians and are willing to sneak on one another. The respondents' description of the current state of social order in prison indicate the state it might be anomie, they report breakdown of social values such as loyalty, trust, or common group interest.

The other important issue is to consider which phenomena are universal in constituting social structure and which are unique only for a prison community. The social structure of micro society (small groups) is formed to some extent by the attributes of individuals, social roles and identities which hierarchical differentiate the position of an individual in group structure. The perception of structure is based on characteristics which individuals attribute to each other and which at the same time are perceived as important in environment they live in. Some elements are universal and also shape the social structure outside the prison walls, they penetrate into the prison world and constitute the inner order (for instance money).

The simplest analysis of the social structure is focused on status attributes: what are the status marks of the social structure in the prison community? Which attributes cause inequality? Which group is superordinate and which subordinate? The perspective which is adopted here is subjective perception of social order and social structure. A reason for that solution was mainly methodological one: the access to objective measures of social structure was impossible during research process[20]. Instead, the perceiving of social structure was examined. Inmates were queried as to main attribute they regard as important for a social position inside a prison community. Quite coherent view of structure emerges from the collected answers because the respondents had very similar opinions about the meaning of some features: over 80% of sample share the same view on what counts in prisons; the most important elements (variables) that matter according to the examined captives are: money, mental strength (tough character) and communication skills (with other inmates). Education was regarded as important by minority (17%) and a large proportion (58%) were of the opinion that education is not important. In the case of some characteristics the judgements among the inmates were divided: the younger the inmates and less educated the more often they regard membership in subculture groups as important status element.

Correlation analysis of qualitative variables proved no significant relations, however contingency tables analysis shows in some cases the slight differences in the frequency of answers: between the two groups of persons socially-orientated and prison-orientated. Each group perceives other thing as important for status. The first group of respondents (who

[20] Prison bureaucracy does not collect data that would be useful to reconstruct social structure. In this case the subjective perception of structure is the way of reconstructing the structural order. However, much more satisfying would be to use 'objective'variables.

worked longer, have children, have better education) regard education and proper relations with prison administration as the main status attributes. The second group respects those elements (values, norms) that are intrinsic for prison realm only and allow to built high (better) social status inside the community of convicts. These prisoners comply with the rules obligatory inside prisons and - at the same time - such attitudes make them difficult to get parole or have better relations with the administration of penitentiary. The inmates form their social status through meaning and prestige they inscribed to the types of crime, length of sentence, time spent in total institutions. Low-status individuals (with low sentence, short time spent in prison) who intend to be promoted to a higher rank in the social structure of convicts also esteem 'prison values' more. Thus, social structure is perceived differently by various inmates depending on connections of particular person to criminal culture.

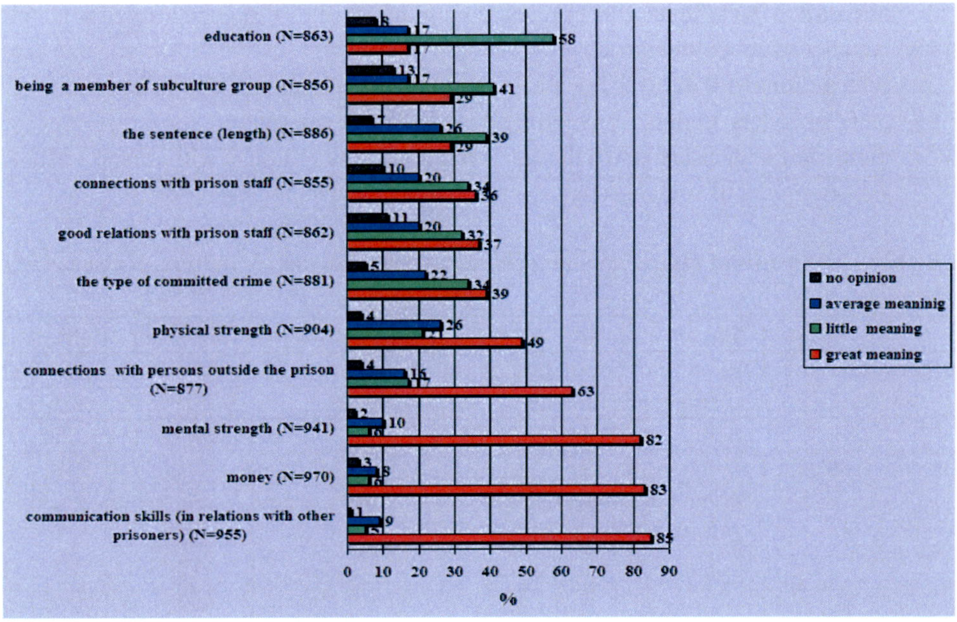

Figure 18. The perception of social structure among the prisoners.

There is a general rule observed by sociologists: the lower is the status of a person in the group the more he/she accepts values and norms of a group if he/she identifies with this group and wants to become its member. For instance, a newcomer to prison has usually low status, the same concerns a person who is sentenced for short-term or stigmatized crimes or low-profit crimes. A person with low status should be more interested in getting promotion and that is why he/she would accept more norms and status element typical for prison reality. In sociological analysis of group behaviour it is called anticipated socialization. Also it is known that for some prisoners normative and value system of 'criminal community' is very attractive as possible carrier path or it is important because both in prison and after doing the sentence they live in criminal population. No matter they are in or outside prison their behaviour and identity is controlled by the same normative system. That is why inmates who committed property crime, who make a living by crime and belong to criminal community also outside penal complex more often regarded the type of crime and membership in subculture groups as meaningful for status in social structure. Whereas prisoners convicted for violent offences (a part of them) think these factors have little importance for their status, they often commit crimes by accident and they do not belong to environment.

In search of deeper understanding how social structure is shaped factor analysis was carried out. Factor analysis detected four groups of variables that differentiate attitudes toward social order in prison and the position of captives inside community. All these groups of factors can be interpreted in such a way that different dimensions of structure evolve in the process of adaptation to prison life. But there are different ways people adopt to prison depending mainly on group influence and values they accept. Considering this, twelve variables that define the status of individuals in social structure were reduced to four groups in factor analysis:

1. **normative structure**: the type of committed crime, sentence (duration), being a member of subculture group.
2. **interactional structure:** mental strength, communication skills in relations with other prisoners, connections with persons outside prison.
3. **dominant order status attributes**: education, good relations with prison staff.
4. **simple model of social structure**: money, physical strength.

Table 12. The groups of status characteristic. Factor analysis. Varimax, Kaiser criterion

	Factor analysis	**ii**	**iii**	**iii**	**iv**
normative structure	the type of committed crime	,788	,082	,055	,118
	the sentence (length)	,773	,030	,226	-,013
	being a member of subculture group	,549	,148	-,054	,081
interactional structure	mental strength	,145	,843	,104	-,003
	communication skills (in relations with other prisoners)	,051	,804	,012	,157
	connections with persons outside prison	,196	,410	,382	,154
dominant order status attributes	education	,006	,092	,838	-,167
	good relations with prison staff	,103	,019	,665	,343
simple model of social structure	money	,002	,037	,117	,877
	physical strength	,333	,332	-,055	,584

The first group called normative structure can be interpreted in terms of 'traditional' reorientation for prison life, where respecting a prison code allows a prisoner to obtain high status, which I discussed earlier. Within this dimension three variables appear to be important such as time spent in prison, connections with criminal subculture and groups, identification with prison roles related to the type of offence and criminal identity (e.g. criminal 'profession'). The acceptance of prison code values is regarded as a way of adaptation to prison life. Again, such a way of perceiving social structure is based on involvement in the system of criminal values and norms.

The second group was called interactional structure because it comprises factors connected with social relations and allows one to establish high position in the community during social interactions: communication skill, mental strength and connections with persons outside prison. Communication skill is an evident feature for building social position. The mental strength is one of the clue features which gives prestige and high esteem in a prison society. Toughness is one of the elements of masculine personality pattern popular in criminal culture. It is crucial because it allows one to cope with conflicts and social pressure during social interactions, it gives an inmate power and supremacy. Any person who surrenders in a conflict situation loses his (her) respect, in other words, mental weakness means low position in social structure, as was demonstrated earlier in this chapter. The newly-arrived inmates are often put to the test of conformity[21] to a group and to a penal institution. Such tests serve to identify the personality of convicts, to attribute the social roles and to stigmatize them. Connections refer to the social capital of inmates (e.g., knowing persons with high social status in society); such relations help to exist inside the prison through financial support, to arrange services or even to settle release from prison. At present, with the advent of organised crime, connections gain new meaning: they give real power to the convicts who belong to an organised group because they get support while serving a sentence.

The third group named **dominant order status attributes** consist of two variables: education and good relations with prison staff. They are drawn from the free community and in fact conformity to dominant values constitutes an order which relates to this larger world outside the prison. The inmates who see education and good relation with custodians as important elements identify themselves with a dominant social order. These inmates are most susceptible to a correctional institution, and if any kind of rehabilitation is possible, they are prone to it.

The fourth group was labelled **simple model of social structure,** and two variables were important here: money and physical strength. The social structure emerges from the elements that have great meaning in a specific society. If we explain a social order we look for fundamental variables that usually are primary resources essential to survive. It appears that in prison they are money and physical strength. As it was mentioned before, money has become a significant status attribute in a society of growing inequalities and it shows in prison and in society as well. Whereas physical strength is much appreciated in masculine culture as the source of potential power and domination.[22]

Taking into account the gathered data, I would claim that the society of inmates in fact consists of several different sub-communities and sub-groups that share different beliefs and values, use different adaptive strategies and form incommensurable status in the social structure. In addition social bonds in society are rather weak. All these arguments allow me to say the society of captives as a whole is not coherent, and rather external administrative coercion sustains the inmates as a whole.

---

[21] Such test are described and discussed in work *Games prisoners play* by M. Kamiński ; this research is based on author's personal experience while serving a sentence of imprisonment.

[22] Here are significant illustation of inmates behavior that indicates the meaning of physical strength: many inmates do physical exercise no matter if it is allowed or not (and it varies in different units); they appreciate the muscular look especially; there is a practice which enables prisoners to achieve that kind of look without do physical exercise: they inject an oil into the muscles which causes inflammatory condition and muscles seem to be 'bigger'.

CONCLUSIONS

The transition in correctional institutions in Poland is not a unique phenomenon. If we look back to the history of prisons, we see that changes are constant features of correctional institutions, and even lately modifications have appeared in many prison systems. The spectacular example is the USA penitentiaries, with growing prison population, developing the penal industry and privatisation of prisons [Shelden 2001].

What I have tried to demonstrate in this chapter then, was to indicate the main changes in prisons in Poland during the transformation from communist regime to democratic state. At the same time, my intention was to explain them as the effect of the linkages between the prison and the social system in which it is embedded. I mostly adopt here a structural and functional perspective for an explanation with regard to the question of the role of culture.

Free market society imposed new economic conditions and democracy introduced a new social and political order which have brought fundamental alteration in the penal system. The most significant for the modification of the penitentiary system are: civil liberty and civil rights along with introducing new regulations in penal institutions, the new profile of prison officers, the appearance of new type of crimes and organised crime. As to transformation of social order, there have been changes in social structure: social class gaps widen. An attempt to open prisons to the community has been successful (otherwise this research would be impossible). The prisons cooperate with many institutions: scientific, religious, humanitarian, etc.; the medical and psychological treatment has improved. The complex set of new social conditions shape a prison—an institution and community.

The task of comparing communist prisons to democratic prisons seems rather complicated because of the multi-dimensional character of the social realm in which the prison system is embedded. However, some features are distinctive.

First, the basic function of a penal system is the same both in a communist and a democratic system: to control society, to employ prison for political ends, furthermore to support the existing social order in the interest of the dominant class. The difference between prisons in the democratic and totalitarian state lies in the degree of discipline, regulation and the forms of control.

Second, the penal system is involved in the present mechanisms of exercising power—the constant change in administration and management after election—which results in the deficiency of cohesive penal policy and absence of continued penitentiary policy by successive governments. In other words, every new government and ministry of justice starts to create the policy 'from the beginning'.

Third, we can observe the transformation of the social cohesion: the level of social cohesion among the prisoners was high in communist prisons, at present it has diminished; furthermore, the social relations are better between staff and prisoners than among prisoners, and there are much more hostile relationships among inmates in democratic prisons than in totalitarian prisons.

Fourth, there is the decline of 'an old type' subculture group and erosion of the traditional convicts' code, which in turn led to the disruption of community social organisation.

Fifth, among the main organisational and infrastructure problems are overcrowding, lack of work and organised leisure activities along with staff shortages. But on the other hand, convicts have more liberty inside the prison (they are allowed to hold tv-sets, computers, the have more contactd with relatives and outside world etc.).

Sixth, there has been significant improvement in the level and quality of education among the staff, especially in the rehabilitation section.

Seventh, the crime fear of public opinion, and the influence of media create an unfriendly social climate for prisoners which is not conducive for liberal penal reforms.

Finally, there is a general question concerning public penal policy and the philosophy of punishment in Polish society which in fact is a part of the debate that has been carried out in western societies on the relevancy of punishment, the influence of imprisonment on individuals and the families of convicts, the social costs of incarceration, plus the function of prison in specific social and economic conditions, etc. Unfortunately, not enough attention is given to these important concerns in Poland.

It is important to understand better the linkages between social order and institution of prison in order to be aware of the consequences of implementation of the specific penitentiary system. If we are to believe we can improve somehow the functioning of social institutions like prisons, this knowledge is the first step towards reorganization.

REFERENCES

Berk R., Kenneth A., Lenihan J, & Rossi H. (1980) Crime and Poverty: Some Experimental Evidence from Ex-Offenders, *American Sociological Review* 45: 766-86.

Centralny Zarząd Służby Więziennej (CZSW) (2008). http://www.sw.gov.pl/. Miesięczna informacja statystyczna grudzień 2008. Monthly Bulletin of Statistics. Ministry of Justice, the Central Directorate of Penal Service (CZSW),

Clemmer D.(1958) *The Prison Community*. New York: Rinehart & Co, Inc.

Crutchfield R.,D. & Pitchford S.R. (1997) Work and Crime: the Effects of Labour Stratification, *Social Forces* 76: 93-118.

Custodial and non-custodial measures. The Prison System. Criminal Justice Assessment Toolkit UNITED NATIONS. New York, 2006. http://www.unodc.org

Franklin T. W., Franklin C.A. & Pratt T.C. (2006) Examining the empirical relationship between prison crowding and inmate misconduct: A meta-analysis of conflicting research results. *Journal of Criminal Justice*, vol. 34 4 01–412.

Garland D. (1990) Punishment and Modern Society. A study. In: *Social Theory*. Oxford: Clarendon Press.

Hagan J. & Peterson R.D (ed.) (1995) *Crime and Inequality*. Stanford : Stanford University Press.

Kaminski M. (2004) *Games Prisoners Play: The Tragicomic Worlds of Polish Prison*. Princeton: Princeton University Press.

Morris, N. & Rothman D, (1995) *The Oxford History of Prisons*. Oxford: Oxford University Press.

Platek M. (1998). Penal practice and social theory in Poland before and after the events of 1989. In Weiss R.P. & South N. (ed.) C*omparing Prison Systems: toward a comparative and international penology*. (pp. 263-288). Amsterdam: Gordon and Breach Publishers.

Quinney R. (1974). *Critique of Legal Order: Crime control in Capitalist Society*. Boston: Little Brown.

Quinney R. (1980) *Class, State and Crime*. New York: Longman.

Reiman J.H. (1998). *The Rich Get Richer and the Poor Get Prison*. Boston: Allyn and Bacon

Rusche G., Kirchheimer O. (1968,). *Punishment and Social Structure*. New York: Russell and Russel.

Sampson R. J. & Laub J. H. (1993) *Crime in the Making: Pathways and Turning Point through Life*. Cambridge MA: Harvard University Press.

Shelden R.G. (2001) *Controlling the Dangerous Classes. A critical introduction to the history of Criminal Justice.* Boston: Allyn and Bacon.

South C. R. & Wood J. (2006) Bullying in prisons: the importance of perceived social status, prisonization, and moral disengagement. *Aggressive Behavior*, Volume 32, Issue 5, 490 – 501.

Taveres, C. & Thomas G. (2008). *http://epp.eurostat.ec.europa.eu/cache/ITY_OFFPUB/KS-SF-08-019/EN/KS-SF-08-019-EN.PDF.* Eurostat. Statistics in focus. Population and Social Conditions. *http://www.ojp.usdoj.gov/bjs/pub/pdf/p07.pdf.*

Thorneberry T. P, Christenson R.L. 1984) Unemployment and Criminal Involvement: An Investigation of Reciprocal Causal Structures. *American Sociological Review*, 49: 398-411,

Weiss R.P. & South N. ed. (1998) *Comparing Prison Systems: toward a comparative and international penology*. Amsterdam: Gordon and Breach Publishers.

West H. C. & Sabol W. J. 2007. *Prisoners in 2007.* Bureau of Justice Statistics Bulletin. December 2008. U.S. Department of Justice. Office of Justice Programs U.S. Department of Justice.

Hagan J. & Peterson R.D. ed. (1995) *Crime and inequality*. California: Stanford University Press..

Polish Legal acts: Dz.U.03.14.142 *The Decree of ministry of Justice of 16 January 2003 on qualification of the prison Staff.* ROZPORZĄDZENIE MINISTRA SPRAWIED LIWOŚCI z dnia 16 stycznia 2003 r. w sprawie wymagań w zakresie wykształcenia i kwalifikacji zawodowych, jakim powinni odpowiadać funkcjonariusze Służby Więziennej (Dz. U. z dnia 31 stycznia 2003 r.) Na podstawie art. 25 ustawy z dnia 26 kwietnia 1996 r. o Służbie Więziennej (Dz. U. z 2002 r. Nr 207, poz. 1761.

In: Violent Crime and Prisons: Population...
Ed: Aidan Renshaw and Emelina Suárez
ISBN: 978-1-60741-668-5

Chapter 6

VIOLENCE AND COLLEGE STUDENTS – PREVALENCE, LEGAL AND PSYCHOLOGICAL ISSUES[1]

Dean Lauterbach[2] and Natalie K. Nugent
Eastern Michigan University, USA

ABSTRACT

There is an explicit expectation that universities will educate students and a tacit expectation that they will protect those in their care. Unfortunately, universities are seeing high levels of campus violence. This chapter will discuss the prevalence of violence among college students with an eye toward the legal mandates to warn students of imminent danger and the psychological consequences for exposure to violence among college students. We will conclude with specific recommendation for college counseling centers, which are most likely to encounter trauma-exposed college students.

VIOLENCE AND COLLEGE STUDENTS – PREVALENCE, LEGAL AND PSYCHOLOGICAL ISSUES

Schools were once seen as safe havens for our young; yet, over the last several years there have been high profile mass murders on the campuses of Virginia Tech and Northern Illinois University. High Schools are not immune and the nightly news features high school fights posted on YouTube ("Teacher Beat in Classroom," 2008). Over the last 20 years there has been increased attention devoted to physical, sexual, and emotional abuse, domestic violence, and rape on college campuses. The effect of violence on college students can be dramatic affecting the health and well-being of millions of individuals. Federal legislation now requires that campuses provide information on prevalence of campus crimes to students,

---

[1] The authors would like to thank Dr. Lisa Lauterbach, Ph.D., and Daniel Jones, BA, for their contributions to this chapter.
[2] For additional information on this chapter, please contact the first author: e-mail; Dlauterba@emich.edu, Telephone; 734 487-0785, Address; 507 Mark Jefferson Science Hall, Department of Psychology, Eastern Michigan University, Ypsilanti, MI 48197.

prospective students, prospective employees and all interested parties. This unfunded legislation continues to drain limited university resources. The purpose of this chapter is to discuss the prevalence of violence among college students with an eye toward the legal mandates to warn students of imminent danger and the psychological consequences for exposure to violence among college students. We will begin with a case example of the sexual assault and murder of a Michigan college student and then discuss the legal mandates of universities to inform and protect students. This will be followed by a broader discussion of the prevalence of violence among college students and factors predictive of recovery. Lastly, we will discuss the role of college counseling centers in servicing the needs of traumatized students.

LAURA DICKINSON – A TRAGIC LOSS

By all accounts, Laura Dickinson was the type of person who loved life and had a special respect for others (Menard, 2007). As a child she was shy and retiring but as she grew into a teen, her love of theater and school dances emerged. She worked at three jobs in her home town of Hastings, Michigan. After graduating from high school, Laura attended Grand Rapids Community College where she made the Dean's list. In the fall of 2006, Laura transferred to Eastern Michigan University (EMU), a school with 24,000 students that is within 30 minutes of Detroit. Laura's father warned her to travel with friends, lock her doors, and be careful.

Although not particularly athletic, Laura took advantage of the opportunity to join the novice rowing team at EMU. On the night of December 12th, 2006, Laura went to the rowing team Christmas party. They exchanged gifts and Laura returned to her dorm room at about 11:00pm with two bags of presents. Like many college students, she ended her day by calling her boyfriend and talking for more than an hour.

Several days passed and Laura's parents and her boyfriend were unable to reach her. Since final exams had started, they assumed that she was busily studying. However, after several days, Laura's father began to worry. At about the same time, residents in the adjacent rooms complained of a strong odor and on December 15th, a janitor opened the door to discover Laura dead at the foot of her bed.

The reports released by the university indicated that no foul play was suspected and they believed that Laura's death was likely the result of a heart arrhythmia that had been diagnosed two years earlier. Laura's parents were also told that no foul play was suspected. Stunned by the news that their apparently healthy daughter had died, the Dickenson's buried their daughter on December 21st.

Behind the scenes, a grimmer picture emerged. The physical evidence pointed to foul play. When Laura was found she was partially nude, lying on the floor at the foot of her bed with a pillow over her face, and there were traces of semen on her leg. For the ensuing two months, police reviewed security tapes from her dorm room, and waited for the state crime lab to return DNA test results. The investigation continued behind the scenes while the university remained publicly silent of their suspicions that Laura had been murdered.

On February 23rd, fully two months after Laura's death, Orange Taylor III, a student at EMU, was arrested and charged with 1st degree murder. The community was shocked and angered to learn that the EMU Police had been investigating her death as a homicide. While

Taylor was eventually convicted of first degree murder, assault with intent to commit sexual penetration, first degree home invasion, and larceny in a building, the story attracted the attention of the national media. The Washington Post, ABC News, and local media each covered the story. There are three reasons for the extensive coverage. First, a number of university officials were fired including the president of the university, the vice president for student affairs, and the chief of police ("University Cover Up," 2007). Second, this was a particularly brutal rape and murder, the first homicide on the EMU campus since it was founded in 1849. Third, an independent investigation by the Butzel Long law firm ruled that EMU violated a law known simply as the *Clery Act.* (See Long (2007) for a complete discussion of findings.)

Description of the Clery Act

In 1990 congress enacted legislation known as the "Crime Awareness and Campus Security Act of 1990." It is found in Title II of the Student Right-to-Know and Campus Security Act of 1990. All public and private postsecondary institutions that participate in federal Title IV student aid programs must comply with these regulations. In arguing for the need for the legislation, congress noted that the incidence of violent crime on college campuses has risen steadily over recent years. Moreover, at the time there was no mechanism for the comprehensive collection of data on campus crimes. Only 4.4% of 8,000 postsecondary institutions participating in federal student aid programs voluntarily provide crime statistics directly through the uniform Crime Report of the FBI. While several states were considering the adoption of legislation requiring campuses to report crime statistics, the pending legislation was uneven in scope and standards. Most importantly, congress argued that *students and employees of universities as well as applicants and parents of applicants should be aware of the incidence of campus crime and polices/procedures for crime prevention.* Implicit is the notion that access to crime information will facilitate the types of self-corrections inherent in a free market economy. Armed with accurate information on campus crime statistics, parents and students will make informed decisions to attend schools that boast lower crime rates. These safe universities would assume a competitive advantage in the market place and other less safe institutions would be impelled to take affirmative action to improve their campus safety record.

There were three key elements of the Crime Awareness and Campus Security Act. First, beginning in September 1, 1991 eligible institutions were required to begin collecting information on campus crime statistics and campus security policies of that institution, and beginning September 1, 1992, and each year thereafter, distribute to all current students and employees, and to any applicant for enrollment or employment upon request, an *annual* security report. At a minimum, the annual report had to contain the following information:

A. Policy statements regarding current:
    1. procedures and facilities for students and others to report criminal actions,
    2. security and access to campus facilities,
    3. campus law enforcement,

4. monitoring and recording through local police agencies of criminal activity at off-campus student organizations which are recognized by the institution,
5. possession, use, and sale of alcohol/illegal drugs and enforcement of State underage drinking laws and Federal and State drug laws.

B. Descriptions of:
1. the type and frequency of programs designed to inform students and employees about campus security procedures and practices and to encourage students and employees to be responsible for their own security and the security of others.
2. programs designed to inform students and employees about the prevention of crimes.

C. Statistics concerning:
1. the occurrence on campus, during the most recent school year, and during the 2 preceding school years, of the following criminal offenses reported to campus security authorities or local police: murder, rape, robbery, aggravated assault, burglary, and motor vehicle theft.
2. the number of arrests for the following crimes occurring on campus: liquor law violations, drug abuse violations, and weapons possessions.

The second element is central to the case of Laura Dickinson. Each institution is required to make timely reports to the campus community on crimes considered to be a *threat to other students and employees*. Such reports shall be provided to students and employees in a manner that is *timely* and that will *aid in the prevention of similar occurrences*. The third key element is that, upon the request of the Secretary, each institution shall submit a listing of all required crime statistics. Of note, the initial legislation did not include language on the consequences for non-compliance or the effect that disclosure of information could have on ongoing investigations.

Since its inception, there have been several amendments to the Crime Awareness and Campus Security Act. As part of the *Higher Education Amendments Act of 1998* (Section 486(e) of Public Law 105-244) the official title of the legislation changed to the *Jeanne Clery Disclosure of Campus Security Policy and Campus Crime Statistics Act* [20 U.S.C. 1092(f)] known more commonly as the *Clery Act*. The *Clery Act* is named in memory of a 19-year-old Lehigh University freshman, Jeanne Ann Clery, who was raped and murdered while asleep in her residence hall room on April 5th, 1986. More specific language was provided regarding the need to disclose institutional policies and programs on sexual assault and inform the campus community where information on registered sex offenders may be obtained. Several types of offenses were added to the initial list of six types of events that must be reported and the term "rape" was replaced with the phrase "sexual offenses, forcible or nonforcible." The Department of Education can issue civil fines up to $27,500 per violation for a substantial misrepresentation of the number, location, or nature of the crimes required to be reported.

Returning for a moment to the case of Laura Dickinson, clearly information on the nature of the investigation was not released in a timely manner. However, a clause of the *Clery Act* stipulates that an institution may temporarily withhold information in some cases. However, there must be clear and convincing evidence that the release of information would:

- Jeopardize an ongoing investigation;
- Jeopardize the safety of an individual;
- Cause a suspect to flee or evade detection; or
- Result in the destruction of evidence.

Institutions may withhold *only* that information that could cause an adverse effect, but must disclose such information once the adverse effect is no longer likely to occur. The individual making the judgment to withhold information should document the reason for doing so.

Although the *Clery Act* is relatively brief (5 pages) the scope and implications of this unfunded federal mandate are considerable. The Department of Education (DOE) has developed a comprehensive manual for campus crime reporting, (*The Handbook for Campus Crime Reporting*, 2005). Table 1 highlights key elements of *Clery Act* compliance and was abstracted from the DOE manual. In addition, Appendix B of the DOE compliance manual includes a checklist for *Clery Act* compliance. Lastly, workshops are offered to train relevant parties in procedures necessary to comply with the *Clery Act*.

One measure of the effectiveness of the *Clery Act* is the extent to which schools have complied with the reporting mandates. As a rough gauge of compliance, the websites for schools from three conferences were searched for one or both of the following: reference to the *Clery Act* and information on crime statistics. Three conferences were selected, the Mid-American Conference (which includes Eastern Michigan University), the Big 10 Conference, and the Big 12 Conference. Universities were judged to be compliant if they had a clear reference to the *Clery Act* (or to one of the earlier names for the legislation) and if they reported crime statistics in a way that was consistent with *Clery Act* guidelines. Collapsing across the 35 schools, there was universal compliance with the *Clery Act*[3].

Crime statistics for all college campuses are also available at the Department of Education's website http://www.ope.ed.gov/security/. The search engine within this site allows users to search for crime statistics for individual institutions, for aggregated data for a group of campuses, and to download data for a group of campuses. As an additional check for *Clery Act* compliance for schools in the Mid-American, Big-10, and Big 12 conferences, crime statistics data were obtained from the Department of Education website. Annual crime statistics for all 35 institutions we surveyed were reported to the Department of Education and reported on their website.

The data presented thus far suggests that the *Clery Act* has been largely successful. However, a Stetson Law Review article (Fisher, Hartman, Cullen, & Turner, 2002) reached a far more damning conclusion with respect to overall compliance with the *Clery Act* and particularly with respect to the accuracy of crime statistics provided in all reports[4]. The authors conclude that the *Clery Act* is largely symbolic, serving simply to superficially

[3] Summary data from these 35 universities, including the location where crime information is located, can be obtained from the first author.

[4] It is important to note that this article did not address compliance or effectiveness of several key elements of the *Clery Act* including compliance and adequacy of timely warnings and various statements of policy.

demonstrate that action is being taken on a perceived social problem. Several of the challenges to the institutional compliance and implementation will be briefly outlined.

Table 1. Time line for reporting.

What needs to be disclosed	When does it need to be disclosed	To whom should it be disclosed
Development, disclosure and implementation of all campus security policies	Routinely on an ongoing basis.	All members of the campus community.
Timely warnings to alert the campus community about crimes that pose a serious or continuing threat to safety.	Whenever there is a threat that a crime is ongoing or may be repeated (i.e., as soon as the information becomes available).	All members of the campus community.
*A daily crime log that lists, by date reported, all crimes reported to the campus police or security department.	Updated daily as crimes are reported.	Must be made available for public inspection without exception.
Annual security report containing campus security policy disclosures and crime statistics for the previous three years.	Must be published and distributed annually by October 1. There is no grace period. http://www.ope.ed.gov/security/	Current students and employees individually. Prospective students and employees notified of availability of report.
Report to ED of statistics for Clery Act crimes via designated Web site.	Each fall, on the dates provided by ED in a letter to your institution.	Made available for public inspection.
*A crime log is mandatory for all institutions that maintain a campus police or security department.		

Soon after passage of the Crime Awareness and Campus Security Act there was institutional resistance to the provision of crime statistics. Colleges and universities argued that campus crime records contained information in which individual students could be identified. This would constitute a violation of the Federal Education Rights and Privacy Act (FERPA) (20 U.S.C. § 1232g; 34 CFR Part 99) also known as the Buckley Amendment. Violation of FERPA could entail the loss of federal funds. By the early 1990s, two court cases challenged the notion that FERPA covered campus crime statistics ("*Bauer v. Kincaid*,"; "*Campus Communications v. Criser*,"). In these two cases, the courts ruled that campus crime incident reports and statistics were not protected as educational records (under FERPA).

A second tier of issues clearly compromises institutional compliance with the accurate reporting of crime statistics. In estimating the frequency of occurrence of crime, there are two sources of data: (1) official statistics and (2) victimization-survey statistics. Official statistics include the Uniform Crime Report (UCR) statistics, which includes only data on crimes reported to law enforcement. Victimization surveys are administered to probability samples (i.e., samples representative of the population of interest) that attempt to measure the prevalence and/or incidence of different types of victimization. Victimization surveys include crimes reported to police and unreported crimes.

Prevalence estimates based on the Uniform Crime Reporting practices and population-based victimization surveys [i.e., the National Crime Survey (NCS) and National Crime Victimization Survey (NCVS)] are quite different. A consistent finding across these studies is that a large proportion of victims do not report their victimization to law enforcement officials.

As noted earlier, crime statistics reported in the *Clery Act* rely exclusively on data that are based on official statistics such as those reported in the UCR. In making this choice, lobbyists, the bill's authors, and Congress, ignored data on how best to measure crime prevalence. In particular, they ignored the finding that official statistics, such as the UCR statistics, systematically under-reported crime victimizations because they do not include the substantial number of crime victims who did not report their experiences to law enforcement officials. Thus, the crime statistics published to satisfy the *Clery Act* mandate are incomplete, if not inaccurate. In other words, institutions may comply with the letter of the *Clery Act* but not the spirit of the act.

Results from three national-level student victimization surveys support the fact that very few students report their victimizations to campus law enforcement, security, or to other campus authorities (Fisher, Cullen, & Turner, 2000; Fisher, Daigle, Cullen, & Turner, 2006; Sloan, Fisher, & Cullen, 1997). Furthermore, the statistics mandated by the *Clery Act* overemphasize the seriousness of crimes occurring on campuses. For example, institutions are not required to report the frequency of larceny–theft. However, several studies and the UCR have consistently shown that larceny–theft is by far the most-frequently-occurring crime on campuses. The exclusion of this offense is yet another reason to question the utility of the *Clery Act* to produce statistics that accurately reflect the prevalence and types of campus crime. In their conclusions regarding *Clery Act* compliance, Fisher et al (2002) state that "In the end, the *Clery Act* provides the campus community with the "right to know" crime-statistics information that is questionable at best and, at worst, misleading" (p. 86).

A congressionally-mandated study of the content of the annual security report from 1,015 randomly selected two-year and four-year institutes of higher education covered by the *Clery Act* (Karjane, Fisher, & Cullen, 2002)[5] concluded that overall, compliance varied across the different requirements. For example, the *Clery Act* specifies that the past three years of crime statistics should be included in the annual security report. For colleges and universities that included crime statistics in their annual security report (74.2%), 84.2% included the past three years' statistics. Compliance was lower for the *Clery Act's* stipulation that sexual offenses be divided into forcible and nonforcible offenses. Only 36.5% of colleges and universities were fully compliant with this reporting requirement. Moreover, there was considerable variation in compliance across the different types of schools. The reasons for the uneven compliance are unclear and warrant future investigation.

[5] This governmental report has not been published but can be down loaded at: http://one.center-school.org/search-document-detail.php?ID=173

Violent skirmishes occur when force is threatened or almost used to settle a dominance dispute between a perpetrator and a victim. Lastly, dominance tiffs represent conflictive social acts. It is important to note however, that in this theory violence is defined in its relation to social occurrences.

An alternative taxonomy divides violent or aggressive acts into two components based on the nature of the act committed. Most frequently, these components are referred to as physical and relational aggression (Crick, 1996). Physical aggression or violence is characterized by overt aggressive actions such as hitting, kicking, pushing, or verbal threats and tends to be employed by those motivated to harm others through physical means. This type of violence is much more commonly associated with males (Hess & Hagen, 2006). Relational aggression or violence, on the other hand, is much more common in females (Hess & Hagen, 2006) and is typified by purposeful manipulation with the intent to harm others. Covert aggressive acts, such as social exclusion or rumor spreading, are frequently employed with the intent of causing social harm, disruption to others, or in retaliation for perceived slights, and it is this form of relational aggression that can lead to poor social functioning among girls (Crick & Dodge, 1994; Crick & Grotpeter, 1995). While these two independent versions of violence clearly delineate distinct forms of aggression, they are both consistent with McCann et al's (1988) definition of violence as a stressful event or experience that requires psychological adaptation. For the purpose of this chapter however, the focus will remain on physical violence or aggression.

A third way to conceptualize the nature of physical violence focuses on the potentially reactive nature of some violence. Chase, O'Leary, and Heyman (2001) dichotomize the construct into reactive versus proactive violence. In this model, reactive violence is characterized by responses, whether appropriate or inappropriate given the situation, to perceived threats. These responses are characterized by high physiologica arousal and minimal cognitive processing. In contrast, proactive violence is characterized by deliberate, systematic, goal-directed behavior that occurs in the context of minimal or decreasing physiological arousal and utilizes high degrees of cognitive processing. While there is little doubt that both proactive and reactive violence are important in understanding the nature of violent encounters, for the purpose of this chapter, violence will be addressed from a physical, proactive stand-point.

Overview of Violence Exposure

While colleges and universities are not hotbeds for violence (Bromely, 1995), it is certainly true that a large number of individuals in university settings have been exposed to violence either prior to entering college or while at school (Fisher, Sloan, Cullen, & Lu, 1998). Precollege, violence exposure can include various forms of childhood maltreatment including neglect, physical abuse, and sexual abuse. Additionally, teenagers may experience emotional abuse or physical and sexual assaults at the hands of family members, acquaintances, strangers, or in the context of romantic relationships. The following section provides an overview of the prevalence rates of specific forms of violence in the United States. As college students are increasingly representative of the US residents, understanding the prevalence of exposure to violence prior to college and while in college are both important.

Child Maltreatment

Child Maltreatment as defined by the Center for Disease Control is "any recent act or failure to act on the part of a parent or caretaker which results in death, serious physical or emotional harm, sexual abuse or exploitation or an act or failure to act which presents an imminent risk of serious harm." (*Child Maltreatment Fact Sheet*, 2008) The CDC provides definitions for four specific types of child maltreatment: neglect, physical, sexual and emotional abuse (*Child Maltreatment Fact Sheet*, 2008). Neglect is defined as the failure to meet a child's basic needs, which include housing, food, clothing, education, and access to medical care and is the most common form of child abuse. The second most common form of maltreatment is physical abuse, which is characterized by physically injurious behavior directed toward a child in the form of hitting, kicking, shaking, burning, or other direct or indirect means of showing force. Sexual abuse is defined as engaging a child in a sexual act including fondling, rape, and/or exposing a child to other sexual activities. Finally, the fourth category of child maltreatment, emotional abuse, is characterized by behaviors that harm a child's self-worth or emotional well-being and include behaviors such as name calling, shaming, rejection, withholding love, and threatening. Reports of emotional abuse can be difficult to interpret due to the subjective nature of the concept.

According to the U.S. Department of Health and Human Services, (*Child Maltreatment*, 2006) there were three million reported cases of alleged child abuse or neglect over a period of twelve months (October 1, 2005 through September 30, 2006) concerning over six million children. It was estimated that 905,000 children were victims of child abuse or neglect in the year 2006 (48.2% were boys and 52.5% were girls). This translates into a 12.1 cases per thousand children. Of these 905,000 children, 64.1% experienced neglect, 16.0% experienced physical abuse, 8.8% experienced sexual abuse, and 6.6% experienced emotional abuse. An important takeaway message is that apparently high functioning college students may very well bring with them to college a history of childhood maltreatment.

While these data are useful in understanding the prevalence rates of child abuse and neglect in the general population of the United States, prevalence rates of student victimization are much harder to pinpoint. According to Witchel (1991), it appears that between 19 and 34% of college students have been the victim of childhood sexual abuse. While rates of sexual abuse and incest have frequently been the topic of discussion and research, research suggests that physical abuse, emotional abuse, and neglect are equally damaging, occur more frequently, and should become a focus of further in-depth study (Dunn, 1995).

In a longitudinal study of college women, Graves, Sechrist, White and Paradise (2005) found that 49.6% of college women had been physically abused and 28.4% had been sexually abused at some time during their childhood or adolescence. In a sample of 313 college aged women, Feerick and Haugaard (1999) found that 15% reported a history of childhood physical abuse and 21% reported a history of childhood sexual abuse. The prevalence rates of sexual abuse found in these studies are comparable to that found by Witchel (1991), indicating a somewhat stable trend over the course of a decade.

Intimate Partner Violence

According to the Center for Disease Control, intimate partner violence, many times referred to as domestic abuse or violence, can be subdivided into four categories (*Intimate Partner Violence Fact Sheet*, 2006). These categories include physical abuse, sexual abuse, threats, and emotional abuse. Physical abuse is defined as deliberately hurting one's intimate partner whether by kicking, hitting, burning, or other physical force. Sexual abuse refers to forcing a partner to take part in a sex act when one is non-consenting. Emotional abuse is defined as "threatening a partner or his or her possessions or loved ones, or harming a partner's sense of self-worth." Common examples of emotional abuse include stalking, name-calling, intimidation, or not letting a partner see his or her friends and/or family. Finally, intimate partner abuse in the form of threat refers to using words, gestures, or weapons to indicate to one's partner the desire or ability to initiate physical or sexual violence.

The National Violence Against Women Survey (Tjaden & Thoennes, 2000) concluded that nearly 25% of surveyed women and 7.6% of surveyed men said they were raped and/or physically assaulted by a current or former spouse, cohabiting partner, or date at some point in their lifetime; 1.5 percent of surveyed women and 0.9 percent of surveyed men said they were raped and/or physically assaulted by a partner in the previous 12 months. Prevalence rates of intimate partner violence in the general population have been studied extensively over the past few decades, as the stigma associated with reporting domestic violence has dissipated. However, studies pertaining to specific populations, such as college students, have only recently emerged.

In a study of undergraduate college students, rates of violence (victimization and perpetration) were assessed for male and female students before and during college. In this study, 42.1% of the polled students reported victimization at some point during their lives, with exactly half of these individuals reporting that the victimization occurred at the hands of an intimate partner. Victimization was subdivided into three categories, emotional, physical, and sexual abuse. All forms of abuse were more common before entering college, with 21.1% of undergraduate men and women reporting some form of emotional abuse before entering college. Students reported rates of 12.0% for physical abuse and 11.8% for sexual abuse during college, with more than half of these reported victimizations perpetrated by an intimate partner (Forke, Meyers, Catallozzi, & Schwarz, 2008).

The prevalence and severity of intimate partner violence (domestic violence) has been examined in college students. Gryl, Stith, and Bird (1991) assessed the rates of expressed or sustained violence in current relationships of college students. They found that 32.5 % of college students (men = 38.7%; women = 27.6%) had been the victim of intimate partner violence. Types of behaviors included pushing, shoving, wrestling, slapping, punching, kicking, or "other" forms.

The most comprehensive data on the annual prevalence of intimate partner violence come from surveys conducted by the American College Health Association assessing college student health (ACHA-NCHA) in 2005 and 2006 (American College Health Association, 2005, 2007). The data from these two surveys are fairly consistent and only the most recent data will be presented. In this survey, 94,806 current college students were asked about the occurrence and types of abusive relationships experienced in the past school year. Annual prevalence was highest for emotional abuse (females = 13.9%, males = 9.0%) followed by physical abuse (females = 2.1%, males = 1.4%) and sexual abuse (females = 1.7%, males = 1.1%).

Sexual Assault

Sexual assault, as defined by The National Center for Victims of Crime (NCVC, 2008), includes victimization in the form of rape or attempted rape, any unwanted sexual contact, or the threat of sexual contact or rape. Included in this definition is the notion that sexual assault can be perpetrated by strangers, acquaintances, intimate partners, friends, or family members. Rape is typically the most researched aspect of sexual assault, and as such, prevalence rates are significantly easier to locate than prevalence rates of unwanted sexual contact or threat of such contact. According the Federal Bureau of Investigation's Uniform Crime Report (2005), in 2005, 94,635 individuals reported to their local law enforcement that they had been the victim of a rape. Of course, as mentioned in the discussion of the *Clery Act*, this figure does not accurately reflect the actual numbers of completed rapes, as individuals who have been the victim of a rape are statistically less likely than victims of other crimes to report such an act. While both males and females can be the victims of sexual assault, research conducted by the U.S. Department of Justice, Bureau of Justice Statistics, found that between the years of 1992 and 2000 females were drastically more affected by sexual assault than males, accounting for over 90% of all attempted and completed rapes.

In a study of college women Graves et al. (2005) found that 28.4% of female participants had been sexually victimized in adolescence. Adolescence was defined as the period of life between 14 years old and the age at which each female first entered college. Unfortunately, Graves et al. did not assess whether the perpetrator was a stranger, a friend, an intimate partner, or a family member or caregiver. Thus, it is difficult to know whether individual women in this study should be considered victims of child sexual abuse or sexual assault.

Several nationally representative studies have examined rape prevalence among college students. The National College Risk Health Risk Behavior Survey (Brener, McMahon, Warren, & Douglas, 1999) sampled 4,838 college students and found that 20% of the women studied reported experiencing a rape, with 15% of those women reporting having been raped after the age of 15. Based on interviews designed after the National Crime Victimization Survey, which were conducted with 3,472 randomly selected students across 12 institutions, Fisher et al (1998) found considerably lower estimates. They found reported rates of rape (completed and attempted) of 4.0% on campus and 4.3% off campus. The reported rates of sexual assault (completed and attempted) on and off campus were 12.7% and 8.9% respectively. Fisher et al. go on to suggest that these figures may underestimate of the true prevalence of rape and sexual assault on college campuses. The items used to assess rape and sexual assaults were vague and the reference period (i.e., last 6-9 months) was shorter than previous studies.

The most comprehensive data on the annual prevalence of sexual assaults among college students come from the ACHA-NCHA surveys in 2005 and 2006 (American College Health Association, 2005, 2007). In the most recent survey, 94,806 current college students were asked about the occurrence and types of sexual assaults experienced in the past school year. Annual prevalence was highest for unwanted: sexual touching (females = 10.7%, males = 4.2%) followed by verbal threats of sex (females = 3.9%, males = 2.4%), attempted sexual penetration (females = 3.6%, males = 1.0%), and completed sexual penetration (females = 1.8%, males = 0.7%).

The data indicate that exposure to various forms of violence are fairly common both prior to entering college and while in college. In general population studies, both men and women frequently report being victims of some form of childhood maltreatment. Similarly, rates of domestic violence are quite high in the general population. Lastly, the prevalence of sexual assaults is extremely high with population prevalence estimates among typically approaching 25% when both attempted and completed sexual assaults are included. As noted by previous authors (Brener et al., 1999), college women are at particularly high risk for sexual assaults. Exposure to violence can result in a broad array of psychological, emotional, and developmental challenges. While universities have a tacit responsibility to protect students in the most effective ways possible, including adhering to the aforementioned *Clery Act*, there is no way to ensure that university students will not be exposed to some form of violence. As such, it is important to recognize variables that influence the ability of individuals to adequately cope with violence.

VARIABLES PREDICTIVE OF COPING WITH VIOLENCE

Cognitive Style

Cognitive style in general refers to generalized ways individuals think about the world and personal experiences. More to the point, cognitive style is significantly related to the way in which trauma victims perceive and react to the violent event. Clearly, the phrase cognitive style can be used to indicate a variety of cognitive tendencies. What follows is a brief overview of the topic that highlights three key cognitive variables: (1) cognitive flexibility, (2) rumination, and (3) attributional style when explaining adverse events. A cognitive style characterized by cognitive flexibility seems to play a moderating role in the future development of long-term negative consequences following exposure to a violent encounter (Quota, El-Sarraj, & Punamaki, 2001).

Cognitive rumination literally refers to 'chewing over' or thinking about the circumstances before, during, and following an adverse event. Rumination can be divided into two forms, "intrusive rumination" and "deliberate rumination" (Taku, Calhoun, Cann, & Tedeschi, 2008). Intrusive rumination is characterized by repetitive, negative, and *unwanted* thoughts that occur despite numerous attempts at avoidance. Those individuals with a propensity toward intrusive rumination are at increased risk for future development of depressive symptoms and anxiety following exposure to a violent or traumatic encounter (Phelps, Williams, Raichle, Turner, & Ehde, 2008). By contrast, deliberate rumination is characterized by *purposeful*, repetitive thoughts that tend to focus around a sense of struggle with the traumatic or violent event. Individuals with a propensity toward this form of rumination tend to fare much better (Phelps et al., 2008).

The third cognitive variable we will discuss is attributional style. When confronted with adverse life events, including violence, victims often search for explanations. Put in slightly different terms, victims search for someone or something to blame. This has been referred to as attributional style and there are individual differences in who or what people are likely to blame for adverse events (Abramson, Metalsky, & Alloy, 1989; Abramson, Seligman, & Teasdale, 1978). A cognitive style characterized by a tendency to make attributions that are internal, global and stable is predictive of depression and negative symptomatology following exposure to a trauma. For example, a victim of violence who concludes that she was victimized because she is dumb or unobservant would be at risk to develop symptoms post-event. These attributions are internal (she's saying that she is dumb/unobservant), global (she's not stating that her stupidity/inobservance is limited to a particular location or circumstance) and stable (she's not stating that her stupidity/inobservance is due to a transient set of circumstances). Consistent with this model, Gray, Pumphrey, and Lombardo (2003) found that individuals who were prone to evaluating negative events using internal, global, and stable attributions were more likely to develop posttraumatic stress disorder symptoms.

Relationship between Victim and Perpetrator

The nature of the violence experienced is also significantly related to the manner in which individuals subsequently cope with the experience. One variable related to the nature of the violent event is the relationship between the victim and the assailant. In a study of 790 rape victims Thornhill and Thornhill (1990) found that being raped by a stranger was the most psychological traumatizing. These results have been replicated by Gutner, Rizvi, Monson, and Resick (2006) in a study of 122 victims of a physical and/or sexual assault. Victims who did not know their assailants were more likely to report PTSD symptomatology and were less likely to have these symptoms improve over time. These findings can be difficult to understand in part because stranger assaults tend to be more violent than acquaintance assaults. In other words, relationship status is confounded with level of violence.

Summary of Adaptive Coping Strategies

While many contributing factors have been studied, some emphasis has been placed on the utilization of active coping strategies, which have proven effective in decreasing PTSD symptomotology following a trauma. Active coping strategies include those strategies which seek to change how one thinks or feels about the traumatic or violent occurrence. Active strategies can include, cognitive restructuring, emotional expression, and seeking social support (Gutner et al., 2006), redefining the event, finding meaning in the trauma, changing one's behaviors, and/or focusing on self-blame (Janoff-Bulman, 1985, 1992). Conversely, avoidant strategies, including social withdrawal, dissociation, and problem-solving avoidance tend to be linked to less successful coping and greater risk for the development of PTSD (Gutner et al., 2006). Gutner et al. (2006) interviewed 122 women who had been physically or sexually assaulted to identify successful coping strategies used after the assault. Women who withdrew socially following an assault (an avoidant strategy), were significantly more likely to report an increase in PTSD symptoms. Additionally, the active coping strategy of emotional expression was related to a decrease in PTSD symptomatology (Gutner et al., 2006).

CONCLUSIONS AND RECOMMENDATIONS

While college campuses are not hotbeds for violence exposure there is a clear sense that institutions of higher education have a higher duty to inform and ultimately protect students. This is certainly embodied in the concept of *in loco parentis*. Parents send their children to college with an explicit belief that they will be educated and protected. As tragically illustrated by the case of Laura Dickinson, at times this trust is violated. While the *Clery Act* represents an attempt to protect students by increasing access to information on the prevalence and types of campus crimes, compliance is uneven at best and the data presented are virtually guaranteed to be an inaccurate representation of campus violence.

Critically important in successful coping with violence are individual cognitive and emotional resources. These resources include: (1) a flexible cognitive style, (2) a deliberate rumination style characterized by *purposeful*, repetitive thoughts that tend to focus around a sense of struggle with the traumatic or violent event, and (3) attributions for causality that are external, unstable, and specific. Of course, institutions can not control these variables so what can they control? The clear answer is access to more accurate information and access to adequate counseling resources on campus are no doubt essential to successful coping.

Regarding the first issue, colleges would be advised to exceed the *Clery Act* mandates and provide students with prevalence estimates based not only on UCR-styled data but also on probability surveys of their institution. This should become a routine part of the institutional evaluation process. Institutions choosing to participate in the annual ACHA-NCHA survey have access to both institutional data and comparative national data. Student exposure to violence should be systematically tracked throughout their academic career. College samples are unique in that all members in the universe of consideration can be enumerated and sampled at random. This sampling methodology has certain advantages over stratified and/or clustered samples (West, 2008).

Regarding the second issue, colleges have a responsibility for providing adequate access to well-trained mental health professionals with specific training in the assessment and treatment of victims of violence. The International Association of Counseling Services has established accreditation guidelines for university and college counseling services. Minimum staffing guidelines include a staff to student ratio of 1 therapist to 1,000 to 1,500 students. Thus, a counseling agency responsible for providing all counseling and assessment services for a university with 24,000 students should have between 16 and 24 full-time therapists. This staffing ratio will allow agencies to adhere to other accreditation guidelines (e.g., maximum of 65% of time devoted to direct contact, opportunities for continuing education, outreach to campus, which could be used to present information on crime/victimization).

REFERENCES

Abramson, L. Y., Metalsky, G. I. & Alloy, L. B. (1989). Hopelessness depression: A theory-based subtype of depression. *Psychological Review*, *96*, 358-372.

Abramson, L. Y., Seligman, M. E. P. & Teasdale, J. (1978). Learned helplessness in humans: Critique and reformulation. *Journal of Abnormal Psychology*, *87*, 49-74.

American College Health Association. (2005). American college health association national college health assessment (ACHA-NCHA) Spring 2005 reference group data report (Abridged). *Journal of American College Health, 55(1)*, 195-205.

American College Health Association. (2007). American college health association national college health assessment spring, 2006 reference group data report (Abridged). *Journal of American College Health, 55(4)*, 195-205.

Athens, L. (2005). Violent encounters: Violent engagements, skirmishes, and tiffs. *Journal of Contemporary Ethnography, 34(6)*, 631-678.

Bauer v. Kincaid, 759 F. Supp. 575 (W.D. Mo. 1991).

Brener, N. D., McMahon, P. M., Warren, C. W. & Douglas, K. A. (1999). Forced sexual intercourse and associated health risk behaviors among female college students in the United States. *Journal of Consulting and Clinical Psychology, 67*, 252-259.

Bromely, M. L. (1995). Comparing campus and city crime rates: A descriptive study. *American Journal of Police, 14(1)*.

Campus Communications v. Criser, 9 Fla. Supp. 2d 97 (Fla. 8th cir. 1986).

Chase, K. A., O'Leary, K. D. & Heyman, R. E. (2001). Categorizing partner-violent men within the reactive-proactive typology model. *Journal of Consulting and Clinical Psychology, 69*, 567-572.

Child Maltreatment. (2006). Retrieved December 1, 2008. from http://www.acf.hhs.gov/programs/cb/pubs/cm06/cm06.pdf.

Child Maltreatment Fact Sheet. (2008). Retrieved December 1, 2008. from http://www.cdc.gov/ncipc/pub-res/cmfactsheet.pdf.

Crick, N. (1996). The role of over aggression, relational aggression, and prosocial behavior in the predition of children's future social adjustment. *Child Development, 67*, 2317-2327.

Crick, N. & Dodge, K. A. (1994). A review and reformulation of social information processing mechanisms in children's social adjustment. *Psychological Bulletin, 115(74-101)*.

Crick, N. & Grotpeter, J. K. (1995). Relational aggression, gender, and social-psychologcal adjustment. *Child Development, 66*, 710-722.

Feerick, M. M. & Haugaard, J. J. (1999). Long-term effects of witnessing marital violence for women: The contribution of childhood physical and sexual abuse. *Journal of Family Violence, 14(4)*, 377-398.

Fisher, B. S., Cullen, F. T. & Turner, M. G. (2000). *The sexual victimization of college women.* Retrieved December, 1, 2008. from http://www.ncjrs.gov/pdffiles1/nij/182369.pdf.

Fisher, B. S., Daigle, L. E., Cullen, F. T. & Turner, M. G. (2006). Reporting sexual victimization to the police and others: Results from a national-level study of college women. In C. R. Bartol & A. M. Bartol (Eds.), *Current perspectives in forensic psychology and criminal justice* (pp. 149-159). Thousand Oaks, CA: US: Sage Publications.

Fisher, B. S., Hartman, J. L., Cullen, F. T. & Turner, M. G. (2002). Making campuses safer for students: The Clery Act as symbolic legal reform. *Stetson Law Review, 32(1)*, 61-89.

Fisher, B. S., Sloan, J. J., Cullen, F. T. & Lu, C. (1998). Crime in the ivory tower: The level and sources of student victimization. *Criminology, 36(3)*, 671-710.

Forke, C. M., Meyers, R. K., Catallozzi, M. & Schwarz, D. F. (2008). Relationship violence among female and male college undergraduate students. *Archives of Pediatric and Adolescent Medicine, 162(7)*, 634-641.

Graves, K. N., Sechrist, S. M., White, J. W. & Paradise, M. J. (2005). Intimate partner violence perpetrated by college women within the context of a history of victimization. *Psychology of Women Quarterly, 29*, 278-289.

Gray, M. J., Pumphrey, J. E. & Lombardo, T. W. (2003). The relationship between dispositional pessimistic attributional style versus trauma-specific attributions and PTSD symptoms. *Journal of Anxiety Disorders, 17*, 289-303.

Gryl, F. E., Stith, S. M. & Bird, G. W. (1991). Close dating relationships among college students: Differences by use of violence and by gender. *Journal of Social and Personal Relationships, 8(243-264).*

Gutner, C. A., Rizvi, S. L., Monson, C. M. & Resick, P. A. (2006). Changes in coping strategies, relationship to the perpetrator, and posttraumatic distress in female crime victims. *Journal of Traumatic Stress, 19(6)*, 813-823.

The Handbook for Campus Crime Reporting. (2005). Retrieved December 1, 2008. from http://www.ed.gov/admins/lead/safety/handbook.pdf.

Hess, N. H. & Hagen, E. H. (2006). Sex differences in indirect aggression: Psychological evidence from young adults. *Evolution and Human Behavior, 27(3)*, 231-245.

Intimate Partner Violence Fact Sheet. (2006). Retrieved December 1, 2008. from http://www.cdc.gov/ncipc/dvp/ipv_factsheet.pdf.

Janoff-Bulman, R. (1985). The aftermath of victimization: Rebuilding shattered assumptions. In C. R. Figley (Ed.), *Trauma and its wake: The study and treatment of post-traumatic stress disorder.* New York: Brunner/Mazel.

Janoff-Bulman, R. (1992). *Shattered assumptions: Towards a new psychology of trauma.* New York, NY: Free Press.

Karjane, H. M., Fisher, B. S. & Cullen, F. T. (2002). Campus sexual assault: How America's institutions of higher education respond, *Final Report, NIJ Grant #1999-WA-VX-0008.* Newton, MA: Educational Development Center, Inc.

Long, B. (2007). Executive summary of the report of the independent investigation into Eastern Michigan University's response to the death of student Laura Dickinson. Retrieved December 1, 2008, from http://www.emich.edu/regents/Butzel_Long_investigation/BL_execsum.pdf

McCann, I. L., Sakheim, D. K. & Abrahamson, D. J. (1988). Trauma and victimization: A model of psychological adaptation. *The Counseling Psychologist, 16*, 531-594.

Menard, J. (2007, May 10). EMU slaying probe reopens wounds: Loved ones struggle to cope with loss of student amid investigation of school's handling of the case. *The Detroit News.*

Phelps, L. F., Williams, R. M., Raichle, K. A., Turner, A. P. & Ehde, D. M. (2008). The importance of cognitive processing to adjustment in the 1st year following amputation. *Rehabilitation Psychology, 53(1)*, 28-38.

Quota, S., El-Sarraj, E. & Punamaki, R. (2001). Mental flexibility as a resiliency factor among children exposed to political violence. *International Journal of Psychology, 36*, 1-7.

Sloan, J. J., Fisher, B. S. & Cullen, F. T. (1997). Assessing the Student-Right-to-Know and Campus Securty Acto of 1990: An analysis of the victim reporting practices of college and university students. *Crime and Delinquency, 43(2)*, 148-168.

Taku, K., Calhoun, L. G., Cann, A. & Tedeschi, R. G. (2008). The role of rumination in the coexistance of distress and posttraumatic growth among bereaved Japanese university students. *Death Studies, 32*, 428-444.

Teacher Beat in Classroom by a Student [Video]. (2008). Retrieved December 15, 2008, from http://www.youtube.com/watch?v=xyAhbbjaZ34&feature=related

Thornhill, N. W. & Thornhill, R. (1990). An evolutionary analysis of psychological pain folowing rape: II. The effects of stranger, friend, and family-member offenders. *Ethology and Sociobiology, 11(3)*, 177-193.

Tjaden, P. & Thoennes, N. (2000). *Extent, nature, and consequences of intimate partner violence: Findings from the national violence against women survey.* Retrieved December 1, 2008. from http://www.ncjrs.gov/pdffiles1/nij/181867.pdf.

University officials accused of covering up killing lose jobs. (2007, July 17). *The Washington Post.*

West, B. T. (2008). Statistical and methodological issues in the analysis of complex sample survey data: Practical guidance for trauma researchers. *Journal of Traumatic Stress, 21(5)*, 440-447.

Witchel, R. (1991). College student survivors of incest and other child sexual abuse. *New directions for Student Services, 54*, 63-76.

In: Violent Crime and Prisons: Population... ISBN: 978-1-60741-668-5
Ed: Aidan Renshaw and Emelina Suárez

Chapter 7

VIOLENT CRIME ON TELEVISION: CONTENT AND IMPACT

Amir Hetsroni *

The Department of Communication, Ariel University Center of Samaria, Israel
The Department of Communication, Yezreel Valley College, Israel

ABSTRACT

So profound is the belief in the potency of television to nurture crime, so that when asked to select measures that would significantly reduce violent crime, Americans choose restrictions on the presentation of crime and violence on television more frequently than they suggest firmer gun control regulations (Lichter, Lichter & Rothman, 1994, p.30).

This chapter will describe the presentation of violent crime on the home screen through the years. I will review the major findings of studies measuring the impact of viewing crime shows, go over the characteristics of people who are attracted to these programs, and talk about the public discourse regarding their impact on our society. Here are the sections of the chapter:

1. Theoretical frameworks to studying the contents and effects of TV crime
2. The presentation of violent crime on TV
3. The message of TV crime: Does it pay off and does it curb potential harmful effects off-screen?
4. The Audience of TV crime
5. Effects of TV crime on individuals and society
6. TV crime and public policy

AUTHOR'S BIO

Dr. Amir Hetsroni is a Senior Lecturer in the Department of Communication at Ariel University Center of Samaria and at Yezreel Valley College – both in Israel. He holds a Ph.D.

* Correspondence: 31 Erez St., Carmei Yosef, 99797, ISRAEL, Tel. 972-8-9286602; E-mail: amirhetsroni@gmail.com; amirh@yvc.ac.il

in communication from the Hebrew University of Jerusalem. His research concerning the presentation of sex, violence and death in popular TV programming and advertising and applications of cultivation theory and media system dependency theory to studying the effects of the presentation of these contents have appeared in journals such as *Journal of Communication*, *Journal of Advertising*, *Communication Monographs*, *Sex Roles* and others. He is co-author of the book *Sex differences: Summarizing more than a century of scientific research* (published by Routledge in 2008).

INTRODUCTION

Since the inception of commercial television broadcasting in the early 1950s, the home screen has been swept with a long line of screened and non-screened programs portraying violent crime. From the *Naked City* and the *Untouchables* in the 1950s and 1960s to the *Sopranos* and *Rescue 911* in the 1990s and 2000s, viewers have been exposed to excessive amounts of violent attacks, interpersonal and collective aggression, gunshots, gory images and even death (Roman, 2005). Even though the direct behavioral effect of prolonged routine exposure to TV violence is not conspicuously large by social science standards (see Bushman & Anderson, 2001; Paik & Comstock, 1994), the academic establishment, along with public figures and public opinion, have been treating the appearance of and the report on violent crime on television broadcasts as a serious problem. Three out of four Americans think that there is a relationship between violence on television and the national crime rate (Saad, 2007), and a majority of the public feel that television crime shows, violent films and television news items about crime contribute a lot to the seemingly high US murder rate (Potter, 2003). Epidemiologists have asserted that television violence is responsible for no less than 10,000 homicide cases in the USA alone (Centerwall, 1989). The late Senator John Pastore has argued that television violence is "a public health risk" (see Cole, 1996, p.15). Newton N. Minow, former Chairman of the Federal Communications Commission (FCC), the federal agency in charge of broadcasting regulation, said the following in a text selected by rhetoric experts as one the twenty-five speeches that changed the world:

> I invite you to sit down in front of your television set when your station goes on the air and stay there, for a day, without a book, without a magazine, without a newspaper, without a profit and loss sheet or a rating book to distract you. Keep your eyes glued to that set until the station signs off. I can assure you that what you will observe is a vast wasteland... mayhem, violence, sadism, murder, western bad men, western good men, private eyes, gangsters, more violence (Minow, 1961, cited in Minow & LaMay, 1999, p.95).

1. Theoretical Frameworks to Studying the Contents and Effects of TV Crime

The history of media research begins in the period leading up to World War II. Television was not yet present, but radio and cinema had a substantial grip in our culture, and raised the attention of sociologists, psychologists and criminologists, who questioned the amount of crime carried mostly by films and the impact of exposure to this mediated presentation of crime. Much of the scholarship exhibited concern about the consequences of this exposure (Lowery & DeFleur, 1995). A popular metaphor used in that period for the effect of media was "hypodermic needle", connoting the idea that the media inject messages to mass audiences that lack any power to resist (Lasswell, 1935). The content of messages gave another reason for concern, as even in those days the silver screen had already been saturated with crime and violence. Scholars were worried that if watching films in the theater house once or twice a week can be considerably influential – television might pose an immense risk (Lowery & DeFleur, 1995). However, a long series of studies, commencing in the 1950s, have acknowledged the fact that television's direct contribution to actual crime is very modest. Currently, the dominant paradigm in investigating the impact of media on crime emphasizes reality reconstruction, the idea that - more than being a direct cause of crime - television provides us with knowledge about crime and its context, and we act in light of this knowledge (Weimann, 2000). This paradigm contends that understanding of the world is gained by studying its shared meanings, which are not directly and entirely dependent on empirical validity, but are strongly influenced by the interaction with mediating sources of knowledge, which disseminate information. The main sources are personal experience, significant others (peers, family, friends, acquaintances) institutions and groups (school, unions, churches, virtual communities) and the mass media. The last construe a symbolic reality, which is not necessarily identical to the actual social reality. For example, only 2% of the people have a criminal record, but more than 10% of the protagonists in TV drama are criminals (Hetsroni & Tukachinsky, 2006). The mass media are the least influential source of knowledge, because people tend to believe their own eyes and count on their dear ones, before they attend to the media. However, in topics which are not highly familiar to the public at large, and when non-media sources depend on the media for gaining information – the role of the mass media in construing people's vision of the world increases (Ball-Rokeach & DeFluer, 1976). The media may also assist in legitimizing ways of handling life problems, such as crime. For example, the success of *Crime Stoppers* programs on television - shows that reward viewers for providing information that helps to catch criminals - can change the image of police informants from "tellers" to people who fulfill a civic duty (Pfuhl, 1992).

In sum, more than the media disperse crime or prevent crime, they make us aware that crime is either dispersed or prevented. This knowledge may guide our activities, but of course the media are not always a major guideline of human behavior.

2. The Presentation of Violent Crime on TV

With the exception of specialty news channels, most of the TV content that is carried by commercial broadcasters can be defined as "fictional-entertainment" (or "infotainment" in the case of some of the reality programs). Very soon after commercial broadcasting had taken off, researchers were already noticing the ubiquitous presence of crime in the medium's offerings. Even in the 1950s, when television was still epitomized by relatively innocent plotlines (Lichter et al., 1994), nearly one fifth of the protagonists in prime-time programs were criminals or law enforcers (Head, 1954; Smythe, 1954). These numbers, which are several times higher than comparable population figures, have persisted throughout the decades (Dominick, 1973; Maguire, 1988; Diefenbach & West, 2001).

Television drama has been introducing two types of criminals: The professional deviant who lives a life of crime and the established denizen who turns to crime to maintain or improve his standard of living (Lichter & Lichter, 1983). The first type enjoys non-recurring roles in police drama, courtroom drama and medical drama. His personality is rarely analyzed in depth, and his partaking in the program is mostly limited to his involvement in the crime scene. The second type of criminal has leading roles and multifaceted personality. His decision to choose crime as a profession constitutes a significant part of the plot and receives an explanation, if not a justification. A good example is the character of Toni Soprano in *The Sopranos* – a godfather who runs a criminal organization as a family business. The TV criminal of this type tends to belong to the upper or middle class. He is often presented as a businessman whose pursuit of profit leads to performing illegal actions.

In sharp contrast with reality – where convicted criminals over-represent people under the age of 25, and in particular young blacks – on television the vast majority of criminals are white males aged 30 to 40 years old (Lichter & Lichter, 1983; Brown, 2001). This over-representation of Caucasians in criminal roles sends, perhaps unintentionally, a somewhat utopian message about the behavioral nature of minorities.

Women are under-represented among TV felons, just as they are under-represented in the criminal population in the real world. While the ratio of males to females in leading and supporting roles in drama and comedy has been – according to different studies – approximately one to two (Greenberg & Collette, 1997; Greenberg, Simmons, Hogan & Atkin 1980), among criminal characters this ratio has fluctuated between one to ten (in 1968) and one to three. Over the decades, there was a slight increase in the share of female criminals, but this change is minor in size and does not conceal the lingering unequivocal message of popular TV programs: criminal behavior is not a viable option for women as it is for men (Hetsroni, 2007). This is part of a generally conservative worldview of gender roles, typical of popular programming, which finds expression in the portrayal of family life, occupations and child rearing (Greenberg & Collette, 1997).

In terms of occupation, television criminals are seldom identified in any way other than as criminals or law enforcers who crossed the line (Dominick, 1973). More than one third of the criminal characters are gangsters, thieves or own an organized crime network. Second in share, come law enforcers (policemen, lawyers etc.) who switched sides. Businessmen and free occupations e.g. doctors, architects make up the third major source of criminal characters (Lichter & Lichter, 1983). Blue collar occupants are rarely depicted as criminals, even though in the real world this group contributes abundantly to the population of thieves and unarmed robbers (Maguire, 1988). However, since petit crime is rarely seen on the screen, one can say that actually the exclusion of blue collar occupants from the pool of criminal protagonists is realistic in its way. Economically speaking, TV criminals tend to be rich people: From boss Hogg in *Dukes of Hazzard* in the 1970s to Toni Soprano in *The Sopranos* in the 2000s not much as changed on television content (Roman, 2005), which continues to contradict real world statistics according to which most of the criminals are of the lowest economic tires (Lichter & Lichter, 1983; Maguire, 1988). The twisted racial-economic TV portrayal of criminals stretches on to convicts: Prison cells in TV drama are full of older rich white males, while in the real world many inmates are poor young blacks. One aspect where the TV picture does resemble the real world is the tendency towards recidivism in criminality: Most of the people who are arrested on the screen, just like most of the people who are arrested by the police, have been arrested before (Lichter & Lichter, 1983).

Crime on television is carefully contemplated in 60% of the cases. Greed, revenge and mental illness serve as primary motives (Lichter et al., 1994). It is difficult to compare this finding with real world statistics, since there is no official notation of criminal motivations for all crimes. However, the FBI does publish statistics regarding motives and circumstances surrounding homicides. On television, murders are meticulously planned, whereas in real life murder is most often a crime of passion, a result of momentary annoyance such as reaction to hostile argument (Surrete, 1998). As for the victims of TV criminals – they are portrayed as passive and helpless with an over-representation of white people in general and young white females in particular. This demography resembles the viewers' fear of being subject to crime more than it represents actual victimization risk (Scheingold, 1984).

What are the crimes that are most often depicted in TV drama? Table 1 summarizes the most frequent crimes according to different studies.

While the numbers have fluctuated over the years, murder is a highly frequent crime across the board and property crime is a rare occurrence. This contradicts official statistics, which point at property crime, particularly theft and larceny, as the most frequently reported crime, subject to over 80% of the cases known to the police (Maguire, 1988). The implied message to viewers is that violent crime (murder, armed robbery, aggravated assault) and not property crime is what people face more often in daily life.

Table 1. The Most Frequent Crimes in TV Drama.

Crime	Dominick (1973)	Lichter & Lichter (1983)	Maguire (1988)	Brown (2001)
Homicide	22%	24%	48%	79%
Armed Robbery	6%	18%	2%	3%
Aggravated Assault	29%	8%	12%	6%
Rape	0%	2%	1%	1%
Fraud/White collar crime	6%	3%	1%	0%
Theft and non-violent property crime	0%	5%	1%	2%

News programs present a picture of crime that bears a lot of similarities to what is shown in fictional programming, but the news has few unique nuances. Just as in drama, the news, too, present homicide as the most frequent crime, but in contrast with drama the news present a somewhat larger share of white collar crime (often in relation to political scandals) and sensational sex related crime (Sheley & Ashkins, 1981). A distinctive example of sensational coverage of crime, which packs together politics and sex, is the New York State governor Elliot Spitzer use of escort service and his alleged use of campaign money to pay for the service. In 2008, this affair took an unprecedented share of local and national news airtime, although the crime itself was classified as no more than misdemeanor in the eyes of the law. The extensive coverage of sensational crime has to do with its rarity, as the media prefer to report on the unusual and leave the expected out of the screen. Murder makes up only 0.2% of the crime known to the police, but it is the subject of more than a quarter of crime news stories, because it is dramatic and infrequent (Graber, 1980; Surette, 1998).

Crime journalism is torn between two models of operation: The *market model* and the *manipulative model*. Both models screen, process and present information according to its news worthiness, and both of them construe the news magazine in a way that emphasizes recent news and leaves an impression of thematic consonance between the items. However, while in the market model newsworthiness is determined largely by public interest and journalists act as objective reporters, in the manipulative model stories are selected not according to public interest but according to the interests of PR (public relations) agencies that purposefully use the media to shape public opinion in order to meet the needs of their clients (Tuchman, 1972). Of course, the police and the justice system put efforts to publish "success stories". This increases the chances of resolved crime stories to get published. These stories are prepackaged by PR agencies, so that the broadcaster's task in assembling the report is minimal. In broadcasters' jargon such stories receive the unflattering title "garbage crime". They are aired only when the station has nothing better to air (Surette, 1998). At a higher level, we find news stories that report on crime, where noted public figures and celebrities are involved, either as offenders or as victims. To cover these stories, termed "OJ felonies" (in the name of O.J. Simpson), journalists search for additional information, beyond what is supplied by the police, the defense attorney etc. Thus, the news reporter becomes a significant *gatekeeper* of information (Berkowitz, 1990). Overall, most of the crime remains unreported: in a study of local news, only 15 of 1,741 felonies investigated by the police over a three month period were mentioned in the news (Fedler & Jordan, 1982). Nonetheless, crime and justice items still make up a prominent share of the news – ten to fifteen percent in local news programs and around 20% national news magazines (Graber, 1980).

The typical treatment of crime does not refer to it as “a social problem” but covers criminal incidents as discrete events. Thus, the implied message is that responsibility for committing the crime resides almost exclusively with the individual criminal (Surette, 1998). Who are the criminals according to crime news? Like in entertainment programming, crime news bring to fore greedy businessman as perpetrators of white collar crime, and present professional predators and organized crime moguls as responsible for violent transgression of the law, but in contrast with TV drama - the news frequently present bureaucrats and civil servants as criminals who breech public trust (Terry, 1984). The most ignored group of criminals in TV news are poor young men, who do not belong to any criminal organization but do commit property crime which is sometimes violent but more often not (Surette, 1998). The victims, according to television crime news, tend to be females, who are considerably young or exceptionally old, and/or of high social status. This mode of portrayal, which contradicts real life circumstances, where most of the victims of violent crime are males, assists in construing a narrative of crime as an intended action in of strong men to exert power on physically weak women (Meyers, 1994).

The criminal justice system is described mostly as a punitive organization. Since crime is presented as an individual choice, the function of the system is to punish the sinners and correct the deviants. The system is evaluated according to its success in doing so, namely changing the criminal habits of individuals (Graber, 1980).

Finally, a new sub-genre, infotainment, which emerged in the 1990s, blurs the line between news magazines and entertainment programming. Shows such as *Cops* and *Rescue 911* present actual crimes in a realistic light - sometimes in reenactments, sometimes as dramatized stories, and sometimes in documentary-style stories. These programs tend to concentrate on bizarre violent crime, and present stereotypical portraits of predatory evil criminals and helpless victims. The gruesome is shown as the mainstay of modern life

(Jermyn, 2006). The content of these shows is often an over-exaggeration of crime drama, but the apparent realism makes it more credible.

3. The Message of TV Crime: Does It Pay off and Does It Curb Potential Harmful Effects Off-Screen?

Does crime pay? Statistically speaking, the answer in the real world is commonly yes, since around two thirds of the cases reported to the police remain unresolved. Television is a totally different sphere. On the screen, nearly 60% of the crimes are solved (Lichter & Lichter, 1983). The juridical procedure in the real world is a multi-step saga, where many of the phases are less than dramatic, and where most of the cases end in a non-ceremonial deal between the prosecution and the defense. Television concentrates on cases that do reach a verdict, and highlights the more dramatic phases of the juridical procedure. In past decades, episodes of police or courtroom drama nearly always ended in a conviction of the criminal. Current programs such as *Law and Order* and *Boston Legal* do leave an open-end from time to time, or let the criminal sneak out unpunished (Roman, 2005), but the conviction rate of TV criminals remains impressively high. This sends a clear message to the audience: Crime does not pay off, since law enforcers put things in order (Stark, 1987). Here is the place to emphasize: While crime shows and cop shows may be about law and order, in practice they are light on law and heavy on order (Lichter et al., 1994). This tone has led to a number of concerns about the message and its implications. On the one hand, concerns are about unrealistic expectations that viewers may develop about the ability of the police; on the other hand, the programming' dismissal of negative police behaviors such as overuse of guns and lack of consideration of detainees' rights may encourage disregard of human rights in the name of security (Surette, 1998). Generally, the media portray the justice system as a malfunctioning organization, saved occasionally by lonesome heroes (attorneys, private detectives, police officers) whose actions go against the mainstream. However, paradoxically, it is the presentation of the justice system as malfunctioning that encourages expectations for harsh punishment as the only effective way to avoid dealing with the same criminals once and again (Bortner, 1984).

Does this "moral lesson" to the viewers have an impact on potential criminals as well? Since evidence from laboratory experiments shows that violent behavior can be learned through observational imitation of behavior shown on the screen (Bandura, 1994), it makes sense that the message repeatedly transmitted in crime drama will have a curbing effect on the tendency to commit crimes, but evidence from the real world is weak and inconsistent. Studies of inmates have failed to detect a heavy diet of violent media among felons convicted of violent crime (Goldstein, 1973). The offenders themselves seldom cite the media as a motivating source for their actions, but they do mention television as a source of information about crime techniques, although not in great frequency (Pease & Love, 1984). *Copycat* offenses, which are one to one imitations of crimes that had been reported in the media a short while before the commission of the acts, that some see as a direct media effect, are actually very rarely linked to the media – when examined from the criminals' perspective (Heller & Polsky, 1976). Naturally, we cannot entirely rule out the possibility that criminals are unaware that their behavior actually imitates TV presentations of similar acts, but at the conscious level the "lessons" taught by television about crime have no considerable effect on criminals' willingness and tendency to commit a crime in the real world.

4. The Audience of TV Crime

Since exposure to the media is a prerequisite for any media effect, the following section is dedicated to describing the viewership of crime programs and to analyzing the place of these shows in the stations' lineup.

Figure 1 shows the percent of crime drama and action-adventure programming that depict crime and law enforcement in the prime-time lineup of the major networks (ABC, CBS, NBC, FOX) between 1970 and 2006. The classification of the programs is based on descriptions appearing the TV Guide directory (TV Guide, 2006).

On average, over the years, about 20-25% of all prime-time shows have focused on crime and law enforcement. There were two golden eras - the mid 1970s, when police drama such as *Starskey & Hutch* and *Kojak* and action-adventure series like *Charlie's Angels* and *Dukes of Hazard* were major staples of prime-time, and the mid 1980s, when the *A-Team* adventures and *Magnum P.I.* investigations dominated the airwaves, but the overall pattern points at a rather steady presence of crime programming with periodical ebb and flow. This pattern fits media researchers' view of the popularity of the TV genre as a process initiated when the success of a specific program brings about the production of copycats, until the public becomes fed up with the lookalikes. It is then that a different genre emerges as popular, and so on and on with a limited number of genres that interchangeably switch roles in leading the programming (Comstock & Scharrer, 1999).

Rating wise, over the years, crime dramas have not been among the industry's most notable blockbusters, nor were they considered to be the most enjoyed programs in the eyes of the general public (Diener & DuFour, 1978). Partly, the reason for that could be the scheduling of crime drama in the later part of the prime-time slot (10pm - 11pm), when many viewers are already sleeping and others are excruciatingly tired. However, this scheduling is not arbitrary. On the one hand, it is a political gesture, on the part of the broadcasters, to please conservative lobby groups, who oppose screening violent programming at an earlier hour, when young children are watching (Signorielli, 2005); on the other hand, it is an effective economic move in light of the characteristics of the genre's viewership: men above the age of 50 or in the age bracket of 18-24, often high school or college dropouts, and frequently blacks (Comstock, Chaffee, Katzman, McCombs & Roberts, 1978). Economically speaking, this cluster does not constitute the most sought for population, but programs that attract these viewers are nonetheless desired by advertisers, who target young males and elderly men, particularly in light of the fact that the audience for most of the non-violent successful TV programs is dominated by middle aged women (Comstock & Scharrer, 1999). The distinctive demographic composition of crime drama viewership can explain the lingering presence of the genre on the small screen despite moderate ratings. It can also explicate why crime drama is regarded a niche product in the universe of popular programming. The niche status has even been strengthened recently with the proliferation of cable channels such as *Spike*, which target less-educated males and concentrate on crime programming.

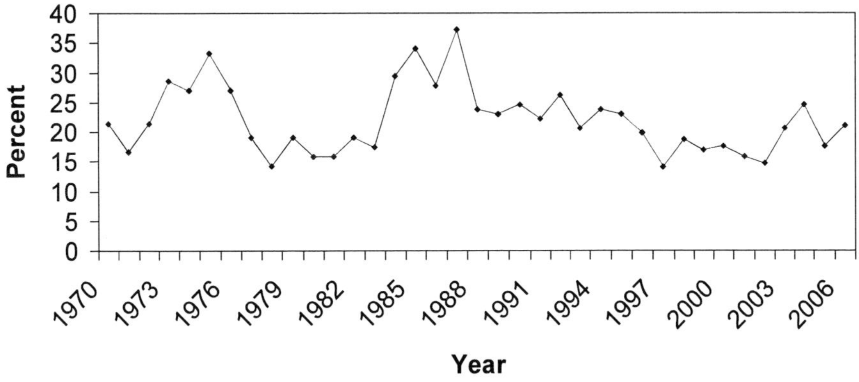

Figure 1. Percent of Network Prime-Time Programs featuring Crime.

5. Effects of TV crime on individuals and society

The surreptitious and unexpected nature of crime in the real world makes isolating and assessing the direct impact of single factors, such as television, impractical in most of the cases. As a result of that, most of the conclusions regarding the influence of television on crime level are indirect, historical or derived from artificial laboratory experiments. A popular approach among researchers is to treat crime as an expression of violence, and to suggest that an intensive televised depiction of violence brings about aggression among the viewers (through observational learning), which in turn results in increased amounts of crime. This proposition suffers from a number of deficiencies. First, even though crime is routinely presented on television broadcasts, which target large numbers of viewers, and although these viewers normally have no alternative source that exposes them to such crime – in practice over 90% of the crime on the street is not violent and consists of offenses rarely shown on television. Evidence from historical aggregate crime rate studies indicates that the introduction of commercial broadcasting in the USA was associated with an immediate increase in the rate of property crime but not an increase of violent crime (Hennigan, Heath, Wharton, Del-Rosario, Cook & Calder, 1982). One study was able to point at an increase in the level of violent crime – but only 10 to 15 years after television was introduced (Centerwall, 1989). The author's suggestion that the criminals needed a number of years to absorb the message does not sound convincing, as he disregards a more plausible explanation that connects the rise in violent crime in America in the 1960s with the political turmoil of the era. Further shadow of doubt on the relationship between the level of violent crime in society and the depiction of violent crime on television is cast by the fact that the level of violent crime in America decreased steadily throughout the 1990s, even though violence remained present on the screen throughout the decade (Potter, 2003). Another study examined the patterns of 140,000 US homicides from 1973 to 1979, which took place before and after TV news reports about prizefights, murder acquittals, life sentences and executions, and found out that the number of homicides showed a significant increase several days after the TV report (Philips & Hensley, 1984). However, this research disregarded the fact that gang crime and homicides happen as ebb and flow due to factors such as gang rivalry and revenge that have nothing to do with the media. Furthermore, the effect detected in that study, although statistically significant, was very modest in size. This is typical of studies that assess the impact of TV crime on actual crime in the real world and are able to attribute no more than one percent of the variance to television viewing (Bushman & Anderson, 2001; Paik & Comstock, 1994). This pattern of very small effects casts a serious doubt on the practical significance of television as a cause of crime.

Laboratory experiments found greater effects, but they often used amateur films as stimuli and operationalized criminal intention as the willingness to administer an imaginary shock to a research confederate - a twisted definition by all means. Furthermore, even lab studies revealed that televised depictions of violence do not affect all the viewers in the same way. A number of factors – from momentary frustration to hypermasculine personality - play into the media's effect (Comstock, 1983).

Only one mass-scale work took a longitudinal approach. Eron and Huesmann (1980) surveyed young people in two different time periods: when they were nine years old and when they were thirteen years old. The researchers detected a positive correlation between the kids' preference for violent programming, when were nine years old, and their violent behavior four years later, but they also found out a positive correlation between the kids' violent behavior in primary school and their violent behavior as teens. As a result of that, it is difficult to determine if the violence at a later life stage was caused by earlier media exposure, or whether the subjects' aggressive nature motivated them to act violently as teens and to consume violent media as kids. Even more perplexing is the lack of correlation between the teens' tendency to act violently and their media diet as adolescents.

Very few studies lab studies employed actual broadcasts as stimuli. A rare exception is the work of Liebert and Baron (1972), who assessed the effects of watching *The Untouchables* on the aggressive behavior of five to nine year old boys and girls. The researchers found out that – in comparison with kids who watched a non-violent film - the kids who watched the crime series were more willing to hurt other children. Yet, even here the operationalization of criminal intention through questionnaires seems notably artificial.

The despair from detecting behavioral effects of significant size that can be unequivocally ascribed to watching crime on television led the scientific community to look for a different kind of impact - the shaping of worldview and opinions. Given the emphasis television puts on violent crime, and since most of the Americans see violent crime as a serious problem that is becoming more and more severe (in contrast with what official statistical reveal - see Saad, 2007), it is not surprising that researchers were able to establish a significant correlation between perceiving violent crime as a serious problem and media consumption (Doppelt & Manikas, 1990). The most popular explanation of this correlation is provided by Gerbner's *cultivation theory*. According to Gerbner and his colleagues, television is a successful storyteller and most of its tales involve and revolve around violence and crime. Due to the ubiquitous role of television in our culture and the repetitive nature of the programs, there is – according to Gerbner – a uniform effect of seeing the world in TV eyes that increases in size as viewing increases. For instance, heavy television viewers are more likely than light viewers to think that 5% of the workforce is employed in law enforcement occupations, when the actual figure is around 1%. Television viewing inflicts the public to see the world as dangerous surroundings. This effect is empirically measured by the *mean world index* - a set of questions (Do you think most people would try to take advantage of you if they got a chance or would they try to be fair?"; "Would you say that most of the time people try to be helpful, or that they are mostly just looking out for themselves?"; Generally speaking, would you say that most people can be trusted or that you can't be too careful in dealing with people?), to which the answers elicited by heavy television viewers more often than by light viewers point at mistrust, fear and suspicion. Indeed, cultivation's greatest contribution to our knowledge about the impact of televised crime is not attributing criminal behavior to television viewing, but relating exposure to the programming to fear of crime (Gerbner, Gross, Morgan, Signorielli & Shanahan, 2002). Fear of crime pushes heavy viewers to support further spending on crime control despite their general reservation from expanding government expenditure (Dowler, 2003). Heavy viewing dilutes pre-existing differences between people who define themselves as liberals and persons who define themselves as conservatives and brings everyone to adopt a strict punitive view about crime. The dilution of pre-existing differences between viewers is called *mainstreaming* (Gerbner, Gross, Morgan & Signorielli, 1982). The main problem with cultivation, as with nearly all the attempts to point at significant effects of exposure to televised crime, is the small size of the effect: 1% of the variance (Potter, 1993). Another problem is that although the effect is robust to demographics and personality traits, it works better with general fears of crime is less able to account for specific worries (Heath & Gilbert, 1996).

6. TV Crime and Public Policy

Very early in the history of commercial broadcasting, politicians have expressed concern over TV portrayal of crime and commented that something ought to be done about this. In 1952, the Commerce Committee of the House of Representatives held the first political hearing on the subject – seeking to determine whether television programs contained offensive material or emphasized crime and violence. Throughout the next decade, several congressional and senate hearings followed, culminating in the conclusion that further research is needed to determine whether television viewing is dangerous to society and individuals (Donnerstein & Linz, 1995; Signorielli, 2005). However, for politicians and officers appointed to serve in the FCC, the answer appeared to be very simple:

> Millions of television receivers are pouring an unending stream of crime, violence, outright murder, brutality, unnatural suspense and horror into the living rooms of America... The suggestions that there is no discernible relationship between these programs and the recent appalling increase in juvenile delinquency, in my opinion, flout common sense (Testimony of FCC officer before the US Senate Judiciary Committee on Juvenile Delinquency in the United States, 1955 – cited in Surette, 1998, pp.116-117).

In the 1960s and 1970s, the US Surgeon General appointed two committees to scientifically investigate the relationship between TV violence and violence in American society. Both of the committees reached the conclusion that there is probably a connection between the two, but that relationship is not very strong and is heavily mitigated (Signorielli, 2005). The broadcasters have kept on claiming that the research findings are not conclusive, and that the study conditions are too artificial to bear enough resemblance to the real world (Donnerstein & Linz, 1995). No longstanding regulatory decision was made (Signorielli, 2005). In the 1980s, the political-public discourse regarding the operation of the TV industry revolved around market deregulation, and the issue of televised crime and violence was left mostly off the table. The 1990s saw renewal of the debate expressed in congressional and senate hearings and further research that eventually led the "advisories compromise", which became part of the *1996 Telecommunication Act*: According to this compromise, the broadcasters agreed to add marking advisories to violent programs that viewers can use as a guideline to avoid exposure to violent shows (Potter, 2003). This arrangement has been criticized both technically (suggesting that the advisories are not self explanatory) and substantially (suggesting that they may incite a forbidden fruit desire to see violence – especially among kids – see Kunkel, Farinola, Farrar, Donnerstein, Biely, & Zwarun, 2002). Nonetheless, politicians are still hesitant to enforce external censorship on the entertainment industry that covers them in news programming and to expurgate artistic expressions that are legally protected by the First Amendment.

As we just noticed, the ability of politicians to change the mode of presentation of crime on television is limited. Does it mean that television portrayal of crime is strong enough to have an impact on public policy? This issue has not been heavily investigated, but there is evidence that the answer can be positive in some cases. Any criminologist is familiar with the *echo effect* – the tendency of law enforcers to treat defendants in unpublicized cases harshly, if the media have been demanding such treatments for defendants in publicized cases (Surette, 1998). At the macro level, a study by Fishman (1978) has shown that extensive media coverage of crimes against the elderly resulted in the creation of new enforcement squads specializing in the protection of old people. The direct exposure of policy makers and law enforcers to the media makes them susceptible to direct influence, regardless of what public opinion has to say, but further research is needed to determine how sizable the impact of TV crime on public policy is.

REFERENCES

Ball-Rokeach, S. J. & DeFleur, M. L. (1976). A dependency model or mass-media effects. *Communication Research*, *3*, 3-21.

Bandura, A. (1994). Social cognitive theory of mass communication. In J. Bryant, & D. Zillman (Eds.), *Media effects: Advances in theory and research* (2nd edition) (pp. 61-90). Hillsdale, NJ: Lawrence Erlbaum.

Berkowitz, D. (*1990*). Refining the gatekeeping metaphor for local television news. *Journal of Broadcasting & Electronic Media*, *34(1)*, 55-68.

Bortner, M. A. (1984). Media images and public attitudes toward crime and justice. In R. Surette (Ed.), *Justice and the Media* (pp. 15-30). Springfield, IL: Thomas.

Brown, J. D. (2001). A comparison of fictional television crime and crime index statistics. *Communication Research Reports*, *18(2)*, 192-199.

Bushman, B. J. & Anderson, C. A. (2001). Media violence and the American public: Scientific facts versus media misinformation. *American Psychologist*, *56(6-7)*, 477-489.

Centerwall, B. S. (1989). Exposure to television as a risk factor for violence. *American Journal of Epidemiology*, *129*, 643-652

Cole, J. (1996). *The UCLA television violence monitoring report*. LA: UCLA Center for Communication Policy.

Comstock, G. (1983). Media influences on aggresson. In A. Goldstein, & L. Krasner (Eds.), *Prevention and control of aggression* (pp. 241-272). Elmsford, NY: Pergamon Press.

Comstock, G. & Scharrer, E. (1999). *Television: What's on, who's watching and what it means*. San Diego: Academic Press.

Comstock, G., Chaffee, S., Katzman, N., McCombs, M. & Roberts, D. (1978). *Television and human behavior*. NY: Columbia University Press.

Diefenbach, D. L. & West, M. D. (2001). Violent crime and Poisson regression: A measure and a method for cultivation analysis. *Journal of Broadcasting & Electronic Media, 45(3)*, 432-445.

Diener, E. & DuFour, D. (1978). Does television violence enhance program popularity? *Journal of Personality and Social Psychology, 36*, 333-341.

Dominick, J. R. (1973). Crime and law enforcement on prime-time television. *Public Opinion Quarterly, 37(2)*, 241-250.

Donnerstein, E. & & Linz, D. (1995). The media. In J. Q. Wilson, & J. Petersilia (Eds.), *Crime* (pp. 237-264). San Francisco: Institute for Contemporary Press.

Doppelt, J. & Manikas, P. (1990). Mass media and criminal justice decision making. In R. Surette (Ed.), *The media and criminal policy* (pp. 129-142). Springfield, IL: Thomas.

Dowler, K. (2003). Media consumption and public attitudes toward crime and justice: The relationship between fear of crime, punitive attitudes, and perceived police effectiveness. *Journal of Criminal Justice and Popular Culture, 10(2)*, 109-126.

Eron, L. D. & Huesmann, L. R. (1980). Adolescent aggression and television. *Annals of the New York Academy of Sciences, 347*, 319-331.

Fedler, F. & Jordan, D. (1982). How emphasis on people affects coverage of crime. *Journalism Quarterly, 17*, 474-478.

Gerbner, G., Gross, L., Morgan, M. & Signorielli, N. (1982). Charting the mainstream: Television's contributions to political orientations. *Journal of Communication, 32(2)*, 100-127.

Gerbner, G., Gross, L., Morgan, M., Signorielli, N. & Shanahan, J. (2002). Growing up with television: Cultivation processes. In J. Bryant, & D. Zillman (Eds.), *Media effects: Advances in theory and research* (2nd edition) (pp. 43-67). Hillsdale, NJ: Lawrence Erlbaum.

Goldstein, M. (1973). Exposure to erotic and violent stimuli and sexual deviance. *Journal of Social Issues, 29*, 197-219.

Graber, D. (1980). *Crime news and the public*. NY: Praeger.

Greenberg, B. S. & Collette, L. (1997). The changing faces on TV: A demographic analysis of network television's new seasons, 1966-1992. *Journal of Broadcasting & Electronic Media, 41(1)*, 1-13.

Greenberg, B. S., Simmons, K. W., Hogan, L. & Atkin, C. K. (1980). The demography of fictional TV characters. In B. S. Greenberg, *Life on television: Content analyses of U.S. TV drama* (pp. 99-128). Norwood, NJ: Ablex Publishing Corporation.

Head, S. W. (1954). Content analysis of television drama programs. *Quarterly of Film, Radio and Television, 9*, 175-194.

Heath L. & Gilbert, F. (1996). Mass media and fear of crime. *American Behavioral Scientist, 39(4)*, 379-386.

Heller, M. & Polsky, S. (1976). *Studies in violence and television*. NY: American Broadcasting Company.

Hennigan, K., Heath, L., Wharton, J. D., Del-Rosario, M. L., Cook, T. D. & Calder, B. J. (1982). Impact of the introduction of television on crime in the United States: Empirical findings and theoretical implications. *Journal of Personality and Social Psychology, 42(3)*, 461-477.

Hetsroni, A. (2007). Forty years of violent content on prime-time network programming: A longitudinal meta-analytic review. *Journal of Communication, 57(4)*, 759-784.

Hetsroni, A. & Tukachinsky, R. H. (2006). TV world estimates and real world estimates: A new scheme for cultivation. *Journal of Communication, 56(1)*, 133-156.

Jermyn, D. (2006). *Crimewatching: Investigating real crime TV.* London: IB Tauris.

Kunkel, D., Farinola, W. J. M., Farrar, K. M., Donnerstein, E., Biely, E. & Zwarun, L. (2002). Deciphering the V-chip: An examination of the television industry's program rating judgments. *Journal of Communication, 52(1)*, 112-138.

Lasswell, H. D. (1935). *World politics and personal insecurity: A contribution to political psychiatry*. NY: McGraw-Hill.

Lichter, L. S. & Lichter, S. R. (1983). *Prime time crime*. Washington, DC: Media Institute.

Lichter, S. R., Lichter, L. S. & Rothman, S. (1994). *Prime time: How TV portrays American culture*. Washington, DC: Regnery.

Liebert, R. M. & Baron, R. A. (1972). Short term effects of television aggression among institutionalized boys: Fact or artifact? In G. A. Comstock, E. A. Rubinstein, & J. P. Murray (Eds.), *Television and social behavior, Vol. 5: Television's effects – Further explorations* (pp. 351-358). Washington DC: Government Printing Office.

Lowery, S. A. & DeFleur, M. L. (1995). *Milestones in mass communication research: Media effects* (3rd edition). White Plains, NY: Longman.

Maguire, B. (1988). Image vs. reality: An analysis of prime-time television crime and police programs. *Crime and Justice, 11(1)*, 165-188

Meyers, M. (1994). News of battering. *Journal of Communication, 44*, 47-63.

Minow, N. & LaMay, C. (1999). *Abandoned in the wasteland: Children, television and the First Amendment*. NY: Hill and Wang.

Paik, H. & Comstock, G. (1994). The effects of television violence on antisocial behavior: A meta-analysis. *Communication Research, 21(4)*, 516-546.

Pease, S. & Love, C. (1984). The copycat crime phenomenon. In R. Surette (Ed.), *Justice and the Media* (pp. 199-211). Springfield, IL: Thomas.

Pfuhl, E. (1992). Crimestoppers: The legitimization on snitching. *Justice Quarterly, 9(3)*, 505-528.

Philips, D. & & Hensley, J. (1984). When violence is rewarded or punished: The impact of mass media stories on homicide. *Journal of Communication, 34(3)*, 101-116.

Potter, W. J. (1993). Cultivation theory and research: A conceptual critique. *Human Communication Research, 19*, 564-601.

Potter, W. J. (2003). *The 11 myths of media violence*. Thousand Oaks, CA: Sage.

Roman, J. (2005). *From daytime to primetime: The history of American television programs.* Westport, CT: Greenwood Press.

Saad, L. (2007. October 22). *Perceptions of crime problem remain curiously negative*. Retrieved December 13, 2008, from http://www.gallup.com/poll/102262/Perceptions-Crime-Problem-Remain-Curiously-Negative.aspx

Scheingold, S. (1984). *The politics of law and order*. White Plains, NY: Longman.

Sheley, J. & Ashkins, C. (1981). Crime, crime news and crime views. *Public Opinion Quarterly*, *45*, 492-506.

Signorielli, N. (2005). *Violence in the media: A reference handbook*. Santa-Barbara, CA: ABC-CLIO

Smythe, D. W. (1954). Reality as presented by television. *Public Opinion Quarterly*, *18*, 143-156.

Stark, S. (1987). Perry Mason meets Sonny Crocket: The history of lawyers and the police as television heroes. *University of Miami Law Review*, *42*, 229-283.

Surette, R. (1998). *Media, crime, and criminal justice: Images and realities* (2nd Edition), NY: Wadsworth Publishing.

Terry, W. (1984). Crime and the news: Gatekeeping and beyond. In R. Surette (Ed.), *Justice and the media* (pp. 31-50). Springfield, IL: Thomas.

Tuchman, G. (1972). Objectivity as strategic ritual. *American Journal of Sociology*, *77*, 660-679.

TV Guide (2006). *Guide to TV*. NY: Barnes & Noble Publishing.

Weimann, G. (2000). *Communicating unreality: Modern media and the reconstruction of reality*. Thousand Oaks, CA: Sage.

In: Violent Crime and Prisons: Population… ISBN: 978-1-60741-668-5
Ed: Aidan Renshaw and Emelina Suárez

Chapter 8

PSYCHOPATHY AND VIOLENCE: PARSING THE HETEROGENEITY OF AGGRESSION AND AGGRESSORS

Shayne Jones, James Ray and Casey Williams
University of South Florida, USA

ABSTRACT

Psychopathy is a construct that has been robustly linked to violent behavior. Yet, violence encompasses a wide variety of behaviors, which potentially masks more nuanced relationships. In this chapter, we review the theoretical and empirical literature between psychopathy and different manifestations of criminal behavior and aggression. In doing so, we demonstrate that psychopathic individuals are more likely to engage in (1) violent than non-violent criminal behavior and (2) both proactive and reactive types of aggression. These empirical findings are then discussed in the context of a recent theoretical development that explains these patterns. Finally, we discuss how a more detailed understanding of both individual characteristics and behavioral outcomes may yield more promising treatment approaches.

INTRODUCTION

The term violence is a heterogeneous construct. For example, in the criminal law, violent crimes include such disparate acts as murder, rape, assault, robbery, battery, and arson (United States Department of Justice, 2008). Although these crimes are categorized as violent, they are quite distinct and the specific categories are somewhat arbitrary from a theoretical standpoint. In addition, while most acts of violence are proscribed by the law, not all are. Thus, what is needed is a more encompassing construct that captures a fuller range of violent behavior that has some theoretical and empirical rationale that distinguishes among the various manifestations. One such construct is aggression. For instance, aggression is a more encompassing term, which includes not only the aforementioned criminal acts, but also acts that are not necessarily criminally proscribed. Buss and Perry (1992) suggested there are four manifestations of aggression – physical aggression, verbal aggression, anger, and hostility. In most cases, only physical aggression is legally prohibited. Crick and Grotpeter

(1995) identified relational aggression (purposefully damaging one's peer relationships and social standing through manipulation) as an important variant of aggressive behavior. Thus, aggression is a more nuanced, meaningful conceptualization that captures the breadth and variety of dangerous actions perpetrated by individuals.

In addition to the various manifestations of aggression, there may be unique underlying causes of such behaviors. Although numerous explanations have been advanced, one important factor that has been repeatedly linked to aggressive behaviors is psychopathy. Psychopathy is a personality disorder characterized by specific interpersonal, affective, and behavioral dimensions (Farrington, 2005). Importantly, psychopathic individuals engage in higher levels and more varieties of aggressive behavior than non-psychopathic individuals. This suggests that a more refined and complete understanding requires a focus on both the aggression and the aggressor.

This chapter explores these issues in-depth, with a focus on the following. First, the construct of psychopathy is thoroughly defined. Second, the literature linking psychopathy and aggression (including criminal behavior) is reviewed. Third, theoretical origins of this disorder are discussed, with a particular emphasis on how underlying neurological systems provide an explanation of why and how psychopathy is related to aggression. Finally, there will be a review of treatment of psychopathy. In the broadest sense, our goal is to demonstrate that parsing the heterogeneity of aggression and aggressors can yield invaluable insights that not only better explain aggression, but may lead to a reduction in such behavior.

Psychopathic Personality Disorder

Psychopathy is a personality disorder characterized by specific interpersonal, affective, and behavioral deficits. One of the most widely used and respected instruments designed to assess psychopathy is the Psychopathy Checklist-Revised (PCL-R; Hare, 2003), which possesses a two-factor structure, comprised of four facets. Factor 1 represents the interpersonal and affective features of psychopathy. Interpersonally, psychopathic individuals are superficial, charming, manipulative, and grandiose. Affectively, such individuals are unable to experience deep emotions, are callous and unremorseful, and fail to accept responsibility for their actions. Factor 2 denotes the behavioral and antisocial facets. Behaviorally, psychopathic individuals act impulsively and irresponsibly, are parasitic, and lack realistic long-term goals. The Antisocial facet includes early behavioral problems, juvenile delinquency, parole violation, and criminal versatility.

Although the two-factor model has predominated, some have argued that psychopathy is best represented by the Interpersonal, Affective, and Behavioral facets. Using a variety of statistical techniques, Cooke and Michie (2001) found that the items from the Antisocial facet failed to converge with the other items. Instead, it has been argued that antisocial behavior is a manifestation (or outcome) of psychopathic traits as opposed to an indicator of the disorder (Cooke, Michie, Hart, & Clark 2004). Nonetheless, Hare (2003; Hare & Neumann, 2006) persuasively argued that antisocial behavior is an important and necessary component of psychopathic personality disorder. An extended discussion of this issue is beyond the scope of this chapter, and a resolution to this issue is still forthcoming. What is noteworthy, however, is that some argue that the most defining element of psychopathy is the affective deficit (Blair, Mitchell, & Blair, 2005). As will be discussed below (see *Neurological Underpinnings*), this is an important consideration as it may explain why psychopathic individuals differ from their non-psychopathic counterparts in how they aggress.

Although there are a variety of measures used to assess psychopathy, Fulero (1995) dubbed the Psychopathy Checklist (PCL: Hare, 1991) as the gold standard for assessing this disorder. Because the PCL and its derivatives (the Psychopathy Checklist-Revised [PCL-R], Hare 2003; the Psychopathy Screening Version [PCL: SV], Hart, Cox, & Hare, 1995; the Psychopathy Checklist: Youth Version [PCL: YV], Forth, Kosson, & Hare, 2003) have such widespread application, familiarity, and validity, the vast majority of studies reviewed in this chapter are based on them. Thus, the term psychopathy throughout this chapter, unless otherwise indicated, is referring to PCL-defined psychopathy. Moreover, despite recent discussions of the facets of psychopathy, the most common utilization has relied on the two-factor model described above. As such, we will refer primarily to Factors 1 and 2 when distinguishing the different components of psychopathy.

PSYCHOPATHY AND OFFENDING

There is a large literature examining the relationship between psychopathy and offending (i.e., criminal and delinquent) behavior. Numerous reviews document this relationship (see Patrick, 2006). Perhaps the most revealing studies, however, are the meta-analyses that explored the quantitative relationship between psychopathy and offending across numerous empirical investigations.

One meta-analysis conducted by Salekin and colleagues focused on violent and nonviolent recidivism, and was based on 18 studies yielding 29 effect sizes (Salekin, Rogers, & Sewell, 1996). They found the average effect size of psychopathy on recidivism was .68. For violent recidivism, the average effect size was .79 (range: .42-1.92), while for general recidivism it was .55 (range: .24-.93). They also examined the relationship between psychopathy and deviant sexual arousal and sexual sadism. Only three studies explored these relationships, but the effect sizes ranged from .47-.77. This meta-analysis offers three important findings. First, psychopathy was moderately related to a variety of offenses. Second, it was more strongly related to violent recidivism than nonviolent recidivism. Third, the relationship held across different offender samples (e.g., mentally ill, sexual sadists). Thus, this study demonstrated the importance of psychopathy in understanding and predicting violent recidivism.

A subsequent meta-analysis (Leistico, Salekin, DeCoster, & Rogers, 2008), based on much more data (95 non-overlapping studies; 15,828 participants), confirmed and extended early findings. In this study, the authors included a broader class of antisocial outcomes (e.g., recidivism, institutional maladjustment), examined whether the two factors of psychopathy were differentially related to these outcomes, and explored what factors may moderate the relationship between psychopathy and antisocial behavior. They found that average effect size for the total psychopathy score was .55, slightly lower than the previous meta-analysis (discussed above). Yet, this still represented a moderate relationship. Notably, they found Factor 2 was more strongly related to antisocial behavior (median weighted d = .60) than Factor 1 (median weighted d = .38). They also found several moderators, including sex

(Factor 1 effect sizes were stronger when more females were included), race, and country in which the study was conducted (Total and Factor 2 scores were stronger among Caucasians and studies carried out in the United States). However, one study that explicitly examined whether there were differences between Caucasians and African-Americans on psychopathy failed to find any substantive difference, particularly when the core psychopathy traits (i.e., Factor 1) were explored (Skeem, Edens, Camp, & Colwell, 2004). Thus, the meta-analysis conducted by Leistico et al. confirmed the moderate relationship between psychopathy and antisocial behavior, but also demonstrated that this relationship was stronger when focusing on Factor 2, and may be somewhat dependent on study characteristics.

Other meta-analyses corroborate these findings. Grann, Langstrom, Tengstrom, & Kullgren (1999) assessed the relationship between psychopathy and recidivism (within 5 years) among a Swedish sample of offenders with personality disorders (N=352). They found those scoring high on psychopathy (≥26) were nearly twice as likely to violently recidivate as those scoring below that threshold. Thus, despite the stronger effect sizes noted among North American samples, this study indicated the psychopathy-violence relationship had cross-cultural support. They also noted that Factor 2 was a better predictor of such behavior, although Factor 1 remained a significant predictor. A meta-analysis conducted by Walters (2003) found Factor 2 scores to be superior in their prediction of institutional maladjustment and recidivism. On this point, he noted other studies that used multivariate techniques to understand how Factors 1 and 2 uniquely related to antisocial behaviors. Across six such studies, four failed to find that Factor 1 significantly related to antisocial behavior after controlling for Factor 2. Although this pattern suggests that Factor 1 scores may not play much of a role in understanding and predicting antisocial behavior, it is important to note that Factor 1 and Factor 2 are moderately correlated (r = .50; Hare, 2003), making it difficult to disentangle their unique effects.

Although some of the aforementioned meta-analyses included age as moderator and failed to find the effect sizes significantly differed among younger and older samples, a recent meta-analysis that focused specifically on psychopathy assessments among adolescent samples is more revealing. Edens, Campbell, & Weir (2007) found psychopathy was related to both general (weighted $r = .24$) and violent (weighted $r = .25$) recidivism, but not sexual recidivism. They also found Factor 2 bore stronger relations with recidivism than Factor 1. Interestingly, and somewhat contradictory to those studies highlighted above, psychopathy was not related to recidivism among adolescent females (although there were relatively few studies that included females, thus precluding any definitive conclusions). Although these findings generally support the research noted above – namely that psychopathy is related to recidivism – the effect sizes are lower in magnitude and appear to be less generalizable (at least with respect to gender) among younger samples than older (i.e., adult) samples. This suggests that psychopathy, at least as measured by Hare's psychopathy checklists, may not be as potent a factor in predicting recidivism among youth compared to adults. It is worth noting, however, that the effect of psychopathy on recidivism was comparable to the Youth Level of Service/Case Management Inventory (YLS/CMI; Hoge & Andrews, 2002), which was specifically designed to assess risk among adolescent populations.

Although these findings demonstrate that psychopathy is related to antisocial behaviors that are legally proscribed, this class of behaviors is relatively crude and may mask more nuanced manifestations of aggression. Therefore, in the following section we will explore the relationship between psychopathy and aggression, with a focus on different types of aggression.

Psychopathy and Aggression

In general, individuals diagnosed as psychopathic are more aggressive than those who are not psychopathic (Hare, 1993; Stafford & Cornell, 2003). However, this relationship is more complex when considered in a more nuanced way. For instance, while psychopathy is a unidimensional construct, it is comprised of different facets. Moreover, there appear to be different manifestations of aggression, with one of the most recognized distinctions being between proactive and reactive aggression. Bandura (1983) described aggression as a learned behavior that is goal-motivated. More specifically, aggression is used as a means to an end, and is based, in part, on principles of operant conditioning. Thus, aggressive behavior is shaped by patterns of reinforcement. For example, if a person uses aggression to successfully obtain money or sex, such behavior is more likely to be repeated in future encounters. This form of aggression is considered proactive or instrumental aggression. On the other hand, Berkowitz (1988, 1993) suggested that aggression can manifest as a result of negative stimuli or provocation that produces negative affective states. For example, if an individual is insulted or ridiculed by a peer, this may lead to frustration and anger, which serves as the impetus for retaliation. This is often referred to as reactive or hostile aggression.

While others have criticized the utility and existence of distinct forms of aggression (Bushman & Anderson, 2001), empirical evidence supports the dichotomy. For example, various measures that distinguish between the two types of aggression have been developed. Dodge and Coie (1987) developed a teacher-rating instrument that proved useful in assessing proactive and reactive aggression among children (Brendgen, Vitaro, Tremblay, & Lavoie, 2001; Dodge et al., 2003). In addition, Raine et al. (2006) developed a self-report measure of aggression called the Reactive-Proactive Aggression Questionnaire that distinguished between the two forms among children. Subsequently, this measure was adapted and found to have good reliability and validity among an adult sample (Miller & Lynam, 2006). Cornell, Warren, Hawk, Stafford, Oram, and Pine (1996) developed another commonly used instrument for assessing proactive and reactive aggression. Their measure classifies offenders as nonviolent, reactive, or proactive based on official reports and institutional records of individuals. In addition to conceptual differences between reactive and proactive aggression, the existence of distinct forms of aggression has been upheld by findings of unique relationships with external correlates. For example, proactive aggression more closely related to externalizing behaviors such as delinquency and drug abuse than reactive aggression (Miller & Lynam, 2006). Conversely, reactive aggression associated much higher with internalizing behaviors such as anger, frustration, and depression than proactive aggression (Vitaro, Brendgen, & Tremblay, 2002). In addition, reactive aggression had a stronger association with neuroticism, while proactive aggression had a stronger association with antagonism (Miller & Lynam, 2006). Thus, while there remain disputes surrounding the uniqueness of proactive and reactive aggression, there exists both theoretical and empirical evidence supporting the distinction.

Beyond the evidence highlighted above, psychopathy appears to play a role in the specific manifestation of aggression. Research in this area focuses on differential relationships between psychopathy and the two distinct forms of aggression (e.g., Cornell et al., 1996; Murrie et al., 2004; Stafford & Cornell, 2003). Conceptual notions of psychopathy (e.g., Cleckley, 1988, Hare, 1993) suggest that psychopathic individuals act without emotion, engaging in a disproportionate amount of proactive or instrumental aggression compared to non-psychopathic individuals. Accordingly, it has been shown that violent offenses committed by psychopathic individuals tend to be out of utility (e.g., material gain) and lacking emotion, whereas non-psychopathic individuals use of violence is often in response to provocation leading to a negative emotion (e.g., anger, frustration; Williamson, Hare, & Wong, 1987) within that individual. Cornell et al. (1996) and Murrie et al. (2004) assessed whether individuals scoring high on psychopathy were more likely characterized as reactive or proactive violent offenders. Their findings suggest that individuals characterized as psychopathic are more likely to be proactive, violent offenders than non-psychopathic individuals. Relatedly, Stafford and Cornell (2003) found psychiatric patients scoring high on psychopathy were more likely characterized by their primary case manager as engaging in proactive aggression compared to those with low psychopathy scores. These findings support the conceptual notion that psychopathic individuals tend to engage in calculated, less emotionally-based forms of aggression. However, these studies did not examine if facets of psychopathy have differential relationships with the two types of aggression.

Woodworth and Porter (2002) examined the role of psychopathy in predicting different types of homicide (purely reactive, reactive/instrumental, instrumental/reactive, and purely instrumental). Individuals scoring high on the PCL-R were more likely to engage in instrumental homicide. However, Factor 1 scores were predictive of the level of instrumentality used, while Factor 2 scores were not. In another study conducted by Porter and Woodworth (2007), Factor 1 scores also predicted higher rates of instrumental use of violence compared to Factor 2 scores among offenders incarcerated for homicide. The use of deception was also examined by comparing self-reported descriptions of the event that led to their conviction with official accounts of the homicide. Self-reported accounts by psychopathic individuals were more likely to be inconsistent with police records. Specifically, psychopathic individuals were more likely to use deception than non-psychopathic individuals, describing their behavior as more reactive compared to official records. It was also shown that deception was more likely to be used by those scoring high on Factor 1 as opposed to those scoring high on Factor 2. This latter finding underscores the importance of obtaining objective, third-party information to designate whether the behavior was proactive versus reactive in nature.

Vitacco et al. (2006) examined psychopathy among a group of juvenile offenders using the PCL: YV (PCL: Youth Version; Forth et al., 2003). Although they examined the two-, three-, and four-factor models of psychopathy, the most revealing results stemmed from the four-factor model. Specifically, the interpersonal component of psychopathy was positively associated with instrumental violence, whereas the antisocial component was negatively associated with instrumental violence. Neither the affective nor lifestyle facets demonstrated unique relations with instrumental violence. Falkenbach et al. (2008) also found that individuals scoring high on Factor 1 were more likely to engage in mixed (instrumental and reactive) aggression, whereas those scoring high on Factor 2 were more likely to engage in solely reactive aggression.

Few other studies have examined the relationship between specific facets of psychopathy and aggression. However, these studies attempted to examine this relationship using other measures of psychopathy along with more objective measures of aggression. For example, Reidy, Zeichner, Miller, and Martinez (2007) examined the relationship between scores on Levenson's Self-Report Psychopathy scale (LSRP; Levenson, Kiehl, Fitzpatrick, 1995) and a laboratory test of aggression - Response Choice Aggression Paradigm (RCAP; Zeichner, Frey, Parrot, & Butryn, 1999). Factor 1 scores associated with both reactive and instrumental types of aggression, whereas Factor 2 scores associated with reactive aggression only. Orstrov & Houston (2008) examined differences between psychopathy as measured by the Psychopathic Personality Inventory (PPI; Lilienfeld & Widows, 2005) and aggression based on the Self-report of Aggression and Social Behavior Measure (SRASMB; Morales & Crick, 1998) among a sample of undergraduates. They found that the Fearless Dominance factor of the PPI (i.e., Factor 1) positively associated with proactive physical aggression only. Alternatively, the Impulsive Antisociality factor (i.e., Factor 2) positively associated with both proactive and reactive aggression.

Based on the findings from the studies presented, there is evidence suggesting that aggression is associated with psychopathy, and that there are divergent relationships between the multiple dimensions of the two constructs. However, the overlapping nature of proactive and reactive aggression poses problems for researchers in distinguishing between the two types. Some argue that specific acts of aggression cannot be characterized as either proactive or reactive and that many acts of violence contain elements of both (Bushman & Anderson, 2001; Woodworth & Porter, 2002). Bushman and Anderson (2001) go as far as to say the proactive-reactive dichotomy should be done away with due to a lack of clarity in classifying a given behavior as either reactive or proactive. They point out three problematic areas that arise in classifying acts as either reactive or proactive: the same motive driving different types of aggression, different motives driving the same type of aggression, and mixed motives.

Despite these arguments, future research in this area is needed to further assess the relationship between psychopathy and aggression. While research supports the notion that different facets of psychopathy have discriminating relationships with different types of aggression, it is unclear why. This divergent association may be understood when considering shared external correlates of psychopathy and aggression. For example, Reidy et al. (2007) suggest that this relationship may be explained by the positive association that reactive aggression and the behavioral (i.e., Factor 2) component of psychopathy share with Neuroticism. These relationships, however, may also be accounted for by underlying biological systems; a possibility explored in the following section.

Neurological Underpinnings

As reviewed in the previous section, psychopathy has shown to be a robust correlate of instrumental and reactive aggression. Although there are surely multiple factors that lead psychopathic individuals to engage in both variants of aggression, one promising new perspective underscores the role of neurological systems. Blair et al. (2005) articulated a theory that purports to explain why psychopathic individuals evince both instrumental and reactive aggression. Like others (Barry, Frick, DeShazo, McCoy, Ellis, M., & Loney, 2000),

Blair et al. underscore the importance of the affective deficit in defining psychopathy. This deficit, according to Blair et al., has its origins in a dysfunctional amygdala. The amygdala is a structure in the forebrain, and one of its primary functions is the processing of emotional stimuli. Because the amygdala does not function properly among psychopathic individuals, they have difficulty experiencing emotions. This explains the affective deficit characteristic of psychopathic individuals.

Importantly, amygdala dysfunction will not inevitably lead to instrumental aggression. The manifestation of this dysfunction will be based, in part, on one's social experiences. One of the most important developmental milestones is the ability to inhibit aggressive behaviors (Tremblay, 2003). That is, a child does not learn to aggress so much as he learns not to aggress. What is required (among other things) to learn to inhibit aggression is the ability to perceive and appreciate the negative reactions from others. For example, a child who aggresses against another child will likely evoke distress. A parent may display disappointment over the child's aggression. In most instances, the child is able to perceive and accurately interpret these social interactions, and is distressed by those reactions. This will, in turn, help the child to learn more appropriate behaviors. If, however, the amygdala is not sensitive to these cues because of some dysfunction, then the child will not interpret these emotionally negative reactions from others appropriately and will continue to aggress. Over successive interactions, this aggressive child may be reinforced for using aggression to achieve some goal (i.e., instrumental aggression). As Blair et al. (2005) indicate, adults and children with psychopathic traits have difficulty processing sad and fearful facial cues; the very cues that inhibit the use of aggression among most individuals. Thus, this lack of inhibition, coupled with a history of reinforcement, increases the likelihood of instrumental aggression.

Yet, psychopathic individuals also engage in reactive aggression. Here, the underlying neurological mechanisms are the same for non-psychopathic individuals who engage in reactive aggression. Blair et al. (2005) argue that this heightened level of reactive aggression can be traced to orbital, medial, and verntrolateral frontal cortex dysfunction. The origins of this dysfunction are myriad, but genetics likely play some role. Also important is the role of experience, particularly early in the life course. When external stimuli initiate the basic threat circuitry, all individuals may display reactive aggression. However, early abuse and exposure to violence may alter the sensitivity of this system such that lower threats are required to initiate the system. Thus, even lesser or ambiguous threats may lead the individual to typically react aggressively.

Because this neurological dysfunction is not unique to psychopathic individuals, it can explain why both psychopathic and non-psychopathic individuals evince reactive aggression. Moreover, this demonstrates why it is important to distinguish between instrumental and reactive aggression. Individuals who engage in excessive antisocial behavior are a heterogeneous group. This heterogeneity, however, masks important distinctions: namely, instrumental and reactive aggression. That is, excessive use of reactive aggression is relatively common among extremely antisocial individuals. Yet, there is a subgroup that expresses more severe, persistent forms of both instrumental and reactive aggression – psychopathic individuals. Thus, while they share some overlap with non-psychopathic aggressive individuals (in terms of reactive aggression), psychopathic individuals represent a unique group because they are more likely to engage in instrumental and reactive aggression.

TREATMENT OF PSYCHOPATHY

Despite the compelling theoretical perspectives recently advanced, most of the research examining them is still in its infancy. The clinical implication of this is that these perspectives have not been able to advance a specific type or form of intervention or prevention. Instead, the treatment of psychopathy has been examined in the context of more commonplace psychological treatments. As noted above, psychopathy demonstrates robust relations to antisocial and aggressive behaviors. And, while this disorder is quite rare (afflicting approximately less than 1 percent of the population; Blair et al., 2005), psychopathic individuals are responsible for a disproportionate amount of crime. Thus, prevention and treatment are vitally important. Unfortunately, the treatment of this recalcitrant disorder remains a challenge.

The debate over effective treatment and the general question of whether it is possible to *cure* psychopathy is longstanding. As mentioned above, psychopathic individuals possess characteristics that may present an enormous challenge in the context of treatment. For instance, they demonstrate a penchant for manipulating others (including therapists), an inability to form emotional attachments, and learning deficits (Skeem, Monahan, & Mulvey, 2002). Given these characteristics, it is not surprising that the predominant view on the treatability of psychopathy has been less than optimistic. Instead, it has been suggested that psychopathic individuals require incapacitation rather than rehabilitation (Cleckley, 1941; Karpman, 1946). Others have proposed treatment modalities including psychotherapy (Corsini, 1958; Lipton, 1950; Rodgers, 1947; Rosow, 1955; Schmideberg, 1949; Showstack, 1956; Thorne, 1959), therapeutic communities (Hare, 1970), and cognitive-behavioral therapy (Andrews & Bonta, 1994; Brown & Gutsch, 1985; Lochman, 1990; Rottenberg, 1975; Serin & Kuriychuk, 1994; Seto & Barbaree, 1999; Templeman & Wollersheim, 1979; Wong & Hare, 2005). Despite the many types of treatment aimed at this disorder, much of the research suggests treatment is typically unsuccessful for psychopathic adults (Hare, 1970; McCord, 1982; Ogloff, Wong, & Greenwood, 1990; Rice, Harris, & Cormier, 1992; Richards, Casey, & Lucente, 2003; Seto & Barbaree, 1999). Nonetheless, the debate continues because not all research has yielded such discouraging results.

A meta-analysis conducted by Salekin (2002) showed a positive effect of treatment in reducing psychopathic traits and recidivism. Specifically, Salekin suggests that the most effective treatment includes intense cognitive-behavioral and psychoanalytic techniques that involve the offender's family. Skeem et al. (2002) found civil psychiatric patients scoring high (>13) on the PCL: SV were able to benefit from treatment, especially intensive treatment. They also suggest possible methodological issues behind studies are the reason that they have found no treatment effects. For example, Skeem and colleagues point out that most studies use heterogeneous groups that include individuals with Antisocial Personality Disorder (American Psychiatric Association [DSM-IV], 1994) rather than the less prevalent disorder of psychopathy. They also emphasize that there are virtually no controlled studies, and those that are controlled usually include bogus or inappropriate treatment techniques that lack efficacy in general (regardless of one's level of psychopathic traits) (Harris et al., 1994; Rice et al., 1992). In addition, psychopathic individuals within these studies may have received less treatment time than others due to time spent in punishment for bad behavior (Skeem et al, 2002). This is important given research showing that less or short-duration treatment is related to recidivism (Gretton, McBride, Hare, & O'Shaughnessey, 2000; Salekin, 2002; Skeem et al., 2002). For example, these studies showed that individuals who finished treatment programs were less likely to recidivate, and generally longer amounts of treatment were related to a decreased likelihood of future offending.

Other researchers suggest that studies showing successful treatment outcomes (Salekin, 2002; Skeem et al., 2002) are in fact methodologically unsound. For instance, Harris and Rice (2006) state that the meta-analysis conducted by Salekin (2002) is plagued with biased misinterpretation. They assert that studies included in the meta-analysis are unable to explain the relationship between treatment and psychopathy, since they lack control groups as well as objective measures of psychopathy. Additionally, studies examining the effectiveness of therapeutic communities not only demonstrated the absence of treatment effects, but have shown *higher* rates of recidivism for psychopathic compared to nonpsychopathic individuals. Rice et al. (1992) found that rather than providing an environment fostering empathy and responsibility, therapeutic communities actually increased violent recidivism for psychopathic individuals compared to control groups. The authors proposed that this iatrogenic effect may be due to the possibility that psychopathic individuals learn more ways to simulate actual emotions in order to aid in manipulating others.

Some general conclusions can be drawn from these contrasting results. The most apparent is that more research is needed with an emphasis on addressing the methodological issues that have prevented more definitive conclusions. Controlled studies utilizing random assignment and objective measures of psychopathy are crucial in order to draw confident conclusions. Future research should include forensic as well as community samples, paying special attention to specific traits within a population. This is important because the evidence is equivocal regarding which traits may be more related to recidivism and negative treatment outcomes. As indicated above, Factor 2 appears to be more consistently related to antisocial outcomes. However, Hare, Clark, Grann, & Thornton (2000) found that high scores on Factor 1 of the PCL-R were related to recidivism. Lastly, some studies have suggested that treatment should focus on changing skills and behaviors rather than relatively immutable personality traits (Harris & Rice, 2006; Skeem et al., 2002). This is in line with research showing that treatment is more effective when focusing on individual criminogenic needs and dynamic risk factors (Kraemer, Kazdin, Offord, & Kessler, 1999). Although the current evidence does not portray the treatment of psychopathy in a positive light, it seems reasonable that more stringent research may generate new insights that yield promising results.

Future Directions

As argued throughout this chapter, understanding violence in general, and aggression in particular, is a complex task. One must consider both the heterogeneity of offenders (or aggressors) and behaviors (e.g., proactive versus reactive aggression) in order to more fully appreciate and understand the origins of and motivations for violence. As we have articulated, psychopathy is a useful construct for understanding this heterogeneity. Psychopathic individuals represent a smaller, more homogeneous class of offenders that engage in both proactive and reactive aggression at elevated rates. Non-psychopathic individuals, in contrast, appear much more likely to display only reactive aggression. Yet, there remain many unresolved issues to more fully elaborate these relationships.

First, it is unclear how different facets of psychopathy are related to specific manifestations of aggression. Some research supports the notion that Factor 2 is more related to aggression, while other studies draw a link with Factor 1. Moreover, some research indicates that the facets within each of these two factors may be more revealing. As Vitacco et al. (2006) suggest, such a focus can inform the more general debate of whether antisocial behavior is an indicator or consequence of psychopathy. Second, more theoretical and empirical research needs to be conducted that focuses on how best to differentiate among the different variants of aggression, and even whether there are pure types. The focus need not be limited to the proactive-reactive categorization. Other researchers have proposed relational aggression as a specific type of aggression (Crick & Grotpeter, 1995). Relational aggression is more common among females than physical aggression (which is predominantly carried out by males). Moreover, psychopathy appears to have different external correlates among females (Verona & Vitale, 2005). Thus, future research may reveal that while psychopathic females are not especially prone to physical aggression, they may be highly likely to engage in relational aggression.

The unresolved questions are not mere academic issues; instead, they have important practical implications. More research on the relationships between specific traits and forms of aggression may better inform violence risk assessment. In addition, and as discussed above, prevention and treatment efforts are undoubtedly influenced by psychopathic traits. Just as importantly, different treatment modalities or techniques may be necessary depending on the type of aggression exhibited by the person. For instance, the reduction of proactive aggression will likely need to focus on altering the contingencies such that punishment outweighs the reinforcement. For reactive aggression, cognitive-behavioral treatments focusing on anger management and the processing of social cues would be required. However, the prospects for differential application and utilization of treatment based on individual characteristics and specific behaviors can only be achieved with well-informed, nuanced, and methodologically-sound research.

REFERENCES

American Psychiatric Association. (1994). *Diagnostic and statistical manual of mental disorders* (4th Ed.). Washington, DC: Author.

Andrews, D. & Bonta, J. (1994). *The psychology of criminal conduct*. Cincinnati, OH: Anderson.

Bandura, A. (1983). Psychological mechanism of aggression. In R. G. Geen, & E. I. Donnerstein (Eds.), *Aggression: Theoretical and empirical reviews* (vol. I. pp. 1-40)/ New York: Academic Press.

Barry, C. T., Frick, P. J., DeShazo, T. M., McCoy, M. G., Ellis, M. & Loney, B. R. (2000). The importance of callous-unemotional traits for extending the concept of psychopathy to children. *Journal of Abnormal Psychology*, *109*, 335-340.

Berkowitz, L. (1988). Frustrations, appraisals, and aversely stimulated aggression. *Aggressive Behavior*, *14(11)*, 3-11.

Berkowitz, L. (1993). *Aggression: Its Causes, consequences, and control.* New York: McGraw-Hill.

Blair, J., Mitchell, D. & Blair, K. (2005). *The psychopath: Emotion and the brain.* Malden, MA: Blackwell.

Brendgen, M., Vitaro, F., Tremblay, R. & Lavoie, F. (2001). Reactive and proactive aggression: Predictions to physical violence in different contexts and moderating effects of parental monitoring and caregiving behavior. *Journal of Abnormal Child Psychology, 21,* 293-304.

Brown, H. & Gutsch, K. (1985). Cognitions associated with a delay of gratification task: A study with psychopaths and normal prisoners. *Criminal Justice and Behavior, 12,* 453-462.

Bushman, B. J. & Anderson, C. A. (2001). Is it time to pull the plug on the hostile versus instrumental aggression dichotomy? *Psychological Review, 108,* 273-279.

Buss, A. H. & Perry, M. (1992). The aggression questionnaire. *Journal of Personality and Social Psychology, 63,* 452-459.

Cleckley, H. (1941). *The mask of sanity.* St. Louis, MO: Mosby.

Cleckley, H. (1988). *The mask of sanity* (5th Ed.). Augusta, GA: Cleckley, E.

Cooke, D. J. & Michie, C. (2001). Refining the construct of psychopathy: Towards a hierarchical model. *Psychological Assessment, 13,* 171-188.

Cooke, D. J., Michie, C., Hart, S. D. & Clark, D. A. (2004). Reconstructing psychopathy: Clarifying the significance of antisocial behavior in the diagnosis of psychopathic personality disorder. *Journal of Personality Disorders, 18,* 337-356.

Cornell, D. G., Warren, J., Hawk, G., Stafford, E., Oram, G. & Pine, D. (1996). Psychopathy in instrumental and reactive violent offenders. *Journal of Consulting and Clinical Psychology, 64(4),* 783-790.

Corsini, R. (1958). Psychodrama with a psychopath. *Group Psychotherapy, 11,* 33-39.

Crick, N. R. & Grotpeter, J. K. (1995). Relational aggression, gender, and social-psychological adjustment. *Child Development, 66,* 710-722.

Dodge, K. A. & Coie, J. (1987). Social-information processing factors in reactive and proactive aggression in children's peer groups. *Journal of Personality and Social Psychology, 53,* 1146-1158.

Dodge, K. A., Lansford, J. E., Burks, V. S., Bates, J. E., Pettit, G. S., Fontaine, R. & Price, J. M. (2003). Peer rejection and social information-processing factors in the development of aggressive behavior problems in children. *Child Development, 74(2),* 374-393.

Edens, J. F., Campbell, J. S. & Weir, J. M. (2007). Youth psychopathy and criminal recidivism: A meta-analysis of the Psychopathy Checklist Measures. *Law and Human Behavior, 31,* 53-75.

Falkenbach, D., Poythress, N. G. & Creevy C. (2008). The exploration of subclinical psychopathic subtypes and the relationship with types of aggression. *Personality and Individual Differences, 44(4),* 821-832.

Farrington, D. F. (2005). The importance of child and adolescent psychopathy. *Journal of Abnormal Child Psychology, 33,* 489-497.

Forth, A. E., Kosson, D. S. & Hare, R. D. (2003). *Hare Psychopathy Checklist: Youth Version.* North Tonawanda, NY: Multi-Health Systems Inc.

Forth, A. E., Kosson, D. S. & Hare, R. D. (2003). *Hare Psychopathy Checklist: Youth Version technical manual.* Toronto, Ontario, Canada: Multi-Health Systems.

Fulero, S. M. (1995). Review of the Hare Psychopathy Checklist – Revised. In J. C. Conoley, & J. C. Impara (Eds.), *Twelfth mental measurements yearbook* (pp. 453-454). Lincoln, NE: Buros Institute.

Grann, M., Langstrom, N., Tengstrom, A. & Kullgren, G. (1999). Psychopathy (PCL-R) predicts violent recidivism among criminal offenders with personality disorders in Sweden. *Law and Human Behavior*, *23*, 205-217.

Gretton, H., McBride, M., Hare, R. & O'Shaughnesssey, R. (2000). *Psychopathy and recidivism in adolescent offenders: A ten-year follow-up.* Paper presented at the annual meeting of the Association for the Treatment of Sexual Abusers, San Diego, CA.

Hare, R. D. (1991). *The Psychopathy Checklist – Revised.* Toronto, ON: Multi-Health Systems Inc.

Hare, R. D. (2003). *Hare Psychopathy Checklist – Revised* (2nd Ed.). North Tonawanda, NY: Multi-Health Systems Inc.

Hare, R. D. & Neumann, C. S. (2006). The PCL-R assessment of psychopathy. In C. J. Patrick (Ed.), *Handbook of psychopathy* (pp. 58-88). New York: Guilford.

Hare, R. D. (1970). *Psychopathy: Theory and Research.* New York: Wiley.

Hare, R. D. (1993). *Without Conscience: The disturbing world of the psychopaths among us.* New York: The Guilford Press.

Hare, R. D., Clark, D., Grann, M. & Thornton, D. (2000). Psychopathy and the predictive validity of the PCL-R: An international perspective. *Behavioral Sciences and the Law*, *18*, 623-645.

Harris, G. T. & Rice, M. E. (2006). Treatment of psychopathy: A review of empirical findings. In C. J. Patrick (Ed.), *Handbook of psychopathy* (pp. 555-572). New York: Guilford.

Harris, G., Rice, M. & Cormier, C. (1994) Psychopaths: Is a therapeutic community therapeutic? *Therapeutic Communities*, *15*, 283-299.

Hart, S., Cox, D. & Hare, R. D. (2005). *Manual for the Psychopathy Checklist: Screening Version* (PCL: SV). Toronto, CA: Multi-Health Systems Inc.

Hoge, R. & Andrews, D. (2002). *Youth Level of Service/Case Management Inventory.* Toronto: MHS.

Karpman, B. (1946). Psychopathy in the scheme of human typology. *Journal of Nervous and Mental Disease*, *103*, 276-288.

Kraemer, H., Kazdin, A., Offord, D. & Kessler, R. (1999). Coming to terms with the terms of risk. *Archives of General Psychiatry*, *54*, 337-343.

Leistico, A. M. R., Salekin, R. T., DeCoster, J. & Rogers, R. (2008). A large-scale meta-analysis relating the Hare measures of psychopathy to antisocial conduct. *Law and Human Behavior*, *32*, 28-45.

Levenson, M. R., Kiehl, K. A. & Fitzpatrick, C. M. (1995). Assessing psychopathic attributes in a noninstitutionalized population. *Journal of Personality and Social Psychology*, *68*, 151-158.

Lilienfeld, S. O. & Widows, M. R. (2005). *Psychological Assessment Inventory*-Revised (PPI-R). Lutz, FL: Psychological Assessment Resources.

Lipton, H. (1950). The psychopath. *Journal of Criminal Law, Criminology, and Police Science*, *6*, 399-411.

Lochman, J. (1990). Modification of childhood aggression. In A. M. Hersen, R. Ersler, & P. Miller (Eds.), *Progress in behavior modification* (p.23). New York: Academic Press.

McCord, J. (1982). Parental behavior in the cycle of aggression. *Psychiatry, 51*, 14-23.

Miller, J. & Lynam, D. (2006). Reactive and proactive aggression: Similarities and differences. *Personality and Individual Differences, 14*, 1469-1480.

Morales, J. R. & Crick, N. R. (1998). *Self-report measure of aggression and victimization.* Unpublished measure.

Murrie, D. C., Cornell, D. G., Kaplan, S., McConville, D. & Levy-Elkon, A. (2004). Psychopathy scores and violence among juvenile offenders: A multi-measure study. *Behavioral Sciences and the Law, 22*, 49-67.

Ogloff, J., Wong, S. & Greenwood, A. (1990). Treating criminal psychopaths in a therapeutic community program. *Behavioral Sciences and the Law, 8*, 81-90.

Orstrov, J. M. & Houston, R. J. (2008). The utility and forms of functions of aggression in emerging adulthood: Association with personality disorder symptomatology. *Journal of Youth and Adolescence, 37(9)*, 1147-1158.

Patrick, C. J. (2006). *Handbook of psychopathy*. New York: Guilford.

Porter, S. & Woodworth, M. (2007). "I'm sorry I did it ... but he started it": A comparison of the official and self-reported homicide descriptions of psychopaths and non-psychopaths. *Law and Human Behavior, 31(1)*, 91-107.

Raine, A., Dodge, K., Loeber, R., Gatzke-Kopp, L., Lynam, D., Reynolds, C., Stouthamer-Loeber, M. & Liu, J. (2006). The reactive-proactive aggression questionnaire: Differential correlates of reactive and proactive aggression in adolescent boys. *Aggressive Behavior*, 32, 159-171.

Reidy, D. E., Zeichner, A., Miller, J. D. & Martinez, M. (2007). Psychopathy and aggression: Examining the role of psychopathy factors in predicting laboratory aggression under hostile and instrumental conditions. *Journal of Research in Personality, 41*, 1244-1251.

Rice, M., Harris, G. & Cormier, C. (1992). An evaluation of a maximum security therapeutic community for psychopaths and other mentally disordered offenders. *Law and Human Behavior, 16*, 399-411.

Richards, H., Casey, J. & Lucente, S. (2003). Psychopathy and treatment response in incarcerated female substance abusers. *Criminal Justice and Behavior, 30*, 251-276.

Rodgers, T. (1947). Hypnotherapy and character neuroses. *Journal of Clinical Psychopathology, 8*, 519-524.

Rosow, H. (1955). Some observations on group therapy with prison inmates. *Archives of Criminal Psychodynamics, 1*, 866-897.

Rotenberg, M. (1975). Psychopathy, insensitivity, and socialization. *Professional Psychology, 6*, 283-292.

Salekin, R. (2002). Psychopathy and therapeutic pessimism: Clinical lore or clinical reality? *Clinical Psychology Review, 22*, 79-112.

Salekin, R. T., Rogers, R. & Sewell, K. W. (1996). A review and meta-analysis of the Psychopathy Checklist and Psychopathy Checklist-Revised: Predictive validity of dangerousness. *Clinical Psychology: Science and Practice, 3*, 203-215.

Schmideberg, M. (1949). The analytic treatment of major criminals: Therapeutic results and technical problems. *International Journal of Psychoanalysis, 30*, 197.

Serin, R. & Kuriychuk, M. (1994). Social and cognitive processing deficits in violent offenders: Implications for treatment. *International Journal of Law and Psychiatry, 17*, 431-441.

Seto, M. & Barbaree, H. (1999). Psychopathy, treatment behavior, and sex offender recidivism. *Journal of Interpersonal Violence, 14*, 1235-1248.

Showstack, N. (1956). Treatment of prisoners at the California Medical Facility. *American Journal of Psychiatry, 112*, 821-824.

Skeem, J. L., Edens, J. F., Camp, J. & Colwell, L. H. (2004). Are there ethnic differences in levels of psychopathy? A meta-analysis. *Law and Human Behavior, 28*, 505-527.

Skeem, J., Monahan, J. & Mulvey, E. (2002). Psychopathy, treatment involvement, and subsequent violence among civil psychiatric patients. *Law and Human Behavior, 26*, 577-603.

Stafford, E. & Cornell, D. G. (2003). Psychopathy scores predict adolescent inpatient aggression. *Assessment, 10(1)*, 102-112.

Templeman, T. & Wollersheim, J. (1979). A cognitive-behavioral approach to the treatment of psychopathy. *Psychotherapy: Research and Practice, 16*, 132-139.

Thorne, F. (1959). The etiology of sociopathic reactions. *American Journal of Psychotherapy, 13*, 310-330.

Tremblay, R. E. (2003). Why socialization fails: The case of chronic physical aggression. In B. B. Lahey, T. E. Moffitt, & A. Caspi (Eds.), *Causes of conduct disorder and delinquency* (pp. 182-224). New York: Guilford.

United States Department of Justice, Federal Bureau of Investigation. (September 2008). Crime in the United States, 2007. Retrieved (December 1, 2008), from http://www.fbi.gov/ucr/07cius.htm.

Verona, E. & Vitale, J. (2005). Psychopathy in women. In C. J. Patrick (Ed.), *Handbook of psychopathy* (pp. 415-436). New York: Guilford.

Vitacco, M. J., Neumann, C. S., Caldwell, M. F., Leistico, A. & Van Rybroek, G. J. (2006). Testing factor models of the Psychopathy Checklist: Youth Version and their association with instrumental aggression. *Journal of Personality Assessment, 87*, 74-83.

Vitaro, F., Brendgen, M. & Tremblay, R. E., (2002). Reactively and Proactively aggressive children: Antecedent and subsequent characteristics. *Journal of Child Psychology and Psychiatry, 43(4)*, 495-505.

Walters, G. D. (2003). Predicting institutional adjustment and recidivism with the Psychopathy Checklist factor scores: A meta-analysis. *Law and Human Behavior, 27*, 541-558.

Williamson, S. E., Hare, R. D. & Wong, S. (1987). Violence: Criminal psychopaths and their victims. *Canadian Journal of Behavioral Science, 19*, 454-462.

Wong, S. & Hare, R. D. (2005). *Guidelines for a psychopathy treatment program*. Toronto, ON, Canada: Multi-Health Systems.

Woodworth, M. & Porter, S. (2002). In cold blood: Characteristics of criminal homicides as a function of psychopathy. *Journal of Abnormal Psychology, 111*, 436-445.

Zeichner, A., Frey, F. C., Parrott, D. J. & Butryn, M. (1999). Measurement of laboratory aggression: A new response choice paradigm. *Psychological Reports, 82*, 1229-1237.

In: Violent Crime and Prisons: Population...
Ed: Aidan Renshaw and Emelina Suárez

ISBN: 978-1-60741-668-5

Chapter 9

EFFECTS OF SEX AND STATUS DIFFERENCE OF TARGET AND AGGRESSOR ON ADOLESCENTS' ASSESSMENT OF THE TARGET IN SCENARIOS OF AGGRESSION

***María de la Paz Toldos-Romero**
Escuela de Negocios y Humanidades. Instituto Tecnológico de Estudios Superiores de Monterrey (ITESM), Campus Guadalajara, Jalisco (México)

ABSTRACT

This study aims to explore adolescents' assessment of the target in hypothetical scenarios of aggression and to establish any sex differences in adolescent perceptions of the target of these scenarios. An instrument with eight different hypothetical scenarios of aggression was designed. This instrument manipulates the sex of the aggressor, the sex of the target, and the status difference (same vs. different) between the aggressor and the target in each scenario. The instrument was administered to a sample (N = 653) of adolescents aged 14 to 18. A multifactorial repeated-measures design with a 2 x 2 x 2 analysis of variance (ANOVA) was used. Results showed a significant interaction between sex of aggressor, sex of target, and status difference of aggressor and target ($F_{1,560} = 20.329$, $p = .000$). More specifically, results showed that (i) when the aggressor was male, the subjects assessed a female target more positively than a male target, regardless of status difference; (ii) when the aggressor was female, the subjects assessed a male target more positively than a female target, regardless of status difference; (iii) the subjects assessed a target more positively in the scenarios where the aggressor and target were of different sexes; (iv) the subjects assessed a target more positively when the aggressor and the target were of different status; (v) the subjects assessed a target more positively in the scenarios in which the target was a student, either male or female; (vi) compared with females, males assessed the target more positively when the aggressor was a female, when the target was a male, and when the target was a male with unequal status in the relationship; and (vii) females assessed the target more positively when the aggressor was

* Correspondence to: María de la Paz Toldos , Escuela de Negocios y Humanidades. Instituto Tecnológico de Estudios Superiores de Monterrey (ITESM), Campus Guadalajara, Jalisco (México), Avda. General Ramón Corona 2514, Col. Nuevo México, 45201 Zapopan, Jalisco, México, E-mail: mariadelapaz.toldos@itesm.mx

a male and when the target was a female. These findings are discussed in terms of important attitude changes in overcoming the sexist stereotype toward a female target in a situation of aggression within the family; nevertheless, this stereotype has not been completely overcome in other scenarios where aggression takes place.

1. INTRODUCTION

Numerous studies in aggression research have established a classification of various types of aggression in terms of its form and behavior (e.g., Björkqvist et al., 1992; Crick and Grotpeter, 1995; Lagerspetz et al., 1988; Salmivalli et al., 2000; Underwood, 2003). Moreover, there has been a great deal of research on sex differences in these different types of aggressive behavior (e.g., Archer, 2000; Archer, 2004; Benson, 1993; Björkqvist et al., 1992a-1992c; Campbell, 1999; Capaldi and Crosby, 1997; Eagly and Wood, 1991 Maccoby and Jacklin, 1974; Richardson and Green, 1999, Toldos, 2005), in most cases with inconsistent results, few of which are generalizable.

As a result, there is a significant amount of research looking at the perceptions of aggressive interactions between males and females and how they are perceived differently by observers. These studies have examined the effects of the sex of the target and the aggressor on perceptions, attributions, and assessments of the aggressive behavior in real or hypothetical situations. Some research found diverse results as a function of the variables used in the study. For example, in some studies the researchers arranged the observation so that observers were unable to decipher the sex of the aggressor and the target. In some of these studies the results indicate that when the sex was unknown, the subjects viewed the aggression between two boys as the least aggressive, as their behavior was more likely to be attributed to rough-and-tumble play than to intentional harm. However, the subjects viewed such behavior by girls as aggression rather than as play (Condry and Ross, 1985). On the other hand, in similar studies the sex of the children was made clear to observers, and when the sex of the aggressor and the target was known, subjects rated boys and girls as equally aggressive; nevertheless, boys' aggression was seen as more intentional and masculine (Ostrov et al., 2005; Susser and Keating, 1990).

Researchers such as Harris and Knight-Bohnhoff (1996) also examined whether the variables of sex of aggressor and sex of target affected the perception of violent behavior. In their study they manipulated the sex of the aggressor and the sex of the target across experimental groups using sequences of vignettes that described aggressive interactions. They found that subjects considered the act to be more aggressive when the aggressor was a male, the male aggressor was assessed worse than the female aggressor, and the aggressive behavior toward a female was perceived as less desirable than the same aggressive behavior toward a male target.

Marks and Nelson (1993) conducted another study in which students watched four videos of vignettes that showed interactions involving sexual harassment between professors and students.

For each vignette, the sex of the initiator of the behavior and the type of behavior was manipulated. The results showed that the behavior of female professors who initiated sexual harassment behavior toward a male student was perceived as more appropriate than the same behavior initiated by male professors toward female students in identical situations.

In a Spanish study, Perles and Moreno (2000) analyzed how verbal provocation on the part of the target, the explicit description of violent behavior, and the sex of the target influenced the evaluation of the social image of the female victim of aggression on the part of her husband or boyfriend. The researchers found that the female was evaluated higher in all of the dependent variables, even when she started the aggression but ended up being the target. The researchers showed that when the target was a female, the importance and violence of the incident was considered greater, the target was assessed more positively, her behavior was comprehended, the severity of the physical and psychological harm was considered greater, and the responsibility of the male for the incident was considered greater. When the target was a male, it was found that subjects considered that he had more responsibility for the incident, that the aggression was caused by his personality characteristics, that he wanted to be punished, and that his behavior was more provocative.

Research has also indicated that women and men tend to hold different social representations of aggression (see Archer and Haign, 1997a, 1999; Archer and Parker, 1994; Campbell and Muncer, 1987; Campbell et al., 1991) and that they differ in their perceptions of the seriousness and importance of the incident, as well as in their perceptions of the motivations of the participants involved (Fitzgerald et al., 1995; Frazier et al., 1995; Hutchinson et al., 1994; McCaul et al., 1990; McCormick, 1994). Thus Campbell et al. (1991) propose that the sex of the subjects has a significant relationship with the social representation of the violence, although the narrative and meta-analytical review have indicated a number of variables in which the magnitude of these sex differences is enhanced, diminished, or eliminated (Eagly and Steffen, 1986; Frodi et al., 1977; White, 1983). Authors such as Pierce and Harris (1993) find sex differences in the perception of the target, the image perceived by females being the most favorable in all the variables. They also observed that males tended to consider the aggressor less responsible for the incident and to justify the use of force when the female target of the aggression had demonstrated verbally provocative behavior. In sexual harassment scenarios between teachers and students, Marks and Nelson (1993) found that females perceived the behavior as harassment and as inappropriate more often than males did, although some types of harassment were interpreted by females as more appropriate than when these same types were interpreted by males.

In this same line, Harris and Cook (1994) found that schoolgirls considered an aggressive incident much more violent than boys did, and that the mistreatment of a wife was more serious than the same incident in which the target was a husband. They also found that women sympathized more with the target despite the similarity between the target and the aggressor. Harris and Knight-Bohnhoff (1996) also found that women considered incidents of aggression much more serious than men did. Galen and Underwood (1997) showed examples of real-life social aggression to a group of adolescents in which girls rated the aggressors as angrier than boys did.

It has been found in other studies that males, both adults and adolescents, tend to justify aggression, blaming the target to a greater extent than females do (Caron and Carter, 1997; Falchikov, 1996; Keltikangas and Lindeman, 1997; Monson et al., 1996; Pakaslati and Keltinkangas, 1997; Toldos, 2006; Workman and Freeburg, 1999). Kristinasen and Giulietti (1990) found that males looked down on and blamed the target more, and their attitudes toward women were less favorable. Females, on the other hand, had positive attitudes toward the female target. Locke and Richman (1999) found that females, assessing relationships between husband and wife, blamed the husband for the abuse and sympathized more with the wife. The subjects had more positive views of the women and more strongly disapproved of violence toward the women. Hillier and Foddy (1993) found that females blamed or held accountable an abusive husband more and an abused wife less compared with males, who blamed the target more than females did.

All of these studies, to cite only a few, are in keeping with the idea that violent situations between men and women are perceived differently by observers. The studies also agree that there are differences between males and females in the perception and evaluation of violent behavior. Furthermore, the sex of those who intervene in a violent situation is crucial and can produce different results for the variables that we are trying to measure. In this sense, the study that is presented next is based principally on some of the studies cited previously, but extends the research by one more variable and makes some modifications. Although there is a significant amount of research looking at adult perceptions of aggressive interactions between adults or children and of the effects of the sex of the aggressor, target, and observer, fewer studies have examined adolescents' perceptions of aggression involving adolescents. Most of the above studies consisted of adult subjects viewing very young children or other adults engaging in real-life or hypothetical situations of aggression. Therefore, I propose that adolescent observers may have different perceptions regarding situations of aggression than adult observers do.

Furthermore, to my knowledge no study has included variables different from the sex of the aggressor, the sex of the target and the sex of the observers. So I examined the effects of another variable, the status difference between the target and the aggressor (same vs. different). And lastly, I extended the situations where violence can take place, using situations in which adolescents could easily identify themselves. These situations were scenarios of aggression that adolescents had documented in a pilot study. The adolescents had been part of the situations, directly or indirectly, or had heard of the situations from others. In this way, not only are situations of aggression within the family or between equals at school included, but situations of aggression between equals in places of leisure and situations of aggression with teachers are included as well.

Therefore, the aim of this study is to establish whether adolescent boys and girls differ in their perceptions of male and female targets as a function of sex and status difference in different hypothetical scenarios of aggression. More specifically, the study examines the adolescents' assessment of the target in hypothetical situations of aggression enacted by peers and adults, as well as sex differences in this assessment.

On the basis of past research and the theoretical considerations discussed earlier, it was predicted that female targets would be assessed more positively than male targets in all the scenarios of aggression. In the situations initiated by a male aggressor, it was predicted that the target would be assessed more positively than in those situations initiated by a female aggressor. And it was predicted that the subjects would assess a target more positively in the scenarios where the aggressor and the target were of different sexes. For the variable of status difference, it was predicted that the subjects would assess a target more positively when the target and the aggressor were of different status. Furthermore, following the trend revealed in previous research, it was predicted that females would assess the target more positively in a wider range of situations than males would.

2. Method

2.1. Subjects

The subjects in this study consisted of a sample of 653 students (337 boys and 336 girls). The mean age was 15.45 (SD = 1.01) and the age range was 14 to 17 (males: M = 15.51, SD = .97; females: M = 15.56, SD = 1.05). The study was carried out in four high schools in Madrid, Spain, situated in two zones of the city with different socioeconomic status (medium-low vs. medium-high) and different type of education (private-religious vs. public-nonreligious). In each high school, five classes from each grade were randomly selected for inclusion in the study. Each class ranged from 20 to 30 students.

2.2. Procedure

Consent was obtained from the school authorities and all subjects received parental permission to participate before the data was collected. No parents denied permission for their children to participate in the study, and no students refused to participate. Before administration of the questionnaire, subjects were provided with the objective and instructions to fill out the questionnaire. The measures were administered by the researcher in a counterbalanced order at class level in order to control the effects of fatigue of the subjects. The questionnaire was completed during two sessions in the subjects' normal classrooms.

2.3. Instrument

An instrument with eight scenarios describing an episode of aggression was designed to measure the assessment of the target. In a previous pilot study (N = 60), different scenarios of aggression were used with an open-answer questionnaire. But in a focus group during this pilot study, I detected that the adolescents were unfamiliar with some of the scenarios of aggression and I could not get enough information. Also, the adolescents told me that the scenarios were unreal and strange for them. So I asked them to talk about situations in which they had been involved directly or indirectly, or aggressive situations they had heard about. Thus, I decided to select this information about aggressive situations that were closer to the adolescents. Afterwards, eight short scenarios were specifically created for the current study respecting the experimental conditions and the three independent variables (sex of aggressor, sex of target and status difference) for this study.

The subjects were presented with the eight scenarios that depicted a protagonist (adolescent, student, adult, or teacher) in a social interaction with another person (adolescent, student, adult, or teacher) in which the two became involved in a dispute that ended in aggressive behavior. This hypothetical interaction culminated with one individual in each pair (the aggressor) acting in an aggressive manner toward the other (the target), yelling, arguing, or insulting the other person. The scenario was kept as brief and neutral as possible in order to adapt it to the various male-female combinations and to the real situations where adolescents could be involved. The scenarios were left unfinished to allow the subjects to imagine what would happen afterward.

Scenarios	Sex of the Aggressor	Sex of the Target	Status
1. A male is aggressive toward a female in a domestic context	Male	Female	Same
2. A female is aggressive toward a male in a domestic context	Female	Male	Same
3. A male teacher is aggressive toward a female student	Male	Female	Different
4. A female teacher is aggressive toward a male student	Female	Male	Different
5. A male student is aggressive toward a male teacher	Male	Male	Different
6. A female student is aggressive toward a female teacher	Female	Female	Different
7. A male adolescent is aggressive toward another male adolescent at a bar	Male	Male	Same
8 A female adolescent is aggressive toward another female adolescent at a bar	Female	Female	Same

Figure 1. Experimental Conditions.

The sex and status difference in each scenario were manipulated in a 2 x 2 x 2 design, totaling eight versions. There were four different scenarios that described an episode of aggression and each one was used twice with the only difference being the sex of the aggressor and of the target. In order to control a possible order effect, the scenarios were counterbalanced in two sessions. In the first test session, roughly 50% of the subjects completed four of the eight scenarios while the other half completed the other four. In the second test session, which took place after a period of rest, the subjects completed the four scenarios that had not been completed previously. Figure 1 presents the eight experimental conditions.

There was one question relating to the assessment of the target in each of the eight scenarios of aggression. The item consisted in asking subjects to rate their evaluation of the target by circling a number on a Likert scale ranging from 1 (negative) to 5 (positive). When a subject circled a number bigger than 3, the subject was considered to assess the target more positively in that scenario, but a lower score meant that the target received a negative assessment. The reliability of the questionnaire (α = .61) was fairly good considering the number of items (only one item of each scenario for a total of eight items).

3. Results

In order to assess the effects of the manipulations, the scenarios were analyzed with a 2 (sex of aggressor [male, female]) by 2 (sex of target [male, female]) by 2 (status difference [same, different]) multifactorial repeated measures design with the subjects' sex as an intergroup factor. I obtained the main effect of the three dependent variables (sex of aggressor, sex of target, and status difference) and the interaction between these variables (sex of aggressor x sex of target; sex of aggressor x status difference; sex of target x status difference; and sex of aggressor x sex of target x status difference) and also the interaction with these and the sex of the subjects. The differences in the main simple effects were analyzed with confidence intervals previously corrected by the Bonferroni procedure. All the analyses were carried out with the statistical software package SPSS 12.0 for Windows.

The mean scores for males and females on the dependent variable measured for each experimental condition are presented in Figure 4. Results showed a significant main effect of the *sex of the aggressor* on the assessment of the target ($F_{1,560} = 4.536$, $p = .034$), which indicates that the subjects assessed a target more positively in the scenarios where the aggressor was male. Also, the interaction with the sex of subjects was significant ($F_{1,560} = 9.122$, $p = .003$), with females scoring the target higher than males when the aggressor was a male (females: $M = 3.51$, SD = .04; males: $M = 3.47$, SD = .05). Males, compared with females, assessed the target more positively when the aggressor was a female (males: $M = 3.50$, SD = .05; females: $M = 3.35$, SD = .05)

There were no significant effects of the *sex of the target* on the assessment of the target ($F_{1,560} = 2.242$, $p = .135$) but there was a significant interaction between the sex of the target and the sex of the subjects ($F_{1,560} = 7.955$, $p = .005$), with males scoring the target higher than females when the target was a male (males: $M = 3.51$, SD = .05; females: $M = 3.36$, SD = .05) and females scoring the target higher than males when the target was a female (females: $M = 3.50$, SD = .05; males: $M = 3.46$, SD = .05)

The effect of the *status difference* on the target's assessment was also significant ($F_{1,560} = 31.768$, $p = .000$) The subjects assessed a target more positively when the aggressor and the target had different status. There were no significant effects between the status difference and the sex of the subjects ($F_{1,560} = .059$, $p = .808$).

Furthermore, results showed a significant interaction between the *sex of the aggressor* and the *sex of the target* ($F_{1,560} = 370.514$, $p = .000$). The subjects assessed a target more positively in the scenarios where the aggressor and the target were of different sexes. When the aggressor was a male and the target was a female, subjects assessed the female target more positively than when the aggressor was a female or when the target was a male. Moreover, when the aggressor was a female, the subjects assessed the male target more positively than the female target. However, there was no significant interaction with the sex of the subjects ($F_{1,560} = .607$, $p = .436$).

A significant interaction was found between the *sex of the aggressor* and the *status difference* ($F_{1,560} = 17.438$, $p = .000$), and aggression by a female against a target of different status was more positively assessed than aggression by a male. There was no significant interaction between these variables and the sex of the subjects ($F_{1,560} = 2.327$, $p = .128$).

Results showed no significant interaction between the *sex of the target* and the *status difference* ($F_{1,560} = 2.925$, $p = .088$), but there was a significant interaction with the sex of the subjects ($F_{1,560} = 1.719$, $p = .190$), with males scoring the target higher than females when the target was a male with different status (males: $M = 3.62$, SD = .05; females: $M = 3.52$, SD = .05)

As Figures 2 and 3 show, there was a significant interaction between the three independent variables, *sex of aggressor x sex of target x status difference* ($F_{1,560} = 20.329$, $p = .000$). These results indicate that a female target was assessed more positively than a male target when the aggressor was a male, and a male target was assessed more positively than a female target when the aggressor was a female, regardless of status difference. In other words, when the aggressor was male, the subjects assessed a female target more positively than a male target, regardless of the status difference between aggressor and target, and when the aggressor was female, the subjects assessed a male target more positively than a female target, regardless of the status difference between aggressor and target. There was no significant interaction with the sex of the subjects ($F_{1,560} = .212, p = .645$).

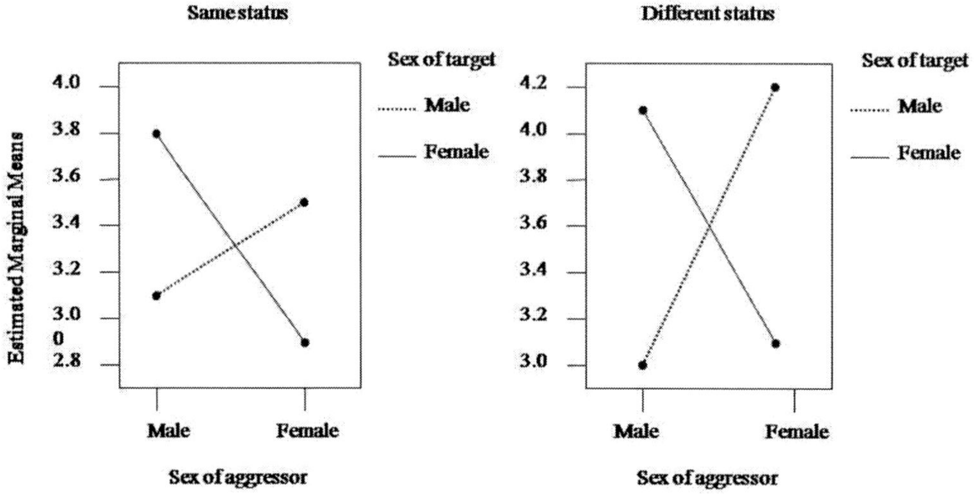

Figures 2 & 3. Significant interaction between sex of aggressor x sex of target x status difference.

Scenario	Males		Females		All		Order of Assessment
	M	*SD*	*M*	*SD*	*M*	*SD*	
Domestic setting							
1. A male is aggressive toward a female	3.70	1.28	3.93	1.20	3.82	1.24	3.
2. A female is aggressive toward a male	3.68	1.26	3.34	1.27	3.51	1.28	4.
Teacher toward student							
3. A male teacher is aggressive toward a female student	3.99	1.27	4.09	1.06	4.04	1.17	2.
4. A female teacher is aggressive toward a male student	4.16	1.16	4.07	1.12	4.11	1.14	1.
Student toward teacher							
5. A male student is aggressive toward a male teacher	3.10	1.48	2.99	1.38	3.04	1.43	7.
6. A female student is aggressive toward a female teacher	3.15	1.50	3.06	1.40	3.11	1.45	5.
Adolescents in a bar							
7. A male is aggressive toward another male	3.11	1.51	3.04	1.43	3.07	1.47	6.
8. A female is aggressive toward another female	3.03	1.48	2.94	1.40	2.98	1.44	8.

Figure 4. Assessments of the Target Made by Male and Female Subjects for the Eight Experimental Conditions. Means and Standard Deviations.

If we compare the mean scores in all the scenarios (see Figure 4), we can observe in which of them the subjects assessed a target more positively. The subjects scored the target from highest to lowest in the following order: experimental conditions 4, 3, 1, 2, 6, 7, 5, and 8. These results show that the situations in which subjects assessed the target more positively were when a female teacher was aggressive toward a male student and when a male teacher was aggressive toward a female student. In the eight scenarios of aggression, the situations in which the subjects assessed the target most positively were those in which the teachers were aggressive toward the students. These scores were followed by the situations in which a male was aggressive toward a female and a female was aggressive toward a male in a domestic setting, a female student was aggressive toward a female teacher, a male adolescent was aggressive toward a male adolescent, and a male student was aggressive toward a male teacher. The situation in which the subjects assessed the target worst was that in which a female adolescent was aggressive toward a female adolescent in a bar.

In addition, we can observe in Figure 4 that the subjects assessed a target more positively in the scenarios in which the aggressor and target were of different sexes (scenarios 1, 2, 3 and 4), and the subjects assessed a target with a lower status more positively than a target with a higher status (scenarios 3 and 4)

4. Conclusion

The results show some consistency with the hypotheses of the study and with previous research, but only partially. One of the hypotheses of this study—that the target's assessment would be more positive in the scenarios where the aggressor and target were of different sexes—was supported. A significant interaction was found between the sex of the aggressor and the sex of the target, and between the sex of the aggressor x the sex of the target x status difference. These results indicate that when the aggressor was male, the subjects assessed a female target more positively than a male target, regardless of status difference, and when the aggressor was female, the subjects assessed a male target more positively than a female target, regardless of status difference. In the eight scenarios of aggression, the subjects assessed a target more positively in the scenarios in which a female teacher was aggressive toward a male student, a male teacher was aggressive toward a female student, a male was aggressive toward a female in a domestic setting, and a female was aggressive toward a male in a domestic setting. It seems that the variable of status difference in interaction with the sex of the aggressor and target was not as relevant as when it was analyzed separately. The main effect of status difference was significant and the results confirmed the hypothesis. It was predicted that the subjects would assess a target more positively when the target and the aggressor were of different status; the results confirmed this. In all the scenarios of aggression, when a teacher was aggressive toward a male or female student, subjects assessed the student more positively. There was also a significant interaction between status difference and the sex of the aggressor: in a situation of aggression by a female against a target of different status, the target was more positively assessed than when the aggression was by a male (e.g., a female teacher was aggressive toward a male student and a female student was aggressive toward a female teacher).

Also, the results showed significant main effects for the sex of the aggressor, which confirm that in the situations initiated by a male aggressor the target was assessed more positively than in those situations initiated by a female aggressor. These results are consistent with prior work that suggested that the male aggressor was assessed worse than the female aggressor and that the female target was more positively assessed when the aggressor was a male (Harris and Knight-Bohnhoff, 1996).

However, the hypothesis that a female target would be assessed more positively than a male target in all the scenarios of aggression was confirmed only partially. In the four different scenarios that were used twice, with the only difference being the sex of the aggressor and of the target (domestic setting, teacher toward a student, student toward teacher, and adolescents in a bar), female targets were more positively assessed in the following scenarios: (a) a male was aggressive toward a female in the context of domestic violence; and (b) a female student was aggressive toward a female teacher. But in the other scenarios, the male targets were more positively assessed than the female targets (a male student and a male adolescent in a bar). The target was poorly assessed in following situations: (a) a female was aggressive toward another female in a bar; and (b) a male student was aggressive toward a male teacher. The subjects assessed a target more positively in the scenarios in which the target was a student, either male or female. These results are inconsistent with prior work that suggests that female targets are more positively assessed than males targets (Harris and Knight-Bohnhoff, 1996; Perles and Moreno, 2000)

Furthermore, the results confirm sex differences in social representations of aggression, in which females assessed the target more positively than males did when the aggressor was a male, and males assessed the target more positively when the aggressor was a female. Females, compared with males, assessed the target more positively when the aggressor was a male and when the target was a female. On the other hand, males assessed the target more positively than females did when the target was a male with different status. These results are consistent with prior work that suggests that females have more positive attitudes toward a female target (Harris and Cook, 1994; Locke and Richman, 1999; Pierre and Harris, 1993). And studies found that females assess the target more positively when the aggressor is a male (Hillier and Foddy, 1993), and that males assess the target worse when the target is a female (Caron and Carter, 1997; Falchikov, 1996; Keltikangas and Lindeman, 1997; Monson et al., 1996; Pakaslati and Keltinkangas, 1997; Toldos, 2006; Workman and Freeburg, 1999). However, although it was predicted that females would assess the target more positively in a wider range of situations than males would, there was no significant interaction between the sex of the aggressor, the sex of the target, and status difference with the sex-of-subject variable. The only situations in which females assessed the target more positively than males did were when a male was aggressive toward a female in a domestic setting and when a male teacher was aggressive toward a female student.

In summary, all of these results indicate that in situations of domestic violence between a man and a woman, the woman is assessed more positively, suggesting that there exists an overcoming of the sexist stereotype of women victims of masculine violence as being guilty of provoking the violence. This could indicate that the efforts undertaken in Spain in the last several years through prevention and intervention campaigns to eradicate violence against women and change sexist attitudes has had positive results. Nevertheless, it appears that the sexist stereotype that women have had as being guilty of provoking the violent situation has not been completely overcome by adolescents. Of all of the situations of violence in this study, the worst-evaluated target was an adolescent target of another adolescent in a leisure situation. This result is related to another study conducted with the same sample of adolescents in which it was found that it was precisely in situations of violence between two adolescent females that violence was most justified by subjects (Toldos, 2006) and that the target was considered to be guilty of provoking the incident (Toldos, 2002). The results involving the differences in representations of violence between male and female adolescents also indicates that adolescent females do not value the target in all situations and, in comparison with adolescent boys, evaluate an adolescent female worse when she is the target of another adolescent female. These finding are alarming if we take into account that the index of violence has increased in Spain between adolescent females and toward their male counterparts.

Furthermore, there was another finding that is important to consider: of all the situations of violence, students who were assaulted by their teachers were the most positively evaluated by the subjects. These results need to be taken into account in future studies and intervention programs for youth given that they could be related to the justification of violence against teachers that has occurred in Spain in the last several years.

These results warn of the necessity to carry out interventions that permit the overcoming of the sexist stereotype toward women of any age and in all environments. Also, education programs need to be oriented to contribute to the rejection of violence in general and violence toward women specifically. At the same time, programs must be started to prevent violence among adolescents and against authority, a trend that has a worrying level of acceptance among adolescents.

Of course, this study has limitations. In the situations of violence used in the study, the aggressor's behavior was only *verbally* violent. Therefore, it would be interesting in future studies to use scenarios in which other forms of violence take place. Also, the combinations of sex of aggressor and sex of target should be expanded in order to analyze the perception of adolescent violence between two adolescents of different sexes. Variables different from those already studied could be included, or the variable of status difference could be better defined, since it appears that status difference is not as important as the variety of scenarios of aggression tested in the study. Thus it would be enriching to include more scenarios of aggression (e.g., situations of aggression between adolescents in school, between acquaintances and strangers, in organizational contexts, and so forth) and use only scenarios in which at least one of the protagonists is an adolescent. Finally, it would be interesting to include predictor variables that could influence the perceptions and representations of the adolescents when observing situations of aggression.

5. References

Archer, J. (2000). Sex differences in aggression between heterosexual partners: A meta-analytic review. *Psychological Bulletin*, *126*, 651-680.

Archer, J. (2004). Sex differences in aggression in real-world settings: A meta-analytic review. *Review General Psychology*, *8*, 291-332.

Archer, J. & Haigh, A. M. (1997a). Do beliefs about aggressive feelings and actions predict reported levels of aggression? *British Journal of Social Psychology*, *36*, 83-105.

Archer, J. & Haigh, A. M. (1999). Sex differences in beliefs about aggression: Opponent's sex and the form of aggression. *British Journal of Social Psychology, 37*, 71-84.

Archer, J. & Parker, S. (1994). Social representations of aggression in children. *Aggressive Behavior, 2*, 101-114.

Benson, P. L. (1993). *The troubled journey: A portrait of 6th-12th graders*. Minneapolis, MN: Search Institute.

Björkqvist K., Lagerspetz K.M. J. & Kaukiainen A (1992). Do girls manipulate and boys fight?. Developmental trends in regard to direct and indirect aggression. *Aggressive Behavior, 18*, 117-127.

Björkqvist, K., Österman, K. & Kaukiainen, A. (1992). The development of direct and indirect aggressive strategies in males and females. In K. Björkqvist, & P. Niemelä (Eds.), *Of mice and women aspects of female aggression* (pp. 51-64). San Diego, CA: Academic Press.

Campbell, A. (1999). Staying alive: Evolution, culture, and women's intrasexual aggression. *Behavavior Brain Sciences, 22*, 203-252.

Campbell, A. & Muncer, S. (1987). Models of anger and aggression in the social talk of women and men. *Journal for the Theory of Social Behavior, 17*, 489-512.

Campbell, A., Muncer, S. & Coyle, E. (1991). Social representation of aggression as an explanation of gender differences: A preliminary study. *Aggressive behavior, 18*, 95-108.

Capaldi, D. M. & Crosby, L. (1997). Observed and reported psychological and physical aggression in young at risk couples. *Social Development, 6*, 184-206.

Caron, S. & Carter, B. (1997). The relationships among sex role orientation, egalitarianism, attitudes toward sexuality and attitudes toward violence against women. *The Journal of Social Psychology, 137, 5*, 568-587.

Condry, J. C. & Ross, D. F. (1985). Sex and aggression: The influence of gender labels on the perception of aggression in children. *Child Development, 56*, 225-244.

Crick, N. R. & Grotpeter, J. K. (1995). Relational aggression, gender, and social-psychological adjustment. *Child Development, 66*, 710-722.

Eagly, A. H. & Steffen, V. J. (1986). Gender and aggressive behavior: A meta-analytic review of the social psychological literature. *Psychological Bulletin, 100, 3*, 309-330.

Eagly, A. H. & Wood, W. E. (1991). Explaining sex differences in social behavior: A meta-analytic perspective (Special issue). *Personality and Social Psychology Bulletin, 17*, 306-315.

Falchikov, N. (1996). Adolescent attitudes to abuse of women: Are wives and non marital partners viewed differently? *Journal of Interpersonal Violence, 11, 3*, 391-409.

Fitzgerald, L.F., Swan, S. & Fischer, K. (1995). Why didn't she just report him?. The psychological and legal implications of women's responses to sexual harassment. *Journal of Social Issues, 51*, 117-138.

Frazier, P. A., Cochran, C C. & Olson, A. M. (1995). Social science research on lay definitions of sexual harassment. *Journal of Social Issues, 51*, 21-37.

Frodi, A., Macaulay, J. & Thome, P.R. (1977). Are women always less aggressive than men?. A review of the experimental literature. *Psychological Bulletin, 84*, 634-660.

Galen, B. R. & Underwood, M. K. (1997). A developmental investigation of social aggression among children. *Developmental Psychology, 33*, 589-600.

Harris, M.B. & Cook, C.A. (1994). Attributions about spouse abuse: It matters whom the batterers and victims are. *Sex Roles, 29, 9/10*, 629-644.

Harris, M.B. & Knight-Bohnhoff, K. (1996). Gender and Aggression I: Perceptions of Aggression. *Sex Roles*, *35*, *1/2*, 1-25.

Harris, M.B. & Knight-Bohnhoff, K. (1996). Gender and Aggression II: Personal Aggressiveness. *Sex Roles*, *35*, *1/2*, 27-42.

Hillier, L. & Foddy, M. (1993). The role of observer attitudes in judgments of blame in case of wife assault. *Sex Roles*, *29*, *9/10*, 629-644.

Hutchinson, R.L., Tess, D.E., Gleckman, A.D., Hagans, C.L. & Reese, L.E. (1994). Students' perceptions of male sexually aggressive behavior as a function of educational level and gender. *Sex Roles*, *30*, *5/6*, 407-422.

Keltikangas, L. & Lindeman, M. (1997). Evaluation of theft, lying and fighting in adolescence. *Journal of Youth and Adolescence*, *26*, *4*, 467-483.

Kristiansen, C. M. & Guilietti, R. (1990). Perceptions of wife abuse: effects of gender, attitudes toward women, and just-world beliefs among college students. *Psychology of Women Quarterly*, *14*, 177-189.

Lagerspetz K. M. J., Björkqvist K. & Peltonen T. (1988). Is indirect aggression typical of females? Gender differences in aggressiveness in 11 to 12 year old children. *Aggressive Behavior*, *14*, 403-414.

Locke, L. M. & Richman, C. L. (1999). Attitudes toward domestic violence: Race and gender issues. *Sex Roles*, *40*, *3/4*, 227-247.

Maccoby, E. E. & Jacklin, C. N. (1974). *The Psychology of Sex Differences*. Stanford, CA: Stanford University Press.

Marks, M. A. & Nelson, E. S. (1993). Sexual harassment on campus: Effects of professor gender on perception of sexually harassing behaviors. *Sex Roles*, *28*, *3/4*, 207- 217.

McCaul, K. D., Veltum, L. D., Boyechko, V. & Crawford, J. (1990). Understanding attributions of victim blame for rape: Sex, violence, and foreseeability. *Journal of Applied Social Psychology*, *20*, 1-26.

McCormick, N. (1994). *Sexual salvation: Affirming women's rights and pleasures*. Westport, CO: Praeger Publishers.

Monson, C., Byrd, G. & Langhinrichsen, J. (1996). To have and to hold: perceptions of marital rape. *Journal of Interpersonal Violence*, *11*, *3*, 410-424.

Ostrov, J. M., Crick, N. R. & Keating, C. F. (2005). Gender-biases perceptions of preschoolers' behaviour: How much is aggression and prosocial behavior in the eye of the beholder?. *Sex Roles*, *53*, 394-398.

Pakaslati, L. & Keltinkangas, J. (1997). The relationships between moral approval of aggression, aggressive problem solving strategies and aggressive behavior in 14 years old adolescents. *Journal of Social Behavior and Personality*, *12*, *4*, 905-924.

Perles, F. & Moreno, M. P. (2000). Influencia de la provocación, la descripción de la agresión y el sexo en la percepción social de las víctimas de violencia familiar. *Revista de Psicología Social Aplicada*, *10*, *1*, 97-113.

Pierce, M. C. & Harris, R. J. (1993). The effect of provocation, race, and injury description on men's and women's perceptions of a wife-battering incident. *Journal of Applied Social Psychology*, *10*, 767-790.

Richardson, R. & Green, L. (1999). Social sanction and threat explanations of gender effects on direct and indirect aggression. *Aggressive Behavior*, *25*, 425-434.

Samivalli, C., Kaukiainen, A. & Lagerspetz, K. (2000). Aggression and sociometric status among peers: Do gender and type of aggression matter. *Scandinavian Journal of Psychology*, *41*, 17-24.

Susser, S. A. & Keating, C. F. (1990). Adult sex rol orientation and perceptions of aggressive interactions between girls and boys. *Sex Roles*, *23*, 147-155.

Toldos, M. P. (2002). *Adolescencia, Violencia y Género.* Tesis Doctoral. Universidad Complutense de Madrid.

Toldos, M. P. (2005). Sex and Age differences in self-estimated physical, verbal and indirect aggression in Spanish adolescents. *Aggressive Behavior*, *31*, *13-23.*

Toldos, M. P. (2006). Effects of sex and status of target and aggressor on adolescents' justification of aggression. In K. Österman, & K. Björkqvist (Eds.), *Contemporary research on aggression* (pp.64-68). Abo Akademy University, Vasa, Finland.

Underwood, M. K. (2003). *Social aggression among girls*. New York: Guilford Press.

White, J. W. (1983). Sex and gender issues in aggression research. In R. G. Geen, & E. I. Donnerstei (Eds.), *Aggression: Theoretical and Empirical Reviews* (vol. 2, pp 1-26). New York: Academic Press.

Workman, J. E. & Freeburg, E. W. (1999). An examination of date rape, victim dress, and perceiver variables within the context of attribution theory. *Sex Roles*, *41 (3/4)*, 261-277.

In: Violent Crime and Prisons: Population…
Ed: Aidan Renshaw and Emelina Suárez
ISBN: 978-1-60741-668-5

Chapter 10

LOVE, WARMTH AND SEXUAL GRATIFICATION OR, RATHER, MANIPULATION OF POWER AND ABUSE: FEMALE INMATES' ATTITUDES TOWARD SAME-SEX SEXUAL RELATIONSHIPS IN A MAXIMUM-SECURITY PRISON

Tomer Einat
Department of Criminology, Bar-Ilan University, Ramat Gan, Israel.

ABSTRACT

Research on same-sex sexual relationships among female inmates has been a neglected topic until recently. This article examines female inmates' attitudes toward same-sex sexual activity in prison, and analyzes the link between female inmates' viewpoints of same-sex sexual relationships in prison and the length of imprisonment, ethnicity, and the prevalence of such conduct.

Main findings: (a) Most female inmates express negative attitudes towards same-sex sexual relationships in prison; (b) `short-timers` and 'long-timers' define and perceive same-sex sexual relations in prison differently; (c) ethnicity does not affect female inmates' attitude toward same sex sexual relationships.

INTRODUCTION

To date, there have been relatively few studies examining same-sex sexual relationships in female prisons (Hensley, 2000; Girshick, 1999; Owen, 1998; Pollock, 1998; Greer, 2000). Both early and current research found that many female prisoners participate consensually in same-sex sexual couple relationships and/or "pseudo-families" (Giallombardo, 1996; Larsen & Nelson, 1984; Owen, 1998; Pollock, 1998; Propper, 1982; Struckman-Johnson & Struckman-Johnson, 1999; Ward & Kassebaum, 1965).[1] Such relationships were found to

[1] For a comprehensive review of these studies, see Alarid (1996, 2000) and Koscheski, Hensley, Wright and Tewksbury (2002).

form a significant aspect of the female prison subculture (Pollock, 1998), to be associated with economical and sexual manipulation and victimization (Greer, 2000; Owen, 1998; Pollock, 1998), and to fulfill lost familial roles including daughter, wife, father, cousin and grandmother (Owen, 1998). Therefore, the study of such relations may deepen our understanding of female prison culture and inmate behavior (Tewksbury & West, 2000) and, more importantly, help reduce unwanted sexual conduct behind prison walls and the related health problems, which have severe implications for prisoners, institutional staff, and the general public (Hensley, 2000; Maruschak, 1999; Struckman-Johnson et al., 1996). Although some attention has been paid to the research of same-sex sexual activity in female prisons (Alarid, 2000; Owen, 1998; Pollock, 1998; Struckman-Johnson et al. 1996), one research topic has received almost no academic attention: Female inmates' attitudes toward same-sex sexual relationships in prison (Hensley, 2000; Girshick, 1999). The present research seeks to fill this gap in our understanding of same-sex-sexuality in female prisons. Specifically, the aims of the study were: (a) to study female inmates' perceptions of same-sex sexual activity in prison, (b) to examine the relationships between female inmates' attitudes toward same-sex sexual relationships in prison and the prevalence of such conduct, (c) to explore the connection between female inmates' definition of same-sex sexual relations and length of imprisonment, and (d) to analyze the link between female inmates' ethnicity and attitudes toward same-sex sexual activity in prison.

LITERATURE REVIEW

By design, prisons are single-gender institutions. According to Sykes (1958) and Faith (1993), deprivation of heterosexual relationships constitutes one of the most significant 'pains of imprisonment' for male and female inmates. The replacement of heterosexual relationships (at least temporarily) with same-sex sexual ones and their permanent psychological impact on female prisoners has been documented (Chesney-Lind & Rodriquez, 1983; Fletcher et al. 1993; Giallombardo, 1966; Koscheski et al. 2002; Larsen & Nelson, 1984; Owen, 1998; Pollock, 1998; Ward & Kassebaum, 1965). To date, the majority of criminological and penological literature refers to two main categories of same-sex sexual relationships in female prisons: Play families (Giallombardo, 1966; Heffernan, 1972; Owen, 1998) and homosexual relationships (also called: "same-sex sexual relationships"; Koscheski et al. 2002; Owen, 1988; Propper, 1982; Ward & Kassebaum, 1965).[2]

In 1965, Ward and Kassebaum studied the sexual behaviors of adult female inmates at the California Institution for Women in Frontera. Their study revealed that 50% of prisoners had engaged in "some form of overt sexual experience at least sometime during their sentence" (p.92). Giallombardo's (1966) study in the West Virginia Women's Federal Reformatory examined sexual relationships as well as membership and relationship of inmates involved in pseudo-families within the prison facility. Interviews with the inmates, staff, and the associate warden led Giallombardo to estimate that approximately 86% of the women had had a homosexual experience of some type during their incarceration. In addition,

2 In contrast to this, Bosworth (1999) argued that relying on these typologies of female inmates' adaptations is problematic because they are based on traditional gender stereotypes of female behavior and do not acknowledge the full range of female experiences and identities.

the researcher had discovered that many inmates participated in pseudo-marriages as well as make-believe family networks. Giallombardo (1966) concluded that these dyad and kinship relationships evolved as a result of the female prisoners' psychological, physiological or sociological deficiencies.

Heffernan's (1972) study of 100 female inmates in the Women's Reformatory of the District of Columbia in Occoquan Virginia, focused on the involvement of inmates in pseudo-families as well as "game-playing" within the prison facility.[3] The study, which was based on structured interviews and surveys, found that 71% of the population was involved in sexual relationships, but only 50%-60% of the inmates were involved in a marriage. Pseudo-families at Occoquan were viewed by the interviewees as a critical element of social order within the facility. Membership within these make-believe families supplied the inmate with a sense of stability, emotional and economic support, and access to information during their incarceration. These types of relationships were therefore favored and accepted.

Nelson (1974) conducted a study of homosexual behavior in female correctional facilities in New Jersey and Pennsilvania. Based on 119 questionnaires and thirty-four interviews, Nelson (1974) concluded that homosexual behavior was considered to be the norm in both prison facilities, and that pseudo-family networks were prevalent at both prisons. Psychological security and sexual gratification were the important factors listed for voluntarily participation in such conduct

An additional study, conducted by Propper (1976) of four female juvenile institutions and three coed juvenile institutions, focused on homosexual behavior in correctional institutions. The research revealed that 14% of the inmates were "going with" or married to another inmate. Additionally, 10% of the females reported passionately kissing another girl, 10% wrote love letters to another girl, and seven percent reported sexual behavior beyond just hugging and kissing (Propper, 1976, 1978, 1981, 1982). Propper (1981) concluded that same-sex-sexual relationships were affected by cultural, personality, and biological variables prior to incarceration, as well as physical and emotional satisfaction within the prison facility. While examining pseudo-families, Propper (1982) found that 49% of the respondents reported membership in a make-believe family. Furthermore, she found that make-believe family networks consisted of basically sexless relationships (sister/sister, mother/daughter), and that membership in such families was not associated with the potentiality of homosexual behavior. Affiliation with these families occurred mainly for the purpose of a sense of confidence, companionship, fondness, attention, status, esteem, and acceptance. Hopper (1980) revealed different findings in his study on 176 female inmates in the Florida Correctional Institution in Lowell, Massachusetts, including: the existence of two separate pseudo-families in prison: the conventional family – a sexless family unit centering on security, companionship, and affection and, an additional smaller family unit revolving around traditional initiatives as well as homosexual relationships. Hopper suggested that membership into this second type of family "provided an outlet of new sexual partners for females who were predisposed to homosexual behavior" (Koscheski et al. 2002, p. 127). A large number of studies indicated that pseudo-families did not always include sexual relationships, and that these nonsexual relationships tended to provide more security, support, guidance, and love (Owen, 1998; Pollock-Byrne, 1990).

---

[3] The term "played" was used by the inmates to distinguish those females who were involved in conjugal roles from those who were not

In 1998, Owen conducted a three-year quasi-ethnographic study of the Central California Women's Facility (CCWF). Her study revealed that 30%-60% of the prisoners engaged in same-sex sexual behavior and that there was a complex system of interpersonal relationships among the inmates which were based on emotional, practical, material, sexual, and familial foundations. She also discovered that the prison families and dyads crossed both racial and ethnic boundaries. Pseudo-families at CCWF consisted of older women (both in terms of their time served and their actual age) assuming the role of mothers and/or mentors, younger inmates taking the role of the "kids", and more aggressive, dominant women assuming the role of dad or brother. These designations, however, were flexible and could change over time. Many entered into the prison family because they had either no family or a disruptive family on the outside.

Greer (2000) examined sexual relations, make-believe families and friendship in a Midwestern state female correctional facility. The results of this study, based upon semi-structured interviews with approximately 14% (n=35) of the prison's population, revealed that fifteen women had been involved in or were currently involved in a sexual relationship with another woman. Reasons given for participation in this type of relationship included game playing, economic manipulation, loneliness, the need for companionship, and genuine affection. Moreover, Greer (2000) discovered that make-believe families did not exist at this facility. She concluded that modern inmates have everyday, ongoing relationships with their families on the outside as well as access to media coverage of local and world events and, thus, pseudo-families that were traditionally formed as a proxy for the family on the outside (ibid.) have become unnecessary.

Hensley, Tewksbury and Koscheski (2002) conducted a study of consensual sex among female inmates. The purpose of their study was two-fold: (a) to address same-sex sexual behavior within a female correctional facility, and (b) to predict which female inmates were most likely to participate in five same-sex sexual behaviors (kissing, touching, receiving oral sex, performing oral sex, and a fifth variable constructed as a composite of the first four to measure the rate of homosexual behavior) based on several demographic and incarcerated-related variables. Hensley and colleagues (2002) reported that although the subcultures and behaviors of incarcerated women have changed, at least one third of the female inmates participating in their study continued to be same-sex sexually active during incarceration. The most significant variables in the models that predicted consensual same-sex sexual activity while incarcerated were age, amount of time served, and religion, with age showing the greatest influence on female inmates' same-sex sexual behavior. Women under the age of thirty-four were more likely to have engaged in all five types of behavior. Women who had served longer prison sentences were more likely to have engaged in same-sex sexual activities with another inmate than women who had served shorter periods of time.[4] Additionally, women who reported a non-Protestant religious affiliation were more likely to have performed oral sex on another inmate than those who reported a Protestant religious affiliation.

Keys (2002) also referred to the amount of time served and argued that female inmates, particularly those who had served long sentences and lost contact with their families and children, remarked on the key functions that a prison family performs.

[4] Race, however, was a statistically significant predictor of only two forms of same-sex sexual behavior (touching another inmate in a sexual way and receiving oral sex).

Finally, Hensley (2000) conducted an exploratory research regarding differences between male and female inmates' attitudes toward homosexuality in prison. The study, which was based on 256 anonymous surveys, revealed that gender, same-sex sexual conduct during incarceration, race, and remaining sentence time, had statistically significant effects on inmates' attitudes toward same-sex sexual relationships in prison. Specifically, incarcerated men were more likely than incarcerated women to have homophobic attitudes. Inmates who had engaged in same-sex sexual conduct during incarceration were less likely to have homophobic attitudes than those who had not. Those who had longer remaining sentence times were more likely to have negative attitudes toward homosexuality compared with those with shorter remaining sentence times. Finally, black inmates were more tolerant of same-sex sexual conduct compared with white inmates.

As indicated by the research described above, same-sex sexual relationships in female-prison facilities are common and function as a means of coping with 'imprisonment pains', thus enabling inmates to serve their prison time with the least amount of psychological discomfort. In addition, thus far relatively few studies have researched this topic – in general and female inmates' attitudes toward it – in particular. The challenge for researchers is therefore to find ways to produce valid and reliable research concerning same-sex sexual relationships in female-prisons and to increase our understanding of its nature, implications and consequences in female prison subculture.

METHOD

In order to both explore the way female inmates look at same-sex sexual relationships in prison and to attach meaning to the experience, the researchers used a flexible design. This methodology allowed access to contents that are not predicted a priori, as well as examination of the research subject matter from the standpoint of the research sample (Briggs, 1986; Silverman, 1993). Qualitative methodology and the phenomenological semi-structured interview were used to collect and analyse data from the participants. The final stage of the analysis is a description of the main trends that emerge from the findings (Stake, 1995).

Participants

The participants were 46 adult female prisoners from a single Israeli female prison, Neve Tirza.[5] The ethnic ratio of inmates at Neve-Tirza prison participating in this study was comprised of approximately 65.2% Jews and 34.8% [Israeli] Arabs. All participants were literate females. The mean number of years of education for the inmates was approximately 12 (*SD*=2.60) and the mean age was approximately 37 years (*SD*=12.32). Most interviewees (approximately 46%) were single, just about 24% were divorced and approximately 26% were married. Most female inmates (59%) had children. Approximately, thirty percent had been in jail previously; the mean number of incarcerations was approximately 2.2 (*SD*=2.70),

[5] Initially, 48 women-inmates were recruited to the study but 2 chose to drop out after being informed about the purpose of the study and its procedures.

and the mean number of months served in prison was approximately 62 months (*SD*=84.70). (See appendix A).

Procedure

The researchers met the warden, the vice warden and the head of the educational department at the Neve-Tirza prison facility. During the initial meetings, the researchers described the type and purpose of the research project and requested the assistance of the staff in notifying as many female inmates as possible about the study, as well as encouraging them to voluntarily participate in it. In the course of the following month, the researchers met with all inmates willing to participate, and explained the nature and objectives of the study, requested voluntary participation, and guaranteed anonymity. Female inmates willing to participate in the study signed an informed consent form serving as an official agreement provided by the Israel Prison Service. This agreement included a statement from the inmate declaring their voluntary agreement to participate, and acknowledging that they may withdraw from the study at any time. In the ten months that followed, 140 hours of in-depth semi-structured interviews were conducted with 46 prisoners all of whom volunteered to take part in the study without payment. Interviews were held in the education wing of the prison facility during the afternoon hours, each session lasting approximately 2 hours.

Appendix A. Descriptive Analysis of Participants' Type of Crime and Length of Time Served (*n* = 46).

Characteristics	Number	Percentage
Type of Crime[6]		
Substance abuse	13	28
Drug trafficking	14	30
Burglary	8	18
Violent	7	16
Murder/Accomplice manslaughter	7	16
Fraud/Forgery	9	20%
White collar crime	3	7%
Others	6	13%
Length of time served		
Less than 1 year	7	15%
1 to 5 years	25	43%
more than 5 years	14	26%

The prisoners were encouraged to share their experiences and attitudes with the interviewer in a setting conducive to a sense of interpersonal involvement. Given that definitions of same-sex sexual relationships vary considerably (Hensley et al. 2002), the interviewees were asked to refer to advances (invited or uninvited) made by and directed at female inmates that included oral sex (receiving or performing), genital folding or penetration

[6] The groups under the "Type of Crime" category are not mutually exclusive; therefore the total number of inmates exceeds the sample size (i.e., participants may have committed multiple offenses).

of the vagina or anus of another person by a hand, finger, or other object (U.S. Department of Justice, 2005). All interviews were audio-recorded with the consent of the interviewees.[7]

Research Tool

The phenomenological semi-structured interview was chosen as the most appropriate research tool to achieve the main research objectives. This type of interview is based on general guidelines to ensure that all those interviewed are subject to similar stimuli, thereby allowing a common base for data analysis (Briggs, 1986; Porgebin, 2003). The design of the interview was tentative and was modified in correspondence with new findings that emerged from the flexible method of questioning (Rubin & Rubin, 1995).[8]

In addition, a "self-report personal-details" questionnaire was distributed to all interviewees. The questionnaire included demographic questions, criminal histories and age of criminal onset of the participants' "first-degree" family members.

Data Analysis

In view of their essentially qualitative nature, the data were subjected to content analysis (Strauss & Corbin, 1990; Weber, 2001), which is generally applied to narrative texts such as transcribed interviews and published works. This type of analysis seeks to expound what can be learned through respondents' understanding of events and through close examination of the content and language of texts. The objective is to uncover aspects of meaning by examining the data qualitatively. In effect, content analysis is used to examine how respondents view and understand certain issues, as well as to help examine and understand their beliefs.

In order to analyze and code the data, interviews were studied extensively. Themes within the inmates' responses emerged naturally, though careful attention was paid so that weight was not given to any preconceived themes that the researcher may have harbored. The transcript data was, therefore, analyzed thematically first, and, only after themes were identified, examined in light of the questions already identified.

The analysis is based upon the frequency with which themes appear in the data, indicating the respondents' attention to these particular subjects in certain situations, and the intensity with which they relate to these subjects (Pogrebin, 2003). In this research, intensity was measured by the level of importance that the respondents ascribed to the respective topics, based on the words they used to refer to them. The analysis is, then, essentially thematic and based on categorization of content areas.

---

[7] Preference was given to recording rather than taking notes during the conversation because: (a) detailed note-taking can distract both researcher and interviewee and disrupt the conversation; (b) it is mentally exhausting to listen closely to everything said while taking accurate notes; (c) it is important to keep data collection and analysis separate and avoid premature conclusions before all of the data are in, and taking notes requires the researcher to make judgments about what is important during the interview; and (d) like any other research effort, it is desirable to keep the original data complete and intact, so that both the researcher and other interested researchers can refer to it, if necessary Doyle, 2001).

[8] The main advantage of such an interview is that it enables the interviewee to correct misunderstandings and vagueness in the course of the interview. This flexibility contributes to the quality and credibility of the interview (Rubin & Rubin, 1995).

RESULTS

Nearly all interviewees described their attitudes toward same-sex sexual relationships in prison. Approximately 67% of the Jewish and Muslim inmates (65.2% and 34.8% of the research population respectively) expressed negative attitudes towards same-sex sexual relationships in prison, 13% had positive attitudes and 20% reported experiencing relatively neutral feelings toward participation in such relationships (see Appendix C). These respondents indicated that although they did not wish to become involved in intimate relationships with other women, they did not judge those individuals who did choose to engage in such activity harshly.

Appendix B. Motivation for Participation in Same-Sex-Sexual Relationships in Prison (n = 46).

Motivation	Number	Percentage
Economic manipulation	31	67%
Love	8	17%
Sex	31	67%
Fear	1	0.5%

Note: Since female inmates may have multiple motivations for participating in same-sex sexual relationships in prison, the total number of interviewees exceeds the sample size, and the total percentage goes beyond 100%.

Appendix C. Israeli Female-Inmates' Type of Attitudes toward Same-Sex-Sexual Relationships in Prison (n = 46)

Motivation	Number	Percentage
Positive attitudes	6	13%
Negative attitudes	31	67%
Neutral attitudes	9	20%

Interestingly, although 90% of the respondents described same-sex sexual relationships among women as being extremely prevalent, only 13% of them held positive attitudes towards this type of relations.

Negative Attitudes toward Same-Sex Sexual Relations in Prison

Prisoner *SY*, a twenty-one-year-old female, comments: "I would never ever like to have lesbian relationships…god forbid. There are many other sexless ways to receive warmth and a hug".

YH, a fifty-eight-year-old woman, now serving a long first term of incarceration, expresses this point of view: "Many girls here are disgusting…lesbians…having [same-sex] sexual relations in my cell…I'm shocked…it makes me sick…revolting".

R, a prisoner in her early forties, suggests: "Girls [inmates] who have same-sex sexual relationships in prison have reached the lowest possible level...even if one has to serve a long sentence, she can release [her sexual needs] by writing letters and books" (Similarly, these attitudes are documented in Einat's (in press) findings regarding rape and consensual sex in male Israeli prisons (i.e. all male inmates have stated that same-sex sexual relationships are dishonourable and that prisoners participating in them are morally disgraceful).

Lastly, *A*, a forty-four female inmate serving a life prison term, states her negative attitude toward same-sex sexual relationships in prison: "One thing that many people and prisoners say about a newcomer is that she will be corrupted in prison...and this is one of the main reasons why inmates who never had same-sex sexual experiences on the outside begin having [sexual] lesbian relationships inside [the prison facility]. I believe these girls have weak characters and such relations are repulsive".

Neutral Attitudes Concerning Same-Sex Sexual Relationships in Prison

AZ, a young female inmate, talks about her feelings on the subject of same-sex sexual relationships in prison: "I really do not know why so many girls [inmates] have lesbian relationships in prison, but I have to say that it does not bother me or surprise me at all. I accept any kind of conduct in prison and if the [lesbian] girls enjoy [having same-sex sexual relationships] than it's fine with me...let them enjoy".

HA, a middle-class woman, supports the feelings mentioned above: "I judge no one. I'm apathetic towards sex in prison".

An additional point of view, relating to the neutral attitudes toward same-sex sexual relationships in prison, is expressed by *SI*, a middle-age Muslim inmate serving her first [and relatively long] prison term: "In Savion wing [housing non-drug-addicted inmates] the lesbian sexual relationships are nice...with honor and warmth, but in the other two "dirty" wings [housing ex-addicted females] it is horrible...revolting, dishonorable. Personally, I do not support or oppose [sexual] lesbian relations in prison and I never had any experience in lesbianism".

Positive Attitudes Regarding Same-Sex Sexual Relations in Prison

Thirteen percent of the participants expressed positive attitudes to same-sex sexual relations. For instance, a forty-year-old Jewish inmate and a twenty-one-year-old Jewish inmate [correspondingly], serving their first term of imprisonment, expressed positive attitudes toward same-sex sexual relations in prison:

Prisoner *EA*: "I never had and will never have same-sex sexual relationships in prison...mainly because for me it symbolizes a kind of breakdown...it's like saying to yourself that you will never ever marry in the future. However, I support these kinds of relationships because I know they help many inmates and make them happy. Once, I was even a matchmaker".

Inmate *N*: "I won't lie to you...I'm a bisexual, and I believe that it's the right of every woman to choose what kind of [sexual] life she wishes. On the outside, same-sex sexual relations between women are gentle and pleasant".

DISCUSSION

This study presents Israelis female inmates' attitudes toward same-sex sexual relationships in prison.

Before discussing the results of this study, we acknowledge that they must be interpreted in light of their main limitations: (1) The validity of the inmates responses and (2) Sample size.

(1) As mentioned previously, all data were collected by phenomenological semi-structured interviews. Since several studies have indicated that same-sex sexual relationships in female prisons are underreported due to reluctance of becoming a 'snitch', shame, and fear of being stigmatized as a 'canteen whore' (Eigenberg, 1994; Einat, In Press; Greer, 2000; Koscheski et al. 2002; Owen, 1998: 21-22), it is possible that other sophisticated data-collection techniques (i.e., written self-reports; interviewing past and future prison intelligence officers) as well as more convenient settings for interviews (i.e., outside the prison facility) may have revealed more detailed data, as well as additional findings that were not revealed in the present work.

(2) The results of this research are based on interviews with only 25% of the total population of the women-inmates in the prison facility. Hence, the researchers cannot be sure that the attitudes towards same-sex sexual relationships in prison as well as the incentives to take part in them stated in this paper truly represent the perspectives and attitudes of the total female-inmate population.

Despite these limitations, the researchers believe that the results of this study add to the existing knowledge base regarding the attitudes towards same-sex sexual relationships in female prison facilities.

One significant finding of this study relates to the negative attitudes of most Israeli female inmates toward same-sex sexual relationships in prison. 67% of the interviewees demonstrated negative attitudes toward same sex sexual relationships, perceiving them as a form of prostitution and those who participate in them as 'canteen whores'. Only 13% of the research participants expressed positive attitudes toward this type of relationships while 20% of the participants reported experiencing relatively neutral feelings toward participation in such relationships. Interestingly, these findings stand in contrast to the actual same-sex sexual behaviour among Israeli female inmates in prison (Einat & Chen, in press). Eighty five percent of the female inmates admit participating, at least once, in same-sex sexual relationships in prison, and eighty nine percent of the Israeli female inmates' population, regardless of whether or not they approve of such behaviour, consider same-sex sexual relationships a fairly significant aspect of prison subculture and describe them as being extremely prevalent (*ibid.*). These findings strengthen Keys's (2002) argument that same-sex sexual behavior among female inmates and prisoners' attitudes towards such relationships are not congruent and, in some cases, stand in contrast. This suggests that such sexual conduct in prison may be an outcome of the prison atmosphere and/or economical necessity rather than female inmates' sexual preference/tendencies. Moreover: The tremendous prevalence of same-sex sexual relationships in the only Israeli female prison facility in spite of negative inmate attitudes toward them may reflect the beginning of a new era in the general thoughts and feelings regarding female prison sexual relationships. Following Festinger's (1957) dissonance cognitive theory and Kelman's arguments regarding the ability of behavior to change attitude when there is a conflict between these two variables (i.e. behaviour and attitudes), it can be postulated that same-sex sexual relations will continue to take place in the future, and that the female inmates' attitudes toward them will become more and more positive.

A second important finding of this study relates to the definition of same-sex sexual relationships in prison. Female inmates who define same-sex sexual relations as prostitution are mainly `short-timers` (sentenced to 1 year- 5 years). In contrast, `long-timers` (sentenced to more than 5 years) tend to characterize these relationships as an expression of love and companionship and, therefore, participate in these relationships in a sincere and long-lasting manner. These findings correlate with the findings of Hensley et al., (2002) revealing that women who had served longer prison sentences were more likely to have engaged in same sex sexual activities with another inmate than women who had served shorter sentences. Our findings therefore indicate that perception of, and participation in same-sex sexual relations in female prisons are linked to the length of imprisonment.

An additional important finding of this study concerns the link between ethnicity and attitudes toward same-sex sexual relationships in prison. More than two thirds of the Jewish and Muslim female prisoners participating in this study expressed negative attitudes toward same-sex sexual relationships in prison but, at the same time, 90% (n=27) of the Jewish prisoners and 81.25% (n=13) of the Muslim inmates admit to participating, at least once, in them. Since most female inmates share the `attitude-conduct` conflict, regardless of ethnicity, it could be proposed that ethnicity does not affect their attitude and behavior with regard to same sex sexual relationships and, more importantly, that ethnicity is a minor predicting factor of same-sex sexual conduct in the current Israeli female prison subculture.

The findings of this study may have a contribution in providing correctional administrators and staff with theoretical and practical knowledge concerning the role of same-sex sexual relationships in prison. For example, since same-sex sexual relationships are perceived as negatively affecting the maintenance, control, safety, health and secure environment of the prison (Gartner, & Miller, 2000; Greer, 2000; Huggins, Capeheart & Newman, 2006; Krebs, 2002; McGaughey & Tewksbury, 2002; Maruschak, 1999; Saum et al., 1995; Tyndall, Lik, Montaner & Wood, 2005), correctional administrators must continue to strive to forbid all forms of such relations in female-prisons. In the words of one long-timer interviewee: 'even if one has to serve a long sentence, she can release [her sexual needs] by writing letters and books".

As a final note, it should be emphasised that female prison sexual relationship research in Israel and worldwide is incomplete and fails to adequately address the policy needs of correctional authorities. We know very little about how female-prisoners create characterisations of sexuality and very few studies have concentrated on similarities or differences in sexual terms and roles in prisons in different countries or regions. There is a lack of accurate data regarding sexual victimisation and manipulation of female prisoners by correctional officers, and there is no gender-oriented research regarding the resemblance or dissimilarities in meanings, functions and implications of same-sex sexual relationships in male and female prisons. The existing literature on female prison sexual relationships hardly touches upon any of these areas. There is a great need for additional research that addresses these issues, so that we can begin to explore the answers to these types of questions.

REFERENCES

Alarid, L. F. (1996). Female inmates subcultures. In J. W. Marquart, & J. R. Sorensen (Eds.), *Correctional contexts: Contemporary and classical readings* (pp.134-139). Los-Angeles: Roxbury.

Alarid, L. F. (2000). Sexual assault and coercion among incarcerated women prisoners: Excerpts from prison letters. *The Prison Journal, 80 (4)*, 391-406.

Bosworth, M. (1999). *Engendering resistance: Agency and power in women's prisons*. Brookfield, VT: Ashgate.

Briggs, C. L. (1986). *Learning How to Ask: A Sociolinguistic Appraisal of the Role of the Interview in Social Science Research*. Cambridge, UK: Cambridge University Press.

Chen, G. (2008). Patterns of Crime and Substance Abuse among Israeli Ex-Addict Female Inmates. *Asian Journal of Criminology* (In Press).

Chesney-Lind, M. & Rodriquez, N. (1983). Women under lock and key: A view from the inside. *The Prison Journal, 63*, 47-65.

Chesney-Lind, M. (1986). Women and crime: The female offender. *Signs, 12(1)*, 78-96.

Chesney-Lind, M. (2006). Patriarcy, crime and justice: Feminist criminology in an era of backlash. *Feminist Criminology, 1(1)*, 6-26.

Einat, T. Inmate Harassment and Rape: An Exploratory Study of Seven Maximum and Medium Security Male Prisons in Israel. *The International Journal of Offender Therapy and Comparative Criminology* (In Press).

Einat, T. Rape and Consensual Sex in Male Israeli Prisons: Are There Differences with Western Prisons? *The Prison Journal* (In Press).

Faith, K. (1993). *Unruly women: The politics of confinement and resistance*. Vancouver: Press Gang Publishers.

Festinger, L. (1957). *A theory of cognitive dissonance*. Evanston, IL: Row, Peterson.

Fletcher, B., Shaver, L. D. & Moon, D. (Eds.), (1993). *Women prisoners: A forgotten population*. Westport, CT: Praeger.

Giallombardo, R. (1966). *Society of women: A study of a woman's prison*. New York: Wiley.

Giligan, C. (1982). In a Different Voice: *Psychological Theory and Women's Development*. Harvard University Press

Girshick, L. B. (1999). *No safe haven: Stories of women in prison*. Boston: Northeastern University Press.

Greer, K. R. (2000). The changing nature of interpersonal relationships in a women's prison. *The Prison Journal, 80*, 442-467.

Heffernan, E. (1972). *Making it in prison: The square, the cool, and the life*. New York: John Wiley and Sons, Inc.

Hensley, C. (2000). What have we learned from studying prison sex. *Humanity and Society, 24(4)*, 348-360.

Hensley, C. R., Tewksbury, R. & Koscheski, M. (2002). The characteristics and motivations behind female prison sex. *Women and Criminal Justice, 13*, 125-139.

Hopper, C. (1980). A study of homosexuality and surrogate families in an institution for women. *American Journal of Sociology, 37*, 247-253.

Irwin, J. (1980). *Prisons in Turmoil.* Boston: Little, Brown.

Irwin, J. & Austin, J. (1997). *It's about time: America imprisonment binge* (2nd ed.) Belmont, CA: Wadsworth.

Irwin, J. & Cressey, D. (1962). Thieves, convicts and the inmate culture. *Social Problems, 10*, 145-147.

James, J. (1980). Women's Liberation and the Female Delinquent. *Journal of Research in Crime and Delinquency, 17(2), 230-244.*

Kelman, H. C. (1974). Attitudes are alive and well and gainfully employed in the sphere of action. *American Psychologist, 29*, 310-324.

Koscheski, M., Hensley, C., Wright, J. & Tewksbury, R. (2002). Consensual sexual behavior. In: C. Hensley (Ed.), *Prison sex: Practice and policy*. Boulder, London: Lynne Rienner Publishers.

Larsen, J. & Nelson, J. (1984). Women, friendship, and adaptation to prison. *Journal of Criminal Justice, 12(5)*, 601-615.

McGaughey, D. & Tewksbury, R. (2002). Masturbation. In C. Hensley (Ed.), *Prison sex* (pp. 133-142). Boulder, CO: Lynne Rienner Publishers.

Morash, M., Haarr, R. & Rucker, L. (1994). A comparison of programming for women and men and US prisons in the 1980s. *Crime and Delinquency, 40(2)*, 197-221.

Nelson, C. (1974). *A study of homosexuality among women inmates at two state prisons*. PhD. dissertation, Temple University.

Obergoot-Salev, R. (2001). Coping of inmates in Israel prison-the pseudo-family. *Unpublished Master's Thesis*. Ramat-Gan: Bar-Ilan University.

Owen, B. (1998). *"In the mix": Struggles and survival in a women's prison*. Albany: State University of New York Press.

Pogrebin, Mark. (2003). *Qualitative Approaches to Criminal Justice Perspectives from the Field*. Newbury Park, CA: Sage Publications.

Pollock, J. M. (1998). *Counseling women in prison*. Thousand Oaks, CA: Sage.

Pollock-Byrne, J. M. (1990). *Women, prison, and crime*. Belmont, CA: Wadsworth.

Propper, A. M. (1976). *Importation and deprivation perspectives on homosexuality in correctional institutions: An empirical test of their relative efficacy*. PhD. dissertation, University of Michigan, Ann Arbor

Propper, A. M. (1978). Lesbianism in female and coed correctional institutions. *Journal of Homosexuality, 3(3)*, 265-274.

Propper, A. M. (1981). *Prison homosexuality: Myth and reality*. Lexington, Mass: Lexington Books.

Propper, A. M. (1982). Make-believe families and homosexuality among imprisoned girls. *Criminology, 20(1)*, 127-138.

Rubin, H. & Rubin, I. (1995). *Qualitative Interviewing: The Art of Hearing Data*. Thousand Oaks, CA: Sage.

Saum, C., Surratt, H., Inciardi, J. & Bennett, R. (1995). Sex in Prison: Exploring the Myths and Realities. *The Prison Journal, 75/4*, 413-430.

Silverman, D. (1993). *Interpreting qualitative data: methods for analyzing talk, text, and interaction*. Thousand Oaks, CA: Sage.

Stake, R. E. (1995). *The Art of Case Study Research*. Thousand Oaks, CA: Sage Publications.

Strauss, A. & Corbin, J. (1990). *Basics of Qualitative Research: Grounded Theory Procedures and Techniques*. Newbury Park, CA: Sage Publications.

Struckman-Johnson, C. J. & Struckman-Johnson, D. L. (November, 1999). Pressured and forced sexual contact reported by women in three Midwestern prisons. Paper presented at the annual meeting of the Society for the Study of Sexuality and the American Association of Sex Educators, Counselors, and Therapists, St. Louis, Mo.

Struckman-Johnson, C. J. et al., (1996). Sexual coercion reported by men and women in prison. *The Journal of Sex Research, 33(1)*, 67-76.

Sykes, G. M. (1958). *The society of captives: A study of a maximum security prison.* Princeton, NJ: Princeton University Press.

US Department of Justice. (2005). *Sexual violence reported by correctional authorities, 2004.* Washington, DC: Bureau of Justice Statistics.

Ward, D. & Kassebaum, G. (1965). *Women's prison: sex and social structure*. Chicago: Aldine.

Weber, R. P. (2001). *Basic Content Analysis*, 2nd Edition. Newbury Park, CA: Sage Publications.

In: Violent Crime and Prisons: Population...
Ed: Aidan Renshaw and Emelina Suárez
ISBN: 978-1-60741-668-5

Chapter 11

WOMEN AND THE PAINS OF IMPRISONMENT: DOES GENDER MATTER?

Olga Themeli
Department of Psychology, University of Crete, Greece.

ABSTRACT

It is well known that, internationally, women's delinquency is lower than the one of men's. However, the last ten years it is observed that women's participation in criminality appears to be on the increase and is mainly detected at specific crimes. This increase can be related to the expansion of opportunities resulted from the new roles adapted by women, as well as to the wider exposure of their actions following their way into public life for professional and social reasons. This exposure enhances the possibilities of their taking part in the mechanisms of the criminal justice award system.

1. INTRODUCTION

The involvement in the long arm of the correctional system is labelling the person who is deprived of its freedom, ignoring dramatically, and often in an ostentatious way, every other attribute this person may have. Thus, the attribute of the "prisoner" predominates, engulfing pitilessly any other quality, feature or characteristic of the imprisoned person such as gender, age, nationality, physical or mental illness etc.

It is commonly accepted that the assignment of roles and positions in the base of gender discrimination, reproduces the differences, and by extension the inequalities inside specific socially isolated groups. The confined female population appears to be dealt with differently both by society in general and science in particular. For example, an important lack of bibliography is ascertained with reference to that related to men, more negative stereotypes and prejudices and finally application of less measures coping with their problems.

All researchers have drawn the common conclusion that women experience the pains of imprisonment more vividly than men and that their diverse needs – because women's needs are significantly diversified compared to the needs of men – are not taken into consideration as far as the prison system is concerned. In other words, it is all about a system which is concentrated and adjusted to the needs of men and which systematically ignores women's needs, thus resulting to their complete break down. High rates of mental illness, substance use and self-destructing behaviour constitute the ultimate proof.

2. "PRISON" IS OF MALE GENDER

Prison, the most representative total institution, affects in a catalytic way the female personality, rendering women a particularly vulnerable social group needing immediate clinical / counselling intervention. Jail subculture, overpopulation, high rate of mental illness, excessive stress, fear and insecurity, still time and shutting down from the family and general social environment, institutionalisation, withdrawal and the "pains of imprisonment" in general, prevent every effort to ameliorate the conditions of confinement and aggravate the life of the incarcerated.

Gender, age, nationality and former experiences of confinement constitute parameters that affect the way which every inmate perceives and deals with the number of stressful factors, but also the effect that these factors have on the mental health of the incarcerated.

Gender constitutes an important parameter regarding the experience of stress. According to Lindquist & Lindquist (1997), higher levels of stress are noted among imprisoned women than men. Women refer more stressful factors arising from the jail environment, while at the same time they are far more affected by them. One more significant difference between imprisoned women and men is the issue of maternity, since the majority of female inmates are mothers. Parting their children consists one of the main causes of anxiety and stress (Lindquist & Lindquist, 1997; Griffith & Steptoe, 2000).

It has been characteristically said that prisons have been made by men for men (Tomasevski, 1993). The prison service has mostly been devised with male prisoners in mind. Still, the irony is that the prison system is less tolerant to women's misbehaviour (Mc Clean 1994). Hence, women are more frequently punished in comparison to men when they break prison rules and regulations, which in particular are formed only on the basis of male gender (Dobash et al., 1986).

At this point, it is worth noticing that, internationally, the number of inmates is considerably increasing in the last years. It is also worth noting that the spread of imprisoned women is startling. It is estimated that after the eighties, the incarcerated women population has gone up to 20% (Bureau of Justice Statistics, 2000). Researchers point out that the annual raising of the number of women entering jail institutions in the USA is up to 11,2 %, while as far as men is concerned the matched percentage is 6,1 % (Dalaire, 2007). Given that in Europe as well, the vast number of female inmates in many countries is increasing, sometimes faster than the size of the imprisoned male population (e.g. in England and Wales the male population has gone up to 50% between 1992 and 2002, whereas the matched female has reached 173 %), it is in fact necessary to meet the needs of female prisoners.

Bibliography, in its entirety, argues that the high percentages of mental and physical illness, excessive stress, fear and insecurity, still time, shutting down from the family and general social environment as well as institutionalisation block considerably the adjustment process of women in a freedom depriving environment, which has been essentially created for men (Heidensohn, 1985).

3. PRISON AND "FEMALE" PROBLEMS

In Europe, women represent on an average, approximately the 4.5 % to 5.0% of the whole prison population. It could be assumed that since women are far less than men, they would be more privileged compared to them or they would at least be treated more favourably. Unfortunately, however, the opposite is happening. Their small number is the cause for a series of isolations which generate more adverse conditions for the period of their imprisonment and make subsequently difficult their social reintegration. The deprivations experienced by the female population are probably more intense than those experienced by men. The most important of these deprivations are loss of liberty, goods and services, heterosexual relations, autonomy and personal security (Sykes, 1958).

In surveys, women state that institutional adjustment for them is more difficult compared to men. In addition, they appear to be more affected by the loss of "privacy" (Pollock – Byrne, 1992), as well as by the rejection from their family (Dobash, Dobash & Gutteridge, 1986). Furthermore, women often have to deal with sexual abuse and misconduct by correctional staff (Moss, 1999). The need for emotional support regarding the abovementioned problems appears to be of utmost importance for the female population (Toch, 1975). The regular recourse in homosexual relationships is based on their effort to find love and support, in comparison with the male population that primarily seeks satisfaction of its sexual urge (Bowker, 1981; Pogrebin & Dodge, 2001).

Central issues that disturb women are health problems, substance use, hospitalisation, their children and their professional and social reintegration.

3.1. Health Conditions

Women involved with the Criminal Justice System are usually arrested for less serious crimes and originate from homes where they have experienced unpleasant situations such as poverty, victimisation and substance use. They have low educational level, lack of information regarding prevention and limited access to the mental health system. For this reason, their health is already aggravated at the time they go to jail.

Jail institution, as it is today, not only is an inadequate solution with reference to encountering women who have acute and chronic physical and mental illnesses, but also isolation and the feeling of weakness that come along with imprisonment, may contribute in illness outbreaks. Although the correctional staffs have a duty to maintain order and security, prison continues to be a hostile environment that may have a negative affect on persons who have been prone to violence and misuse in the past. International survey results provide evidence that prison is inevitably connected to serious disorders of mental as well as physical health of the incarcerated population. Indicatively there are references of serious conditions of the cardiac, the respiratory or the gastro – enteric system. Patients with chronic and incurable diseases are also presented with high rates. The past decades, a dramatic increase of patients – carriers of HIV is underlined alongside with diseases, such as meningitis, tuberculosis and hepatitis, which, even though they have been significantly reduced within the general population of well – governed societies, in prison they spread like an epidemic (Conix, 2000 ; Hammet, Harmon & Maruschak, 1999 ; Malinowska, 2002). It is also worth noticing that the average life time of the incarcerated population is lower than the equivalent of the general population.

As far as women are concerned, bibliography as a whole sustains that female prisoners seem to be agitated with frequent problems of their physical as well as of their mental health. It has been found that the imprisoned female population has triple possibilities to complain about weakness in health compared to the general female population (Marquart, Brewer & Mullings, 1999). Sexually transmitted diseases, obstetrical problems, obesity, kidney trouble, dental problems, dermatological problems, but also chronic health conditions (AIDS, tuberculosis, hypertension, anaemia, hepatitis, cardiac etc) seem to trouble female inmates with great frequency (Smith, Simonian & Yarussi, 2006). These conditions emerge in high levels among users of narcotic substances.

According to surveys, particularly the imprisoned female population is presented with higher levels of sexually transmitted diseases (STD's) and gynaecological inflection compared to the general population (Fogel & Belyea, 1999). In addition to that, the percentage of imprisoned women with HIV is estimated to be 30 times higher than the equivalent of women outside prison (DeGroot, 2000). In many cases, the cause of these problems has to be looked for in the particular way of life, which comprised sexual abuse, substance use and prostitution. The non timely treatment of the abovementioned conditions is responsible for some types of cancer, infertility, infections and birth defects (Messina & Girella 2006 ; Smith, Simonian & Yarussi, 2006).

Female prisoners, however, are mainly facing problems with their mental health. Besides, it is known worldwide that prisons are disease – breeding and have been turned into an out of the ordinary type of mental institution.

International bibliography provides evidence that the indicator for arresting mentally disturbed is higher than the one applied to the mentally healthy population (Teplin, 1984). Studies have shown that persons with history of mental problems are 67 times more likely to be arrested than persons whose behaviour does not imply the presence of a mental condition (Teplin, 2000). Even when these individuals demonstrate a faulty behaviour, they are often charged with offences of greater socio-moral demerit (Monohan & Steadman, 1994).

In the past decade, *"criminalisation of the mentally ill"* has led a substantial number of women, among others, to jail. For this reason, it should not be impressive that a significant proportion of women had already been diagnosed with a mental disorder prior to their imprisonment (Jordan et al., 1996). Older women in particular seem to have addressed to mental health services more frequently (Marquart et al., 2001).

According to research data, over half of the detainees had got in touch with with the mental health and psychiatric system prior to their imprisonment; very few though followed and completed a therapeutic program (Scott, 2004).

Among the rest of the detainees, the more common types of psychological problems are depression and stress (Sacks, 2004). The psychological distress experienced by the inmates is very high. Rates of high to severe psychological distress in female prisoners were estimated to be 150% greater than those in the community (Hurley & Dune, 1991).

Epidemiological studies of mental disorder in women prisons have shown high rates of psychiatric morbidity. Maden, Swinton and Gunn (1994) found that 58% of female inmates had at least one psychiatric diagnosis cooperated with 38% in a matched male population. Among these diagnosis, reference is made to high rates of personality disorders, mental handicap, drug abuse and alcohol.

Teplin, Abram and McClelland (1996) have concluded that over 80% of women inmates met the criteria of one or more chronic mental disorders. The indicators for all these disorders were significantly higher than those of the general population. Furthermore, Jordan and his colleagues (1996) have found that the 64% of the incarcerated met the criteria of a serious psychiatric disorder. Fazel and Danesh (2002), provided evidence that 4% of female inmates are agitated with psychosis, 12% are presented with major depression and 42% with personality disorders. Parsons, Walker and Grubin (2001) have recovered that 59% of female remand prisoners had at least one mental disorder, excluding substance abuse.

Finally, a high percentage suffers from post traumatic stress disorder (PTSD). Specifically, 78% - 85% of the incarcerated female population referred that it had experienced a severe traumatic event (Resnick et al., 1993). It is worth mentioning that post traumatic disorder is the second most common diagnosis between imprisoned women after substance misuse (Teplin, Abram & McClelland, 1996).

There is no doubt that the high PTSD indicator is connected with high rates of abuse. International literature has shown that child abuse in particular is quite common among the incarcerated. Bond & Semann (1996) have demonstrated in their study that half of the inmates had a history of sexual abuse and tree quarters of this population had a history of physical abuse by their companion. Sable and his colleagues (1999) have underlined in their later study that pregnant prisoners had, compared to the general population, double possibilities to have endured physical or sexual abuse and triple possibilities to have suffered both types of victimisation.

According to a Home Office study (1997), with a sample of 234 women prisoners, one third had suffered sexual abuse during childhood, one fifth had been sexually victimised during their early days as well as their adolescence and one third were bullied in prison. According to other studies, 23% to 48% of the imprisoned refer such experiences (Greenfield, 1991; Singer et al., 1995). Similar study has shown that almost every woman (98%) have suffered a traumatic event, while 71% has been a victim of family violence. It does not have to be high lightened that these severe traumatic experiences render the experience of incarceration more intense (Covington, 2007).

It is common ground that female inmates are ill with much more chronic diseases than men, physical as well as mental. Limited access to healthcare as well, plays an important part to the deterioration of this situation. Many of the abovementioned illnesses require the necessary medication, regular medical examinations and hygiene care on a daily basis. We should remind again that prison services are devised with male prisoners in mind, ignoring systematically women's special needs. Thus, the life of a woman in prison might, among other things, not only be humiliated, but also be put in significant danger.

3.2. The Substances

Female inmates consist of a group with high rates not only of victimisation but also of substance addiction. Jail population can be considered as a high risk group with regards to substance use: substance users are over-represented in prisons and a considerable number of detainees has been convicted for drug related offences (mainly for drug possession), which illustrates that substances constitute a serious and prolonged predicament featuring in the life of women with offensive behaviour.

Many studies on the subject of gender differences among users have demonstrated that women face further and more serious problems through their period of life than men. Employment problems, mental health problems and family problems are some of them (Byqvist, 1999 ; Davis & DiNitto, 1996). Additionally, it is not only the nature of the problems that differs, but also the cause that leads the two genders into substance use. International bibliography provides evidence that the majority of women ends up with drugs in order to endure psychological pain (Corcoran & Corcoran, 2001), at the same time as it points out that women are commonly drawn into use as well as antisocial behaviour by their partners (Kassebaum, 1999; Robles et al, 1998). Furthermore, survey results confirm that it was highly likely for these women to have grown up in homes where a member of the family was performing substance use. As far as emotional relationship is concerned, it is 7 times more possible for women to have married a user, than men. Especially in rough relationships, the expectation for an enhanced communication, may lead these women to drugs (Kim, 2003).

Peter and his colleagues have proven that female population is more psychologically vulnerable than male population, mainly because it has experienced higher levels of depression and suicide ideation. Authors have assumed that these inter-gender differences are probably connected to the fact that women are far more often victims of physical, mental and sexual abuse during childhood. This assumption is consistent with the standpoint according to which women in prison lose control of their life mostly due to the violence and the following disappointments that they go through.

Social exclusion has been considered a significant psycho – oppressive factor regarding addictive substance misuse. The majority of women have faced major barriers in search of employment before imprisonment, whereas they often gained less than men for the same occupation (Peters et al., 1997). In these cases, substance misuse often is intended for escaping the problems of poverty that come along with bad employment conditions.

For all the above reasons, researchers draw attention to the need for application of specially devised programs adjusted to the needs and demands of the female population. In these cases, programs are proposed that aim not so much at confrontation – like in the case of men – as at providing support, at bracing self esteem and finally at offering skills that will be proven useful to their life after prison (Pelissier et al., 2003 ; Laundry, 1997).

3.3. Self – Destructing Behaviour

It is noteworthy that, whereas suicide holds the tenth position among the causes of death in the general population, it holds the first position among prisoners. Surveys' data provide evidence that the indicator of suicides in prison is four to eleven times higher that the equivalent in the community (Hayes & Blaauw, 1997; Dooley, 1990).

Although there is plenty of international bibliography regarding the study of the self – destructing phenomenon inside male prisons, respective studies about female inmates is particularly limited (Liebling, 1994).

Besides, until recently prevailed the myth that the risk of suicide threatened only the male inmates (Liebling, 1994). However, the remarkable increase of the female incarcerated population in the last years has drawn the interest for more systematic study of this particular field (Pollock – Byrne, 1992; Deakin & Spencer, 2003).

It has been recovered that a significant proportion of female inmates had attempted to commit suicide before their imprisonment (Cullen, 1985). Researchers have illustrated that at least half the female prisoners in the sample had attempted to commit at least one self – destructing act prior to the deprivation of their freedom (Borril et a.l, 2003). Heney (1990) noticed that 60% of female inmates were self – injured in prison, using principally sharp objects. Women seem to commit more often acts of self – destruction rather than suicides and they commit suicides by choosing less violent means than men (Kerkhof & Arensman, 2000).

Particularly vulnerable to the risk of suicide are women pending trial, drug addicts and mentally ill detainees. Along with gender, youth and minority population origin comprise factors that complicate the adjustment to incarceration conditions.

Already since 1975, Toch had argued that one in nine females would suffer a self – destructive break-down while incarcerated. Adopting self – destructing behaviours that may even end to the suicide of women in jail, can be easily explained when bearing in mind all that has been previously said about high rates of mental health illness, experiences of abuse prior to their imprisonment, poverty and financial difficulties as well as the problems of social isolation. It could be supported that suicides in prison mainly show the sad consequences of the function of a mechanism that is totally unsuitable for women, whose goal seems to be their psychological extinction (Themeli, 2006). One of the most painful matters that troubles women in prison, prolongs their psychological pain and leads faster to their psychological destruction is parting their children.

3.4. Maternity

Separating the child from the mother is a particularly painful experience for the incarcerated woman. It is fair enough to say that it could be considered the most dreadful viewpoint of jail.

Two thirds of imprisoned women are mothers of at least one child below eighteen (Caddle & Crisp, 1997; Henriques, 1996). The vast majority of female inmates, who it should be noted that they became mothers at a younger age compared to women of the general population, were raising their children themselves before imprisonment. Separation has unpleasant consequences to them as well as to their children. Agony and stress of imprisoned mothers reaches a peak when it comes to matters concerning their children.

Often, the distress about the ability of the father to effectively undertake the care of the minor children in the period of their absence, extends the existent condition, whereas in a more difficult position are found those inmates who, due to the absence of any relatives, the custody of their children is engaged by social services. It is worth noting that the children will have to change their way of life – within the first year of partition – at least once (Myers et al., 1999).

Three quarters of the children (75%) are forced to abandon their permanent residence at the time of their mother's imprisonment. Grandparents undertake their care at 55% of the cases, their father at 20%, 15% ends up to the hands of relatives or friends, while 10% seeks the aid of social service (Mumola, 2000). Distress regarding the regaining of their children's custody after their release from prison, often worsens their already adverse condition (Pogrebin & Dodge, 2001).

Women experience emotions of despair, helplessness, guilt and shame. On the other side, the correctional system offers limited emotional support and stands in the way of conserving the mother – child relationship. Another common obstacle in the communication of women with their children is the great distance where the prison is situated. Studies mention that a significant number of women did not receive any visit from their children all through their imprisonment. An additional cause is the negative attitude of relatives towards the jail environment since they believe that it would rather harm than benefit the children or that the mother is a bad influence to the child. But even when obstacles are set aside, standardised visits in the prison ground protract anguish and emotional pressure of the mother as well as the child. The impersonal, cold and noisy visiting rooms discourage any effort of substantial communication (Bloom & Steinhart, 1993).

Unfortunately, stereotypic behaviours against women intensify the existing conditions (Schram, 1999). A particularity of female prison is that they are attributed one more social blame, stigma is referred to their parental ability. They are worried whether they will be accused as bad mothers, they are afraid whether their children will forget them and they send objects and handmade articles and they try to prove that they are close to them. They live with the agony of the potential deprivation of their children's custody.

Still, prisoners that have failed as citizens might be successful parents and, in particular, their success as parents might turn them into better citizens. Studies show that good family bonds are necessary at the time of release from prison, mainly because the existence of a stable family environment, where they will return, is a powerful anti – motive against reversion. Finally, a particularly vulnerable group to the pains of imprisonment is pregnant inmates as well as women who have their children with them in prison until a certain age (Wismont, 2000 & Birmingham et al., 2006). The needs can not often be satisfied due to the lack of adequate and appropriate building installations. The physiology of women is not taken into consideration and there is absence of special hygiene conditions or medical care, especially as far as women in gestation or in childbed are concerned.

4. Conclusion

Often, the necessary conditions regarding the exercise, protection and preserving of the whole of the legal interest of the imprisoned population, are not ensured in the incarceration area. Thus, the abolition of the legal interest of freedom carries along that of health, communication and education.

The consequences of prison are more intense on female inmates who are deprived of their freedom in a system that is concentrated and adapted to the needs of men. Although women who are imprisoned are much fewer than men, from many aspects they endure worse behaviour. Jail itself creates circumstances of pain, punishment, isolation and misery and it constitutes the foundation of painful conditions for the imprisoned women. Entering prison is a traumatic event. Many women experience this procedure as a passageway from dignity to humiliation and shame, which leaves them with indelible wounds.

The endorsement of a completed social policy that will take into consideration the special needs of women is of utmost importance. Their imprisonment should consist of an "ultimum refugium" and should be applied only when all other solutions have been use up (imposition of alternative penalties).

When deprivation of freedom is unavoidable, successful social integration of women should be planed during as well as after imprisonment with the cooperation of social services and other analogous institutions, so as to reassure the uneventful passage from prison to freedom. Special attention should be paid to psychological preparation and to the provision of social support for the time of release.

International human rights standards are clear that providing equality for female prisoners *does not mean simply treating men and women in the same way*. Equality does not mean lack of respect to differentiality (to different needs).

REFERENCES

Birmingham, L., Coulson, D., Mullee, M., Kamal, M. & Gregoirer, A. (2006). The mental health of women in prison and baby units. *The Journal of Forensic Psychiatry and Psychology*, *17(3)*, 393-404.

Bloom, B. & Steinhart, D. (1993). *Why punish the children? A reappraisal of the children of incarcerated mothers in America*. San Francisco: National Council on Crime and Delinquency

Bond, L. & Semaan, S. (1996). At risk for HIV infection: Incarcerated women in a county jail in Philadelphia. *Women & Health*, *24*, 27-45.

Borill, J., Burnett, R., Atkins, R., Miller, S., Briggs, D., Weaver, T. & Maden, A. (2003). Patterns of self-harm and attempted suicide among white and black/mixed race female prisoners. *Criminal Behavior and Mental Health*, *13(4)*, 229-240.

Bowker, L. H. (1981). Gender differences in prisoner subcultures. In L. H. Bowker (Ed.), *Women and crime in America* (pp. 409-419). New Yoork: Macmillan.

Bureau of Justice Statistics. (2000). *Incarcerated parents and their children. Washington,* DC: U.S. Department of Justice.

Byquist, S. (1999). Criminality among female drug users. *Journal of Psychoactive Drugs*, *31(4)*, 353-362.

Caddle, D. & Crisp, D. (1997). *Mothers In Prison*. Research Findings No.38, Home Office Research and Statistics Directorate, London.

Conix, R. (2000). Tuberculosis in prisons in countries with high prevalence. *British Medical Journal*, *320*, 440-442.

Corcoran, M. & Corcoran, J. (2001). Retrospective reasons for the initiation of substance use: Gender and ethnic effects. *Journal of Ethic and Cultural Diversity in Social Work*, *10(1)*, 69-83

Covington, S. (2007). Women and the Criminal Justice System. *Women's Health Issues*, *17*, 180-182.

Cullen, J. E. (1985). Prediction and Treatment of self-injury by female young offenders. In D. P. Farrington, & R. Tarling (Eds.), *Prediction in Criminology*. (pp. 135-148). Albany, NY: State University of New York Press.

Dallaire, D. H. (2007). Children with incarcerated mothers: Developmental outcomes, special challenges and recommendations. *Journal of Developmental Psychology*, *28*, 15-24.

Davis, D. R. & DiNitto, D. M. (1996). Gender differences in social and psychological problems of substance abusers: A comparison to non-substance abusers. *Journal of Psychoactive drugs*, *28(2)*, 135-145.

Deakin, J. & Spencer, J. (2003). Women Behind Bars: Explanations and Implications. *Howard Journal of Criminal Justice*, *42(2)*, 123-136.

DeGroot, A. (2000). HIV infection among incarcerated women: Epidemic behind bars. *The AIDS Reader, 10,* 287-295.

Dobash, R. P., Dobash, R. E., & Gutteridge, S. (1986). *The Imprisonment of Women.* New York: Basil and Blackwell Publishers.

Dooley, E. (1990). Prison suicide in England and Wales, 1972-1987. *British Journal of Psychiatry, 156,* 40-45.

Fogel, C. I., and Belyea, M. (1999). The lives of incarcerated women: Violence, substance abuse, and at risk for HIV. *Journal of the Association of Nurses in AIDS Care, 10*, 66-74.

Greenfeld, L., & Snell, T. (1999). *Women offenders. Bureau of Justice Statistics* (NCJ-175688). Washington, DC: U.S. Department of Justice.

Griffith, J., & Steptoe, A. (2000). Prison. In G. Fink (Ed) *Encyclopedia of Stress* (pp. 241-246). California: Academic Press.

Hall, J. (1998), Death from Natural Causes in Prisons. *Prison Service Journal, 124*: 7-8.

Hammett, T. M., Harmon, P. & Maruschak, L. M. (1999). *HIV/AIDS, STDs, and TB in Correctional Facilities.* Washington: U.S. Department of Justice

Hayes, L. M. & Blaauw, E. (1997). Prison Suicide: A Special Issue. *Crisis: The Journal of Crisis Intervention and Suicide Prevention*, *27(3)*, 146-147,

Heidensohn, F. M. (1985). *Women and Crime*. London: MacMillan.

Heney, J. (1990). *Report on self-injurious behaviour in the Kingston Penitentiary for Women.* Submitted to Correctional Services Canada. Ottawa: Supply and Services Canada.

Henriques, Z. W. (1996). Imprisoned mothers and their children: separation – reunion syndrome and dual impact. *Women and Criminal Justice*, *8*, 77-95.

Home Office (1997). *Thematic review: women in prison.* London: Home Office.

Hurley, W. & Dunne, M. (1991). Psychological Distress and Psychiatric Morbidity in Women Prisoners. *Australian and New Zeeland Journal of Psychiatry*, *25*, 461-470.

Jordan, B. K., Schlenger, W. E., Fairbank, J. A. & Caddell, J. M. (1996). Prevalence of psychiatric disorders among incarcerated women: Convicted felons entering prison. *Archives of General Psychiatry*, *53*, 513-519

Kassenbaum, P. A. (1999). *Substance Abuse Treatment for Women Offenders.* Rockville, MD: Center for Substance Abuse Treatment.

Kerkhof, A. & Arensman, E. (2000). Attempted suicide and deliberate self-harm: epidemiology and risk factors. In M. G. Gelder, J. J. López-Ibor, & N. Andreasen, (Eds.), *New Oxford Textbook of Psychiatry* (pp.1039-1043). Oxford University Press.

Kim S. (2003). Incarcerated women in life context. *Women's Studies International Forum*, *26(1)*, 95-100.

Landry, M. J. (1997). *Overview of addiction treatment effectiveness*. Washington, DC: Substance Abuse and Mental Health Services Administration.

Langan P. N. & Pelissier M. M. B. (2001). Gender differences among prisoners in drug treatment. *Journal of Substance Abuse*, *13*, 291-301.

Liebling, A. (1994). Suicides Amongst Women Prisoners. *Howard Journal of Criminal Justice*, *33(1)*, 1-9.

Lindquist, C., H. & Lindquist, C. A. (1997). Gender differences in distress: mental health consequences of environmental stress among jail inmates. *Behavioral Sciences and the Law*, *15*, 503-523.

McClellan, D. (1994). Disparity in the discipline of male and female inmates in Texas prisons. *Women and Criminal Justice*, *5*, 71-97.

Maden, T., Swinton, M. & Gunn. J. (1994). Psychiatric Disorder in Women Serving a Prison Sentence. *British Journal of Psychiatry*, *164*, 44-54.

Malinowska, K. (2002). Harm reduction in prisons is crucial to the reduction of HIV in Easter Europe and the former Soviet Union. *International Journal of Drug Policy*, *13*, 1-3.

Marquart, J. W., Brewer, V. E. & Mullings, J. L. (1999). Health risks as an emerging filed within the new penology. *Journal of Criminal Justice*, *27(2)*, 143-154.

Marquart, W. J., Brewer, E. V., Simon, E. P. & Morse, V. E. (2001). Lifestyle factors among female prisoners with histories of psychiatric treatment. *Journal of Criminal Justice*, *29*, 319-328.

Messina, N. & Grella, C. (2006). Childhood trauma and women's health outcomes in a California Prison population. *American Journal of Public Health*, *96*, 1842-1848.

Monohan, J. & Steadman, H. J. (1994). *Violence and Mental Disorder: Developments in Risk Assessment*. Chicago, University of Chicago Press.

Moss, A. (1999). Sexual misconduct among staff and inmates. In P. Carlson, & J. Garrett (Eds.)*, Prison and jail administration (pp.189-196).* Gaithersburg, MD: Aspen Publishers.

Mumola, C. J. (2000). *Special report: Incarcerated parents and their children.* Washington , DC: U.S. Department of Justice, Bureau of Justice Statistics (NCJ 182335).

Myers, B. J., Smarsh, T. M., Amlund-Hagar, K. & Kennon, S. (1999).*Children of incarcerated mothers. Journal of Child and Family Studies*, *8*, 11-25.

Parsons, S., Walker, L. & Grubin, D. (2001). The Prevalence of Mental Disorder in Women Serving a Prison Sentence. *British Journal of Psychiatry*, *164*, 44-54.

Pellisier, B. M., Camp, S. D., Gaes, G. G., Saylor, W. G. & Rhodes, W. (2003). Gender differences in outcomes from prison-based residential treatment. *Journal of Substance Abuse Treatment*, *24*, 149-160.

Peters, R. H., Strozier, A. L., Murrin, M. R. & Kearns, W. D. (1997). Treatment of substance-abusing jail inmates. *Journal of Substance Abuse Treatment*, 14, 339-349.

Pogrebin, R. M. & Dodge, M. (2001). Women's accounts of their prison experiences. A retrospective view of their subjective realities. *Journal of Criminal Justice*, *29*, 531-541.

Pollock-Byrne, J. M. (1992). *Women in prison: why are their numbers increasing?* In: P. J. Benekes, & A. V. Merlo (Eds.), Corrections: dilemmas and directions (pp. 79-95). Cincinnati, OH: Anderson Publishing.

Resnick, H. S., Kilpatrick, D. G., Dansky, B. S., Saunders, B. E. & Best, C. L. (1993). Prevalence of trauma and posttraumatic stress disorder in a representative national sample of women. *Journal of Consulting and Clinical Psychology*, *61*, 984- 991.

Richie, B. (1996). *Compelled to crime: the gender entrapment of battered black women.* New York: Routledge.

Robles, R., Marrero, C. A., Matos, T. D., Colon, H. M., Cancel, L. I. & Reyers, J. C. (1998). Social and behavioural consequences of chemical dependence. In C. L. Wetherington, & A. B. Roman (Eds.), *Drug addiction research and the health of women* (pp. 197-122). Rockville, MD: National Institute on Drug Abuse.

Sable, M. R., Fieberg, J. R., Martin, S. L. & Kupper, L. L. (1999). Violence victimization experiences of pregnant prisoners. *American Journal of Orthopsychiatry*, *69*, 392-397.

Schram J. P. (1999). An exploratory study: Stereotypes about mothers in prison. *Journal of Criminal Justice*, *27(5)*, 411-426.

Scott, S. (2004). Opening a can of worms? Counselling for survivors in UK women's prisons. In G. Aitken, & C. Heenan (Eds.), Women in prison and secure psychiatric settings - whose needs whose dangerousness? *Feminism and Psychology, 14,* 256-261.

Singer, M. I., Bussey, J., Song, L. Y. & Lunghofer, L. (1995). The psychosocial issues of women serving time in jail. *Social Work*, *40*, 103-113.

Smith, B. V., Simonian, N. & Yarussi, J. (2006a). The health concerns of incarcerated women – Part1: Profiles, chronic diseases, and conditions. *Women, Girls & Criminal Justice*, *7*, 33-34, 39-45.

Sykes, G. M. (1958). *The society of captives: a study of a maximum security prison*. Princeton University Press.

Teplin, L. A. (2000). *Keeping the peace: Police discretion and mentally ill persons*. National Institute of Justice Journal, *244*, 8-15.

Teplin, L. A. (1984b). Managing disorders: Police handling of the mental ill. In L. A.Teplin (Ed.), *Mental health and criminal justice* (pp.157-175). Beverly Hills, CA: Sage.

Teplin, L. A., Abram, K. M. & McClelland, G. M. (1996). Prevalence of psychiatric disorders among incarcerated women: Pretrial jail detainees. *Archives of General Psychiatry*, *53*, 505-512.

Themeli, O. (2006). Gender Issues and Considerations for Preventing Self Harm in Women's Prisons. In D. E. Greg (Ed.), *Preventing Suicide and Other Self Harm in Prison* (pp. 187-194). New York: Pelgrave MacMillan.

Toch, H. (1975). *Men in Crisis.* Chicago: Aldine

Tomasevsky, K. (1993). *Women and human rights.* London: Zed Books.

Walker, L. (1989). *Terrifying love: why battered women kill and how society responds*. New York: Harper and Row, Publishers

Wismont M. J. (2000). The lived pregnancy experience of women in prison. *Journal of Midwifery & Women's Health*, *45(4)*, 292-300.

In: Violent Crime and Prisons: Population...
Ed: Aidan Renshaw and Emelina Suárez
ISBN: 978-1-60741-668-5

Chapter 12

HIV-Positive Prisoners and Institutional Segregation: A Legal and Health Analysis

Bronwen Lichtenstein*
Department of Criminal Justice, University of Alabama, USA

Abstract

HIV-positive inmates in the United States have often been segregated in an attempt to prevent the spread of HIV/AIDS in the nation's prisons. Not surprisingly, this practice generated considerable litigation, including in Alabama where segregation for HIV-positive inmates still exists today. Using Foucault's (1995) theory of carcereal power, this article analyzes two class action lawsuits that failed to overturn Alabama's policies of mandatory HIV testing and segregated medical care and housing for HIV-positive inmates. Case One (*Harris v. Thigpen)* challenged the power of the penitentiary, but was unsuccessful because the court deferred to prison authority regarding prison conditions. Case Two (*Leatherwood v. Campbell*) similarly failed in challenging segregated housing for HIV-positive inmates, but did pave the way for modest improvements in housing and medical care. These cases demonstrate how the power of the penitentiary expanded during the HIV/AIDS epidemic in Alabama through legislative fiat, judicial deference, and offender classifications that were deployed to discipline and punish HIV-positive prisoners on the basis of epidemiologic tropes about violence, deviance, and contagion.

Introduction

In 1996, I received permission from officials at Alabama's Julia Tutwiler Prison to interview HIV-positive women prisoners for an epidemiological study funded by the Centers for Disease Control and Prevention. The Southeast was becoming an epicenter for HIV/AIDS, and we sought to understand how to prevent HIV transmission among at-risk men and women in the region. I arrived at Tutwiler Prison for the first round of interviews with research approvals and tape recorder in hand. A full-body search later, I was ushered into the

* Corresponding author: 430 Farrah Hall, Tuscaloosa, AL 35487-0320, Phone: (205) 348 7782, Fax: (205) 348 7178, Email: blichten@bama.ua.edu

warden's office where he invited me to sit down and then told me that he had changed his mind ("I get a lawsuit a week and I don't want any more trouble. I'm sorry, but you'll have to go home"). This was my first encounter with southern prisons and the legal struggles over HIV-related segregation. At the time of my visit, HIV-positive inmates in Alabama had been housed in separate quarters since HIV testing and segregation had become law. HIV-positive prisoners have been in litigation over these policies ever since the passage of the law in 1987.

The segregation of HIV-positive prisoners is defined as partial or total separation from other prisoners in housing, medical care, or programs (Maruschak, 2003). The trend toward segregating HIV-positive inmates in U.S. prisons began in the early 1980s in order to prevent HIV transmission to other prisoners (American Federation for AIDS Research [amfAR], 2002; Maruschak, 2005). By the mid-1980s, three-fourths of US prisons housed some or all HIV-positive prisoners in separate living quarters (Hammett & Daugherty, 1991). Not surprisingly, this practice prompted litigation from seropositive prisoners throughout the United States who asserted that segregation was a form of punishment (Gostin, Porter, & Sandomire, 1990). By the 1990s, however, prison officials had begun to reintegrate HIV-positive inmates after knowledge about HIV transmission improved, public fears about contagion abated, prisons became more crowded, and HIV-positive prisoners sued under the Civil Rights Act of 1964, the Americans with Disabilities Act of 1990, and §504 of the Rehabilitation Act of 1973 (Knepper, 1995). By the turn of the new century, Alabama was the last state in the nation to segregate HIV-positive inmates in housing, medical care, daily activities, programs, and work placements that were generally available to other prisoners (Greenspan, 2005).

The purpose of this article is to explain how and why Alabama maintained its "last in the nation" policy of segregating HIV-positive prisoners despite ongoing litigation over the matter, and regardless of the integration of such inmates in other states. To place these issues in sociolegal context, I analyzed court transcripts, briefs, and reports from two class action lawsuits (*Harris v. Thigpen*, 727 F. Supp. 1564 (M.D. Ala 1990; *Leatherwood v. Campbell*, CV 02-BE-2812-W, 2002). I also interviewed a prison official who was involved in the litigation. The two lawsuits represent the major litigation brought by HIV-positive prisoners after the Alabama Code § 22-11A-17(a) (1987) mandated segregated housing, medical care, and programs for inmates with HIV/AIDS. The central legal issue in these cases involved the power of the state to define HIV-positive inmates as medico-legal deviants in order to justify segregation from other prisoners, versus the right of disabled persons to be protected from such exclusions. Seropositive inmates were framed as medically unique in legal arguments on both sides, that is, in defendants' claims that HIV-positive inmates were a special class of deviants, and in plaintiffs' claims about being a protected class of citizen based on medical status.

Theorizing the HIV-Positive Prisoner Through Litigation

As conceptualized by Michel Foucault (1995), the carcereal system consists of state authorities (e.g. the legislature, judiciary, and criminal justice system) and disciplinary actors (e.g., physicians, psychologists, and criminologists) who function interdependently to define, monitor, and control social behavior. Social deviance is defined, in part, through the exercise of disciplinary knowledge in which categories of deviance or criminality are created, classified, and expanded with increasing sophistication. According to Foucault, this classification system is used to assign lawbreakers to the penitentiary, which operates as a complex arrangement of boot camps, juvenile halls, drug courts, rehabilitation centers, jails, and prisons. As a central actor in this system, the U.S. judiciary increasingly upholds the authority of the state through adjudications that defer to established precedent and the regulatory authority of the penitentiary. This development has led to less judicial oversight of penal affairs, and judges have tended to confer absolute authority to the penitentiary by "assuming the complexities and peculiarities of those institutions [are] best dealt with by prison authorities" (Kantor, 2006, p.11).

The judicial record in decisions involving AIDS litigation is a case in point. U.S. courts have been "extremely deferential to correctional officials" (Best, 1991, p. 43), and have generally upheld the segregation of HIV-positive inmates through legislative mandates (Jonsen & Stryker, 1993). On a broader basis, the federal judiciary has upheld the right of prison officials to make administrative decisions concerning any health risk, citing precedents such as Estelle v. Gamble (1976) for cases that predated the moral panics over contagion in the AIDS era (Gostin, Porter, & Sandomire, 1990; Jonsen & Stryker, 1993; Knepper, 1995). In Estelle v. Gamble (1976), the U.S. Supreme Court decided that an injured inmate could not make Eighth Amendment claims of cruel and unusual punishment unless prison authorities were intentionally indifferent to his or her medical plight (Kantor, 2006). Following Estelle v. Gamble (1976), most judicial decisions regarding medical care for HIV-positive prisoners have rejected plaintiffs' claims of cruel and unusual punishment "[d]espite [judges'] lack of medical or public health credentials" (Kantor, 2006, p. 11). The Prisoner Reform Litigation Act [PRLA] (1995), which sought to prevent so-called frivolous lawsuits over prison conditions, further limited the judiciary's ability to intervene in cases involving HIV-positive prisoners (Fleury-Steiner, 2008). Thus, the judiciary deferred to prison administrators over HIV-related segregation even as budget shortfalls and overcrowding placed severe limits on "separate but equal" medical care and housing for seropositive inmates. In Alabama, the carcereal archipelago (i.e., the state legislature, courts, and penal system) operated as mutually reinforcing constituencies whose authority superseded plaintiffs' claims until *Leatherwood,* which threatened the status quo by concluding that medical care for HIV-positive inmates was constitutionally inadequate. In this article, my analysis of how the state exercised control over HIV testing and segregation in housing, medical care, and activities, begins by describing *Harris*, the first class action lawsuit to be appealed by HIV-positive inmates in Alabama.

CASE ONE: HARRIS V. THIGPEN, 1990

Background

Harris was filed by the American Civil Rights Union (ACLU) on behalf of Carmen Harris, an inmate in the Julia Tutwiler Prison for women. The plaintiffs represented all HIV-positive inmates at Tutwiler and the Limestone Correctional Facility for men, and the case was heard by Judge R.E. Varner in the United States District Court for the Middle District of Alabama. This protracted litigation was heard, appealed, remanded, and re-appealed over a

14-year period from 1987 to 2000. During this time, the original lead plaintiff died of HIV/AIDS (Harris), a subsequent lead plaintiff (Onishea) was released from prison, and a third prisoner (Davis) replaced Onishea as the lead plaintiff when the case was appealed to the U.S. Supreme Court. Figure 1 presents a timeline for all litigation involving *Harris*.

1987 Alabama State Legislature
Ala. Code § 22-11A-17(a) "All prisoners must be tested, then segregated if HIV-positive"

1. Middle District of Alabama (Varner)

1990 (District Court)
Harris v. Thigpen
727 F. Supp. 1564
Class action lawsuit over HIV testing, housing segregation, and access to programs.
Denied, appealed.

2. Northern District of Alabama (Bowdre)

2002
Leatherwood v. Campbell
Class action lawsuit over medical negligence.
Settled for improved housing and medical care.

11th Circuit Court of Appeals

1991
Harris v. Thigpen
941 F.2d 1495
Affirmed in part, vacated in part
1997
Onishea v. Hopper
(Substituted for Harris, deceased).
126 F.3d 1323
Appeal after remand.
Denied, appealed.
1998
Onishea v. Hopper
133 F.3d 1377
Granted rehearing en Banc.
Opinion vacated.
1999
Onishea v. Hopper
171 F.3d 1289
Denied, appealed.

U.S. Supreme Court
2000
Davis et al. v. Hopper
Denied Certiorari.

Figure 1. Major litigation involving HIV-positive Alabama prisoners

Harris tested the scope of penal authority, with the plaintiffs arguing that prison officials had overstepped their authority in segregating HIV-positive inmates in housing, medical care, and daily activities. The trial judge denied that segregation amounted to cruel and unusual punishment and decided that correctional authorities had absolute authority over their domain.

The plaintiffs then appealed to the United States Court of Appeals for the Eleventh Circuit (*Harris v. Thigpen*, 941 F. 2d 1494, 1991) on the grounds that they were: 1) denied proper medical care in violation of the Eighth Amendment ("medical negligence"), 2) segregated from other prisoners in violation of the Fourteenth Amendment ("cruel and unusual punishment") and 3) excluded from integrated activities in violation of §504 of the Rehabilitation Act of 1973 ("discrimination against disabled persons"). The appellate court denied the first two claims, and remanded the third claim to the lower court judge for further findings of law and fact. The plaintiffs' subsequent brief to the lower court asserted that lack of access to programs meant that they were unduly stigmatized, could not be rehabilitated prior to release, and had longer sentences than seronegative inmates who generally participated in work-release programs. The lower court again rejected the plaintiffs' claims on the basis that prison officials had absolute jurisdiction over their domain and that prisoner rights could be infringed on this basis. The plaintiffs then filed a second appeal to the Eleventh Circuit (*Onishea v. Hopper*, 126 F.3d 1323 (11th Cir. 1997). *cert. denied, Davis v. Hopper*, 528 U.S. 1114 (2000)) which failed on similar grounds, as did an appeal to the U.S. Supreme Court (*Davis v. Hopper*, 528 U.S. 1114 (2000) (denying certiorari)).

HIV/AIDS, Dangerousness, and the Contagion of Carcereal Power

The discursive basis for *Harris* was the Alabama statute that required HIV testing and segregation in state prisons. Lower court and upper court decisions in *Harris* indicated that seropositive inmates were characterized as both sexually deviant and medically dangerous in Alabama's justifications for segregation. In suing the Alabama Department of Corrections, the plaintiffs rejected these characterizations and sought to be integrated on the basis of constitutional rights as disabled persons. In arguments for and against defining HIV/AIDS as contagion ("absolute risk") or infectiousness ("less risk"), the Alabama courts ultimately deferred to prison officials on the matter, and adopted the discourse of contagion. The following section describes how the disciplinary regime of the penitentiary was reinforced in *Harris* through sociolegal constructions of HIV/AIDS as a modern plague.

The plaintiffs' arguments against mandatory HIV testing and segregation were threefold. They charged that: 1) HIV-positive inmates had been labeled as sociomedical deviants, 2) segregation had resulted in unequal treatment and additional time served, and that 3) "wall-within-walls" sequestration held no escape from daily tedium or stigma. True to Foucault's theoretical claims about classificatory systems being used for coercive means, the state argued that prisoners *per se* were unpredictable and violent, that "aggressive" homosexuals were especially violent because of rape, biting, or vengeful attacks on uninfected inmates, and that segregation was necessary in order to control this dangerous class of inmates. Official briefs provided numerous examples of violence, same-sex activity, and injection drug use among prisoners to justify claims about dangerousness and the potential for attacks by or on HIV-positive inmates. According to these briefs, HIV-positive prisoners possessed a particularly lethal weapon – their contagiousness – which could be used with devastating effect against other inmates in "I'll take you with me" scenarios of attack and revenge. The means for making prisoners docile were presented in terms of surveillance and control through compulsory segregation.

Judge Varner accepted the defendants' arguments by agreeing that HIV-positive inmates were a particularly dangerous class of felon, by stating that the court was required to determine whether integration would pose significant health and safety risks, and by finding in favor of the defendants based on the "any risk is too much risk" standard. The role of contagion in framing the judge's decision was evident in statements about the transmissibility of HIV/AIDS ("[e]xchange of bodily fluids by homosexual rape or of blood resulting from fights is particularly hazardous in prison settings," *Harris* 727 F. Supp. at 1582), and also in beliefs about the venality of inmate-patients (e.g., "'If a correctional officer has been incapacitated in an accident [an inmate] with contempt for that officer could purposely implant, while the guard remains unconscious, blood containing HIV organisms from the HIV+ inmate's open wounds,'" *Onishea v. Hopper*, 126 F.3d 1323 (11th Cir. 1997) quoting *Onishea v. Herring*, No. 87-V1109-N, slip op. at 152 (M.D. Ala. Dec 29, 1995)).

Plaintiffs refuted the state's characterizations by claiming that prejudice was the sole reason for the practice of segregation. Their briefs stated that "Compelling seropositive prisoners to live in segregated units like leper colonies [means they are] publicly branded through the fact of their segregation, as carriers of a dread, socially unacceptable and fatal disease," *Harris v. Thigpen*, 941 F.2d 1495, 1500 n.6 (11th Cir. 1991). Plaintiffs further argued that the state's motives for segregation not only had racial overtones (most of the segregated prisoners were African-American), but also resulted from political pressure to deal with a sexual epidemic through penal quarantine. This influence was acknowledged later by a senior prison official who stated that, "AIDS is perceived as God's wrath, and our policies were grounded in ignorance, fear, and hysteria. Alabama legislators were reactive to public opinion, regardless of the facts" (Prison Official: Personal communication, September 23, 2008).

On appeal (*Harris v. Thigpen*, 941 F2d 1495 (11th Cir. 1991)), the majority of the Eleventh Circuit agreed with the trial judge that the risk of contracting the virus was too great to allow HIV-positive prisoners to integrate, and restated the lower court's "any risk is too much risk" standard in justifications for segregated housing. In using the *Turner* rule[1] as the legal basis for their decision, the majority stated that, "The Court determined that the standard of review for evaluating prisoners' constitutional claims should be one of reasonableness: when a prison regulation or policy 'impinges on inmates' constitutional rights, the regulation is valid if it is reasonably related to legitimate penological interests,'" *Harris v. Thigpen,* 941 F.2d 1495, 1515 (11th Cir. 1991) (quoting *Turner v. Safley*, 462 U.S. 78, 85 (1987)). The appellate court concluded that deferring to prison wardens was indeed justified because "[r]egardless of how much evidence is presented, no court will ever be as qualified as prison officials to judge the particular needs of a penal institution," *Onishea v. Herring*, No. 87-V1109-N, slip op. at 461 (M.D. Alabama Dec. 29, 1995)). This decision ended the case against segregated housing and medical care in Alabama prisons.

The appellate court then turned to access to programs, and directed Judge Varner to consider if any activities involving minimal physical contact (e.g., religious services) could safely be integrated. In so directing, the judges dismissed the defendants' claim that contagiousness was a legitimate basis for blanket exclusions and concluded that the Rehabilitation Act existed to protect "handicapped contagious prisoners from sweeping

[1] In Turner v. Safley, 482 U.S. 78 (1987), the U.S. Supreme Court ruled that penal concerns such as prison security could be used to override prisoners' First Amendment rights.

deprivations based on prejudice, stereotypes or unfounded fear" (*Harris v. Thigpen*, 941 F.2d 1495, 1527 (11th Cir. 1991). The court cited epidemiologic evidence that HIV/AIDS could not be transmitted through casual contact, indicating that medical knowledge (and judicial acceptance of that knowledge) had advanced to the point where HIV/AIDS was considered infectious rather than contagious – an important distinction in considering the state's claims of epidemiologic threat in low-contact situations. Carcereal authority thus should be weighed against plaintiffs' claims for reasonable accommodations if they were sufficiently docile (i.e., non-violent) to be integrated into the daily life of the penitentiary.

Judge Varner was directed to take two factors into account in this assessment. In the first instance, "minimal contact" activities should be identified for integration purposes. In the second instance, the prison classification system should be used to help distinguish between "high risk" and "low risk" plaintiffs in terms of their psychological characteristics and behavior. For the latter, the Eleventh Circuit recognized that officials' claims about dangerousness should be individualized according to the inmate's disciplinary career. The judges also noted that prison officials routinely assessed the behavioral characteristics of HIV-negative prisoners for drug rehabilitation and anger management programs, work-release placements, and other activities. They concluded that the same system could be used to reclassify low-risk HIV-positive persons who did not pose a threat to prison health and order.

Judge Varner would have none of it. As noted by Judge Kravitch on the Eleventh Circuit, "Even a cursory review of the district court's order reveals Judge Varner's unwillingness to put aside the conclusion he reached after the first trial" (*Onishea v. Hopper,* 126 F.3d 1323, 1342 (11th Cir. 1997)). Judge Varner again invoked the *Turner* rule by stating that legitimate penological interests such as security could be used to infringe First Amendments rights (i.e., "the right to petition the government for redress of grievances"). The judge also restated his original decision to uphold the "any risk" standard by reiterating his belief that prisoners were inherently volatile, untrustworthy, and unpredictable, and by concluding that, "[p]rison officials must always 'prepare for the worst' and 'expect the unexpected'" *Onishea v. Hopper,* 171 F.3d 1289, 1301 (11th Cir. 1999) (quoting *Onishea v. Herring*, No.87-V1109-N, slip op. at 57, 58 (M.D. Ala. Dec. 29, 1995)). Highly-charged statements from defendants' briefs were used to support his stance, including this quote about same-sex activity and food contamination: "[Sexual activities include] high-risk behavior committed by two Limestone kitchen workers who engaged in homosexual sex in the kitchen bakery beside a mixing bowl of peanut butter and jelly" (*Id.* at 1294). The judge deployed the language of difference in stating that HIV-positive inmates, "[m]ay have controlling impulses vastly different from those of healthy inmates who may be more concerned about the penal aspects of their future" (*Id.* at 1309).

The plaintiffs' second appeal to the Eleventh Circuit (*Onishea v. Hopper*, 171 F.3d 1289 (11th Cir. 1999)) claimed that they had a constitutional right to be integrated into prison programs. The case was heard by a panel of three judges who agreed with the plaintiffs, vacated the lower court decision, and recommended reassignment of the case to a different lower court judge. By this time, the idea of HIV/AIDS as contagion had lost discursive power after therapeutic advances had transformed AIDS from a fatal disease into a more manageable condition. Nevertheless, intersecting discourses of contagion and carcereal power remained powerful rhetorical devices in shaping the outcome of the litigation. For instance, the legacy of contagion remained a cornerstone of defendants' briefs and, ultimately, was sealed in final judgments after the *en Banc* court vacated the panel's recommendation and denied the plaintiffs' appeal. Trial fatigue was evident in the judges' deliberations and in the court's recognition that, "[t]here is justifiable reluctance to reverse and remand once again for a new trial in this protracted case" (*Id.* at 1315). The majority upheld the defendants' claims in favor of segregation by reiterating that prison officials were uniquely qualified to assess security risks. The final judgment stated that, 1) segregated programs did not represent an exaggerated response to the threat of violence, 2) hiring additional personnel to supervise integrated programs would be an undue financial burden on a cash-strapped system, and 3) classifying prisoners as either high or low risk was irrelevant because prisoners were inherently unpredictable.

It is worth noting that three of the 13 judges who presided on the *en Banc* court dissented from the majority opinion. These judges cited medical evidence in stating that HIV/AIDS could be treated like other infectious diseases and complained that "the only testimony below in support of Alabama's policy consists of the opinions of corrections officials and none comes from any public health entity unconnected with the parties" (*Onishea v. Hopper*, 171 F.3d 1289, 1315 (11th Cir. 1999) (Barkett, J., dissenting)). In support of the plaintiffs' claims for integration, the minority noted how prisoners with infectious diseases such as Hepatitis B or C had not been similarly segregated or excluded from daily activities in US prisons, and concluded that segregation was a particularly severe form of punishment that could not be justified by extant medical evidence.

The plaintiffs' final plea to the US Supreme Court was denied, thus affirming Alabama's right to use contagion as a discursive tool to justify penal segregation. This outcome fails to support Foucault's (1995) premise that deviance is a shifting category that is constructed anew with increasingly sophisticated forms of disciplinary knowledge (e.g. medical information that HIV/AIDS is neither contagious nor untreatable). However, Foucault also claimed that deviance, once defined, is essential to broadening the power and scope of the carcereal archipelago through the classificatory claims of penological actors. In Alabama, the state legislature had expanded the power to discipline and punish through quarantine for inmates who were deemed doubly deviant by virtue of their medico-criminal status. The labeling of HIV/AIDS as a contagious, inevitably fatal disease thus became fixed in correctional policies and was legitimized by broader legal precedent (e.g. *Turner*) and legislative actions such as the PRLA that rendered the Harris courts as docile agents of the state. Alabama's "separate but equal" policies remained until Antonio Leatherwood and other HIV-positive male inmates sued the state in 2002. In this case, the plaintiffs deployed a different set of arguments by challenging the quality of health care and housing for segregated inmates rather than the fact of segregation in health care, housing, and daily activities for HIV-positive men at Limestone.

CASE TWO: LEATHERWOOD V. CAMPBELL, 2002

Background

Leatherwood was filed by the Southern Center for Human Rights (SCHR) on behalf of Antonio Leatherwood and all other HIV-positive men at the Limestone Correctional Facility (Figure 1). The case was heard by Judge Karon O. Bowdre in the Northern District of

Alabama. This litigation differed from *Harris* in several important respects. First, the complaint did not include HIV-positive women at the Tutwiler prison. Second, the plaintiffs narrowed their complaint to address substandard housing and HIV care after a medical audit identified a high number of suspicious deaths over a three-year period. Third, internal state documents revealed that officials knew about the inadequate medical services provided by NaphCare, the prison's health care contractor, and that they were seeking a replacement. Fourth, the judge directed the parties to mediation rather than trial, an important distinction that will be discussed later. Finally, in contrast to *Harris*, medical documentation dominated the proceedings and provided the rationale for a settlement.

Leatherwood is a case study of how three discrete themes (carcereal authority, privatization, and contagion) intersected at critical points in the production of death in the HIV unit. Beginning with carcereal authority, the state initially defended HIV segregation by citing the "undue financial burden," and "need to minimize risk" arguments that had succeeded in Harris. However, the state abandoned this approach after being asked by the Department of Corrections' own medical auditor to explain the deaths of 38 HIV-positive inmates at Limestone over a three-year period. Two issues then had to be resolved over allegations of medical negligence. The first issue concerned the adequacy of treatment services being provided by NaphCare, a co-defendant in the case. The second issue centered on documented evidence of substandard housing in the segregated unit. After these problems came to light during the discovery phase, the plaintiffs focused almost entirely on NaphCare's services, with housing conditions being viewed in this health-related context. The emphasis on medical negligence contrasted with Harris in which privatized HIV care was deemed adequate relatively early in the litigation.

Why did the case involve two defendants (Alabama Department of Corrections and NaphCare) in relation to complaints about medical negligence? This question can be answered by referring to the criminological labyrinth that Foucault (1995) theorized about in *Discipline and Punish.* In the 1970s, this labyrinth had expanded to include outsourcing to private health contractors, a trend that prompted numerous complaints about substandard health care in U.S. prisons from cost-cutting (Jones, 2007; Robbins, 1999). In *Leatherwood*, the auditor identified cost-cutting as a major reason for treatment problems in the segregated unit.[2] As the case progressed, evidence of NaphCare's negligence became indisputable and Judge Bowdre urged the parties to settle after noting that, "At least one [untreated] patient had such severe pneumonia that he suffocated in front of the medical staff" and, "Many male HIV-positive inmates died a horrible death, literally standing on their feet" (Doc. 163, p.7). Nevertheless, the judge also warned the plaintiffs against going to trial because prison litigation reforms such as the PRLA were so absolute that "[t]he class of HIV prisoners at Limestone may not receive any assistance for a very, very long time" (Doc. 163, p. 22). In her summation, Judge Bowdre affirmed that the PRLA was enacted to prevent judicial micro-management of prison systems and that the plaintiffs were likely to lose regardless of the merits of the case.

Two reports were pivotal to settlement of the litigation. The medical auditor cited a host of problems including lack of staff for chronic care clinics ("Inmates said they had not seen the doctor in six to eight months"), cost-cutting, negligence, and poor infection control. The

[2] The medical auditor, Roger Childress of Moore and Associates in Montgomery, Alabama, conducted an audit of the Limestone Correctional Facility on October 1, 2002 on behalf of the Alabama Department of Corrections.

report sounded the alarm over deaths among HIV-positive inmates at Limestone ("The number of AIDS deaths is remarkably high … This rate is more than twice the AIDS death rate from the 2001 ACA statistics," Doc 55, p. 41). The auditor recommended a full review of inmate deaths. The second report, commissioned by the plaintiffs, was written by Dr. Stephan Tabet, an HIV specialist. Tabet's 124-page report described the cause and circumstances of each death and provided evidence of deaths from suffocation ("Nursing notes in the chart documented that the patient stated, 'I am afraid to go to sleep. Please stay and talk to me and watch me' … The patient suffocated to death"), starvation ("He was begging for sandwiches … burst into tears during evaluation … This patient was literally starving to death. Patient died of HIV wasting") and neglect (e.g., "Patient had a 75-pound weight loss and, in fact, he had not been on antiretroviral medications because he was told they were not available to him"). Tabet summarized his findings as follows:

In almost all instances the death was preceded by a failure to provide proper medical care or treatment. Consistently, patients died of preventable illness. Patients with serious diseases experienced serious delays in medical care or were not treated at all. Chronic care clinics are unheard of at Limestone. Life-threatening laboratory results were treated routinely instead of urgently. Other tests such as radiographs showing pneumonia were commonly not assessed until many days later. Because of a broken, severely stressed or often non-existent medical system, patients are needlessly dying and suffering from AIDS-related complications and other illnesses that could be prevented. The conditions at Limestone Prison are unsafe for both the incarcerated and for the staff. There is a sense of hopelessness and helplessness among the patients at Limestone – to a degree that I have not witnessed prior" (Tabet Report, p.113).

Tabet's evidence was accepted by the court and the parties moved to settle. The magistrate's final report concluded that, "Dr. Tabet's deceased HIV prisoner mortality reviews demonstrate that the inadequate medical treatment is unconstitutional" (Doc 163, p.7).

Housing was addressed as a health problem in both reports. The auditor described the AIDS unit as an "[o]ld, leaky warehouse that had formerly housed Alabama's chain gangs" (Doc 55, p. 33) and concluded that housing conditions for inmates in Dorm 16 (the segregated residential unit) and The Infirmary (the hospital unit) were deplorable and a threat to health. Plaintiffs' briefs charged that the unit was overcrowded, and photos of triple cells and double bunks in close proximity were displayed in an Appendix. Dorm 16 was described as being poorly ventilated, moldy, structurally unsound, and infested with mosquitoes and rat and bird droppings ("rats climb into the inmates' beds at night"). Chronic overcrowding in unsanitary conditions had led to outbreaks of disease including "an epidemic of painful boils that plagues HIV+ inmates at Limestone" (Doc 1, p. 8). In the settlement, prison officials agreed to implement an infection control plan using CDC guidelines for treating tuberculosis, boils (*staphylococcus aureus*) and other infections, and to conduct monthly pest control inspections to reduce the threat of disease from insects, birds, and rodents. As part of the settlement, HIV-positive inmates were transferred from the dormitory to a less crowded but still segregated cellblock. The following section describes how the plaintiffs used reverse discourse in order to challenge penological praxis over segregated activities. In so doing, they deployed the concept of "dangerousness" to emphasize the harm they had endured in the segregated unit. This tactic made a clear distinction between the state's characterization of the inmates as an extremely dangerous class of deviants and the life-threatening conditions of the segregated unit for immune-compromised inmates.

Until Leatherwood, contagiousness was a rhetorical device to justify placing HIV-positive inmates in substandard living quarters at Limestone prison. These living quarters consisted of a converted warehouse that was originally assigned for male chain gangs after "tough on crime" Governor Fob James resurrected the gangs as a public shaming device in the mid 1990s (Allen & Abril, 1997).[3] The chain gangs ceased to exist after lawsuits were filed over the wrongful death of an inmate who was shackled to another prisoner, but allegations of racial discrimination also played a role in their demise because so few whites were subjected to this form of punishment (see Austin v. James, 1998). The warehouse was then used for storage until designated for HIV-positive inmates (it was subsequently condemned for human habitation after *Leatherwood*). In racialized parallel, most of the HIV-positive inmates in Dorm 16 were African Americans, and historical connections between chain gangs, racial discrimination, and segregated confinement provided the contextual backdrop to both the lawsuit and settlement in *Leatherwood* even though legal arguments and reports were framed in careful, race-neutral terms (see Fleury-Steiner, 2008).

The theme of contagion appeared in plaintiff's briefs as a plague of boils "as large as golf balls" that caused fever, illness, and extensive scarring in many residents. Legal briefs, experts' reports, and the final settlement described how infected inmates had sought treatment, were denied treatment, and had attempted self-care by "[s]oaking themselves in garbage cans filled with bleach and water" (Doc1, p. 8). The discourse of contagion, successfully used by prison officials in Harris to justify segregation, was reversed in *Leatherwood* in which plaintiffs became victims rather than vectors in the case. Disciplinary knowledge about HIV/AIDS was deployed in this reversal, with medical experts on both sides attesting to the life-threatening conditions of Dorm 16 for immune-compromised inmates. As a strategy for change, the use of reverse discourse in *Leatherwood* led to improvements in housing and health care although segregated housing and infirmary were (and still are) justified by prison officials in these terms, "We separate all prisoners with serious medical conditions. The dialysis patients go to St. Clair, the end-of-life patients go to Hamilton, TB patients are housed in the infirmary, and HIV patients go to Limestone and Tutwiler. The other [state] systems won't call it segregation, but they all do it because it makes budgetary sense" (Prison Official: Personal communication, September 23, 2008).

Leatherwood demonstrated how contagion, cost-cutting, and health care converged in the maltreatment of segregated inmates. NaphCare's ethos of neglect was evidenced by the lack of physicians, nursing staff, medicines, laboratory tests, specialist care, dietary food, and record-keeping. Indeed, understaffing was so chronic that, "HIV-positive inmates provide medication to one another, carry each other to the HCU on stretchers, provide end-of-life treatment to dying inmates, and provide CPR to one another" (Doc 55, p. 13). The inmates certainly provided surplus labor for NaphCare in the absence of paid staff, but their exploitation also signified how the contractor's "out of sight out of mind" practices were tacitly sanctioned by the state. In this respect, prison officials were responsible for relegating the inmates to a back region in which, "The leadership has no understanding about what the

[3] In the mid-1990s, I observed the chain gangs working on an embankment beside U.S. Highway 20/59 while driving to Montgomery, Alabama. Most prisoners were African Americans who were being supervised by an armed, white male correctional officer mounted on a horse.

medical staff is doing and the medical staff does not communicate with the Alabama Department of Corrections. The analogy I would use is that the head of the institution (the Warden) has been severed from the body [NaphCare]" (Tabet Supplement, p. 43).

The threat of contagion was also deployed to minimize contact with the prison's untouchables. For example, HIV-positive inmates were required to administer food and medicine to their dying peers and to dispose of the corpses in order to maintain a *cordon sanitaire* between medical staff and the deceased. Plaintiffs' briefs noted that, "[The physician] often refuses to touch HIV-positive inmates when treating and diagnosing skin infections and other illnesses" (Doc 1, p. 11). This aversion to touching continued for the duration of the inmate's sentence or until he had expired. In one notable case, "An HIV-positive inmate was dying. The NaphCare staff laid a mattress on the floor of Dorm 16. No covering was placed over the mattress. The dying HIV-positive inmate was placed by [another inmate] on the mattress where he died shortly thereafter" Doc 1, p. 10). Plaintiffs' briefs noted that, "This grim and lonely death for HIV-positive inmates demonstrates a clear lack of minimal end-of-life medical treatment" (Doc 1, p. 11). Contrary to Foucauldian understandings that rules for punishment eschew bodily harm in the modern penitentiary, these events -- as confirmed by audit, medical reviews, and judge's report -- indicated that willful neglect was the *modus operandi* of private employees in their role as medical surrogates of the state.

Leatherwood also exemplified how Foucault's microphysics of power ensured that carcereal power was exercised over inmates through surveillance, architecture, and daily disciplines and routines. Segregation certainly operated as a panoptical device in the notorious and highly visible Dorm 16. Rules and routines were the bureaucratic means by which to deny access to medical care. The emergency response system, for example, required seven steps that began with contacting a correctional officer, who then contacted a superior officer (who then contacted a physician) in a stepwise process until permission was granted to phone 911. After that, the prison was placed in lockdown until the patient had been carried into the ambulance. Court documents revealed that the process was overly bureaucratic, subject to failure at each step, and that "[t]he slow response in medical emergencies has contributed to the death of several HIV-positive inmates" (Doc 55, p.13).

Bureaucratic barriers were also evident in relation to non-emergency care. Inmates were required to file "sick-call" slips with the contractor ("A sick HIV-positive inmate can be forced to wait from several days to several weeks to see a nurse or doctor. Some sick-call slips are not answered at all" (Doc 55, p. 11) and to pay for health care visits ("The excessive charging of a $3.00 payment for medical services, which are often not even provided, discourages many patients from seeking essential medical treatment" (Doc 55, p.19). Inmates were required to line up for pill-call regardless of health condition, time of day, or temperature so that, "They are forced to interrupt their much-needed sleep at 3:00 am each early morning to standing in a pill line outside, often in cold, wet weather or sweltering heat . . . Many of these AIDS patients are too sick or unable to stand long enough to wait in line" (Tabet Report, p. 111). The prisoners were also discouraged from filing grievances over the lack of medical treatment, as exemplified by: "Dr. S. told [plaintiff] that if he continued to file grievance forms [over untreated boils] that she would have him locked up in the disciplinary dorm" (Doc 1, p. 17). The court concluded that these rules were obstructive or coercive, or both. In terms of the microphysics of power, this regime constituted a form of punishment that was non-rehabilitative, life-threatening, and sometimes fatal.

HIV SEGREGATION AND DISCIPLINARY POWER

Litigation over mandated HIV testing and segregated housing for Alabama prisoners consisted of failed legal challenges in *Harris v. Thigpen* (1990) and subsequent appeals in *Onishea v. Hopper* (1998) and *Davis V. Hopper* (2000). By contrast, *Leatherwood v. Campbell* (2002) focused exclusively on health care and housing after both the defendants and plaintiffs produced evidence of medical negligence. At time of writing, this two decade-long process has yielded only modest improvements in medical care and housing at The Limestone Correctional Facility and integration into general activities has stalled over concerns about space limitations and security (see Fleury-Steiner, 2008). Access to work release programs was granted recently for some inmates, however, suggesting that the changes wrought by Leatherwood settlement had further salutary effects for prisoners at Limestone. By contrast, the women at Tutwiler were more successful in gaining earlier access to general activities, perhaps because their numbers were few enough to make accommodations less daunting (Hunter, 2008). The iconography of HIV-positive male inmates as dangerous (and their higher numbers relative to women at Tutwiler) is likely to play a role in the non-integration for men, as evidenced by rules that male HIV-positive inmates have to be escorted if they leave the segregated unit (Hunter, 2008).

Alabama's stance on segregation is consistent with the politics of a "tough on crime" state whose carcereal apparatus is, as Foucault's theory suggests, a coercive theater in which the prisoner-deviant is punished according to his or her disciplinary character. The state's characterization of HIV-positive prisoners as vengeful and sexually deviant provided discursive justification for double exile from the free world and other prisoners. This spacial distribution was the manifestation of two laws of the land – one that consisted of the penal code and the other that required quarantine in the case of epidemiologic threats to public health. This double-classification meant that HIV-positive prisoners were on display as both spectacle and warning, much like death row prisoners whose exemplary punishment consists of mandatory assignment to a separate housing unit until execution. In the case of HIV/AIDS, the classificatory system became a means to an end in the form of the prisoner's release or death, whichever came first.

Foucault's (1995) argument that carcereal systems are omnipotent and self-reproducing helps to explain why Alabama resisted desegregation in the face of costly legal challenges. After all, *Harris* and *Leatherwood* demonstrated how prison operatives could resist judicial intervention in most respects (i.e., apart from modest progress toward integrated programs) if or when cases went to trial. In keeping with this theme, Western (2006) noted how the penal state became all-powerful in the late 20th century United States, and Fleury-Steiner (2008) wrote about how infectious diseases such as Hepatitis, Tuberculosis, and HIV/AIDS became associated with criminalized behavior (e.g. drug addiction) during the same period. As I have suggested in this article, the discursive basis for HIV-related segregation in Alabama involved moral panics over a new and deadly disease that converged with the conservative politics of the U.S. south and the rise of the carcereal state. This historicity was the driving force in Alabama's legislative stance on HIV-related segregation and allowed the practice to continue, despite being abandoned elsewhere for administrative, budgetary, or medical reasons (Best, 1991; Jacobs, 1995; MacDougall, 1998).

The character of the judiciary in relation to *Harris* and *Leatherwood* is worthy of note. *Harris* was heard and reheard by a lower court judge whose denigration of HIV-positive inmates (and unwavering belief in the penultimate power of the penitentiary) prompted repeated complaints by plaintiffs' attorneys in the case. The appeals court attempted to modify the lower court findings on two occasions, but the final ruling favored the defendants by invoking Judge Varner's "any risk is too much risk" standard in relation to epidemiologic catastrophe. The court's summation, in fact, reiterated state and lower court arguments almost verbatim. This restatement served to institutionalize HIV/AIDS as a contagious disease because of legal processes that, in Foucauldian terms, converged and gradually produced the blueprint of a general method. By convincing the parties to settle, the judge in *Leatherwood* did not seek to challenge the status quo on segregation. State policies on HIV-related segregation were thus established as legal fact in the south even though US courts in other Circuits generally declined to follow Harris in similar cases (e.g., *Powell v. Schriver,* 175 F.3d 107 (2nd Cir. N.Y. 1999); *Owens v. O'Dea,* 1998 U.S. App. (6th Cir. Ky. May 27, 1998).

CONCLUSION

What theoretical conclusions should be drawn from Harris and Leatherwood? As social theorists from Karl Marx to Michel Foucault have contended, the courts are not only a disciplinary mechanism and integral to the penal economy, but also a forum through which legislative power "speaks" in the legitimizing discourse of the powerful. In the case of HIV-positive prisoners in Alabama, this discursive legitimacy has been promulgated through the state's moral politics and racialized images of the criminal, the deviant, and the diseased. These cultural representations help to explain the disparity between Alabama and other states in relation to carcereal power and HIV-related policies. It is likely that HIV-positive prisoners will continue to experience discrimination and the state will continue to cite security concerns in order to justify housing and other forms of segregation. The question for the future is whether or not legal challenges can, at last, be fought successfully on the grounds that HIV/AIDS is neither contagious nor a certain death sentence, or whether legal barriers such as the PRLA will prevent further litigation. I predict that Alabama's "last in the nation" status will persist in some form for two additional reasons: 1) because segregation has been enshrined in law and praxis for the past 30 years, and 2) because, as I argue elsewhere (Lichtenstein, 2005), HIV stigma is so powerful in the US south that reforms are unlikely for people who are already typecast as exemplary deviants in terms of violence, drug use, prostitution, and other forms of criminality.

REFERENCES

Allen, H.E. & Abril, J.C. (1997). The new chain gang: corrections in the next century. *American Journal of Criminal Justice, 22*, 1-12.

American Federation for AIDS Research [amfAR]. (2002). Project aims to end segregation of HIV-positive inmates. Retrieved July 30, 2008 from: http://www.amfar.org/cgi-bin/iowa/programs/publicp/z.record.html?record=150

Best, T. E. (1991). *Harris* v. *Thigpen*: Segregating HIV-positive inmates in the Alabama correctional system. *Mercer Law Review, 43*: 1263-1290.

Fleury-Steiner, B. (2008). *Dying inside: The HIV/AIDS ward at Limestone Prison.* Ann Arbor, MI: Michigan University Press.

Foucault, M. (1995). *Discipline & Punish: The Birth of the Prison.* 2nd Edition. NY: Vintage.

Gostin, L. O., Porter, L., & Sandomire, H. (1990). *AIDS litigation project: A national survey of federal, state, and local cases before courts and human rights commissions.* Washington, DC: Department of Health and Human Services, Public Health Service.

Greenspan, J. (2005). No justice for Alabama's HIV-positive prisoners. Retrieved September 15, 2008, from: http://www.workers.org/2005/us/alabam-0818

Hammett, T. M., & Daugherty, A. L. (1991). *1990 Update: AIDS in correctional facilities.* U.S. Department of Justice, Office of Justice Programs. Washington, DC: Nat. Inst. of Justice.

Hunter, D. (2008, March 17). Integration of Limestone HIV inmates stalled, timeline sought. Associated Press. Retrieved October 29, 2008 from http://www.aegis.com/news/ap/2008/AP080343.html

Jacobs, S. (1995). AIDS in correctional facilities: Current status of legal issues critical to policy development. *Journal of Criminal Justice, 23*, 209-221.

Jones, D.J. (2007). A cruel and unusual system: The inherent problems of the practice of outsourcing health care of prisons and jails. *Chicano/Latino Law Review, 27.* Retrieved on January 2, 2009, from: http://ssrn.com/sol3/cf_dev

Jonsen, A. R., & Stryker, J. (1993). Editors: *The social impact of AIDS in the United States.* Washington, DC: National Academy Press.

Kantor, E. (2006). HIV transmission and prevention in prisons. Retrieved September 12, 2008, from: http://hivinsite.ucsf.edu/InSite?page=kb-07-04-13

Knepper, K. (1995). Responsibility of correctional officials in responding to the incidence of the HIV virus in jails and prisons. *New England Journal on Criminology and Civic Confinement*, 21, 45-96.

Lichtenstein (2005). "Stigma as a Barrier to HIV Prevention in the Deep South." Fact Sheet 16, Rural Center for AIDS/STD Prevention/Centers for Disease Control and Prevention.

MacDougall, D.S. (1998). HIV/AIDS behind bars. *Journal of the International Association of Physicians in AIDS Care 4*(4), 8-13.

Maruschak, L. (2005). *HIV in prisons – 2003.* Bureau of Justice Statistics. Washington, DC: US Department of Justice, Office of Justice Programs. Publication no. NCJ210344.

Robbins, I. P. (1999). Managed health care in prisons as cruel and unusual punishment. *The Journal of Criminal Law & Criminology, 90*, 195-238.

Western, B. (2006). *Punishment and inequality in America.* New York: Sage.

CASES CITED

Austin v. James, CV 95-T-637-N, 1998.

Harris v. Thigpen, 727 F. Supp. 1564 (M.D. Ala.1990).

Leatherwood v. Campbell, CV 02-BE-2812-W, 2002.
Owens v. O'Dea, 1998 U.S. App. (6th Cir. Ky. May 27, 1998).
Powell v. Schriver, 175 F.3d 107 (2nd Cir. N.Y. 1999).

DOCUMENTS CITED

Leatherwood v. Campbell, CV 02-BE-2812-W. 2002
No.1. Complaint: Filed 11/18/2002, 1-35.
No.55. Second Amended Complaint: Filed 04/02/2003, 1-43.
No.163. Magistrate Judge's Report and Recommendation: Filed 06/02/2004, 1-28.
(a) Tabet Report: Filed 08/26/2003, 1-124.
(b) Tabet Supplement: Filed 03/11/2004, 1-46.

AUTHOR NOTE

Thanks go to Leigh Ann Shelton, Stanley L. Brodsky, Alisha Powell, Dylan Reeves, Jessica Ammon, Creighton Miller, James Leonard, and the Alabama Department of Corrections for technical assistance in the preparation of this article.

In: Violent Crime and Prisons: Population...
Ed: Aidan Renshaw and Emelina Suárez
ISBN: 978-1-60741-668-5

Chapter 13

COUNSELING IN PRISON: PROBLEMS AND CHALLENGES

Theodoros Giovazolias and Olga Themeli
Department of Psychology, University of Crete, Greece

ABSTRACT

Prison is an institution that strives to combine two different and contradictory goals. On the one hand, its purpose is to isolate individuals that are considered threats to society and to impose an exemplary punishment, and on the other hand it aims at their social reintegration by the means of correction (Haidou, 2002). Watson and his colleagues (2004) are supportive of Haidou's point of view by drawing attention to the fact that prison's objectives are punishment, correction and successful reintegration. Correction requires that the inmate adjusts to the values, the mores, the mentality, and the subculture of prison, thus resulting in the distortion of his/her personal identity and uniqueness (Paterline & Petersen, 1999).

1. INTRODUCTION

According to Goffman (1961) prisons are the most characteristic and representative example of a total institution. A total institution is defined as a place of residence and work in which a large number of individuals who are in the same condition, isolated from society for a considerable amount of time, spend together an enclosed and formally managed daily life. In other words, all aspects of life (e.g. habitation, recreation, work) take place in the same space, under the same sole authority, while every activity of its members has a direct relationship to a number of other individuals, who are subject to the same treatment and are required to perform the same tasks. Moreover, all aspects of one's daily routine are tightly programmed as one activity leads to the other in a strictly set time period, and the whole continuum is imposed from above by a system of strict rules and regulations and by a specific body of officials.

Factors such as jail overpopulation, extreme stress, fear and insecurity, still time, the sudden isolation from family and social environment, institutionalisation, and the "pains of imprisonment" in general, make every attempt to improve prison conditions extremely difficult. When we refer to the pains of imprisonment, we mean the unpleasant circumstances experienced by the prisoner as well as the lack of basic services that the prisoner is obliged to deal with (Paterline & Petersen, 1999). Sykes was the first to provide this definition in 1958 when referring to theses unpleasant conditions (see Riley, 2002) which are noted as deprivation of freedom, by means of physical restriction and social isolation, of social goods and services, of heterosexual relations, and of personal autonomy and security.

The above deprivations cause pain and intense unpleasant feelings to the individuals involved and threaten their sense of personal value and identity (Viggiani, 2007). It has been internationally acknowledged in the literature that prison acts as a catalyst in the personality and mental health of imprisoned individuals, rendering them an especially vulnerable social group (Abramowitz, 2005; Davies, Heyman, Godin, Shaw, & Reynolds, 2006; Wilson, 2004).

2. Prisoners with Mental Health Issues

As we have previously mentioned, prison environment is a difficult, rigid place with few stimuli, high degree of control and lack of privacy, and as such it is a high-risk environment for mental disorders and use of illegal substances (Black, James, Evan, & Rogers, 2007). The poor living conditions of the detainees affect their physical and psychological status, thus resulting in a higher than average rate of mental health conditions of the incarcerated compared to the general population (Friedstad & Hansen, 2005). The percentage of mental illness inside correctional institutions is constantly rising, and it has been suggested that they tend to become the new mental institutions (Abramowitz, 2005).

According to Anthony and McFayden (2005), the involvement itself of an individual with the criminal justice system brings up intense stress and depression, regardless the result of the trial. In Greece, prisoners who need any form of psychiatric intervention are transferred to the Psychiatric Ward of the Korydalos' Correctional Institution (Fotiadou et al, 2006).

According to the WHO (2000, see Black et al, 2007), the frequency of individuals with mental disorders in prisons is very high compared to the general population. In a study of Butler, Allnutt, Cain, Owens and Muller (2005) in Australia, it was found that in a sample of 953 prisoners, 43% of the inmates were suffering from some mental disorder, with women presenting higher rates. These percentages pertain to prisoners who developed a form of mental disorder while inside the prison as well as those with a history of mental illness that became worse during imprisonment.

Relevant studies have found that inmates suffer from major depression (Anthony & McFayden, 2005), schizophrenia, (Black et al., 2007), panic attacks, intense stress and sleeping disorders, psychoses, personality disorders, substance and alcohol abuse, (Friedstad & Hansen, 2005; Kjelsberg et al., 2006) as well as bipolar disorder (Falissaerd et al., 2006), which is very difficult to diagnose because the symptoms may be absent at the time of examination (for this reason it is recommended that the inmate's history with regards to depression and mania should be taken into account).

According to Butler and his colleagues (2005), recently imprisoned persons are more likely to suffer from depression, while former inmates often suffer from post-traumatic stress disorder. Moreover, Birmingham (2003) claims that men tend to suffer more from antisocial behavior and paranoid personality disorder, while women suffer from borderline personality disorder.

In a survey that took place in the prisons of Komotini (Northern Greece) from Fotiadou and her colleagues (2006), it was found that in a sample of 80 inmates, 63 met the criteria of mental disorder. 37% suffered from anxiety disorders, 27.5% suffered from major depression, 12.5% suffered from panic attacks and 2 were epileptic. It is noteworthy that the aforementioned percentage rates are 4 times higher than those of the general population of Greece (Fotiadou et al., 2006).

In addition to that, mentally disordered inmates are often victims of rape by their co-inmates (Abramowitz, 2005), they present higher suicide rates (Black et al, 2007) and a lot of them have a history of mental illness prior to their imprisonment (Fotiadou et al, 2006).

As far as this last point is concerned, studies have demonstrated that many deaths inside prison are due to suicides, mostly by hanging, while most of them occur in the first trimester of imprisonment (Birmingham, 2003), with a great deal of suicides taking place in the first seven days (Shaw & Humber, 2004). Stuart claims that suicidal inmates along with those who possess self – destructive predisposition meet the criteria of the mentally disturbed, with most common disorders being major depression, psychoses and substance misuse. Furthermore, he claims that men are more often liable to commit suicide compared to women (Stuart, 2003).

It is mentioned in the literature that some of the reasons for the manifestation of mental disorders inside prisons are that the inmates are homeless, there is a lack of therapeutic choices in society, lack of psychiatric services for inmates, the refusal of psychiatric institutions to accept former prisoners, and the intolerance of the state towards deviating behavior of the mentally ill (Butler et al., 2005). Diagnosing mental disorders inside correctional institutions is extremely difficult with the use of the existing methods, such as the interview, and this is the reason why more reliable alternative methods are being proposed (Fallisard et al., 2006). According to Wolff (2005), one fourth of prison population with mental disorder suffer from a combination of two or more conditions, the more common being antisocial, narcissistic, paranoid, and avoidance personality disorder as well as alcohol and narcotic substance misuse (Birmingham, 2005).

All the above findings indicate that there is a need for the provision of psychological services within the frame of the prison system. This gap has been fulfilled over the last decades by a sub-branch of counseling psychology, namely 'correctional counseling'.

3. From Counseling Psychology to Correctional Counseling

Counseling psychology, a relatively new branch within the field of applied psychology, takes its place alongside other psychology specialisms within mainstream professional practice, balancing an appreciation of the salience of scientific enquiry and the significance of traditional psychotherapeutic traditions (Leiper, 2002). According to the British Psychological Society (BPS) "It continues to develop models of practice and research which marry the scientific demand for rigorous empirical enquiry with a firm value base grounded in the primacy of the counseling/psychotherapeutic relationship..." (British Psychological Society, 2001).

Counseling psychologists study the underlying psychological principles of, and need to demonstrate competence in, a range of therapeutic approaches across a variety of client groups effecting competent integrative psychotherapeutic practice. They work collaboratively with individuals and groups to empower lifestyle change and personal development (Bor & Watts, 1999).

Over the last two decades "Correctional Counseling", also known as "Inmate Counseling" as a particular branch of Counseling Psychology has shown significant growth. In 1981 Kratkoski published the first specialised textbook on inmates' counseling, where he defined its object as the type of therapy used on inmates of correctional institutions. It utilises the "one-to-one" approach between the client and the counselor or group therapy, and it may involve the prisoner, his family, and the environment in which the prisoner will be directed to after his release (Kratkoski, 1981).

More specifically, "Inmate Counseling", having taken into account both the pathogenic environment of incarceration as well as the special needs of each specific group (those awaiting trial, long term convicts, substance users, women, minors, foreigners, etc) intends to:

- Mobilise and boost the prisoner's confidence so as to develop personal goals
- Cultivate abilities that will help the prisoner to better manage his/her life while serving his/her sentence
- Help the prisoner acquire social skills that will be helpful for his/her life after prison
- Help with the prisoner's learning of ways to deal with disagreeable types of behavior
- Help the prisoner modify behaviors that make his/her life difficult and cause conflict with others
- Boost the prisoner's self - esteem
- Improve the prisoner's self image
- Help the prisoner acquire the ability to take on responsibilities
- Help the prisoner improve decision-making

The work of the correctional psychologist includes the assessment of the inmate's condition, diagnosis, re-integration services, research, counseling, training of prison staff, providing support for the inmate during the whole process of intervention and throughout the duration of his/her sentence (AACP, 1999). More specifically, it is within the psychologist's responsibility to diagnose psychological symptoms, take down the inmate's history, to plan intervention programmes for inmates' substance addiction, to deal with the inmate's socio - economic isolation and lack of social support (Davies et al., 2006), as well as to diagnose, manage, and treat severe mental disorders (AACP, 1999). The correctional psychologist cooperates directly with the prison system or works for it, and it is within his/her competence to plan and apply psychological interventions and programs for inmates (Haag, 2006). Regarding his/her qualifications, he/she must have an academic title (of PhD or at least MSc level) or be specialised in correctional philosophy, he/she must be able to write in a specific judicial style, as well as be competent in projects dealing with the minimisation of relapse and criminal behavior (AACP, 1999)

Regarding Greece, the correctional code, although one of the most progressive in Europe in functional issues concerning the rights of prison inmates, is lacking in provisions relating to the organisation and description of the role of specialised prison staff (Arvanitidis, 2008).

As a result, the competence and specialty of the correctional psychologist are not clearly defined but are mostly considered as a notion under development. It is very characteristic that psychologists in Greek prisons are only required to perform psychometric tests, to write reports, and to suggest suitable work for the inmates (Law 1851/89, ch.14, as this is applied in art. 87 paragraph 3 of Law 2776/99), while at the same time they are required to take part in prison councils thus provided with administrative responsibilities (Ministerial Decision No 58819/7-4-03: Internal Regulation of Detention Institutions). It is also worth noting that the term 'prison psychologist' is a recent development of the Greek prison system, and that until now only 30 prison psychologists have been appointed in the whole country. Moreover, if one considers the fact that in the country's largest detention institute (Korydallos) which numbers 2056 inmates in total (Ministry of Justice 2009, personal communication) there is only one psychologist, it is easily made clear that there is still a very long way to go.

4. The Aims of Correctional Psychology

One of the most basic activities of the correctional psychologist is

a) *crisis intervention*, which must take place the soonest possible, and definitely not later than 24 hours (AACP, 1999). According to Kratkoski (1981) every offender who has been under correctional treatment has already been through a series of crises which include arrest, being kept in custody, court hearings, trial, and finally conviction and punishment. It is most likely that the offender has not seen or been helped by any other specialist during all these crises except from his/her lawyer. Crises usually take place when an inmate becomes victim of homosexual rape, or is informed that a beloved person has died or fallen seriously ill, when he/she is under extreme stress or other psychological problems arising from imprisonment itself. Moreover, crises occur when the inmate is informed of his/her family's financial crisis, when a husband or wife files for divorce, when there is alcohol or substance misuse, in cases of attempting suicide or self-injury. Consulting therapy during times of crisis is unavoidably more intense, more direct, and of a different nature than counseling that is designed on a long term and less stressful basis (Kratkoski, 1981).

Pollock (1998) describes two more types of counseling within the prison frame

b. *Counseling which is directly relevant to the crime* that has been committed. This aims at providing help for inmates who have been driven to committing actions that carry high social and moral demerit and thus experience intense feelings of guilt and remorse (e.g. crimes against life or crimes against sexual liberty etc) as well as to inmates addicted to substances.
c. Personal development *counseling*, which aims at facilitating personal growth. It gives emphasis on specific events of one's life that took place prior to incarceration and that constitute obstacles to the psycho-social development of the person receiving therapy (e.g. family problems, communication problems, low self-esteem, etc).

5. Diagnostic and Therapeutic Tools

Mental health professionals in prisons have at their disposal various widely known psychometric tools in order to diagnose mental disorders. The most common among them are the Minnesota Multiphasic Personality Inventory (MMMPI, MMMPI-2) the Milton Clinical Multiaxial Inventory (MCMI), Rorschach's spot test, the Weschler Adult Intelligence Scale (WAIS) and the Weschler Memory Scale. We should note, however, that these tests are performed in prison established in the United States and Canada, and not in Greece. Various approaches are followed regarding the part of therapeutic intervention, depending on the inmate, his/her personality and his/her values. The cognitive model, the behavioral model and the rational-emotive therapy are some of the more common approaches (Boothby & Clements, 2000).

Therapeutic intervention programmes, as mentioned, take place mainly in the United States, in Great Britain, and in Canada. In Greece such programmes are in a rather primitive stage, as the basic priority of the authorities responsible has been the decongestion of prisons due to overpopulation.

As far as the receivers of mental health services are concerned, in a study of Farell and his colleagues (2006) it was found that individuals with serious mental problems (psychoses) or mental disorders in connection with substance addiction are more likely to receive some form of treatment, so are women compared to men, while foreigners have less chances of treatment.

For prisoners with mental disorders, treatment within the correctional institution, even though it is considered critical and necessary for their integration to society, is not always feasible and viable within the boundaries of their individual needs due to high cost and lack of trained staff. Therapeutic interventions are examined more thoroughly in the next chapter for each category of inmates' problems.

6. Therapeutic Interventions within Prison Environment

The problems that inmates suffer inside the correctional institution differ according to the type of difficulty, its intensity, the time of its onset, but also to the way that it is grasped and lived by each inmate (Abrams, Kim, & Anderson – Nathe, 2005). Therapeutic interventions that are addressed to inmates include programs of individual and group psychotherapy, rehabilitation, management of anger, stress and aggressive behavior, and treatments for transmitted diseases in combination with programs for intervention and prevention of reversion (Day, Bryan, Davey, & Cassey, 2006; Gontkovsky, 2002; Pallone & Hennessy, 2002). Interventions are performed by specialised staff, which includes mental health professionals, counsellors / therapists, social workers, nurses and psychiatrists (Morgan, Kroner, & Mills, 2006).

Group Therapy: Group therapy uses the interactions that are developed inside a group in order for individuals to increase self–knowledge and to alter their behavior. It is focused on helping inmates to adapt to the prison environment and subsequently to reintegrate in society after their release (Pallone & Hanessy, 2002). Its primary benefit lies in facilitating inmates to develop functional relationships with the co-prisoners and it is also believed that the support of the group can help the inmate to cope with the problems rising from imprisonment (Morgan et al., 2006).

Group psychotherapy does not constitute therapy for all conditions. It consists more of an element of a proper integration procedure which effectively prevents relapse. However, combined with other forms of treatment, such as cognitive – behavioral, education, professional education, it has a positive effect on the inmates' prosocial behaviour (Morgan & Winterowd, 2002). It is noteworthy that in prisons of Norway, one mental health specialist is in charge of 9 inmates (Kjelsberg et al., 2006).

Group therapy is particularly effective with regards to prisoners that have committed sexually related crimes such as rape, where through role – playing efforts are made so they develop a empathic responses and take control over functions that are related to offensive behavior (Day et al., 2006). Moreover, group therapy includes "therapeutic discourses", which are addressed to substance and alcohol addicts, where, through a psycho-educational way, they aim at informing inmates about the bio chemical composition of substances and the measures of sensitization and desensitisation (Pallone & Henessy, 2002).

Personal Counseling: It includes interventions that attempt to reinforce the self – image, its understanding by the imprisoned and the interest for personal contact with others, the ability of the individual to regain his/her abilities and to reinforce a more positive and productive way of thinking (Bye & Schillinger, 2005). In personal counseling programs, emphasis is given to the individual's adjustment to the prison environment, his/her relationships with its co-inmates, hiw/her emotional and behavioral problems and his/her learning of new skills (Kjesberg et al., 2006; Gontkovsky, 2002). It is mainly applied to individuals with issues of stress, anger and aggression management, as well as to young offenders (Bye & Schillinger, 2005).

It provides techniques for "thought control" and methods of changing the way of thinking before the criminal act by the means of mechanisms such as the system of exchangeable rewards, positive reinforcements and observation (Abrams et al., 2005). Gognitive skills are taught to the imprisoned so as to be familiar with appropriate reactions at the time they would manifest a criminal behavior (Tung & Farrington, 2006). Bye & Schillinger (2005) argue that the inmate's way of thinking constitutes a primary target with regards to an effective reintegration program.

Cognitive – behavioral programs have been developed in several countries such as the United States, Canada, Scandinavian, Great Britain, and they are applied with positive results thus contributing to the decrease of offence repetition (Tong & Farrington, 2006; Kjesberg et al., 2006; Pollack, 2005; Bye & Schillinger, 2005). Cognitive – behavioral therapy is applied to prisoners that have committed sexually related crimes, to drug addicts, to gang members, to prisoners with problems of anger and aggressive behavior management and young offenders (Abrams et al, 2005; Bye & Schillinger, 2006; Di Placido, Simon Wiite, Gu & Wong, 2006; Kjesberg et al., 2006; Morgan et al., 2006; Pallone & Henessy, 2002; Pollack, 2005; Tong & Farrington, 2006).

Interventions on a family level: Interventions on a family level emphasize on forming effective parenting skills, on the function of the family and the interactions between its members (Pallone & Henessy, 2002). They are mostly referred to families of young offenders and they include their psychological support by means of psycho–educational methods and reintegration programs through contact with members of their family, their friends and their schoolmates (Abrams et al., 2005).

Additionally, specialised programs for training parents take place inside prisons and it is women who usually take part in them since the number of imprisoned mothers is significantly rising (Pallone & Henessy, 2002). Participation of inmates in therapeutic programs, according to the literature, has a positive effect within the prison environment as well as after their release. Therapies are focusing on the reintegration of the individual through self-knowledge, personal growth and change in the way of thinking. Still, the development of community programs is considered critical after their release with regards to their psychological and social support, as well as in terms of their possible relapse of repeating the offence and substance use.

7. Ethical Issues

It is important to mention that, apart from the type of intervention, the prison psychologist should offer his/her services without discriminations, without being influenced from nationality, colour, religion, gender, sexual orientation or any inefficiency of the detainee (AACP, 1999). Furthermore, the psychologist should take care of the inmate with dignity and protect the confidential files of the inmates (Haag, 2006). In the correctional institutions, the psychologist may face some ethical dilemmas in relation to the inmates' revelations during therapy, which are confidential and may be relevant to an escape plan, bodily harm of him/herself or an other inmate. This ethical dilemma should be dealt with discretion, without betraying the trust of the imprisoned and without agreeing to illegal acts (Haag, 2006). Finally, mental health professionals must balance between offering help to inmates with mental conditions and strict control, security and military structure of correctional institution in order to perform their therapeutic approach (Booner & Vandecreek, 2006).

8. Conclusion

The above juxtaposition makes it clear that the objectives of counseling within the imprisoned population are not different from the related to the general population (Pollock, 1998). However, as it is pointed out, its application in prison is presented with several particularities.

The main issue is not the person per se, but the mutual, regular and dynamic interaction that is exercised between the person and the pathogenic environment that he/she is obliged to reside (Van Wormer, 1999). Its social and cultural baggage is called to co-exist with the subculture of jail and to finally adjust to his/her demands. Conflicts are intense and the arising problems are by and large causally connected to incarceration and sentence serving. On the contrary, counseling outside prison takes place within a frame of liberty that is free from the stressful conditions of imprisonment, which alter the actual problems and significantly obstruct any substantial endeavour of their resolution.

So, it is reasonable to ask whether an intervention program that is applied in the general population could be also applied in prison with the same efficacy. For example, would a counseling – therapeutic intervention be similarly efficient with regards to abused women that live in a status of freedom and to women who have also been violated but live under the conditions of incarceration? Furthermore, how could family counseling become effective within the prison borders or how is it possible to establish the kind of relationship between the counseling provider and the counselee?

Counseling, when taking into account the pathology of the environment, aims at the minimization of pains entailed by the deprivation of freedom, helping at the same time the boosting of self – esteem, the acquisition of necessary skills for non-problematic social reintegration, the mobilisation and reinforcement of personal goals. Despite the unavoidable existence of significant restrictions, counseling in prison acquires particular value since it plays an important role in the protection and respect of human value within a system that by definition crushes it.

REFERENCES

Abramowitz, Z. M. (2005). Prisons and the Human Rights of Persons with Mental Disorders. *Forensic Psychiatry*, *18*, 525-529.

Abrams, S. L., Kim, K. & Anderson-Nathe. B. (2005). Paradoxes of Treatment in Juvenile Corrections. *Child and Youth Care Forum*, *34*, 7-25.

American Association of Correctional Psychology (AACP). (1999). Standards for Psychology Services in Jails, Prisons, Correctional Facilities, and Agencies. *Criminal Justice and Behavior*, *27*, 433-494.

Anthony, D. & McFayden, J. (2005). Mental Health Needs Assessment of Prisoners. *Clinical Effectiveness in Nursing*, *9*, 26-36.

Arvanitidis, A. (2008). Correctional Counseling in Greek Prisons. In S. Vidali, & P. Zagoura (Eds.), *Counseling and Prison* (pp.179-190). Ant. N. Sakkoulas Publishers, Athens [In Greek].

Birmingham, L. (2003). The Mental Health of Prisoners. *Advances in Psychiatric Treatment*, *9*, 191-201.

Black, D., James, M., Evan, R. & Rogers, P. (2007). The Association between a Self-reported History of Mental Health Problems and a History of Parasuicide in a Sample of UK male Prisoners. *International Journal of Nursing Studies*, *44*, 427-434.

Bonner, R. & Vandecreek, D. L. (2006). Ethical Decision Making for Correctional Mental Health Providers. *Criminal Justice and Behavior*, *33*, 542-564.

Boothby, L. J. & Clements, B. C. (2000). A National Survey of Correctional Psychologists. *Criminal Justice and Behavior*, *27*, 716-732.

Bor, R. & Watts, M. (eds) (1999). *The Trainee Handbook: A Guide for Counselling and Psychotherapy Trainees*. London: Sage.

British Psychological Society (2001). *Professional Practice Guidelines: Division of Counselling Psychology*. Leicester: BPS.

Butler, T., Allnutt, S., Cain, D., Owens, D. & Muller, C. (2005). Mental Disorder in the New South Wales Prisoner Population. *Australian and New Zealand Journal of Psychiatry*, *39*, 407-413.

Bye, L & Schillinger, A. D. (2005). Evaluation of a Cognitive Thinking Program. *Journal of Correctional Education*, *56*, 202-215.

Davies, P. J., Heyman, B., Godin, M. P., Shaw, P. M. & Reynolds, L. (2006). The Problems of Offenders with Mental Didorders: A plurality of Perspectives within a Single Mental Health Care Organisation. *Social Sciences and Medicine*, *63*, 1097-1108.

Day, A., Bryan, J., Davey, L. & Casey, S. (2006). The Process of Change in Offender Rehabilitation Programmes. *Psychology, Crime and Law*, *12*, 473-487.

Di Placido, C., Simon, L. T., Witte, D. T., Gu, D. & Wong, C. P. S. (2006) Treatment of Gang Members Can Reduce Recidivism and Institutional Misconduct. *Law and Human Behavior*, *30*, 93-114.

Falissard, B., Loze, J Y., Gasquet, I., Duburc, A., Beaurepaire, C., Fagnani, F. & Rouillon, F. (2006). Prevalence of Mental Disorders in French Prisons for Men. *BMC Psychiatry*, *6*, 33.

Farrell, M., Boys, A., Singleton, N., Meltzer, H., Brugha, T., Bebbington, P., Jenkins, R., Coid, J., Lewis, G. & Marsden, J. (2006). Predictors of Mental Health Service Utilization in the 12 Months Before Imprisonment: Analysis of Results From a National Prisons Survey. *Australian and New Zealand Journal of Psychiatry*, *40*, 548-553.

Fotiadou, M., Livaditis, M., Manou, I., Kaniotou, E. & Xenitidis, K. (2006). Prevalence of Mental Disorders and Deliberate Self-harm in Greek Male Prisoners. *International Journal of Law and Psychiatry*, *29*, 68-73.

Friestad, C. & Hansen, I. L. S. (2005). Mental Health Problems among Prison Inmates: the Effect of Welfare Deficiencies, Drug Use and Self-Efficacy. *Journal of Scandinavian Studies in Criminology and Crime Prevention*, *6*, 183-196.

Goffman, E. (1961). *Asylums. Essays on the social situation of mental patients and other inmates*. New York: Anchor.

Gontkovsky, T. S. (2002). The Psychology of Aggression: a Critique of Correctional Approaches to Treating Violent Behavior. *Administration and Policy in Mental Health*, *29*, 525-528.

Haag, M. A. (2006). Ethical Dilemmas Faced by Correctional Psychologists in Canada. *Criminal Justice and Behavior*, *33*, 93-109.

Haidou, A. (2002). The Correctional System: Theoretical and Practical Issues. Athens: Nomiki Vivliothiki Publishers [in Greek].

Kjelsberg, E., Hartvig, P., Bowitz, H., Kuisma, I., Norbech, P., Rustad, A., Seem, M. & Vik, T. (2006). Mental Health Consultations in a Prison population: a Descriptive study. *BMC Psychiatry*, *6*, 27.

Kratcoski, C. P. (1981). *Correctional Counselling and Treatment*. Monterey, California: Duxbury Press.

Leiper, R. (2002). Assessing needs for psychological therapies in the context of the national Service framework for mental health. *Counselling Psychology Review*, *17(4)*, 11-19.

Ministry of Justice (2009). *Inmates Statistical Table*, personal communication.

Morgan, D. R. & Winterowd, L. C. (2002). Interpersonal Process-Oriented Group Psychotherapy with Offender Populations. *International Journal of Offender Therapy and Comparative Criminology*, *46*, 466-482.

Morgan, D. R., Kroner, G. D. & Mills, F. J. (2006). Group Psychotherapy in Prison: Facilitating Change Inside the Walls. *Journal of Contemporary Psychotherapy, 10,* 1-8.

Pallone, J. N. & Hennessy, J. J. (2002). Rehabilitation Services for Criminal Offenders. *Journal of Offender Rehabilitation*, *37*, 459-480.

Paterline, A. B. & Peterson, M. D. (1999). Structural and Social Psychological Determinants of Prisonization. *Journal of Criminal Justice*, *27*, 427-441.

Pollack, S. (2005). Taming The Shrew: Regulating Prisoners Through Woman-Centered Mental Health Programming. *Critical Criminology*, *13*, 71-87.

Pollock, J. M. (1998). *Counseling women in prison*. London: Sage Publication

Riley, J. (2002). The Pains of Imprisonment: Exploring a Classic Text with Contemporary Authors. *Journal of Criminal Justice Education*, *13*, 443-461.

Shaw, J. & Humber, N. (2004). Prison Mental Health Services. *Psychiatry*, *3(11)*, 22-24.

Stuart, H. (2003) Suicide Behind Bars. *Forensic Psychiatry*, *16*, 559-564.

Tong, J. S. L. & Farrington, P. D. (2006). How effective is "Reasoning and Rehabilitation" Programme in Reducing Re-offending? A Meta-analysis of Evaluations in Four Countries. *Psychology, Crime and Law*, *12*, 3-24.

Van Wormer, K. (1999). The Strengths Perspective: A Paradigm for Correctional Counselling, *Federal Probation*, *63(1)*, 51-58.

Viggiani, N. (2007). Unhealthy Prisons: Exploring Structural Determinants of Prison Health. *Sociology of Health and Illness*, *29*, 115-135.

Watson, R., Stimpson, A. & Hostick, T. (2004). Prison Health Care: a Review of the Literature. *International Journal of Nursing Studies*, *41*, 119-128.

Wilson, S. (2004). The principle of equivalence and the future of mental health care in prisons. *British Journal of Psychiatry*, *184*, 5-7.

Wolff, N. (2005). Community Reintegration of Prisoners with Mental Illness: A Social Investment Perspective. *International Journal of Law and Psychiatry*, *28*, 43-58.

In: Violent Crime and Prisons: Population...
Ed: Aidan Renshaw and Emelina Suárez
ISBN: 978-1-60741-668-5

Chapter 14

USING ARTS THERAPIES WITH PRISONERS SUFFERING FROM DRUG ADDICTION

L. Schiltz*
Fondation François-Elisabeth, Luxembourg.

ABSTRACT

Drug addicted prisoners are in a special situation: they are permanently oscillating between consciousness of reality and preservation of their illusory dreams. One goal of arts therapies in prison consists in developing their capacity to elaborate on a symbolic level and in favouring a better equilibrium between their Ego Ideal and their Superego. If there is no restructuring process of this kind, they risk having a relapse as soon as they are released.

Clinical vignettes will illustrate the therapeutic process and the special function of the arts therapist in prison.

We present a comparative study of pictures drawn at the beginning of arts therapeutic treatment. Based on the evolution of the pictorial and literary production, we extract the first indicators of a possible relaunch of the subjectivation process.

Our discussion stresses the possibilities but also the limits of arts therapies in prison. The extracted indicators can be useful for future research.

Keywords: arts therapies, drug addiction, prison, subjectivation, therapeutic process.

1. INTRODUCTION

In this chapter I shall try to answer the following question: Can arts therapies promote the reconstruction of identity with drug addicted prisoners? People belonging to this population are in a special situation: as they are in a state of relative abstinence that they have not chosen but that has been imposed on them, they are permanently oscillating between consciousness of reality and preservation of their illusory dreams. Their identities seem to be essentially fluctuating, as is reflected in the instability of their interpersonal relationships and their behaviour.

2. Identity Fluctuation with Drug Addicted Prisoners

In the population that we are studying, the current personality disorders result from the interaction between the structural problems prior to drug consumption, the long-term effects of the substances themselves and the effects of being part of a marginalized group (Schiltz & al., 2007b).

Figure 1. Drawing reflecting the omnipresence of the drug.

Several authors emphasize the necessity for keeping in mind the flaw in the psychic functioning existing prior to drug addiction (Dulz & Schneider, 1996; Marcelli & Braconnier, 1999; Farges, 2000; Gunderson, 2001). According to Jeammet (1991), these persons' habitual functioning modalities regard the failure of internalising and elaborating mechanisms accompanied by a depletion of the libidinal investment, the prevalence of the Ego Ideal over the Superego and the fundamental emotional instability. According to Therrat and Escande

* 10, rue Gabriel de Marie, L-2131 Luxembourg, Email: lony.schiltz@education.lu

(2003), factors of vulnerability are located either at the side of impulsivity or at the side of narcissistic deficiency.

If we rely on the criteria of categorical psychopathology, we have to refer to the Anglo-Saxon authors citing borderline and narcissistic personality disorders among the risk factors (Gunderson & Gabbard, 2000; Kernberg, Weiner & Bardenstein, 2000). The link between antisocial personality and drug addiction also starts to be better known (Fischer & al. 2003). As a matter of fact, these persons seem to present an increased vulnerability because of their low frustration tolerance. On the other hand, current research has stressed complex interactions between the use of cannabis and schizophrenia (Ametepe, 2003). People presenting a latent psychotic state can use the drug with an aim of self-medication; however, the effect is two-way. The positive symptoms of schizophrenia (delirium, hallucination) can be worsened while the negative symptoms (social inhibition, cognitive deficiency, anhedonia) can be ameliorated (Potin & al., 2003).

Drug addicted people end up developing a behaviour of self-sabotage of their potentialities (Chabrol, 2000) and are quickly trapped in a vicious circle, not only because of the reduction of the social relations, but also because of the effects of the drugs on their personality and cognitive functioning. Let us remember that one has to distinguish between short-term effects - hallucinogenous, euphorising, relaxing or anaesthetizing - and long-term effects: increased irritability, instability, dysphoria, motivational deficiency, disturbances of judgment and memory (Reynaud, 2003), hence changes that in turn have a negative effect on the quality of interpersonal relations (Lindesmith, 2008).

Figure 2. Drawing reflecting a major feeling of guilt.

One of the major problems that any type of therapeutic measure in prison has to face is the weakness of the personalised feeling of guilt and the major presence of archaic guilt (Patrick, 2007).

In his pioneering study on antisocial psychopathy, Flavigny (1977) wrote that these persons felt guilty of their existence but did not feel responsible for the wrongs they really had committed towards other people. A diffuse feeling of unworthiness would push them to sabotage their proper efforts or the ones of people trying to reintegrate them into normal life.

One of the persons described by Flavigny told his educator: "Don't take care of me; I always have to destroy everything."

This latent self-destroying tendency often seen in prisoners suffering from drug addiction can be compared to ordalic behaviour patterns. According to Bergeret (1981), addiction can have the meaning of an unconscious attempt to settle a debt. One gives one's body in pledge to pay for an original fault linked in a fantasmatic way to the simple fact of being born. As a matter of fact, many drug addicts are fully conscious of the danger they face when experimenting with the effects of different substances. Likewise, they entrust themselves to an external power so that it can decide about their fate (Charles-Nicolas & Valeur, 1996; Kalechstein & van Gorp, 2007). Drug dealing linked to the sometimes fatal risks for customers is part of the same ordalic behaviour.

In prison, drug addicted persons are suddenly separated from their habitual opportunities of evasion, even if their abstinence is solely relative, as the drug circuits existing in prison cannot be thoroughly controlled. On the other hand, they are suddenly confronted with strict rules that they do not agree with but that have been imposed on them by the outside world. Promiscuity with companions that they have not chosen either is a source of continuous harassments and vexations, which is added to the psychological stress linked with imprisonment and permanent observation. As they precisely are persons with little self-control and as they have not learned to sustain intrapsychic strains, hetero-aggressive or auto-aggressive acting-out is common in prison.

What is obvious in the psychological assessment made prior to the treatment (Schiltz, 2003) is - in addition to the impulsivity and the low frustration tolerance - the persons' imaginary poverty once they are not under the effect of hallucinogenous substances. On the other hand, they suffer from a particular narcissistic pathology, as they have a tendency to present a grandiose Ego Ideal (Kohut, 1977). In a comparative study that we made with several subgroups living in exclusion or marginalisation, this feature distinguishes them from homeless people and persons living in precarity; those persons also present a pathologic state of the Ego Ideal but in the sense of underdevelopment (Schiltz & Houbre, 2004).

In prison, the arts therapist has a special status: on the one hand, he represents law and order, on the other hand, he must trust in the persons' emotional and cognitive resources, i.e. he must ally with the sane part of their personality. Life in prison provides numerous opportunities to confront with the restrictions imposed by regulations or by other people's rights. It is important to use these opportunities to restore or develop a personalised moral consciousness.

One of the major objectives of arts therapy in prison consists in developing the persons' imaginary and symbolic elaboration capacities, to help them let go of their dreams of omnipotence and to favour a better equilibrium between the Ego Ideal and the Superego. If this restructuring process is failing, they risk having a relapse as soon as they are released.

3. THREE PORTRAITS

We present some short clinical vignettes in order to illustrate typical evolutions of people belonging to our sample but also in order to describe the difficulties that arts therapists working in prison have to face. The prisoners' behaviour in the workshops is often the expression of a false self, at least at the beginning of the treatment. With some prisoners, the psychic dependency is such that they do not show any motivation for a life without drugs (Schiltz & al., 2007a).

3.1. Alphonse

Alphonse is a young man who is well groomed, calm and polite. He would have liked to study sciences, but his mother stopped paying; thus he had to leave college before he graduated. He is still suffering from this. Several affective break-ups and, especially, the break-up with the mother of his child, have contributed to his falling into drugs as well as to a suicide attempt. His own mother had left his father when he was a little boy and his relationship with his mother was never good. He says: "I never got a chance in my life".

Alphonse participates in all the activities in a highly motivated manner except for musical improvisation that he does not like. In fact, he is afraid of being overwhelmed by his repressed feelings. He understands the goal of therapy and wants to lead a "normal" life without drugs when released from prison. He succeeds in describing his fellow prisoners in a subtle manner. Because of his intelligence and his confident presence, the group respects him. He openly expresses his antipathy for the "impostors" among the prisoners.

In fact, this pseudo-maturity corresponds to a façade. In his TAT, his anger, his pessimism and his anxiety appear in a veiled manner in spite of the banal contents of his stories. During work with clay, he created a volcano: "Inside of me, things are fermenting. I could explode at any moment..."

Figure 3. Painting made by Alphonse.

When his stay in prison came to an end, he retreated more and more and told the therapist about his apprehensions when thinking about being outside the protective prison walls. He participated in arts therapeutic sessions during eight months.

3.2. Rolf

Rolf is very impulsive and does not stand frustration at all. Concerning his drug addiction, he often relapsed in spite of several therapies he participated in. He talks a lot about drugs and their effects and says that he cannot imagine life without drugs or at least without substitute medication.

During his childhood and his adolescence, he experienced many traumas. When he was three years old, his mother married a man who was not his father and whom he could not stand. During many years, his sister and he himself suffered from physical abuse and sexual abuse by one of that man's family members.

Rolf blames his real father for having abandoned his children and for not having been able to protect them against the cruelties that his sister and he had to endure from a very young age on. As an adolescent he expressed his aggressions by setting fire to the house of his parents, by manipulating the brakes of his stepfather's car and by attacking him with a knife. After a stay at a psychiatric hospital, Rolf went to live in an institution.

One morning, he found his mother dead due to an overdose of medication. At this time he already took heroin. The day of his arrest, he found the dead body of his best friend, likewise dead due to an overdose of heroin.

Figure 4. Drawing made by Rolf.

In prison, Rolf has transferred his need for affection to animals. Every day, he cleans the henhouse with a lot of dedication.

He does not want to participate in role-plays or in musical improvisation: "I have complexes". On the other hand, he likes painting and modelling and asks for paper and coloured pencils in order to make a large painting. The topic of drugs is ubiquitous in his works. After having verbalised the impact of the drugs in his life, he destroys the works that mentioned it. His arts therapeutic treatment lasted eight months.

3.3. Philippe

When he was young, Philippe travelled through Asia and visited India several times. He is convinced that he has been a Buddhist guru as well as a famous architect in his former lives.

He draws in a "psychedelic" manner, reminding one of the 60s and 70s. He also wrote a book about his adventures in India. He says that he is meditating daily. During these meditations, he would have mystical experiences and see a white light.

At the beginning, Philippe participates in the group music therapy session in a distant manner; but soon he openly shows his pleasure. He attaches a lot of importance to the voice and tries entraining people for singing louder and louder and letting off tension through vocal expression. He often criticizes the arts therapist because she does not sing loud enough. From the beginning he plays the flute and tries to imitate Hindu sounds. Later on, he dances and jumps around the hall playing different instruments at the same time.

Figure 5. Painting made by Philippe.

At other times however he says that he needs more distance from the others: "I am a hermit". He complains about not having enough energy anymore for stimulating the others. He would be tired of always giving some thing without ever getting anything in return. He always gives the impression of having to replenish before meeting the others. His energy does not gush from the source. He participated in arts therapeutic sessions for six months.

4. The Biographic Interview

A rating scale for a semi structured biographic interview was constructed in order to analyze the relationship between traumatic biographic events and the current structural functioning of personality (Schiltz & Schiltz, 2008). In the same perspective, we constructed a rating scale for the analysis of the Rotter Sentences Completion Test (Schiltz, 2006).

Table 1. Significant rank correlations between dimensions of the Biographic Interview and the Rotter Test in the third person (N = 59)

Biographic Interview	Rotter Test: he/she	Rho	Level of Significance
Unique break-up	Isolation	.258	p<.05
Repeated break-ups	Separation anxiety	.308	p<.05
	Guilt	.382	p<.01
	Under developed Ego Ideal	.356	p<.01
Nature of trauma : lost	Goal :having a love affair	-.276	p<.05
Nature of trauma : neglect	Regret	.323	p<.05
	Conflicts with Family	.294	p<.05
	Conflicts with Friends	.360	p<.01
Nature of trauma : maltreatance or violence	Separation anxiety	.359	p<.01
	Under developed Ego Ideal	.260	p<.05
Complete family	Distress	-.260	p<.05
	Regret	-.351	p<.01
Single-parent family	Separation anxiety	.329	p<.05
	Under developed Ego Ideal	.277	p<.05
	Isolation	-.329	p<.05
Enlarged family	Envy	.307	p<.05
	Regret	.403	p<.01
	Isolation	.397	p<.01
Suffering during childhood	Separation anxiety	.351	p<.01
	Under developed Ego Ideal	.315	p<.05
Suffering during adulthood	Regret	.261	p<.05

Table 2. Significant rank correlations between dimensions of the Biographic Interview and the Rotter Test in the first person (N = 59).

Biographic Interview	Rotter Test: I / me	Rho	Level of Significance
Continuous life course	Distress	-.283	p<.05
Repeated break-ups	Distress	.344	p<.01
Nature of trauma : neglect	Distress	.357	p<.01
Nature of trauma : maltreatance or violence	Hatred	.373	p<.01
Complete family	Guilt	-.271	p<.05
Enlarged family	Goal : having a love affair	-.336	p<.01
	Isolation	.260	p<.05
Suffering during childhood	Distress	.333	p<.01
Suffering during adolescence	Distress	.283	p<.05
	Isolation	-.371	p<.01

Significant correlations appear between several types of childhood traumata and actual isolation, underdevelopment of Ego Ideal, conflicting relationships and overwhelming negative feelings. In the answers expressed in the third person (Table 1), there is a stronger presence of nostalgia, regret, separation anxiety, whereas in the first person (Table 2), there is a more direct expression of distress, hatred and guilt.

To explain this discrepancy, we can suppose that an intimate need like longing for tenderness can not be admitted consciously at the beginning of therapy and needs to be suppressed with the help of primary defence mechanisms like splitting and denial. Longing for love and tenderness would be a dangerous threat to the feeling of omnipotence because it means being dependant on another human being. We will find a strong support for this interpretation through the analysis of the pictures drawn by prisoners.

5. Study of the Artistic Creation

The study of the artistic production was done in three stages: a comparative study of the pictures drawn during the first therapeutic sessions, a follow-up study of the evolution during the arts therapeutic treatment and a long-term follow-up study of the individual evolution after release from prison. The third part was recently started.

5.1. Extraction of a Typology of Pictures

Based on the state of the arts on borderline functioning and on our prior clinical experience with persons belonging to this population, we established a hypothetical typology for the pictures drawn in the first stage of arts therapeutic treatment.

- Type 1: “Nostalgia of the lost paradise”
- Type 2: “Fascination of the powers of evil”
- Type 3: “Graphics and ornamentation”
- Type 4: “Escape into banality”
- Type 5: “Fragmentation and dislocation of forms”

From a total of 52 representative drawings made by prisoners, 96% could be integrated in one of the first four categories. Type 5 was not met in prison, but only with persons living in great precarity. The authors were homeless people suffering from chronic psychosis (Schiltz, 2006; Schiltz & al. 2007a).

5.2. Further Investigation of the Pictorial Production

a. Distribution of the drawings according to type

Half of the creations of our sample belonged to type 3, “graphics and ornamentation”, and little more than one fifth to type 4, “escape into banality”. Types 1 and 2, pointing towards a more authentic expression of feelings, only occurred in one tenth of the creations. Hence, we see that in our sample, drawings and paintings mainly reflect defensive functioning or factual functioning, at least at the beginning of therapy.

b. Structural analysis

A multi dimensional analysis was computed with the help of a rating scale we constructed for the analysis of the pictures (Schiltz,2006,2008) ,in order to identify latent dimensions. By means of optimal scaling techniques (PRINCALS), we extracted grouping criteria for variables and persons. The inspection of the matrix of discrimination measures led to the following proposal of denomination with Cronbach’s α for a three-level solution = .93 :

- Dimension 1: creativity and formal application linked to a positive atmosphere
- Dimension 2: expression of destructive tendencies
- Dimension 3: abstract contents and ornamental graphics

The three dimensions are psychologically plausible and seem to make sense according to the state of the state of the arts regarding our population.

c. Comparison with other excluded populations (Total N = 156)

The same methodology was applied to other clinical subgroups, namely persons living in precarity and refugees. We present a comparative study based on the crossing of some content categories of the rating scale and the majoritarian occurrence in each type (Table 3).

With prisoners suffering from drug addiction, the existential topics of love, sexuality and religion mainly occur within type 3, i.e. accompanied by graphics and ornamentations, which could be interpreted as an indicator of the defensive functioning of this population.

Table 3. Matrix of the mainly occurring existential topics according to type in the three clinical subgroups.

Variable	Drug addicts	Persons living in Precarity	Refugees
Love	Type 3	Type 1	Type 3
Sexuality	Type 3	Type 3	/
Birth	/	Type 3	/
Death	Type 2	Type 2	Type 2
Religion	Type 3	/	Types 1 and 2
Patriotism	Type 1	Type 1	Type 1

6. Longitudinal Study: Exploration of the Arts Therapeutic Process

6.1. General Hypothesis for the Longitudinal Study (N = 45)

The detailed analysis of the changes in the literary and pictorial production could possibly lead to the extraction of general criteria linked to the relaunch of subjectivation and could thus provide tracks for future research.

Table 4. Rank correlations between the delta variables of the rating scales for the stories and the drawings for p< .01.

Rating scales for the stories variables	Rating scales for the drawings variables	Spearman's correlation	Bilateral significance
Religion	Productivity	,695(**)	,000
Conflict children-parents	Nostalgia	,631(**)	,000
Hero	Nostalgia	,668(**)	,000
Conflict with peers	Perseveration	-,599(**)	,000
Wealth of details	Energy of stroke	,587(**)	,001
Nuanced vocabulary	Disruption	,525(**)	,002
Conflict children-parents	Human person	,525(**)	,002
Structuring	Perseveration	-,492(**)	,005
Description	Banal contents	,483(**)	,006
Emotional implication	Home	,483(**)	,006
Nuanced vocabulary	Love	,474(**)	,007
Nuanced vocabulary	Sexuality	,474(**)	,007
Conformism	Positive atmosphere	,469(**)	,008

6.2. Crossing the Literary and the Pictorial Production

We calculated the rank correlations (Spearman's Rho) between the delta values, i.e. the pre-test / post-test differences of the literary and the pictorial creations (Table 4).

The resulting correlations between the two series are psychologically plausible and could reflect a change in the level of mentalisation allowing elaborating the tensions of daily live on an imaginary and symbolic level instead of acting out or directing one's aggressivity towards one's own body.

6.3. Extracting Indicators of a Relaunch of Subjectivation

All along the therapeutic process, we analysed the artistic creation in order to extract formal and content criteria suitable for indicating a positive evolution. The following text shows a beginning of introspection.

"Possessed by heroine

Every day, the shadows lengthened, the days shortened, the circles shrunk, the friends left, loneliness emerged.
Yes, even the angels left at a certain moment.
Because my life had fallen to pieces; it had lost all meaning.
I had the feeling of a frozen emptiness, I felt like stillborn.
In my mouth, I had the bitter taste of decay.
I wanted to end it all, I almost did. I poisoned myself gradually.
But I survived.
I had burned all the bridges. I don't know whether you understand me.
I had longed for a seat near the window, high up in the sky.
But I found myself in the shadow.
I killed every feeling I had inside of me. Everything I owned.

Now that I am sober, everything seems to be clear.
Now that I am sober, I realise where I have been.
I had escaped to another world, to other times.
I escaped from myself and from my brain full of fear, while hauling myself into the never-ending befuddlement of heroin."

In Table 5, a synthesis of the extracted indicators is presented:

The retained criteria have been validated by their significant correlations with behavioural criteria (observational frames for the therapeutic sessions) and with psychometric tests. The validation results were reported in detail elsewhere. (Schiltz & al, 2007a).

Table 5. Operationalising some theoretic concepts linked to the relaunch of subjectivation.

Theoretic concept	Operationalisation through artistic creation
Loosening of defensive functioning	Change in the distribution of types; diversification and occurrence of new types in the pictorial creations
Decrease of splitting	Occurrence of depressive topics in the pictorial and literary creations
Expression of unsatisfied affective needs	Occurrence of feelings of nostalgia in the pictorial and literary creations
Canalisation of archaic aggressiveness	Change in the ratio archaic aggressiveness / elaborated aggressiveness in the texts
Development of a mature narcissism	Change in the features of the Alter Ego in the texts
Maturing in objectal relationship	Vision of the Other as a differentiated and unfathomable being in the texts
Socialisation	Improvement of the communication skills and the listening capabilities during group music therapy
Integration of reality	Appropriate estimation of one's capabilities and limits in self-reported questionnaires
Complex formal work	Integration of musical parameters, creation of complex musical forms during musical improvisation; artistic elaboration in the texts
Equilibrium between Ego Ideal and Superego	Occurrence of humanitarian and social considerations in the texts

(from Schiltz & al. 2007a)

7. Conclusion

The evaluation of arts therapies in prison showed some positive effects, like the decrease of splitting and of over-adaptation, the expression of more authentic feelings, the awareness of the interiorised anger and the development of a better listening capability.

The limitations of the treatment are related to the severity of the psychiatric co-morbidities and to the irreversible effects of drugs (Kalechstein & van Gorp, 2007). On the other hand, the risk of relapse after release is very high, as prison also acts as a protecting cocoon, in spite of its discomfort.

To what extent can arts therapies thus promote the reconstruction of identity with drug-addicted prisoners? At the present time, our results are provisional. The answer to the asked question can only be given after the long-term longitudinal study aiming at the monitoring of the persons during the first three years after their release, at least for those who wish to continue participating in arts therapeutic sessions. That part of the study will include external psychosocial evaluation criteria like rehabilitation in the working environment and also the social and family relationships that the persons will be able to establish after their release.

PRESENTATION OF THE AUTHOR

Lony Schiltz, Doctor of clinical psychology, HDR, head of research unit in Clinical Psychology, Health Psychology and Arts Therapies at the Fondation François-Elisabeth, Luxembourg, head of studies of the postgraduate curriculum in arts therapies at the University of Luxembourg.

Email: lony.schiltz@education.lu

ACKNOWLEDGMENT

This research was partially funded by a grant of the National Research Fund (FNR 02/05/14) in Luxembourg

REFERENCES

Ametepe, L. (2003). Liens entre usage de cannabis et schizophrénie. *La Revue Française de Psychiatrie et de Psychologie Médicale*, *VII*, *70*, 25-35.

Bergeret, J. (1981). *Le psychanalyste à l'écoute du toxicomane*. Paris: Dunod.

Chabrol, H. (2000). Violence faite à soi-même, violence faite à autrui: abord psychopathologique. *La Revue Française de Psychiatrie et de Psychologie Médicale*, *IV*, *43*, 11-13.

Charles-Nicolas, A. & Valleur, M. (1996). Du sens dans la prise de risque: les conduites ordaliques. *Neuropsychiatrie de l'Enfance et de l'Adolescence*, *11*, 324-330.

Dulz, B. & Schneider, A. (1969). *Borderline Störungen. Theorie und Therapie*. Stuttgart: Schattauer.

Farges, F. (2000). Dépendance, abus, usage. In: P. Angel, D. Richard, & M. Valleur. (Eds.), Toxicomanie. (pp. 16-22). Paris: Masson.

Fischer, B., Haydon, E., Kim, G., El-Guebaly, N. & Rehm, J. (2003). Screening for Anti-Social Personality Disorder in Drug Users - A Qualitative Exploratory Study on Feasibility. *International Journal of Methods in Psychiatric Research*, *12*, *3*, 151-156

Flavigny, H. (1977). De la notion de psychopathie. *Revue de Neuropsychiatrie infantile*, *25*, *1*, 19-75.

Gunderson, J. G. (2001). *Borderline Personality Disorder*. Washington DC: American Psychiatric Publishing, Inc.

J. G. Gunderson, & G. O. Gabbard (Eds.), (2000). *Psychotherapy for Personality Disorders*. Washington DC: American Psychiatric Press.

Jeammet, P. (1991). Addiction, dépendance, adolescence: réflexions sur leurs liens, conséquences sur nos attitudes thérapeutiques. In: J. L. Venisse. (éd). Les nouvelles addictions, *Médecine et Psychothérapie*. (pp 10-29). Paris: Masson.

Kalechstein, A. & van Gorp, W. G. (2007). *Neuropsychology and Substance Use. State-of-the-Art and Future Directions.* New York: Taylor & Francis.

Kernberg, P. F., Weiner, A. S. & Bardenstein, K. K. (2000). *Personality disorders in children and adolescents*. New York: Basic Books.

Kohut, H. (1977). *The Restoration of the Self.* New York: International Universities Press.

Lindesmith, A. R. (2008). *Addiction & Opiates.* New Brunswick (NJ) : Transaction Pub.

Marcelli, D. & Braconnier, A. (1999). *Adolescence et psychopathologie.* Paris: Masson.

C. J. Patrick (Ed). (2007). *Handbook of Psychopathy.* New York : The Guilford Press.

Potin, S., Stip, E. & Roy, J. Y. (2003). Schizophrénie et toxicomanie. Une relecture du concept d'automédication. *L'encéphale, 29, 3,* 193-203.

Reynaud, M. (2003). Cannabis : quelques mises à jour. *Synapse, 199,* 16-18.

Schiltz, L. (2003). L'organisation limite de la personnalité à l'adolescence. Considérations diagnostiques et thérapeutiques. Tome 1. Rapport de recherche. Luxembourg: CRP-Santé.

Schiltz, L. (2006). Grilles d'analyse de contenu basées sur l'approche phénoménologico-structurale. *Bulletin de la Société des Sciences Médicales du Grand Duché de Luxembourg, 2,* 265-280.

Schiltz, L. (2008). *Pictures used as a Tool of Treatment and Research.* An integrated clinical and experimental study of people suffering from trauma and deprivation. In: M. Stemmler, E. Lautsch, & D. Martinke. (Eds.), Configural Frequency Analysis (CFA) and other non-parametrical statistical methods : Gustav A. Lienert Memorial Issue. (119-140) Kassel : Pabst Science Pub.

Schiltz, L., Boyer, L., Denis, B., Fack, P., Martiny, C. & Meyer, C. (2007a). L'organisation limite de la personnalité à l'adolescence. Considérations diagnostiques et thérapeutiques. Applications aux adolescents et jeunes adultes en rupture de projet de vie. Tome III: Etudes d'évaluation des ateliers d'art thérapie. Luxembourg: CRP-Santé.

Schiltz, L. & Houbre, B. (2004). Idéal du Moi et Surmoi chez les personnes en situation d'exclusion. *La Revue française de Psychiatrie et de Psychologie médicale, VII, 81,* 21-28.

Schiltz, L., Houbre, B. & Martiny, C. (2007b). Précarité sociale, marginalisation et pathologie limite: Etude comparative de plusieurs groupes de sujets en rupture de projet de vie. *L'évolution psychiatrique, 72,* 453-468 http://dx.doi.org/10.1016/j.evopsy.2007.05.001

Schiltz, L. & Schiltz, J. (2008). Analysing the relationship between traumatic biographical events and the current structural functioning of personality. *Bulletin de la Société des Sciences Médicales du Grand-Duché deLuxembourg, 1,* 175- 188.

Therrat, B. & Escande, M. (2003). Le concept de carence narcissique. *La Revue Française de Psychiatrie et de Psychologie Médicale, VII, 70,* 15-20.

INDEX

A

B

C

D

E

F

G

H

I

J

K

L

M

N

O

P

Q

R

S